T0075033

Applied Computer Vision and Soft Computing with Interpretable AI

This reference text presents the knowledge base of computer vision and soft computing techniques with their applications for sustainable developments.

Features:

- Covers a variety of deep learning architectures useful for computer vision tasks.
- Demonstrates the use of different soft computing techniques and their applications for different computer vision tasks.
- Highlights the unified strengths of hybrid techniques based on deep learning and soft computing taken together that give the interpretable, adaptive, and optimized solution to a given problem.
- Addresses the different issues and further research opportunities in computer vision and soft computing.
- Describes all the concepts with practical examples and case studies with appropriate performance measures that validate the applicability of the respective technique to a certain domain.
- Considers recent real word problems and the prospective solutions to these problems.

This book will be useful to researchers, students, faculty, and industry personnel who are eager to explore the power of deep learning and soft computing for different computer vision tasks.

Applied Computer Vision and Soft Computing with Interpretable AI

Edited by
Swati V. Shinde
Darshan V. Medhane
Oscar Castillo

CRC Press
Taylor & Francis Group
Boca Raton London New York

CRC Press is an imprint of the
Taylor & Francis Group, an **informa** business

A CHAPMAN & HALL BOOK

Designed cover image: Shutterstock

First edition published 2024
by CRC Press
6000 Broken Sound Parkway NW, Suite 300, Boca Raton, FL 33487-2742

and by CRC Press
4 Park Square, Milton Park, Abingdon, Oxon, OX14 4RN

CRC Press is an imprint of Taylor & Francis Group, LLC

© 2024 selection and editorial matter, Swati V. Shinde, Darshan V. Medhane and Oscar Castillo; individual chapters, the contributors

Reasonable efforts have been made to publish reliable data and information, but the author and publisher cannot assume responsibility for the validity of all materials or the consequences of their use. The authors and publishers have attempted to trace the copyright holders of all material reproduced in this publication and apologize to copyright holders if permission to publish in this form has not been obtained. If any copyright material has not been acknowledged please write and let us know so we may rectify in any future reprint.

Except as permitted under U.S. Copyright Law, no part of this book may be reprinted, reproduced, transmitted, or utilized in any form by any electronic, mechanical, or other means, now known or hereafter invented, including photocopying, micro-filming, and recording, or in any information storage or retrieval system, without written permission from the publishers.

For permission to photocopy or use material electronically from this work, access www.copyright.com or contact the Copyright Clearance Center, Inc. (CCC), 222 Rosewood Drive, Danvers, MA 01923, 978-750-8400. For works that are not available on CCC please contact mpkbookspermissions@tandf.co.uk

Trademark notice: Product or corporate names may be trademarks or registered trademarks and are used only for identification and explanation without intent to infringe.

ISBN: 978-1-032-41723-3 (hbk)
ISBN: 978-1-032-41726-4 (pbk)
ISBN: 978-1-003-35945-6 (ebk)

DOI: 10.1201/9781003359456

Typeset in Times
by SPi Technologies India Pvt Ltd (Straive)

Contents

Preface

Computer Vision is the field of studying and developing technology that enables computers to process, analyze, and interpret digital images. Today, Computer Vision applications can be found in several industries, such as industrial robots, medical imaging, and surveillance. On the other hand, soft computing is being used to reduce the limitations caused by problems in data analytics. Moreover, soft computing is emerging as an innovative technological approach with the ability to allow a broad range of applications which can transform human lives in excellent ways.

The diverse perspectives of soft computing involve numerous aspects of interpretable artificial intelligence. Interpretable artificial intelligence incorporates theories, concepts, and techniques of science, internet technology, computer technology, neuroscience, and so on in a highly multidisciplinary way. It also offers a high computational dynamism. In view of the importance of an interpretable artificial intelligence as an emerging trend and technological approach to be followed in multidisciplinary research areas, we are pleased to present a book titled *Applied Computer Vision and Soft Computing with Interpretable AI.*

Researchers and practitioners have contributed to this book by means of chapters that illustrate research results, projects, surveying works, and industrial experiences that describe significant advances in the areas of computer vision, soft computing, and interpretable artificial intelligence. This book is organized in 20 chapters.

It is intended to be a major reference tool for scientists and engineers interested in applying new computational and mathematical concepts to design applications based on interpretable AI. We consider that this book can also be used to obtain novel ideas for new lines of research, or to continue the lines of research proposed by the authors here. We compliment the contributors for writing their comprehensive chapters which not only introduce the several concepts of interpretable AI in a broad context but also help us in understanding the complex applications of it.

We thank all the people who have helped or encouraged us during the production of this book. We would like to thank our colleagues working in Soft Computing and Computer Vision who are too many to mention individually by name. Of course, we need to thank our supporting agencies for their help during this project and thank our institutions for always supporting our work. Finally, we thank our families for their continuous support during the time that we have spent on this project.

Swati V. Shinde
Pune, Maharashtra, India

Darshan V. Medhane
Nashik, Maharashtra, India

Oscar Castillo
Tijuana, Mexico

Preface

Editors

Swati V. Shinde earned her PhD in Computer Science and Engineering at Swami Ramanand Teertha Marathwada University, Nanded. She has 22 years teaching experience and is currently Dean of R&D and Professor of Computer Engineering, Pimpri Chinchwad College of Engineering (PCCoE), Pune. She worked as a HOD-IT for seven years at PCCoE. Her research interests include Machine Learning, Deep Learning, Soft Computing, Artificial Neural Networks, and Fuzzy Logic. She has published more than a hundred research papers in reputed journals. She received six Best Paper Awards at different IEEE conferences and has filed seven research patents. She received a DST research project grant of almost Rs 3,700,000. She also received a research grant from SPPU University, Pune, an International FDP grant from SPPU, and a conference grant from AICTE. She is a certified trainer and ambassador of NVDIA's Deep Learning Institute. She received the Dr. APJ Abdul Kalam Women Achievers Award from IITech Bangalore. She was awarded the Indo Global Engineering Excellence Award by the Indo Global Chamber of Commerce Industries and Agriculture. She also received first prize for her prototype from SERB at IIT Kanpur.

Darshan V. Medhane is Associate Professor and Head of Department of Computer Engineering at Maratha Vidya Prasarak Samaj's KBT College of Engineering, Nashik. Formerly he was Assistant Professor in Computer Science and Engineering at the Indian Institute of Information Technology, Pune (established by MHRD, India). He holds a doctorate from the Vellore Institute of Technology, Vellore. He has 12 years of teaching experience. He has published several research works in reputed peer reviewed journals like *IEEE Transactions* and has many SCI and Scopus indexed papers to his credit. He has published more than twenty books and a number of book chapters. He completed a funded research project sanctioned by BCUD, University of Pune, and another by SEED, Ministry of Science and Technology. He received the Best Student Award for Engineering. He is a reviewer for various journals. He is a member of IEEE and IET. His research interests include Cyber Physical Systems, Computational Intelligence, Evolutionary Multi Objective Optimization, Position Monitoring Systems, Automata Theory, and Distributed Computing Systems.

Oscar Castillo earned a Doctor of Science degree (Doctor Habilitatus) in Computer Science from the Polish Academy of Sciences (with the dissertation "Soft Computing and Fractal Theory for Intelligent Manufacturing"). He is Professor of Computer Science in the Graduate Division, Tijuana Institute of Technology, Tijuana, Mexico. In addition, he serves as Research Director of Computer Science and head of the research group on Hybrid Fuzzy Intelligent Systems. Currently, he is President of the Hispanic American Fuzzy Systems Association and is a past president of the International Fuzzy Systems Association. Professor Castillo is also Chair of the Mexican Chapter of the Computational Intelligence Society (IEEE). He also belongs to the Technical Committee on Fuzzy Systems of IEEE and to the Task Force on "Extensions to Type-1 Fuzzy Systems". He is also a member of NAFIPS,

IFSA, and IEEE. He belongs to the Mexican Research System (SNI Level 3). His research interests are Type-2 Fuzzy Logic, Fuzzy Control, Neuro-Fuzzy, and Genetic-Fuzzy hybrid approaches. He has published over 300 journal papers, 10 authored books, 90 edited books, 300 papers at conference proceedings, and more than 300 chapters in edited books, in total more than 1000 publications (according to Scopus) with an h index of 89, and more than 26,000 citations according to Google Scholar. He has been Guest Editor of several successful special issues in journals such as *Applied Soft Computing*, *Intelligent Systems*, *Information Sciences*, *Soft Computing*, *Non-Linear Studies*, *Fuzzy Sets and Systems*, *JAMRIS*, and *Engineering Letters*. He is currently Associate Editor of *Information Sciences*, the *Journal of Engineering Applications on Artificial Intelligence*, the *International Journal of Fuzzy Systems*, the *Journal of Complex Intelligent Systems*, *Granular Computing*, and *Intelligent Systems*. He was Associate Editor of the *Journal of Applied Soft Computing* and *IEEE Transactions on Fuzzy Systems*. He was elected IFSA Fellow in 2015 and MICAI Fellow in 2016. Finally, he recently received recognition as Highly Cited Researcher in 2017 and 2018 by Clarivate Analytics and Web of Science.

Contributors

Pratik Adhav
Pimpri Chinchwad College of Engineering
Pune, India

Taymaz Akan
Louisiana State University Health
    Sciences Center
Shreveport, LA, USA
and
Istanbul Topkapi University
Istanbul, Turkey

Avadhoot Autade
Pimpri Chinchwad College of Engineering
Pune, India

Mohammad Ali Balafar
University of Tabriz
Tabriz, Iran

Anjali Manish Bari
Bharati Vidyapeeth's College of Engineering
    for Women
Pune, India

Amol Bhawarthi
Cognizant Technology Solutions
Pune, India

Sajal Ranjan Chakravarty
National Institute of Technology Raipur
Raipur, India

Saroj Kumar Chandra
Jindal University
Raigarh, India

Rishabh Dadsena
National Institute of Technology Raipur
Raipur, India

Leena Deshpande
Vishwakarma Institute of Information
    Technology
Pune, India

Satish R. Devane
Savitribai Phule Pune University, MVPS's KBT
    College of Engineering
Nashik, India

Aditya Dhumal
Pimpri Chinchwad College of Engineering
Pune, India

Gavin Dsouza
University of Mumbai, St. Francis Institute
    of Technology
Mumbai, India

Aaishwarya Ashish Gaikwad
Pimpri Chinchwad College of Engineering
Pune, India

Uma R. Godse
MIT Art, Design and Technology University
Pune, India

J. G. Gujar
Sinhgad College of Engineering
Pune, India

Kavita Jatwar
National Institute of Technology Raipur
Raipur, India

Sangita M. Jaybhaye
Vishwakarma Institute of Technology
Pune, India

Deepa A. Joshi
Savitribai Phule Pune University, Dr. D.Y. Patil
    Institute of Technology, Pimpri
Pune, India

Sonali Kadam
Bharati Vidyapeeth's College of Engineering
    for Women
Pune, India

Shreya Kakade
University of Mumbai, Thakur College of
    Engineering and Technology
Mumbai, India

Apeksha Kamath
University of Mumbai, Thakur College of
    Engineering and Technology
Mumbai, India

R. Karthikeyan
Vardhaman College of Engineering Hyderabad
Hyderabad, India

Yumna Khan
University of Mumbai, Thakur College of
    Engineering and Technology
Mumbai, India

Anand Khandare
University of Mumbai, Thakur College of
    Engineering and Technology
Mumbai, India

Ratnesh Kumar
University of Kalyani
Kalyani, Nadia, India

Payal Kunwar
University of Mumbai, Thakur College of
    Engineering and Technology
Mumbai, India

Sagar Lahade
Pimpri Chinchwad College of Engineering
Pune, India

Maheshwar D. Jaybhaye
COEP Technological University
Pune, India

Kalyani Mali
University of Kalyani
Kalyani, Nadia, India

Darshan V. Medhane
Savitribai Phule Pune University, MVPS's KBT
    College of Engineering
Nashik, India

Radhika Menon
Savitribai Phule Pune University, Dr. D.Y. Patil
    Institute of Technology
Pimpri, Pune, India

K. Jairam Naik
National Institute of Technology Raipur
Raipur, India

Amin Golzari Oskouei
Azarbaijan Shahid Madani University
Tabriz, Iran
and
University of Tabriz
Tabriz, Iran

Abhimanyu Babar Patil
Pimpri Chinchwad College of Engineering
Pune, India

Niraj Patil
Vishwakarma Institute of Information
    Technology
Pune, India

Tejas Patil
Vishwakarma Institute of Information Technology
Pune, India

K. Rajeswari
Pimpri Chinchwad College of Engineering
Pune, India

Yash U. Ringe
Savitribai Phule Pune University, MVPS's KBT
    College of Engineering
Nashik, India

Rohan Sawant
Savitribai Phule Pune University, Dr. D.Y. Patil
    Institute of Technology
Pimpri, Pune, India

Aakanksha Sharaff
National Institute of Technology Raipur
Raipur, India

Amruta Sudhakar Shinde
Bharati Vidyapeeth's College of Engineering
    for Women
Pune, India

Ankita Shinde
Vishwakarma Institute of Information Technology
Pune, India

Sandeep R. Shinde
Vishwakarma Institute of Technology
Pune, India

Swati V. Shinde
Pimpri Chinchwad College of Engineering
Pune, India

Pratik R. Sonar
Savitribai Phule Pune University, MVPS's KBT
    College of Engineering
Nashik, India

Kavita Sonawane
University of Mumbai, St. Francis Institute of
    Technology
Mumbai, India

Ulligaddala Srinivasarao
Vardhaman College of Engineering Hyderabad
Hyderabad, India

Masood Ismail Tamboli
Vishwakarma Institute of Information
    Technology
Pune, India

Deepali Ujalambkar
Savitribai Phule Pune University, AISSMS
    College of Engineering
Pune, India

Vedmani A. Vaidya
Vishwakarma Institute of Technology
Pune, India

B. Vasavi
Vardhaman College of Engineering
Hyderabad, India

Sushma Vispute
Pimpri Chinchwad College of Engineering
Pune, India

N. Yogeesh
Government First Grade College
Tumkur, India

1 Improved Healthcare Systems Using Artificial Intelligence
Technology and Challenges

Anand Khandare, Apeksha Kamath, Shreya Kakade,
Yumna Khan, and Payal Kunwar
University of Mumbai, Mumbai, India

CONTENTS

1.1 INTRODUCTION

Artificial intelligence (AI) is a comprehensive branch of computer science which is concerned with the automation and performing of processes that simulate the human brain. AI has transfigured the entire healthcare industry. The significant development of computational power and infrastructure, big data, and various machine learning (ML) and deep learning algorithms has resuscitated interest in AI technology and accelerated its incorporation in various sectors [1]. Surveys conducted suggest that the market size of AI in healthcare was globally valued at USD 10.4 billion in 2021 and is expected to scale up at a compound annual growth rate of 38.4% from 2022 to 2030. According to All The Research, this market value is expected to rise to USD 36.25 billion by the year 2026. In India too there has been an increasing involvement towards research to explore the potential applications of AI in healthcare. Investment in AI research is expected to rise to USD 11.78 billion by 2025 and to generate an additional USD 1 trillion by 2023, thereby boosting India's economy. AI and ML have begun to attract attention due to their success in being able to accurately predict diseases in their nascent stage based on historical health datasets. AI and automation in health care using AI have developed rapidly, particularly for early discovery and problem-solving applications [2].

Though the COVID-19 pandemic has caused extensive social and economic disruption, it has disinterred the potential of AI technologies and positively influenced the demand for it. Appen's State of AI 2020 Report has shown that 41% of companies accelerated their AI strategies and use during COVID-19 [3]. As per the study conducted by the National Center for Biotechnology Information in 2020, AI-based algorithms have been able to accurately detect 68% of COVID-19 positive cases in a dataset of patients who had been diagnosed as negative cases by professionals [4].

For fatal diseases such as cancer, heart related diseases, and diabetes, as well as computed tomography, AI can be utilized to find accurate and effective innovations which will result in enhanced cures of patients who are going through adversity with these diseases. It can also search for possible remedies for such problems. The old methodologies of analysis and deducing critical clinical diagnostics have been superseded by switching to AI technology. Algorithms in AI help to manifest systems which are precise enough by gradually learning from data. This proves fruitful as unknown patterns can be recognized which help to produce a variety of treatments and accurate diagnostic results. Implementation of AI/ML technologies in enhancing patient care, reducing machine runtime, and minimizing care expenses have given an impetus to the growth of AI in the healthcare industry. When it comes to this industry, especially in the matter of life and death, the promise of AI to improve health outcomes is interesting and fascinating. As noted by the global tech market advisory firm ABI Research, the AI market in the healthcare and pharmaceutical industries is expected to increase from USD 463 million in 2019 to more than USD 2 billion over the following five years [5]. AI is developing drastically in the healthcare sector and its uses are becoming a reality in many medical fields and specialties (Figure 1.1).

Though there has been commendable progress in the field of AI research, a plethora of lacunas still exist when it comes to actually implementing this technology in healthcare. Some of the factors include lack of awareness, lack of trust in technology, lack of infrastructure, and lack of medical

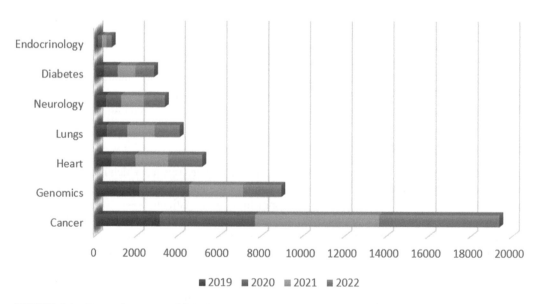

FIGURE 1.1 Research papers published on healthcare in the AI literature. The comparison has been made based on the number of different papers available on the PubMed database.

professionals who are comfortable with technology. This chapter analyzes recent inventions in the domain of AI in healthcare and is aimed at understanding its potential and the risks involved in trying to find solutions to the challenges.

1.2 MOTIVATION

A perfect alliance of increased computer processing speed, a large AI talent pool, and larger data collection libraries has enabled the expeditious development of AI tools and technology within the healthcare sector. AI can use futuristic advanced algorithms to learn features from a large volume of healthcare data, and then utilize the obtained insights to be of service to clinical practice. Also, it can be equipped with learning and self-correcting abilities to improve its accuracy based on feedback. An AI system is capable of assisting physicians by providing up-to-date medical information from journals, textbooks, and clinical practices to inform about proper patient care. Additionally, an AI system can help to reduce diagnostic and therapeutic errors that are inevitable in human clinical practice. Furthermore, an AI system brings out useful information from a large patient population to assist in making real-time inferences for health risk alerts and health outcome prediction.

1.3 LITERATURE REVIEW

Recently, a lot of progress has been made in the field of AI, especially in the healthcare sector, to the point where there have been debates going on as to whether AI will replace medical physicians in the future. AI has great potential in any field owing to its ability to adapt and learn from past mistakes, improvise, and its ability to predict the future when complemented with features like the ability to work in hazardous conditions, perform redundant tasks without fatigue, and all with precision. Currently, the USA is the leading country using AI in healthcare, followed by China and India. In this section, we survey the current AI technologies being used in healthcare or which have the potential for being incorporated in it.

In [6], the authors review the use of AI in healthcare and discuss two major AI categories – ML and natural language processing (NLP) – for performing various healthcare related operations, followed by a survey of applications of AI in stroke care. ML can be used for finding patterns between data and analyzing medical images and other structured data like genetic and electrophysiological (EP) data. NLP can be used for understanding unstructured data primarily in the form of notes and prescriptions to extract information from texts and convert it into a format that can be used by machines ultimately performing ML techniques to gain insights to predict results. For ML, the authors discuss its two major categories: supervised leaning models that include those like support vector machine (SVMs), neural networks (NNs), logistic regression, decision trees, and random forest; and unsupervised learning that works on methods like clustering and principal component analysis (PCA).

In [7], the authors discuss the application of Explainable AI (XAI) methods for elaborating the rationale behind the techniques of AI and the predictions made by it for people, characterized by its increased transparency of processes, liability to stakeholders, result tracing, and overall assistance in improving the performance of models. Nowadays, various AI models exist that are self-explainable and perform predictions quite well, but the challenge with such models is that they put a limit on the models that could be explored and could have otherwise provided better results if not for the lack of explainability of those models. This emphasizes the need for methods like XAI that can explain any AI model. Based on predictions made by a particular AI model, XAI can be used to explain the results and compare them using a clinician's logic. In the case of contradiction, errors can be traced and used for improving the AI model.

In [8], the authors discuss the applications of deep learning in the fields of bioinformatics, medical sensing, imaging, and so on. Unlike traditional NNs, deep learning uses many hidden neurons, which account for its higher quality of abstraction of raw data that helps to perform better operations especially in the field of healthcare by generating features that are usually difficult to elucidate, such as determining DNA or RNA nucleotide sequences and identifying irregularities in cells and tissues. Further, the authors conduct a comparative study of various deep learning architectures along with their pros and cons and discuss the applications of the architecture in healthcare. Though deep learning extensively helps to overcome various complex issues in healthcare, it has some challenges, such as the extensive requirement of data, is highly time-consuming, and can be complex due to its requirement of the optimal estimation of parameters, amongst other things.

In [9], the authors discuss AI in the field of healthcare. They have a particular focus on the healthcare system in India. They discuss the usefulness of AI in helping during the COVID-19 pandemic, which proved to be very useful for contact tracing. It easily assisted in screening the symptoms to identify whether a person was COVID positive or negative. In India there are various healthcare systems. But there is a lack of technology used to enhance the growth of medical treatment. There is a need for proper and accurate data to train AI systems so that they can easily carry out the tasks which are critical for normal human doctors and other medical staff. The government should formulate policies which will be useful for collecting information from patients and the population and to use it to develop a better medical system.

1.4 TECHNOLOGY IN HEALTHCARE

Many industries have been advanced and made efficient using AI, especially healthcare. A previously only imagined industry has now become a truth of everyday life. It is being used by mankind in all possible ways to make life easier. The IT industry is radically evolving and standing out because of AI. The essential division portraying the focus of AI consists in processing detailed facts for managing health systems, automated health records, and the active direction of doctors in their health verdicts [10]. The emerging benefit of AI systems provides a facility to support health professionals, mainly in diagnosis, and which has received mainstream consideration from a research perspective. In the coming years, AI will detect numerous other advanced ailments when it is reorganized with more skill and furnished with more comprehensive facts.

Advancements in healthcare have clear advantages, such as enabling patients to improve their choices and results, and also possible subordinate advantages, such as fewer referrals, cost reduction, and time saving. These could also allow remote data access and endorse employment and maintenance in rural areas [11], in order that this provides a more unbiased scheme of worldwide healthcare in poor-resource situations in high and low-income nations. Some of the technologies of AI that are progressively changing the healthcare industry are mentioned below.

1.4.1 Accurate Cancer Diagnosis

There are AI libraries which are helpful for pathologists. They can precisely diagnose their patients using such tools. The AI library which is useful for them is PathAI. During the diagnosis of a disease like cancer errors are not tolerable; AI helps to overcome such errors and it also provides techniques which can be used in treatment. As a result of advancements taking place in the field of AI, cancer can be detected at an early stage; before the disease becomes established, it can be traced and cured, saving precious life.

1.4.2 Premature Detection of Lethal Blood Diseases

Use of AI to diagnose blood-related diseases which are lethal is of utmost importance, as when done at an early stage enables a timely cure. *Staphylococcus* and other bacteria like *E. coli* in the blood can be easily scanned at a rate which is comparatively faster than manual scanning. This is possible with the use of microscopes which are AI-enhanced [12]. To train the AI to scan and find the harmful bacteria, images of over 25,000 blood samples were used. This helped the model to detect bacteria that were harmful to humans [12]. Machines augmented with the power of AI enabled the identification of the bacteria in samples of blood and, when new samples were provided, the existence of such bacteria was accurately predicted. The accuracy was 95% which helped to reduce the rate of fatality on a large scale.

1.4.3 Customer Service Chatbots

Chatbots are made by using computer technologies like NLP. These chatbots permit patients to raise their doubts regarding appointments, services, payments, etc. Chatbots can help patients with their ailments, medications, and recognize symptoms. This is achievable by the communicating power of chatbots which in turn helps to lower the burden on healthcare professionals.

Chatbots assist in providing solutions of some basic problems, thus allowing healthcare experts to focus on other tasks which are crucial. This use of AI in healthcare is attractive to patients and enables improved cures and treatment, resulting in better outcomes.

1.4.4 Treatment of Odd Diseases

BERG is an AI-based platform founded on biotechnology that works on portraying diseases to increase the pace of developing and producing innovative and advanced vaccines as well as medicines, thus showing a new way forward for healthcare. Interrogative biology and research and development (R&D) are used to enable professionals to innovate and produce robust medical treatments for patients who suffer from rare diseases.

BERG has delivered findings for the therapy of Parkinson's disease [12]. This disease causes disorders in the human brain, giving symptoms like stiffness, vibration, and difficulty in performing easy actions like being steady, walking, or making coordinated movements. The ailments of Parkinson's disease gradually worsen as time passes by. BERG makes use of AI to establish the linkage between a human's body chemicals that were earlier unknown. As a result, the usage of AI is proving to be tremendously helpful in the medical industry and will continue to be so in the coming period.

1.4.5 Automation of Repetitive Jobs

An important role of AI is to automate the performance of repetitive and time-consuming functions in medical and affiliated work. As a result, medical professionals and other workers can utilize the time saved to carry out emergency tasks. An example of this is "Olive". This is a platform based on AI. It mechanizes the process of checking whether judicially unsettled medical claims are eligible; it also conveys the medical data to the respective professionals, etc. Olive can easily incorporate the tools and other necessary software existing in the hospital. Thus, it eliminates the downtime required for integrating a new AI tool.

1.4.6 Handling and Supervision of Medical Records

As the first step in healthcare is to manage, analyze, and compile large amounts of data, such as medical records, data management is the most widely used application of AI and digital automation. Important and costly data may not be visible in a heap of data, but rather be like needles in a haystack. This could lead to huge losses, in billions of dollars, within a year for an industry [12]. Also, if significant data analysis is not done then this can result in the decline of growth in finding new medications and drugs.

Thus, medical firms turn to AI to resist the loss of significant information. AI increases the pace of connecting significant data and extracting useful knowledge which traditionally took many years.

1.4.7 Development of New Medicines

As the healthcare industry advances with technology, the development of new medicines is not far away. Seeking cures and finding drugs are time-consuming and exhaust monitory assets, as trials go on for long periods. The distinct advantage of AI technology is that it helps medical experts to scan previous drugs and utilize them to design a remedy which will be effective against a specific illness. This is how drugs are developed at cheaper cost.

1.4.8 Robot-assisted Surgery

The automation world has been growing rapidly, as has robot-assisted surgery which is gaining admiration nowadays. Various hospitals use robotics which help them and aid them to accomplish tasks which are precision oriented and need monitoring as well as having quick adaptability [13]. This is linked with minimally infectious surgical procedures performed through tiny slits. It is utilized to accomplish medical support like open-heart surgery and tasks that humans cannot accomplish with precision. Mechanical arms, surgical equipment, high-definition video and image capturing cameras, and so on, when integrated into a robot, make it possible to precisely diagnose and cure, resulting in enhanced and efficient surgery.

Operations which are carried out in an environment where AI robots are helping break down complexity and enable tasks to be performed smoothly and increase the recovery rate.

1.4.9 Automation of Medical Image Diagnoses

Applications based on AI make it easy to decode pictures resulting in enhanced analysis. Deep Learning technologies and functionalities are used by AI. This can enhance the speed and accuracy of scanning images obtained from sources like CT scans as well as MRIs. Automated diagnostics of images results in the enhanced accomplishment of tasks by doctors which in turn improves disease recognition in a patient. This tool has proven to be essential to carry on the work of radiologists and similar critical medical task requirements. AI growth in recent years in the field of image processing has been elevated (Table 1.1).

TABLE 1.1

Comparative Study of AI Applications in Healthcare Along with the Technology Used

Healthcare Applications	Technology
Obesity management	NLP, chatbot, SVMs, neuro-fuzzy model, artificial neural network (ANN)
Cardiac arrhythmia	Supervised ML, convolutional neural network (CNN), ANN
Renal disease	CNN, ANN, Random Forest (RF), multivariate logistic regression
Diabetes	Hierarchical recurrent neural network (HRNN), ANN, SVM, evolutionary algorithms
Chemotherapy	Reinforcement learning, supervised ML
Thyroid diseases	SVM, CNN, Koios DS
General surgery	ML, robotics
Prediction of ovarian cancer	Neural networks, supervised ML, Deep Convolutional Neural Network (DCNNs)
In vitro fertilization (IVF)	Multilayer perceptron (MLP), CNN, SVM, Bayesian networks (BNS)
Prediction of male infertility	AutoML Vision, SVM, MLP
Retinopathy	RetmarkerDR, IDx-DR, Eye Nuk
Alzheimer diagnosis	RestNet18, CapsNets, deep neural networks (DNNs)
Identification of genetic patterns and disorders	DeepVariant, domain adaptive neural networks (DANNs), SpliceAI
Mental health	NLP, DL, supervised ML
Drug discovery and design	Machine learning

1.5 CHALLENGES AND SOLUTIONS

Despite the extensive research and progress, the implementation of AI to solve real world problems is often difficult. It often poses ethical issues that need to be addressed [14]. Though these challenges should not be considered as a reason to totally discard AI technologies [15]. Rather, there is a need to understand the risks and challenges involved in the incorporation of AI in healthcare and to try to bridge the gap existing there (Figure 1.2).

1.5.1 AI Bias

AI algorithms require a large amount of data during training. This data basically determines how the model will perform on unseen data. Hence, the data provided should be representative of the target population and should not be biased in that they must represent all classes equally, which for example has been demonstrated in an algorithm for auditory tests for neurological diseases by Winterlight Labs, a Canadian Company [27]. This registered the way a person spoke and analyzed the data to determine the early stage of Alzheimer's disease. The majority of the data collected

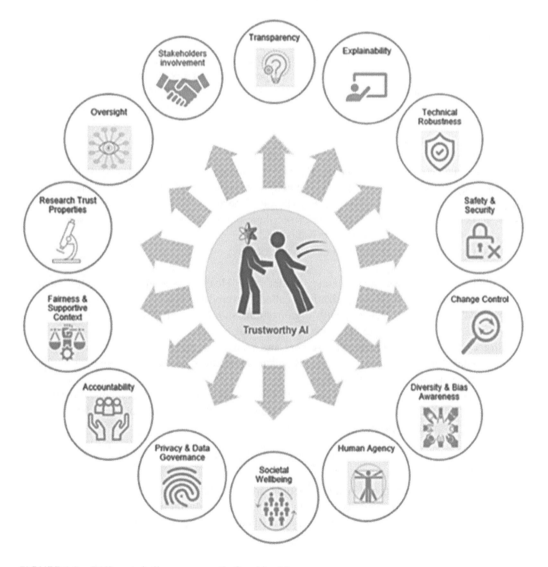

FIGURE 1.2 Different challenges currently faced by AI.

corresponded to native English speakers. The accuracy obtained was greater than 90%; however, the test produced inaccurate results for non-native English. The pauses and mispronunciations were identified as symptoms of the disease. Although the notion of bias is complex, humans too have prejudiced thinking. This necessitates the design of ethical AI systems that help to identify human biases and lead to outcomes that are fair and free from any kind of discrimination.

Some ways in which it is possible to reduce AI bias are:

1. Narrowing the problem definition: This can reduce the number of labels required in the dataset since information that is too general would make it difficult to develop a clear framework for examining the research problem.
2. Improve diversity: This is necessary to ensure that the data represents the maximal diversity of the population in order to include any minority groups that might be left out due to social discrimination such as poor access to healthcare facilities.
3. Understand the end users: This is necessary in order to acknowledge the fact that people come from different backgrounds and hence have different experiences. It is important to anticipate how different people would interact with the technology.

1.5.2 Personal Security

Data concerning the health of a patient is sensitive information since it is linked with the physical and mental well-being of the patient and his or her personal autonomy. Unauthorized disclosure or misuse of healthcare data could lead to a breach of the fundamental rights of patients and psychologically or physically harm them. Since AI models require a huge amount of data for their training there is a possibility that such data collected from patients could be used without their consent. Examples depicting present concerns about privacy breaches include the recent case of Cambridge Analytica, a British consulting firm that used personal data which was collected by Facebook for political advertising, and the case of the Royal Free London NHS Foundation trust that shared the private data of its patients for the development of a medical application without obtaining the patients' consent explicitly [16]. Hence, it is an ethical necessity to respect the confidentiality of patients and ensure that consent is obtained from them before any health interventions as well as before accessing, sharing, or using their private data.

Some ways in which it is possible to ensure security are:

1. Establishing business agreements: Under the Health Insurance Portability and Accountability Act, 1996, organizations called "covered entities" are required to protect patients' health data. Hence, health organizations should establish business agreements with AI vendors that ensure the protection and security of data.
2. Protection of data resources: The servers and computers that store and retrieve patient health data for research purposes must be secure and data should solely remain within the concerned organization's jurisdiction.
3. Data anonymization: Data should be shared with researchers and developers only after they have been properly de-identified. The entities using the data must be bound under ethical laws to prevent attempts at re-identification or reselling.

1.5.3 Transparency

AI is a relatively new term, and a lot of people are still skeptical about its applicability and incorporation in real world scenarios [17]. In healthcare as well, though the performance of AI in the investigation of therapeutic cloning and medical danger estimation has been extremely promising, it is hard to expound the model since the software may learn and evolve over time, quickly repealing algorithmic explanations. This increases problems in the medical world, where clarity and the capability to describe scientific verdicts are very important. Lack of transparency can reduce the credibility of AI models in healthcare. In some cases, AI vendors include clauses in the contract which solely hold the clinical professional responsible in the case of any errors. The burden of lack of knowledge in detecting problems is entirely placed on clinicians, patients, or other consumers, making the former liable and consumers and patients vulnerable. It is very crucial for medical professionals to understand the system before using it since they will be held liable if they ignore any system warnings or alerts. Patients should also be involved in the process so as to allow them to make decisions related to their health themselves without duress or any kind of undue pressure.

Transparency in AI can be ensured through:

1. Using XAI: XAI frameworks are tools that try to explain AI. The concept here is to combine simpler and more sophisticated models. The main emphasis of XAI techniques in healthcare and the medical sector is the functional understanding of the model as opposed to algorithmic understanding that is not so complex [18]. Though XAI frameworks tend to be simple, they are not very accurate. Hence, it is necessary to maintain a balance between explainability and sophistication.
2. Involving clinicians in the process: AI algorithms tend to perform well on certain data but perform poorly on some other. If clinicians are educated about concepts like AI bias, they might be able to identify and provide suitable patient data on which the AI algorithms can be implemented.
3. Divulgence and consent: To be able to accept new technology, people must trust the technology, and in order to build trust, transparency has to be ensured. This means that entities who are impacted by the AI system are aware and have provided consent to be a part of an automated system.

1.5.4 DATA FORMATS

Formats in AI application development are mainly image data formats and image annotation formats. The Digital Imaging and Communication in Medicine (DICOM) format is used by most Picture Archiving and Communication Systems (PACS) to store medical images, which can be converted into other formats like PNG or a TIFF, by groups who collect such images. During such conversion, important DICOM metadata are erased [19]. Image annotation storage is not in a single file format. Current commercial imaging systems that obtain image annotations face a major limitation of reuse for AI development as they do not store annotations in the required format [20].

To solve the problem of data formats the DICOM standards can be adopted.

To save regions of interest in an image, there exists an important image annotation format: DICOM segmentation map format [21]. This is a part of the DICOM standard. Image labels, i.e. radiologic findings or diagnoses, and Annotation and Image Markup (AIM) were developed and incorporated recently into the DICOM-SR standard [20]. DICOM can be used to store data from various medical imaging systems including those from CT scans, MRI or ultrasound (Figure 1.3). This was developed for nongraphic annotations. This standard has been supported by a few AI product vendors and PACS. The adoption of these standards for image annotation data storage will enable sharing, such as multicenter sharing, aggregating, and repurposing, for the study of quantitative imaging biomarkers [19].

DICOM Web Viewer (DWV) is a browser-based DICOM image viewer written in JavaScript and HTML [2].

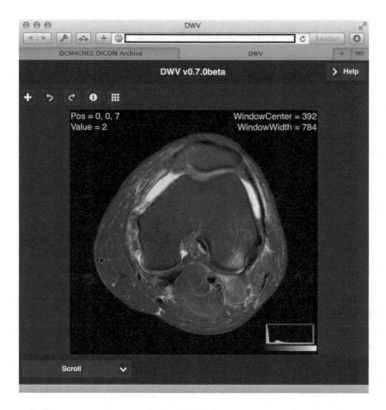

FIGURE 1.3   DICOM web view of Patella (knee cap).

1.5.5   SOCIETAL ACCEPTANCE/HUMAN FACTORS

Generally, many patients show acceptance towards incorporation of new technology and are willing to give it a try. People are open to AI-based diagnosis, but when it differs from that of the doctor, patients tend to start doubting AI technology. Apart from this, medical workers in less developed areas are concerned about whether AI technology will replace them and make them unemployed in the future. Although AI may aid cost saving and reduce the stress that is built into clinics, it may also lead to unemployment by rendering certain jobs redundant and automating them. To date, there are many people who fear that AI in the healthcare sector might lead to unemployment because it has been proved that in certain scenarios it gave better results as compared to humans. This makes more sense when it comes to those healthcare professionals who invested time and money in pursuing a medical education, thereby introducing egalitarian challenges. AI promises to improve several facets of healthcare and medicine but it is still vital to consider the social ramifications of integrating this technology (Figure 1.4 and Table 1.2).

It is understandable that people fear that the development of AI in the healthcare sector might lead to unemployment. But to solve or treat this fear we should keep the following things in mind:

1. If the number of jobs in one sector is decreasing, then at the same time the needs of people are increasing in another sector. To create AI models, we require more and more intelligent brains, i.e., we need people who have knowledge of medicine or technology or both.
2. We need to understand that enhancing the accessibility of data and using them to understand patterns can assist healthcare professionals in taking the right steps towards preventing illnesses at an early stage. Also, real-time data which are characterized by their high velocity can prove to be of great value for informing diagnoses.

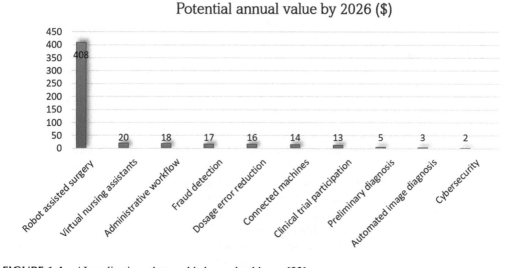

FIGURE 1.4   AI applications that could change healthcare [22].

TABLE 1.2
AI Applications and Its Key Drivers [22]

Application	Key Drivers in Adoption
Robot-assisted surgery	Technological advances in robotic solutions for more types of surgery
Virtual nursing assistants	Increasing pressure caused by medical labor shortages
Administrative workflow	Easier integration with existing technology infrastructure
Fraud detection	Need to address increasingly complex service and payment fraud attempts
Dosage error reduction	Prevalence of medical errors, which leads to tangible penalties
Connected machines	Proliferation of connected machines/devices
Clinical trial participation	Patent cliff; plethora of data; outcomes-driven approach
Preliminary diagnosis	Interoperability/data architecture to enhance accuracy
Automated-image diagnosis	Storage capacity; greater trust in AI technology
Cybersecurity	Increase in breaches; pressure to protect health data

3. Most importantly, we need to remember that AI is just a product developed by humans. It still requires human assistance and surveillance, it may neglect or fail to perceive social factors, it might experience gaps in population information, and it is very susceptible to cyberattacks, owing to the advancement of technology and the rise in instances of extremely proficient and calculated cyberattacks.

From this section we can conclude that, despite the challenges and limitations AI faces, both it and humans are equally important for the development of the healthcare sector in the coming years.

1.6   CONCLUSION AND FUTURE SCOPE

We believe that AI has a paramount role to play in the advancement of healthcare in the future. For example, machine learning, a subset of AI, is the prime mover behind the roll out of precision medicine, which is widely believed to be an indispensable element of the healthcare domain [24, 26]. Although initial efforts at providing diagnosis, disease detection, and treatment guidance are exigent, we expect that AI will eventually master that domain as well. Owing to the rapid advances in AI for medical imaging analysis, there is a possibility that most radiology and pathology images will be examined at some point in the future by a machine. Speech and text recognition are already working for tasks like patient communication and capture of clinical notes, and their usage will escalate gradually [20].

AI plays a crucial role in the domain of biomedicine, not only because of its nonstop advancement, but also due to the connatural multifaceted nature of biomedical glitches and the aptness of AI to resolve such issues. AI has been chasing an extensive series of healthcare requests. In particular, it has been used in signal processing, image processing, and for estimations of variations in functions such as urinary bladder control, epileptic seizures, and stroke predictions. The development of biomedicine involves the innovations emerging from AI. This combination of supply and demand and its relation to development will permit the two fields to be enhanced meaningfully in the foreseeable future, which will eventually ameliorate the life of individuals in society.

The use of AI is associated with a number of moral and social issues pertaining to the lack of transparency and trustworthiness among the general population. Many of these issues are related to those raised by the use of data and healthcare technologies more broadly. A key challenge for the future governance of AI technologies will be ensuring that it is developed and used in a way that is clear and suited to the public interest, whilst driving innovation in the sector.

REFERENCES

1. Senate of Canada. Challenge ahead-integrating robotics, AI and 3D printing technologies into Canada's Healthcare Systems. 2017.
2. Charles Settles, 5 Free DICOM Viewers for Any Practice. October 24, 2019, https://technologyadvice.com/blog/healthcare/5-dicom-viewers/
3. Twisthink. Business disruptions from Covid solved with AI and IOT. https://twisthink.com/how-ai-and-iot-solved-business-disruptions-caused-by-a-global-pandemic/
4. Huang, S., Yang, J, Fong, S. et al. Artificial Intelligence in the diagnosis of COVID-19: Challenges and perspectives, *International Journal of Biological Sciences*. https://www.ncbi.nlm.nih.gov/pmc/articles/PMC8071762/
5. Covid-19 pandemic impact: Global R&D spend for AI in healthcare and pharmaceuticals will increase US$1.5 billion by 2025; ABI Research: The Tech Intelligence Experts. https://www.abiresearch.com/press/covid-19-pandemic-impact-global-rd-spend-ai-healthcare-and-pharmaceuticals-will-increase-us15-billion-2025/
6. Jiang, F., Jiang, Y., Zhi, H., et al. Artificial intelligence in healthcare: past, present and future. *Stroke Vasc Neurol* 2017;2: e000101. doi: 10.1136/svn-2017-000101
7. Pawar, U., O'Shea, D., Rea, S., & O'Reilly, R. (2020). Explainable AI in Healthcare. *2020 International Conference on Cyber Situational Awareness, Data Analytics and Assessment (CyberSA)*. doi: 10.1109/cybersa49311.2020.9139655
8. Ravi, D., Wong, C., Deligianni, F., Berthelot, M., Andreu-Perez, J., Lo, B., & Yang, G.-Z. Deep learning for health informatics. *IEEE J. Biomed. Health Inform* 2017;21(1): 4–21. doi: 10.1109/jbhi.2016.2636665
9. Bajpai, Nirupam, & Wadhwa, Manisha (2021). Artificial Intelligence and Healthcare in India, ICT India Working Paper, No. 43, Columbia University, Earth Institute, Center for Sustainable Development (CSD), New York, NY.
10. Koushik, C.S.N., Choubey, S.B., & Choubey, A. Chapter 7 – Application of virtual reality systems to psychology and cognitive neuroscience research; G.R. Sinha, & J.S. Suri (Eds.), *Computer Modelling, and Cognitive Science JSBT-CI*, Academic Press (2020), pp. 133–147.
11. Greco, L., Percannella, G., Ritrovato, P., et al. Trends in IoT based solutions for health care: moving AI to the edge. *Pattern Recognit Lett* 2020;135: 346–353. doi: 10.1016/j.patrec.2020.05.016
12. Desmond, M. Artificial intelligence in healthcare: AI applications and uses, *Intellipaat Blog*. https://intellipaat.com/blog/artificial-intelligence-in-healthcare/
13. Robotic surgery. *Mayo Clinic*. 2022. https://www.mayoclinic.org/tests-procedures/robotic-surgery/care-at-mayo-clinic/pcc-20394981

14. Komal, G. Sethi, K., Ahmad, N., Rehman, M. B., Ibrahim Dafallaa, H. M. E., & Rashid, M., "Use of Artificial Intelligence in Healthcare Systems: State-of-the-Art Survey," *2021 2nd International Conference on Intelligent Engineering and Management (ICIEM)*, 2021, pp. 243–248. doi: 10.1109/ICIEM51511.2021.9445391

15. Coeckelbergh, M. Health care, capabilities, and AI assistive technologies. *Ethic Theory Moral Prac* 2010;13: 181–190. doi: 10.1007/s10677-009-9186-2

16. Reddy, S., Allan, S., Coghlan, S., & Cooper, P. A governance model for the application of AI in health care. *J Am Med Inform Assoc* 2020 Mar 1;27(3): 491–497. doi: 10.1093/jamia/ocz192. PMID: 31682262; PMCID: PMC7647243.

17. The "inconvenient truth" about AI in healthcare Trishan Panch1,2, Heather Mattie2,3 and Leo Anthony Celi 4,5 npj Digital Medicine 2019;2: 77. doi: 10.1038/s41746-019-0155-4

18. Holzinger, A., Langs, G., Denk, H., Zatloukal, K., & Müller, H. Causability and explainabilty of artificial intelligence in medicine. *Data Min Knowl Discov* 2019;9(4): e1312.

19. Willemink, Martin J., Koszek, Wojciech A., Hardell, Cailin, Wu, Jie, Fleischmann, Dominik, Harvey, Hugh, Folio, Les R., Summers, Ronald M., Rubin, Daniel L., & Lungren, Matthew P. Preparing Medical Imaging Data for Machine Learning PMID: 32068507, PMCID: PMC7104701 NIHMSID: NIHM Radiology. April 2020;295(1): 4–15. Published online 2020 Feb 18. doi: 10.1148/radiol.2020192224 S1582495, www.ncbi.nlm.nih.gov/pmc/articles/PMC7104701/

20. DICOM-Standards-Committee DICOM PS3.3 2019e-Information Object Definitions. NEMA. http://dicom.nema.org/medical/dicom/current/output/chtml/part03/PS3.3.html. Published 2019. [Google Scholar]

21. Fedorov, A., Clunie, D., Ulrich, E., et al. DICOM for quantitative imaging biomarker development: a standards based approach to sharing clinical data and structured PET/CT analysis results in head and neck cancer research. *PeerJ* 2016;4:e2057. [PMC free article] [PubMed] [Google Scholar].

22. Valeriy, Ilchenko. "AI Adoption in Healthcare: 10 Pros and Cons". 07 September 2020 https://www.byteant.com/blog/ai-adoption-in-healthcare-10-pros-and-cons/

23. Davenport, T., & Kalakota, R. The potential for artificial intelligence in healthcare. *Future Health J* 2019;6(2): 94–98. doi: 10.7861/futurehosp.6-2-94

24. Hasani, N., Morris, M. A., Rhamim, A., Summers, R. M., Jones, E., Siegel, E., & Saboury, B. Trustworthy artificial intelligence in medical imaging. *PET Clinics* 2022;17(1): 1–12.

25. Greco, L., Percannella, G., Ritrovato, P., et al. Trends in IoT based solutions for health care: moving AI to the edge; *Pattern Recognit Lett* 2020;135: 346–353. doi: 10.1016/j.patrec.2020.05.016

26. Sunarti, S., et al. Artificial intelligence in healthcare: opportunities and risk for future. *Gac Sanit* 2021;35(S1): S67–S70.

27. Gershgorn, D. If AI is going to be the world's doctor, it needs better textbooks, *Quartz*. September 6, 2018. https://qz.com/1367177/if-ai-is-going-to-be-the-worlds-doctor-it-needs-better-textbooks

2 A Brain MRI Segmentation Method Using Feature Weighting and a Combination of Efficient Visual Features

Amin Golzari Oskouei
Azarbaijan Shahid Madani University, Iran and University of Tabriz, Tabriz, Iran

Mohammad Ali Balafar
University of Tabriz, Tabriz, Iran

Taymaz Akan
USA and Istanbul Topkapi University, Istanbul, Turkey

CONTENTS

2.1 INTRODUCTION: BACKGROUND AND DRIVING FORCES

Brain tumors are one of the most important causes of death in most countries and their prevalence is increasing over time [1, 2]. The position and size of these tumors must be identified in brain MRI images for diagnosis and therapy [1]. A greater understanding of diseases and abnormalities in human organs, including the brain, is being made possible through the development of computer-aided diagnosis systems. Image processing techniques and data mining algorithms are used to analyze brain MRI images in order to identify the precise location, size, and kind of tumor. There has been a lot of recent progress made in this field, but there is still need for improvement due to the overlap between the tissue of healthy and malignant areas and the light intensity distribution, as well as the inherent noise in these images. The area of the brain tumor is preprocessed and segmented in

DOI: 10.1201/9781003359456-2

the first stage of CAD systems; the next step is to choose and extract features and identify the type of disease based on them [3–5].

One of the most crucial phases of image analysis is the preprocessing of brain MRI images, which aims to preserve the sharpness of the boundaries and the details of the brain tissue while minimizing the impact of image noise through the use of techniques like histogram equalization, the application of various filters, and thresholding [6–9].

Image segmentation tries to divide the image into several regions according to predefined criteria [10–13]. These criteria include brightness, type of texture, and color space. Therefore, various methods have been proposed for the segmentation of brain MRI images, including thresholding on image brightness [5, 8, 14], methods based on region growth and active range methods [15], and methods based on unsupervised clustering [9–11, 16–18]. Clustering-based methods are more interesting to researchers due to their simplicity, preserving more image information, time complexity, and easy implementation [12, 19–21].

The k-means [22] algorithm, which groups image pixels into k separate classes, is among the most well-known clustering techniques. This technique has been used to diagnose brain tumors and segment brain MRI images successfully [18]. The fuzzy c-means (FCM) clustering algorithm was also used in tandem with the modified fuzzy segmentation strategy, which is an improved segmentation methodology [23]. In addition, the combination of hierarchical self-organizing neural networks and FCM has been used to improve brain tumor diagnosis and segmentation accuracy [19]. Vector quantization is another clustering method to detect a cancerous mass in these images [24].

However, the problem with existing clustering methods is that they give the same importance to all features [21, 25]; however, the importance of features can be different in each cluster and vary from one testing image to another. So, giving all of the features in each cluster and each image the same weight makes the accuracy much worse [26, 27].

Numerous feature weighting mechanisms have been developed to address this issue. An effective FCM based on the feature-weight entropy regularization approach was proposed in [28] to discover the best feature weights. In [29], a hard clustering method was introduced, in which weights of features are calculated during the clustering procedure.

From 2019 to 2021, for different clustering tasks, some new approaches were introduced. In these methods, the authors used cluster weighting and feature weighting during the clustering process [10, 11, 21, 30]. These methods show good performance for different clustering tasks, especially for image segmentation. These algorithms, however, have a relatively high time complexity.

In most of these methods, only the color features of the image, such as RGB, are used. Using color space alone does not yield a satisfactory result for segmenting MRI images and detecting brain tumors.

Considering the problems of existing algorithms and the need to extract useful features for brain tumor diagnosis, we present an efficient method based on a combination of efficient visual features and FCM clustering. For this purpose, the background area of the images is removed by the new thresholding method, then the useful and efficient features are extracted. We use this new feature space for clustering-based segmentation. The proposed clustering algorithm gives different importance to the extracted features in the segmentation process, which leads to better detection of the tumor region. Finally, to remove some curved edges of the brain and the border between the background and the skull, which are wrongly clustered as tumors, the mode filter is used.

The MRI dataset [31] is used to evaluate and contrast the suggested method with previous clustering techniques. The results show that the proposed segmentation strategy outperformed the competitors.

The remainder of the chapter is as follows. Section 2.2 provides a thorough review of the proposed brain MRI segmentation technique. The experimental findings are provided in Section 2.3. The overall findings and potential next steps are covered in Section 2.4.

2.2   PROPOSED FRAMEWORK

2.2.1   APPROACH OVERVIEW

An overview of the suggested brain MRI segmentation method is shown in Figure 2.1. Preprocessing is the first stage in the segmentation process, as depicted in this figure. The background of the original image is eliminated in this stage. The phase of feature extraction comes next. The suggested clustering method receives the extracted features as input. Post-processing is the last stage.

2.2.2   PREPROCESSING

MRI images contain three general regions: tumor region, non-tumor region, and background. In image segmentation using clustering methods, the background part is recognized as a separate segment, though it does not contain any information. All background pixels have almost constant color intensity. To remove the background part, we use the thresholding technique shown in Relation 2.5.

$$p_{i,j} \text{ is removed if} \begin{cases} p_{i,j} \leq p_{1,1} + 0.02 \\ \quad \text{or} \\ p_{i,j} \leq p_{1,1} - 0.02 \end{cases} \tag{2.1}$$

where $p_{i,j}$ is the ith and jth pixel in normal grayscale color space (range [0, 1]). Figure 2.2 shows the input and output of this thresholding approach.

2.2.3   FEATURE EXTRACTION

The suggested method employs an effective combination of visual features of MRI images, including color and texture, by analyzing the effectiveness of various features used for brain tumor segmentation in MRI images as follows.

1. **Color.** For brain MRI segmentation, the CIELAB and HSV color spaces are employed. The color component of each channel is considered as the specific pixel's color feature. The human visual system interprets differences between colors in CIELAB color space uniformly, hence the distance between any two color components in that space is the same as the difference between those colors as experienced by the human visual system [32]. As a result, the CIELAB color space performs better than other spaces in a variety of machine vision applications [26, 33, 34]. Furthermore, previous research has demonstrated that CIELAB is the appropriate color space for clustering-based segmentation [12, 26, 27, 35].

2. **Texture.** To improve segmentation results, texture components and color information are frequently combined. Results for image segmentation are better when color and texture features are combined than when color features are used alone [36]. In our investigations, the gray-level co-occurrence matrix (GLCM) and the Gabor filter were utilized to identify texture components [37]. These two approaches are very effective and frequently used to extract texture information in a variety of applications [38, 39].

The way the Gabor filter analyzes a picture is similar to how humans perceive images.

The GLCM serves as the method's additional texture feature. Second-order statistics-based GLCM features are simple to use, perform well in terms of time and complexity, and are easy to implement [37]. The spatial correlation of image pixels is taken into account by GLCM [40, 41]. Better segmentation of images can be accomplished with GLCM [42]. After extracting the aforementioned two sets of features for all pixels in the input sample, an 8D feature vector is created and supplied into the clustering stage. This feature vector consists of six color components (HSV and LAB) and two texture components.

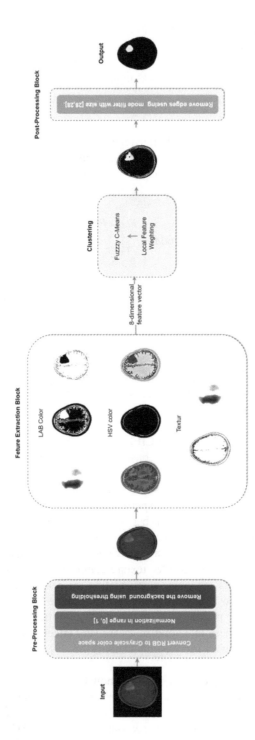

FIGURE 2.1 Diagram of the proposed approach.

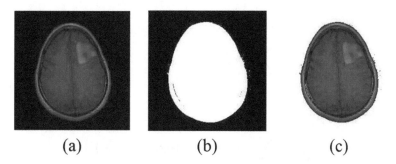

(a)   (b)   (c)

FIGURE 2.2 Preprocessing: (a) input sample, (b) background mask (black pixels are the background area), (c) output image.

2.2.4 Clustering Step

An objective function is required for clustering, which acts as the foundation for setting the clustering algorithm's parameters. The sum of the intra-cluster distances is one of the well-known functions in this area. The Euclidean similarity metric is frequently employed to construct this objective function; however, it is quite noise-sensitive. Additionally, all features are often given the same weight in this criteria.

A new objective function is introduced in the proposed method. This objective function is subjected to the non-Euclidean similarity metric proposed in [29]. Additionally, a certain weight is taken into account for each feature in each cluster. The importance of using a feature weighting Shema is more noticeable in brain MRI segmentation, where different extracted features are usually used.

The objective function employed in the proposed approach is given in Equation (2.2):

$$F(U,C,W) = \sum_{n=1}^{N}\sum_{k=1}^{K} u_{nk}{}^{\alpha} w_{km}^{q}\left(1 - \exp\left(-\gamma_m\left(x_{nm} - c_{km}\right)^2\right)\right) \tag{2.2}$$

In Equation (2.2), N stands for the number of pixels, M for the number of extracted features (in the suggested method, $M = 8$), K for the number of segment areas (tumor and non-tumor area, so $K = 2$), u_{nk} for the degree of membership of the nth pixel to the center of the kth cluster, α for the fuzzification coefficient ($\alpha > 1$), c_{km} for the center of the kth cluster, w_{km} denotes the weight of the mth feature in the kth cluster, q is manually specified (in range $q > 1$ and $q < 0$), and γ_m denotes the inverse of the mth feature's variance. The objective function in Equation (2.3) is assumed to be constrained in the following ways:

$$u_{nk} \in \left[0,1\right], \quad \sum_{k=1}^{K} u_{nk} = 1, \text{ where } \quad 1 \le n \le N \text{ and } 1 \le k \le K; \tag{2.3}$$

$$w_{km} \in \left[0,1\right], \quad \sum_{m=1}^{M} w_{km} = 1 \text{ where } \quad 1 \le k \le K \text{ and } 1 \le m \le M.$$

We can draw the updating policies for u_{nk}, c_{km}, and w_{km} based on (Equations 2.4 to 2.6), respectively:

$$u_{nk} = \cfrac{1}{\sum_{l=1}^{K}\left[\cfrac{\sum_{m=1}^{M} w_{km}^{q}\left(1 - \exp\left(-\gamma_m\left(x_{nm} - c_{km}\right)^2\right)\right)}{\sum_{m=1}^{M} w_{lm}^{q}\left(1 - \exp\left(-\gamma_m\left(x_{nm} - c_{lm}\right)^2\right)\right)}\right]^{\frac{1}{(\alpha-1)}}} \tag{2.4}$$

$$c_{km} = \frac{\sum_{n=1}^{N} u_{nk}{}^{\alpha} \exp\left(-\gamma_m \left(x_{nm} - c_{km}\right)^2\right) x_{nm}}{\sum_{n=1}^{N} u_{nk}{}^{\alpha} \exp\left(-\gamma_m \left(x_{nm} - c_{km}\right)^2\right)} \tag{2.5}$$

$$w_{km} = \frac{1}{\sum_{s=1}^{M} \left[\dfrac{\sum_{n=1}^{N} u_{nk}{}^{\alpha} \left(1 - \exp\left(-\gamma_m \left(x_{nm} - c_{km}\right)^2\right)\right)}{\sum_{n=1}^{N} u_{nk}{}^{\alpha} \left(1 - \exp\left(-\gamma_s \left(x_{ns} - c_{ks}\right)^2\right)\right)}\right]^{\frac{1}{q-1}}} \tag{2.6}$$

Figure 2.3 displays the algorithm's pseudo-code.

Input: Dataset $\chi = \{x_n\}_{n=1}^{N}$, Initial centers $C^{(0)}$, Number of

clusters K (Number of color regions), Number of features M,

Secondary parameters t_{max}, ε, Exponent of feature weight q,

Fuzzy degree α

Output: Membership matrix U, Cluster centers matrix C

1:   set $t = 0$

2:   set $w_{km}^{(0)} = \frac{1}{M}$, $\forall k = 1 \ldots K$, $\forall m = 1 \ldots M$

3:   **repeat**

4:   $t = t + 1$

5:   Update U by (4)

6:   Update C by (5)

7:   Update W by (6)

8:   **until** $\left|F^{(t)} - F^{(t-1)}\right| < \varepsilon$ *or* $t \geq t_{max}$

9:   **return** U, C

FIGURE 2.3   The pseudo-code of the proposed algorithm.

2.2.5 POST-PROCESSING

Some samples of segmented images resulting from the clustering stage are illustrated in Figure 2.4. As shown, some curved edges of the brain and the border between the background and the brain are wrongly clustered as tumors. To remove these edges, we used the mode filter with the size [28, 28]. Figure 2.5 displays the results.

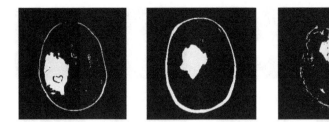

FIGURE 2.4   Some samples of segmented images resulting from the clustering stage.

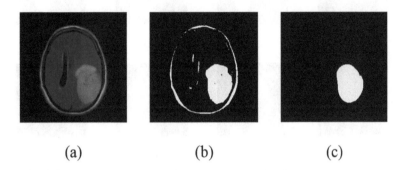

(a)   (b)   (c)

FIGURE 2.5   Post-processing: (a) input image, (b) segmented image, (c) after post-processing.

2.3   EXPERIMENTS

The effectiveness of the suggested technique is assessed in this section. The FCM [43] and the FWCW_FCM [21] were used to compare the results with each other. Parameters ε and t_{max} were set to 10^{-5} and 200, respectively. Both α and q parameters were set to 2. For [21], the required parameters were set as follows: $p_{step} = 0.01$, $p_{init} = 0$, $p_{max} = 0.5$.

2.3.1   DATASET

We utilized the MRI dataset to evaluate the proposed algorithm's performance and compared it with various approaches[1] [44]. The datasets were taken from The Cancer Imaging Archive (TCIA). This is supported by the National Cancer Institute and contains the corresponding medical imaging data for The Cancer Genome Atlas (TCGA) participants. Figure 2.6 displays some of the dataset's images together with their corresponding ground truth.

2.3.2   PERFORMANCE METRICS

Normalized Mutual Information (NMI) [45, 46], Clustering Accuracy (CA) [47, 48], and F-score [49] are the most utilized evaluation metrics in the brain MRI segmentation literature. The higher these values are the better our segmentation results. We also use these metrics to measure the performance of algorithms.

Experiment 1: The Analysis of Extracted Features

In this experiment, to determine the effect of all extracted features, and compare the obtained results using only color space, the performance of the proposed method was evaluated once with all extracted features and once with LAB color space. The statistical results are reported in Table 2.1. Also, the visual segmentation results are shown in Figure 2.7. Post-processing was not applied in this experiment.

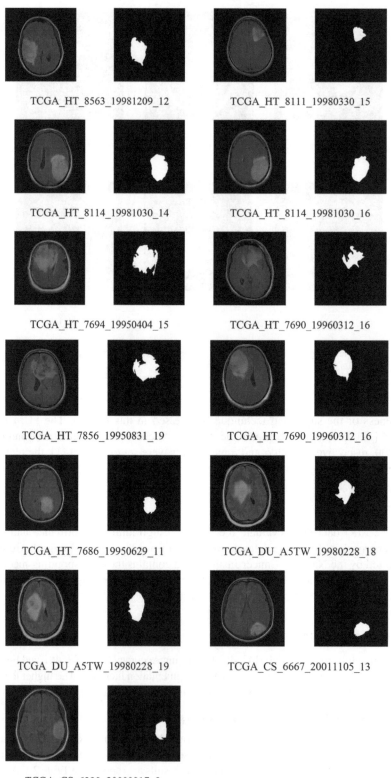

FIGURE 2.6 Magnetic resonance imaging dataset examples with associated ground truth images.

TABLE 2.1

Evaluation of the Suggested Method's Performance Using the LAB Color Space and All of the Obtained Features

Image	Method	Accuracy	F-score	NMI	Runtime
TCGA_CS_6290_20000917_9	LAB	0.9524	0.9749	0.3882	**0.6769**
	All	**0.9543**	**0.9759**	**0.3948**	4.8636
TCGA_CS_6667_20011105_13	LAB	0.9736	0.9863	0.4893	**0.1992**
	All	**0.9792**	**0.9892**	**0.5321**	0.3324
TCGA_DU_A5TW_19980228_18	LAB	0.9501	0.9732	0.4458	**0.3123**
	All	**0.9563**	**0.9766**	**0.4747**	0.6264
TCGA_DU_A5TW_19980228_19	LAB	0.9481	0.9716	0.4850	1.4305
	All	**0.9797**	**0.9891**	**0.6754**	**0.5488**
TCGA_HT_7686_19950629_11	LAB	0.9767	0.9878	0.5552	**0.3668**
	All	**0.9840**	**0.9917**	**0.6230**	0.3759
TCGA_HT_7690_19960312_16	LAB	0.9563	0.9760	0.5698	0.4751
	All	**0.9776**	**0.9879**	**0.6981**	**0.6460**
TCGA_HT_7694_19950404_15	LAB	0.9558	0.9753	0.5680	**0.3956**
	All	**0.9873**	**0.9930**	**0.8077**	0.6254
TCGA_HT_7856_19950831_15	LAB	0.9670	0.9825	0.5524	**0.5588**
	All	**0.9689**	**0.9835**	**0.5641**	0.7995
TCGA_HT_7856_19950831_19	LAB	0.9657	0.9810	0.6450	**0.5802**
	All	**0.9666**	**0.9815**	**0.6543**	0.8542
TCGA_HT_8111_19980330_15	LAB	0.8417	0.9117	0.1811	**0.6859**
	All	**0.9749**	**0.9870**	**0.4251**	1.7588
TCGA_HT_8114_19981030_14	LAB	0.9786	0.9884	0.7033	**0.2320**
	All	**0.9870**	**0.9930**	**0.7762**	0.6089
TCGA_HT_8114_19981030_16	LAB	0.9822	0.9904	0.7193	**0.3011**
	All	**0.9919**	**0.9957**	**0.8318**	0.4857
TCGA_HT_8563_19981209_12	LAB	0.9754	0.9868	0.6360	**0.3738**
	All	**0.9764**	**0.9873**	**0.6456**	0.3919

As shown in Table 2.1 and Figure 2.7, the proposed method has the best performance for all extracted features. For image TCGA_HT_8111_19980330_15, the result of the proposed method with only the CIELAB has less overlap with the main area of the tumor, and the non-tumor area is segmented as a tumor, and due to the low light intensity and the texture of the tumor area, the proposed method with only the CIELAB could not accurately detect the entire tumor area. Also, in the image TCGA_HT_7694_19950404_15, the border of the skull is segmented as a tumor area. This error is mostly due to the high brightness of the tissue surrounding the skull, which in the proposed method with only the CIELAB features, is mistakenly considered to be a part of the tumor. In other images, the overlap percentage of the detected area with the main area is very high. By applying all extracted features in the segmenting process, the accuracy, F-score, and NMI metric rates are improved by an average of 2.09, 1.14, and 16.78% on all testing images. This result demonstrates the effectiveness of the feature combination used in our method.

The execution time is increased by considering all the features. The reason is quite clear. Using the CIELAB color space, the feature space is 3D while using all features, and the feature space is 8D. This increase in dimension causes a high complexity and, as a result, increases the execution time. Although this time has increased, it is negligible because the segmentation accuracy has increased dramatically.

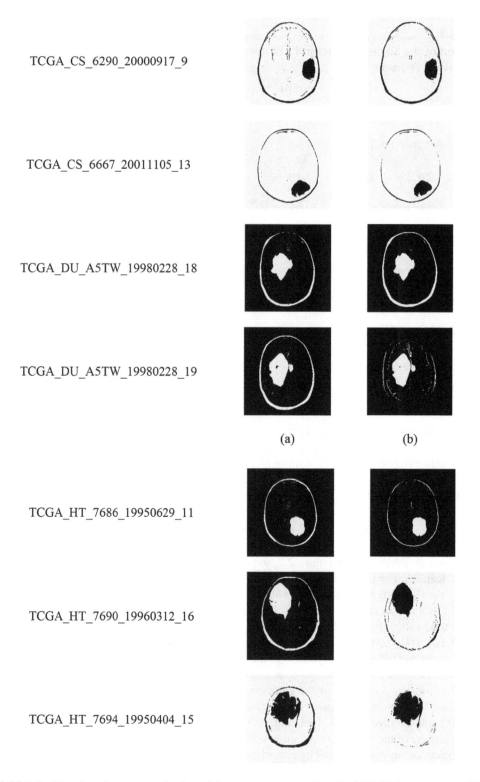

FIGURE 2.7 Visual performance evaluation of the proposed approach with: (a) LAB feature space, (b) all extracted features.

(*Continued*)

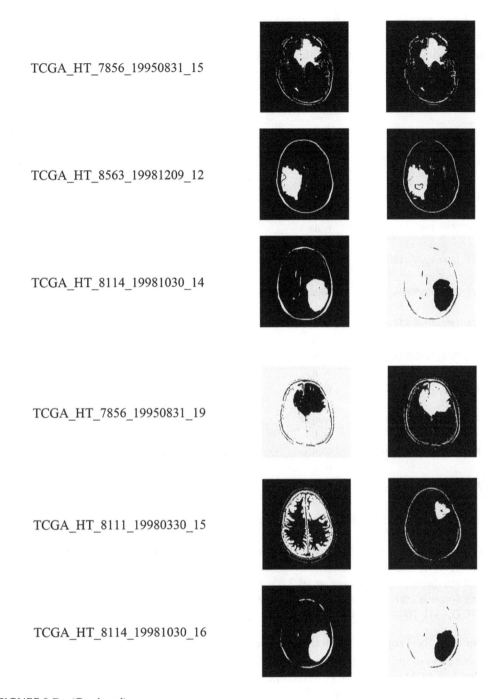

TCGA_HT_7856_19950831_15

TCGA_HT_8563_19981209_12

TCGA_HT_8114_19981030_14

TCGA_HT_7856_19950831_19

TCGA_HT_8111_19980330_15

TCGA_HT_8114_19981030_16

FIGURE 2.7 (Continued)

Experiment 2: The Impact of the Feature Weighting Strategy

In this experiment, the effectiveness of the suggested method was assessed both with and without this technique to ascertain the impact of the feature weighting schema used in our approach. In Table 2.2, the statistical findings are presented. Figure 2.8 also displays the visual segmentation outcomes. This experiment does not use post-processing.

TABLE 2.2

The Suggested Method with and Without Feature Weighting

Image	Method	Accuracy	F-score	NMI	Runtime
TCGA_CS_6290_20000917_9	Without	0.9541	0.9758	0.3808	**0.4613**
	With	**0.9543**	**0.9759**	**0.3948**	4.8636
TCGA_CS_6667_20011105_13	Without	0.9739	0.9864	0.4930	**0.2470**
	With	**0.9792**	**0.9892**	**0.5321**	0.3324
TCGA_DU_A5TW_19980228_18	Without	0.9417	0.9685	0.4332	**0.4635**
	With	**0.9563**	**0.9766**	**0.4747**	0.6264
TCGA_DU_A5TW_19980228_19	Without	0.9468	0.9710	0.4697	**0.3914**
	With	**0.9797**	**0.9891**	**0.6754**	0.5488
TCGA_HT_7686_19950629_11	Without	0.9695	0.9840	0.5044	**0.1893**
	With	**0.9840**	**0.9917**	**0.6230**	0.3759
TCGA_HT_7690_19960312_16	Without	0.9187	0.9544	0.4415	1.1653
	With	**0.9776**	**0.9879**	**0.6981**	**0.6460**
TCGA_HT_7694_19950404_15	Without	0.9400	0.9663	0.4854	0.6246
	With	**0.9873**	**0.9930**	**0.8077**	**0.6254**
TCGA_HT_7856_19950831_15	Without	0.9628	0.9802	0.5253	**0.6431**
	With	**0.9689**	**0.9835**	**0.5641**	0.7995
TCGA_HT_7856_19950831_19	Without	0.9609	0.9783	0.6229	**0.6761**
	With	**0.9666**	**0.9815**	**0.6543**	0.8542
TCGA_HT_8111_19980330_15	Without	0.9283	0.9619	0.3109	**0.6479**
	With	**0.9749**	**0.9870**	**0.4251**	1.7588
TCGA_HT_8114_19981030_14	Without	0.9710	0.9842	0.6486	**0.2688**
	With	**0.9870**	**0.9930**	**0.7762**	0.6089
TCGA_HT_8114_19981030_16	Without	0.9676	0.9825	0.6068	**0.5591**
	With	**0.9919**	**0.9957**	**0.8318**	0.4857
TCGA_HT_8563_19981209_12	Without	0.9702	0.9840	0.6013	**0.3228**
	With	**0.9764**	**0.9873**	**0.6456**	0.3919

The proposed method provides significantly better outcomes with the feature weighting schema. When the feature weighting schema is used, the accuracy, F-score, and NMI metric rates of the suggested approach rise by an average of 2.25, 1.25, and 24.2% on all tested images. The feature weighting formula performs better in some images than others, such as TCGA HT 8114 19981030 16 and TCGA HT 7694 19950404 15.

Experiment 3: The Proposed Method vs. Other Methods

The effectiveness of the suggested strategy was compared with that of other popular clustering techniques (such as FCM and FWCW FCM) in this section. Table 2.3 displays the quantitative assessment of the compared methods. Figure 2.9 depicts a visual analysis of the comparing methods.

The proposed method performs well for all images except 7690_19960312_16, 7694_19950404_15, 8114_19981030_14, and 8563_19981209_12, as shown in Table 2.3 and Figure 2.9. On all testing photos, the accuracy, F-score, and NMI metric rates of the suggested approach average 96.25, 97.96, and 52.52%. The outcomes demonstrate that the suggested algorithm performs better than existing approaches in this area. On all testing images, the accuracy, F-score, and NMI metric rates of the proposed technique are superior to FCM on average by 4.33, 2.40, and 14.27%, and superior to FWCW FCM on average by 5.63, 3.16, and 19.82%.

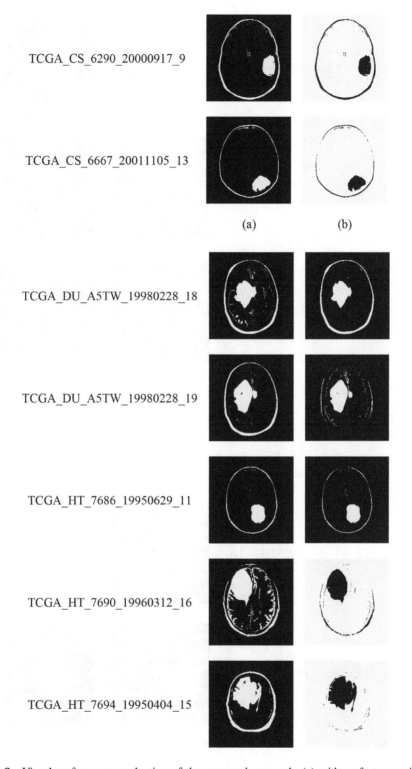

FIGURE 2.8 Visual performance evaluation of the proposed approach: (a) without feature weighting, (b) with feature weighting.

(*Continued*)

TCGA_HT_7856_19950831_15

TCGA_HT_7856_19950831_19

TCGA_HT_8111_19980330_15

TCGA_HT_8114_19981030_14

TCGA_HT_8114_19981030_16

TCGA_HT_8563_19981209_12

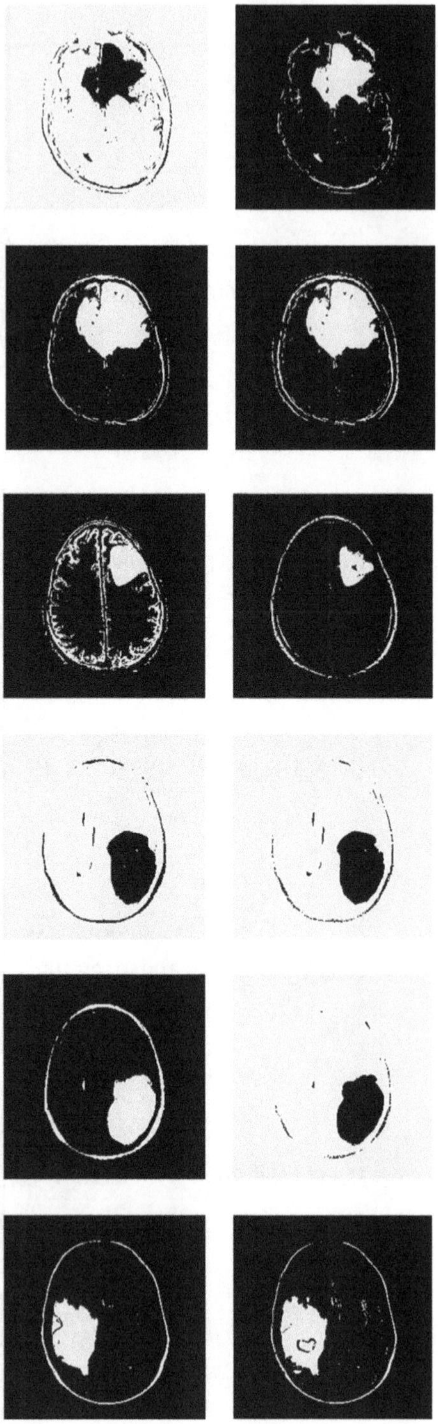

FIGURE 2.8   (Continued)

TABLE 2.3

Performance Comparison of the Suggested Method with Other Cutting-edge Techniques

Image	Method	Accuracy	F-score	NMI	Runtime
TCGA_CS_6290_20000917_9	Our	**0.9543**	**0.9759**	**0.3948**	4.8933
	FCM	0.9248	0.9597	0.3062	21.8726
	FWCW_FCM	0.7921	0.8801	0.1601	**1.7148**
TCGA_CS_6667_20011105_13	Our	**0.9736**	**0.9863**	**0.4893**	**0.3631**
	FCM	0.9694	0.9840	0.4692	36.403
	FWCW_FCM	0.9499	0.9736	0.3507	1.4519
TCGA_DU_A5TW_19980228_18	Our	**0.9501**	**0.9732**	**0.4458**	**0.6328**
	FCM	0.8326	0.9037	0.2414	9.8932
	FWCW_FCM	0.8309	0.9026	0.2415	1.4159
TCGA_DU_A5TW_19980228_19	Our	**0.9468**	**0.9710**	**0.4697**	**0.5496**
	FCM	0.8530	0.9152	0.2907	11.2108
	FWCW_FCM	0.7207	0.8377	0.04140	1.3673
TCGA_HT_7686_19950629_11	Our	**0.9695**	**0.9840**	**0.5044**	**0.3775**
	FCM	0.8633	0.9242	0.2268	11.4227
	FWCW_FCM	0.9369	0.9664	0.3443	1.1964
TCGA_HT_7690_19960312_16	Our	0.9563	0.9760	0.5698	**0.6865**
	FCM	0.9643	0.9805	0.6145	16.9619
	FWCW_FCM	**0.9738**	**0.9857**	**0.6755**	1.433
TCGA_HT_7694_19950404_15	Our	0.9400	0.9663	0.4854	**0.6693**
	FCM	0.9697	0.9832	0.6705	9.9602
	FWCW_FCM	**0.9792**	**0.9885**	**0.7379**	1.2094
TCGA_HT_7856_19950831_15	Our	**0.9689**	**0.9835**	**0.5641**	**0.8172**
	FCM	0.9051	0.9479	0.3349	25.7864
	FWCW_FCM	0.9504	0.9734	0.4560	1.5008
TCGA_HT_7856_19950831_19	Our	**0.9666**	**0.9815**	**0.6543**	**0.9062**
	FCM	0.9621	0.9790	0.6298	12.8267
	FWCW_FCM	0.9515	0.9730	0.5637	1.3891
TCGA_HT_8111_19980330_15	Our	**0.9749**	**0.9870**	**0.4251**	1.863
	FCM	0.8373	0.9091	0.1778	9.0762
	FWCW_FCM	0.8312	0.9053	0.1722	**1.3772**
TCGA_HT_8114_19981030_14	Our	0.9710	0.9842	0.6486	**0.5995**
	FCM	**0.9886**	**0.9939**	**0.7952**	8.4429
	FWCW_FCM	0.9786	0.9884	0.7007	1.4139
TCGA_HT_8114_19981030_16	Our	0.9676	0.9825	0.6068	**0.4708**
	FCM	0.9923	0.9959	0.8391	6.9839
	FWCW_FCM	**0.9784**	**0.9884**	**0.6874**	1.2922
TCGA_HT_8563_19981209_12	Our	**0.9702**	**0.9840**	**0.6013**	**0.3991**
	FCM	0.9273	0.9600	0.4067	42.5038
	FWCW_FCM	0.9666	0.9820	0.5930	1.4643

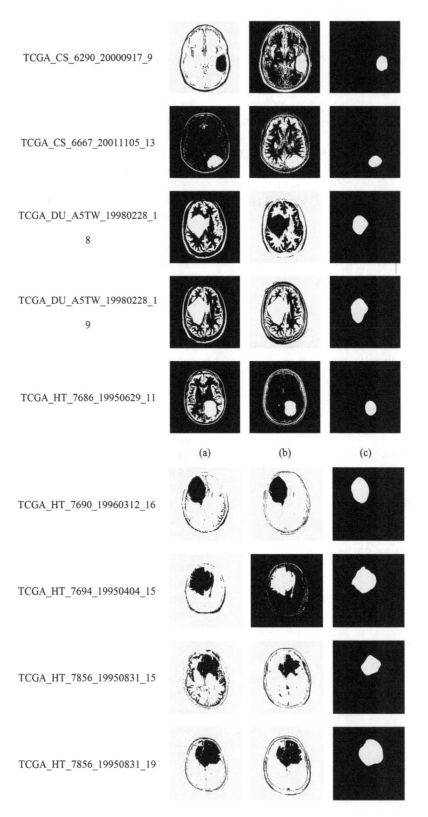

FIGURE 2.9 Visual performance evaluation of the proposed approach with other methods: (a) FCM, (b) FWCW_FCM, and (c) the proposed method.

(*Continued*)

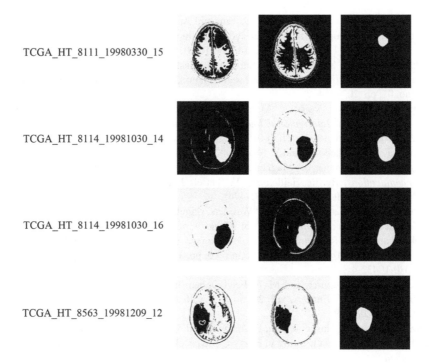

TCGA_HT_8111_19980330_15

TCGA_HT_8114_19981030_14

TCGA_HT_8114_19981030_16

TCGA_HT_8563_19981209_12

FIGURE 2.8   (Continued)

2.4   CONCLUSION

In this research, we have provided an effective technique for identifying brain tumors that combines FCM clustering and effective visual features. For this purpose, the background area of the images was removed by the new thresholding method, then the useful and efficient features were extracted. To obtain better image segmentation, we effectively combined image features such as HSV, CIELAB, and texture. We used this new feature space for clustering-based segmentation. The proposed clustering algorithm gave different importance to the extracted features in the segmentation process, which lead to better detection of the tumor region. Finally, to remove some curved edges of the brain and the border between the background and the skull, which are wrongly clustered as tumors, the mode filter was used. The proposed method was evaluated on the MRI dataset. The accuracy and F-score metric rates of the proposed approach were on average 96.25 and 97.96% on all testing images. In the future, it would be of interest to investigate the application of the proposed method in other medical segmentation images.

NOTE

1   The dataset is available at https://www.kaggle.com/datasets/mateuszbuda/lgg-mri-segmentation

REFERENCES

[1] Z. Liu et al., "Deep learning based brain tumor segmentation: a survey," *Complex & Intelligent Systems*, 2022/07/09 2022, doi: 10.1007/s40747-022-00815-5

[2] S. Das, G. K. Nayak, L. Saba, M. Kalra, J. S. Suri, and S. Saxena, "An artificial intelligence framework and its bias for brain tumor segmentation: A narrative review," *Computers in Biology and Medicine*, vol. 143, p. 105273, 2022/04/01/ 2022, doi: 10.1016/j.compbiomed.2022.105273

[3] E.-S. A. El-Dahshan, H. M. Mohsen, K. Revett, and A.-B. M. Salem, "Computer-aided diagnosis of human brain tumor through MRI: A survey and a new algorithm," *Expert Systems with Applications*, vol. 41, no. 11, pp. 5526–5545, 2014/09/01/ 2014, doi: 10.1016/j.eswa.2014.01.021

[4] M. Balafar, A. Rahman Ramli, M. Iqbal Saripan, S. Mashohor, and R. Mahmud, "Improved fast fuzzy C-mean and its application in medical image segmentation," *Journal of Circuits, Systems, and Computers*, vol. 19, no. 01, pp. 203–214, 2010.

[5] T. Rahkar Farshi and M. Orujpour, "Multi-level image thresholding based on social spider algorithm for global optimization," *International Journal of Information Technology*, vol. 11, no. 4, pp. 713–718, 2019/12/01 2019, doi: 10.1007/s41870-019-00328-4

[6] A. Srivastava, A. Raj Alankrita, and V. Bhateja, "Combination of Wavelet Transform and Morphological Filtering for Enhancement of Magnetic Resonance Images," in *Digital Information Processing and Communications*, Berlin, Heidelberg, V. Snasel, J. Platos, and E. El-Qawasmeh, Eds., 2011// 2011: Springer Berlin Heidelberg, pp. 460–474.

[7] B. Zhang, J. M. Fadili, and J.-L. Starck, "Wavelets, ridgelets, and curvelets for Poisson noise removal," *IEEE Transactions on image processing*, vol. 17, no. 7, pp. 1093–1108, 2008.

[8] T. Rahkar Farshi and R. Demirci, "Multilevel image thresholding with multimodal optimization," *Multimedia Tools and Applications*, vol. 80, no. 10, pp. 15273–15289, 2021/04/01 2021, doi: 10.1007/s11042-020-10432-4

[9] T. Rahkar Farshi, R. Demirci, and M.-R. Feizi-Derakhshi, "Image clustering with optimization algorithms and color space," *Entropy*, vol. 20, no. 4, p. 296, 2018. [Online]. Available: https://www.mdpi.com/1099-4300/20/4/296

[10] A. Golzari Oskouei, M. Hashemzadeh, B. Asheghi, and M. A. Balafar, "CGFFCM: Cluster-weight and Group-local Feature-weight learning in Fuzzy C-Means clustering algorithm for color image segmentation," *Applied Soft Computing*, vol. 113, p. 108005, 2021/12/01/ 2021, doi: 10.1016/j.asoc.2021.108005

[11] A. Golzari Oskouei and M. Hashemzadeh, "CGFFCM: A color image segmentation method based on cluster-weight and feature-weight learning," *Software Impacts*, vol. 11, p. 100228, 2022/02/01/ 2022, doi: 10.1016/j.simpa.2022.100228

[12] T. R. Farshi, J. H. Drake, and E. Özcan, "A multimodal particle swarm optimization-based approach for image segmentation," *Expert Systems with Applications*, vol. 149, p. 113233, 2020/07/01/ 2020, doi: 10.1016/j.eswa.2020.113233

[13] M. Balafar, "Spatial based expectation maximizing (EM)," *Diagnostic Pathology*, vol. 6, no. 1, pp. 1–14, 2011.

[14] T. Rahkar Farshi and A. K. Ardabili, "A hybrid firefly and particle swarm optimization algorithm applied to multilevel image thresholding," *Multimedia Systems*, vol. 27, no. 1, pp. 125–142, 2021/02/01 2021, doi: 10.1007/s00530-020-00716-y

[15] U. Maulik, "Medical image segmentation using genetic algorithms," *IEEE Transactions on information technology in biomedicine*, vol. 13, no. 2, pp. 166–173, 2009.

[16] M. Balafar, A. Rahman Ramli, M. I. Saripan, S. Mashohor, and R. Mahmud, "Medical image segmentation using fuzzy c-mean (FCM) and user specified data," *Journal of Circuits, Systems, and Computers*, vol. 19, no. 01, pp. 1–14, 2010.

[17] M. A. Balafar, A.-R. Ramli, and S. Mashohor, "Brain magnetic resonance image segmentation using novel improvement for expectation maximizing," *Neurosciences Journal*, vol. 16, no. 3, pp. 242–247, 2011.

[18] L.-H. Juang and M.-N. Wu, "MRI brain lesion image detection based on color-converted K-means clustering segmentation," *Measurement*, vol. 43, no. 7, pp. 941–949, 2010.

[19] M. A. Balafar, A. R. Ramli, M. I. Saripan, and S. Mashohor, "Review of brain MRI image segmentation methods," *Artificial Intelligence Review*, vol. 33, no. 3, pp. 261–274, 2010.

[20] L. Feng, H. Li, Y. Gao, and Y. Zhang, "A color image segmentation method based on region salient color and fuzzy C-means algorithm," *Circuits, Systems, and Signal Processing*, vol. 39, no. 2, pp. 586–610, 2020/02/01 2020, doi: 10.1007/s00034-019-01126-w

[21] M. Hashemzadeh, A. Golzari Oskouei, and N. Farajzadeh, "New fuzzy C-means clustering method based on feature-weight and cluster-weight learning," *Applied Soft Computing*, vol. 78, pp. 324–345, 2019/05/01/ 2019, doi: 10.1016/j.asoc.2019.02.038

[22] J. MacQueen, "Some methods for classification and analysis of multivariate observations," in *Proceedings of the Fifth Berkeley Symposium on Mathematical Statistics and Probability*, 1967, vol. 1, no. 14: Oakland, CA, USA., pp. 281–297.

[23] H. Wang and B. Fei, "A modified fuzzy C-means classification method using a multiscale diffusion filtering scheme," *Medical Image Analysis*, vol. 13, no. 2, pp. 193–202, 2009.

[24] H. Kekre, T. Sarode, and K. Raut, "Detection of tumor in MRI using vector quantization segmentation," *International Journal of Engineering Science and Technology*, vol. 2, no. 8, pp. 3753–3757, 2010.

[25] B. A. Pimentel and R. M. C. R. de Souza, "Multivariate Fuzzy C-Means algorithms with weighting," *Neurocomputing*, vol. 174, pp. 946–965, 2016/01/22/2016, doi: 10.1016/j.neucom.2015.10.011

[26] Z. Zhou, X. Zhao, and S. Zhu, "K-harmonic means clustering algorithm using feature weighting for color image segmentation," *Multimedia Tools and Applications* vol. 77, no. 12, pp. 15139–15160, June 01 2018, doi: 10.1007/s11042-017-5096-9

[27] H.-J. Xing and M.-H. Ha, "Further improvements in feature-weighted fuzzy C-means," *Information Sciences*, vol. 267, pp. 1–15, 2014/05/20/ 2014, doi: 10.1016/j.ins.2014.01.033

[28] J. Zhou, L. Chen, C. L. P. Chen, Y. Zhang, and H.-X. Li, "Fuzzy clustering with the entropy of attribute weights," *Neurocomputing*, vol. 198, pp. 125–134, 2016/07/19/2016, doi: 10.1016/j.neucom.2015.09.127

[29] X.-B. Zhi, J.-L. Fan, and F. Zhao, "Robust local feature weighting hard c-means clustering algorithm," *Neurocomputing*, vol. 134, pp. 20–29, 2014/06/25/ 2014, doi: 10.1016/j.neucom.2012.12.074

[30] A. Golzari Oskouei, M. A. Balafar, and C. Motamed, "FKMAWCW: Categorical fuzzy k-modes clustering with automated attribute-weight and cluster-weight learning," *Chaos, Solitons & Fractals*, vol. 153, p. 111494, 2021/12/01/ 2021, doi: 10.1016/j.chaos.2021.111494

[31] P. Arbelaez, M. Maire, C. Fowlkes, and J. Malik, "Contour Detection and Hierarchical Image Segmentation," *IEEE Transactions on Pattern Analysis and Machine Intelligence*, vol. 33, no. 5, pp. 898–916, 2011, doi: 10.1109/TPAMI.2010.161

[32] G. Wyszecki and W. S. Stiles, *Color Science*. Wiley New York, 1982.

[33] K. Wang, L. Li, and J. Zhang, "End-to-end trainable network for superpixel and image segmentation," *Pattern Recognition Letters*, vol. 140, pp. 135–142, 2020/12/01/ 2020, doi: 10.1016/j.patrec.2020.09.016

[34] B. Yuan, L. Han, and H. Yan, "Explore double-opponency and skin color for saliency detection," *Neurocomputing*, 2020/04/25/ 2020, doi: 10.1016/j.neucom.2020.04.089

[35] D.-W. Kim, K. H. Lee, and D. Lee, "A novel initialization scheme for the fuzzy c-means algorithm for color clustering," *Pattern Recognition Letters*, vol. 25, no. 2, pp. 227–237, 2004/01/19/ 2004, doi: 10.1016/j.patrec.2003.10.004

[36] K. Sakthivel, R. Nallusamy, and C. Kavitha, "Color image segmentation using SVM pixel classification image," *World Academy of Science, Engineering and Technology, International Journal of Computer, Electrical, Automation, Control and Information Engineering*, vol. 8, no. 10, pp. 1919–1925, 2015.

[37] A. Humeau-Heurtier, "Texture Feature Extraction Methods: A Survey," *IEEE Access*, vol. 7, pp. 8975–9000, 2019, doi: 10.1109/ACCESS.2018.2890743

[38] M. Gao, H. Chen, S. Zheng, and B. Fang, "Feature fusion and non-negative matrix factorization based active contours for texture segmentation," *Signal Processing*, vol. 159, pp. 104–118, 2019/06/01/ 2019, doi: 10.1016/j.sigpro.2019.01.021

[39] D. Reska and M. Kretowski, "GPU-accelerated image segmentation based on level sets and multiple texture features," *Multimedia Tools and Applications*, 2020/10/03 2020, doi: 10.1007/s11042-020-09911-5

[40] L. Li and Q. An, "An in-depth study of tool wear monitoring technique based on image segmentation and texture analysis," *Measurement*, vol. 79, pp. 44–52, 2016/02/01/ 2016, doi: 10.1016/j.measurement.2015.10.029

[41] C. Sompong and S. Wongthanavasu, "An efficient brain tumor segmentation based on cellular automata and improved tumor-cut algorithm," *Expert Systems with Applications*, vol. 72, pp. 231–244, 2017/04/15/ 2017, doi: 10.1016/j.eswa.2016.10.064

[42] Z. Xing and H. Jia, "Multilevel color image segmentation based on GLCM and improved salp swarm algorithm," *IEEE Access*, vol. 7, pp. 37672–37690, 2019, doi: 10.1109/ACCESS.2019.2904511

[43] J. C. Bezdek, "Objective function clustering," in *Pattern Recognition with Fuzzy Objective Function Algorithms*: Springer, 1981, pp. 43–93.

[44] M. A. Mazurowski, K. Clark, N. M. Czarnek, P. Shamsesfandabadi, K. B. Peters, and A. Saha, "Radiogenomics of lower-grade glioma: algorithmically-assessed tumor shape is associated with tumor genomic subtypes and patient outcomes in a multi-institutional study with The Cancer Genome Atlas data," *Journal of Neuro-Oncology*, vol. 133, no. 1, pp. 27–35, 2017/05/01 2017, doi: 10.1007/s11060-017-2420-1

[45] A. Strehl and J. Ghosh, "Cluster ensembles—a knowledge reuse framework for combining multiple partitions," *Journal of Machine Learning Research*, vol. 3, no. Dec, pp. 583–617, 2002.

[46] A. Golzari Oskouei, M. A. Balafar, and C. Motamed, "EDCWRN: efficient deep clustering with the weight of representations and the help of neighbors," *Applied Intelligence*, 2022/07/05 2022, doi: 10.1007/s10489-022-03895-5

[47] J. C. Bezdek, "A convergence theorem for the fuzzy ISODATA clustering algorithms," *IEEE Transactions on Pattern Analysis and Machine Intelligence*, no. 1, pp. 1–8, 1980.

[48] H. Akramifard, M. Balafar, S. Razavi, and A. R. Ramli, "Emphasis learning, features repetition in width instead of length to improve classification performance: Case study—Alzheimer's disease diagnosis," *Sensors*, vol. 20, no. 3, p. 941, 2020. [Online]. Available: https://www.mdpi.com/1424-8220/20/3/941

[49] M. Aria, E. Nourani, and A. Golzari Oskouei, "ADA-COVID: Adversarial deep domain adaptation-based diagnosis of COVID-19 from lung CT scans using triplet embeddings," *Computational Intelligence and Neuroscience*, vol. 2022, p. 2564022, 2022/02/08 2022, doi: 10.1155/2022/2564022

3 Vision Based Skin Cancer Detection
Various Approaches with a Comparative Study

Kavita Sonawane and Gavin Dsouza
University of Mumbai, Mumbai, India

CONTENTS

3.1 INTRODUCTION: BACKGROUND AND DRIVING FORCES

Melanoma is the difficult-to-treat skin cancer which accounts for nearly 75% of mortalities related to all skin cancer. The estimated five-year survival rate is 99% for patients whose melanomas are detected early; however, survival rate reduce to 63 and 20% when melanomas travel to lymph tissues and finally metastasize to distant organs, respectively. Precise diagnosis of melanomas in the early stage can substantially increase the survival rate.

One of the causative reasons for melanoma is exposure of the skin to ultraviolet radiation. The exposure of the epidermal basal layer often triggers genetic changes (mutations) in pigment-producing melanocytes, leading to aberrant and rampant growth of these cells, finally forming malignant melanoma tumors. Melanomas are mainly formed due to intense and irregular UV exposure which leads to sunburn, particularly in those individuals who are genetically susceptible to the disease.

Commonly, melanomas bear a resemblance to moles which are black or brown in color or can be skin-colored, red, pink, purple, blue, or white. The shape of the mole could be flat, oval, round, or raised in shape, and be less than 6 mm across (approximately the width of a pencil eraser). Moles can appear at the time of birth; however, they might also appear during early or late childhood. Moles which appear in later stages of life need to be checked by a physician.

Once a mole is formed, it usually does not change its size, shape, and color for several years. It is also reported that in a few instances moles may in the end disappear. Generally, most people bear moles, and almost all of them are harmless. But it is very crucial to identify changes in a mole – in terms of its shape, size, and color – which can indicate the onset of a melanoma.

The detection of melanomas by a manual method requires much specialist experience and often comes with inter-observer variations. Therefore, a robust automatic method for the detection of

DOI: 10.1201/9781003359456-3

melanomas will improve the accuracy and efficiency of pathologists. The dermoscopy is a non-invasive skin imaging method, which has been used to enhance the diagnosis of melanomas. Dermoscopy acquires an enlarged and brightened image of a skin region to obtain a clarity of the spots, which in turn improves the visual effect of the skin lesion by eliminating surface reflection.

3.1.1 Problem Formulation and Motivation

Melanoma can be diagnosed earlier by an expert through a visual inspection of pigmented lesions occurring on the surface of skin. However, it can be precisely diagnosed using automated detection with image analysis. Due to the widespread availability of high-resolution cameras, algorithms can definitely improve the ability to screen and distinguish melanoma lesions. Many centers apply effort toward automated analysis. However, a unified, organized, and proportionate effort across institutions has yet to be realized. In addition, low-cost consumer dermatoscope devices for smartphones are beginning to arrive on the market and thus the opportunity for automated dermoscopic assessment algorithms to clearly impact patient care increases.

Melanoma is the deadliest form of skin cancer and accounts for about 75% of deaths associated with skin cancer. These cancerous growths develop when unrepaired DNA damage to skin cells (most often caused by ultraviolet radiation from the sun or tanning beds) triggers mutations (genetic defects) that lead the skin cells to multiply rapidly and form malignant tumors. The estimated five-year survival rate for patients whose melanoma is detected early is about 99 percent. The survival rate falls to 63 percent when the disease reaches the lymph nodes and 20 percent when the disease metastasizes to distant organs.

3.1.1.1 Proposed Solution

The proposed solution aims at helping the dermatologist in diagnosing skin cancer, that is melanoma, with minimal effort and close to the desired accuracy. Along with new machine learning techniques, the effective contribution of the spatial domain bins approach is presented in this chapter.

Imaging techniques like dermoscopy help to eliminates the surface reflection of skin. This aids in the clear visualization of skin levels at depth. Researchers have mentioned that when such techniques are used by expert dermatologists, they provide an improved diagnostic accuracy, as compared to standard photography. This helps in generating the images that require minimal pre-processing.

The proposed system follows two methodologies differentiated by the method of feature extraction. However, the basic block diagram can be represented as in Figure 3.1.

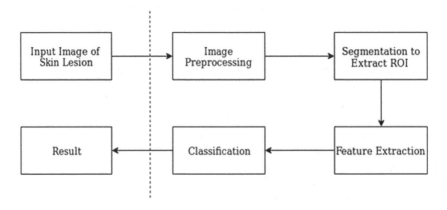

FIGURE 3.1 Block diagram of skin cancer detection and classification.

The proposed system can be explained by four main phases:

1. **Preprocessing**: This will be applied to overcome the problem of noise components in the skin image. The image is enhanced and made ready with the enhanced contents for segmentation to be very easy. Operations such as denoising, hair removal, and deblurring can be applied at this stage.
2. **Segmentation**: Image segmentation can be used effectively to separate the image from its background or foreground image. Mainly it will help here to identify the Region of Interest (ROI). The input at this stage is a preprocessed image, and the output is an image containing only the ROI.
3. **Feature extraction**: The main phase of the system is feature extraction. At this stage all important and desired image contents will be extracted from the image and feature vectors will be generated. These features will be used to represent the image uniquely among all the other images in the database. Thereby, input for this stage is a preprocessed, segmented image and output will be a set of feature vectors to be passed to the next stage. The features include the geometric, color, and texture features of the skin lesion.
4. **Classification**: Classification is carried on in our model using logistic regression. The input for this stage will be the feature sets and output is the classified label, corresponding to an appropriate result, namely the presence of melanoma in the input image.

3.1.1.2 Scope of the Proposed Solution

This is intended to be used by clinical experts and researchers who might want to use it to classify pigmented skin lesion. Clinics can employ the system to provide reports to patients at the earliest opportunity. This will hopefully lead to melanoma being detected at an early stage and thereby reducing the mortality rate. It only classifies melanoma and nevus. It does not include other pigmented skin diseases such as benign keratosis (solar lentigo/seborrheic keratosis, dermatofibroma, and vascular lesion. Basal cell carcinoma, actinic keratosis/Bowen's disease (intraepithelial carcinoma)/lichen planus-like keratosis.

3.1.2 REVIEW OF THE LITERATURE

There are many research contributions reflecting computer-based diagnosis using image processing and analysis to detect melanoma. A conclusive study of all the relevant techniques used in each of the stages is discussed in this section.

The ABCDE rule was used by T. Yamunarani [1] for detecting the usual signs of melanoma:

- **Asymmetry**: Partitioning of the mole or birthmark into two parts, not matching each other.
- **Border**: No clarity of the edges.
- **Color**: The color variations include different shades of skin color and patches of pink, red, white, or blue.
- **Diameter**: The spot size may be larger than the minimum observed values (6 mm) (melanomas may be smaller than this).
- **Evolving**: Mole may have different colors, sizes, or shapes.

Mishra et al. [2] have given an overview of the essential steps for melanoma detection by using dermoscopic images. The process broadly follows four major steps: preprocessing, segmentation, feature extraction, followed by classification. This stage-wise study along with the various contributions from different researchers is presented in the next section.

3.1.2.1   Image Preprocessing and Enhancement

The very first step to be applied is "preprocessing" in order to improve the quality of images by removing the unwanted noise components or other ambiguities in the skin images.

According to Adel et al. [3], the goals of preprocessing can be achieved through three stages: (1) enhancement, (2) restoration, and (3) skin hair removal. Image enhancement refers to bringing out or enhancing the more useful features necessary for our application to further improve the visual presentation of an image along with content enhancement.

Hanon and ALsafy [4] in their paper used contrast enhancement to improve the image visuals so as to obtain more clarity and to achieve better performance. Image borders are sharpened and made more clear, which brings improvement in the segmentation accuracy, thus contributing to the overall accuracy of the model.

In the paper by Kaur and Joshi [5], the color space of images has been converted from RGB to CIELAB in order to measure the color differences effectively. The RGB values must be converted to a device-dependent, absolute color space, which in turn can be converted to the CIELAB color space.

In [3], this step was further categorized as: (1) image scaling, (2) color space transformation, and (3) contrast enhancement. Thereby, images were scaled down to a fixed height and width as per requirements; images from the RGB color space were transformed to CIELAB with CIE-XYZ as an intermediary color space.

i. **Improve Skin Image by Hair Removal**

The presence of thick hairs is considered a common obstruction which misguides segmentation and eventually misleads the result of the classification. Two of the more promising approaches that tackle this challenge are as follows.

In the paper titled "Dull Razor" [6], Lee et al. proposed the following steps to perform hair removal:

1. Locate the dark hair portions by a simple morphological closing operation with a generalized gray scale.
2. Pixels representing hair will be verified by shape as a thin and long structure. These verified pixels will be replaced by a bilinear interpolation.
3. Apply an adaptive median filtering process for obtaining a smoothing effect after step 2.

In the paper by Toossi et al. [7], the proposed hair removal process follows two steps:

1. Apply an adaptive canny edge detector for hair detection and morphological operations for refinement.
2. Repair hair skin texture by a multi-resolution coherence transport inpainting method. This plays a crucial role in the hair removal algorithm.

3.1.2.2   Image Segmentation

Image analysis or pattern recognition can be made simpler by first segmenting the image in the background and foreground by grouping the intensities based on some homogeneity. This can be achieved by different methods.

i. **Segmentation Based on Thresholding**
   - **Simple thresholding**: As the name suggests, this is a very simple technique. Consider one global threshold value as per the desired level of segmentation. While segmenting the image, check if the pixel value is greater than the threshold value, which is assigned one value (if it is white), or another value (if it is black).

     Umbaug et al. [8] used the thresholding parameter of L, where L is the square root of the sum of squares of the RGB component. However, this thresholding method does not account for illumination.

- **Adaptive thresholding**: Alazani et al. [9] implemented segmentation by using adaptive thresholding. The use of a global value as a threshold value will not be appropriate all the time in varying image conditions with different lighting effects in different areas. In such cases, one should go for adaptive thresholding. In this, the algorithm computes the different thresholds of each of the small regions of the same image with varying illumination.

  As seen in Figure 3.2, when the illumination is not constant for the image, adaptive thresholding is more suitable.

- **Otsu's Binarization Method**

  This approach was used by Jain and Pise [10]. The method is named after its inventor, Nobuyuki Otsu. He proposed a segmentation method for implementing thresholding by using the grayscale images to convert in into a binary image. Firstly the image is converted into grayscale. After this, a histogram of the image is obtained. If the gray levels are from 0 to L, we have to decide on t such that we obtain two sets or classes $C0 = \{0,1\ldots,t\}$ and $C1 = \{t+1, t+2,\ldots, L\}$. We have to find t such that we minimize the intra-class variance. This is simply calculated by finding the sum of the variances, multiplied by the weights. As seen in Figure 3.3, the grayscale image is transformed into a binary image by using a cutoff threshold from the histogram.

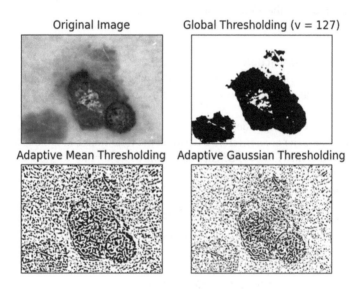

FIGURE 3.2 Comparison of different thresholding methods, sample image: skin lesion.

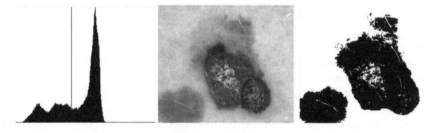

FIGURE 3.3 Binarization using Otsu's method, skin lesion image in the center.

- **K-Means Clustering**

  Saravanan and Sasithra [11] proposed a K-means algorithm for the binarization of the image by setting K to 2. Clustering can be effectively used for classification.

  Let an image of a vector of N measurements describe each image pixel or set of image pixels (i.e., region). The similarity of the measurement vectors and therefore their clustering in the N-dimensional measurement space shows the similarity of the relative or corresponding pixels or pixel regions. This states that clustering in a measurement space may be proved an effective identifier for the similarity of image regions, and can also be used for segmentation as well. K-means, or a generalized version, is one of the wide ranging adaptive texture segmentation approaches. It is simple and equally fast. K-means is initialized from some random selection. In each iteration of the clustering process, each point is assigned to its nearest cluster. Next, the new centroids are computed by averaging the pixels which are part of the same cluster. Cluster centroids are improved in each iteration until they become stable. Based on this we can classify each point into a cluster.

- **Fuzzy C-Means Segmentation**

  Gajbar and Deshpande [12] compared thresholding segmentation with fuzzy C-means segmentation and concluded that the latter is a better algorithm for image segmentation than thresholding as the images are clearer. Using a gray-level co-occurrence matrix (GLCM) they extracted the features from the area obtained by segmenting the image. A feature set is then forwarded to the SVM classifier.

3.1.2.3 Feature Extraction

i. **Geometric Feature Extraction**

The identified geometric features consist of asymmetry, border irregularity, compact index, and diameter. Amran et al. [13] performed feature extraction using various geometric equations:

- Asymmetry: asymmetry Index ➜ $AI = \Delta A \div A * 100$, where A is the area of the total image and ΔA is the area difference between the total image and the lesion area.
- Compact index: measures the density index, the most popular form for estimating obvious 2D objects.
- Compact index ➜ $CI = P24 * A$.

Jain and Pise [10] used the following formulas to extract the features:

- Circularity index: this gives the shape uniformity ➜ $CRC = (4*A)/P2$.
- Irregularity index A: ➜ $IrA = P/A$.
- Irregularity index B: ➜ $IrB = P/GD$.
- Irregularity index C: ➜ $IrC = P*(1/SD – 1/GD)$.
- Irregularity index D: ➜ $IrD = GD – SD$.

Where A is the number of pixels of the skin lesion; B is the number of edge pixels; GD is the greatest diameter or the major axis length, i.e., the length of the largest line passing through the centroid and connecting two boundary points; and SD is the smallest biameter or minor axis length, i.e., the length of the smallest line passing through the centroid and connecting two boundary points.

ii. **Color Feature Extraction**

Ballerini et al. [14] performed color feature extraction by using the mean colors of the skin lesion with their covariance matrix in the RGB color space.

The authors also compared the performance of different color spaces such as RGB, HSV (hue, saturation, value), and CIE Lab. They applied a normalization process to check the performance in these different color spaces. They used a lesion skin image and a healthy skin image from the same patient. After experimenting with the different color spaces, they chose the normalized RGB as it had the best results.

Based on observation with respect to the variations in the color intensities in the lesion area, ad hoc color features were extracted and the ratio computed:

ratio = mean color of region's inner boundary/mean color of region's outer boundary

Assuming the inner region is A and the outer region is B, two ratios were calculated by keeping the ratios of regions A to B as 9:1 and 1:2. This was calculated for all three color spaces HSV, RGB, and CIE.

iii. Color and Texture Feature Extraction

The bins approach is a spatial domain feature extraction technique which was proposed by Kekre and Sonawane [21]. It focuses on color as well as textural features. This novel technique has proved to be best in other medical domain image processing based applications. As per this approach, based on some properties of the image contents, i.e., all image pixels will be segregated into eight bins. This leads to the generation of an eight bin feature vector. Further, textural features in the form of statistical moments are computed for the R, G, and B intensities, owned by all pixels, into each of the eight bins. The bins approach is executed not only in the RGB color space but also in four other color spaces, namely RGB, LXY, L'X'Y, and XYZ.

3.1.2.4 Classification

i. KNN classifier

Ballerini et al. [14] used KNN for the classification of dermoscopy images. The K-NN classifier first finds the K nearest neighbors from a training set then, by further using these K categories, new candidates are labeled; majority voting among the categories of data in the neighborhood is used to decide the class label of any new item.

ii. Support Vector Machine

Celebi et al. [15] performed the classification of dermoscopy images by using a linear SVM kernel. SVMs are popularly known and proven techniques. Derived from statistical theory, it is a kernel based machine learning algorithm.

Compared to other classifiers it has provided a very good, rather balanced performance where the other techniques might have faced the problem of overfitting. The support vector training mainly involves the optimization of a convex cost function. Being a kernel based algorithm, the choice of the appropriate kernel provides a unified framework where it generates different machine learning architectures to support a variety of objectives to be fulfilled – which is one of the advantages of SVM.

iii. Artificial Neural Networks

Ercal et al. [16] and Tu [17] used neural networks to diagnose melanoma from color images. A three-layer neural network was implemented with 14, 7, and 1 neurons in the input, hidden, and output layer. Out of the 14 inputs, 2 were geometric features, i.e., irregularity index and percentage asymmetry; the other 12 were color variances in RGB and their relative chromaticity and color coordinates in different color models.

iv. Convolutional Neural Networks

Convolutional neural networks (CNNs) are also one of the popular deep learning models we are planning to use for training our model. CNN is a class which aids in analyzing visual image datasets. We can see the general block diagram of a CNN in Figure 3.4. Compared to other image classification algorithms, CNN has relatively less focus on pre-processing. It works with smart filters that help in reducing the need of prior knowledge; it also reduces the human effort required for feature designing.

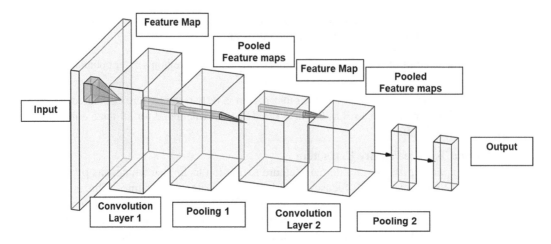

FIGURE 3.4   General block diagram of CNN.

Kwasigroch et al. [18] did a comparative study of three types of CNN. They experimented and tested the performance on the ISIC dataset. The modified VGG19 showed better performance in their studies; however, VGG19 with SVM also showed the same performance. Other research has also reported that ResNet50 gives a much better performance; however, in this particular case, it achieved significantly worse results.

3.1.3 ALGORITHMIC VIEW WITH IMPLEMENTATION DETAILS

Algorithmic View: As depicted in the aforementioned sections above and in Figure 3.5, the system's follows four main phases as pre-processing, segmentation, feature extraction and classification. The algorithmic view of each of them is explained below.

3.1.3.1   Preprocessing

Dermoscopic images are taken in high resolution and good lighting. Hence, the only stage we will be considering for preprocessing is hair removal. We use a simple algorithm to do this:

i. Read color image and convert to grayscale image.
   Convert the RGB color model to grayscale to make operations computationally easier as shown in Equation 3.1:

$$0.30 * R + 0.59 * G + 0.11 * B = \text{pixel value} \tag{3.1}$$

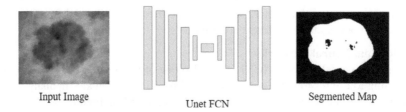

FIGURE 3.5   General flow diagram of FCN Unet.

1. Finding the hair in the input image.
    This step involves applying the dilation and erosion functions and then computing the difference between those that stand out as a morphological gradient.
    The formula for dilation is given by Equation 3.2:

$$(f \oplus b)(x) = \sup\left[f(y) + b(x - y)\right] z \, y \in \mathrm{E} \tag{3.2}$$

The formula for erosion is given by Equation 3.3:

$$(f \ominus b)(x) = \sup\left[f(y) + b(x - y)\right] y \in \mathrm{E} \tag{3.3}$$

where sup is the supremum and inf is the infimum.

2. Isolating the identified hairs.
    Find the blackhat transformations. Closing means a dilation operation followed by erosion. The general forms of blackhat transformations are given by their tophat equivalenting Equation 3.4:

$$T_b(f) = f.b - f \tag{3.4}$$

where "." signifies the closing operation.

3.1.3.2   Segmentation

i. **Otsu's Method**
    This method works quickly when applied to binary segmentation as compared to K-means. However, it works on only one color space (we used grayscale). The algorithm is:
1. Otsu's Based Segmentation:
    In order to minimize the intra-class variance (within class) in Otsu's method we exhaustively search for the threshold. Equation 3.5 defines this as a weighted sum of variances of the two classes:

$$\sigma_w^2(t) = \omega_0(t)\sigma_0^2(t) + \omega_1(t)\sigma_1^2(t) \tag{3.5}$$

where ω_0 and ω_1 are weights and σ_0^2 and σ_1^2 are the variances of the two classes.
The class probabilities are estimated as in Equation 3.6:

$$q_1(t) = \sum_{i=1}^{t} P(i) \quad \text{and} \quad q_2(t) = \sum_{i=t+1}^{l} P(i) \tag{3.6}$$

The class means are given by Equation 3.7:

$$\mu_1 = \sum_{i=1}^{t} \frac{iP(i)}{q_{1(t)}} \quad \text{and} \quad \mu_1 = \sum_{i=t+1}^{l} \frac{iP(i)}{q_{2(t)}} \tag{3.7}$$

2. Generate the binary mask by applying the threshold value.
3. Remove small holes and objects in the binary mask by checking the size of the object if it is less than 10% of the overall size of the object.
4. Apply mask to image.

ii. **K-means**

K-means works on the number of dimensions; as a result we can use it on the RGB image. However, K-means clustering is slower than Otsu's method when used for two clusters. The algorithm is:

1. Find two cluster centers by applying K-means, with K set to 2.
   a. Randomly select "2" cluster centers.
   b. Compute the distance between the centroid of the cluster and each data point.
   c. Now, the data point becomes the member of that if its distance is a minimum of with that cluster among all the cluster centers.
   d. Based on these cluster revisions, now recompute the new cluster center using equation 3.8:

$$v_i = \frac{1}{c_i} \sum_{j=1}^{ci} x_j \qquad (3.8)$$

where c_i represents the number of data points in the ith cluster.

   a. Recompute the distance between the newly obtained cluster centers and each data point.
   b. If no single datapoint is reassigned to the new cluster then stop, else goto step(c).
2. Classify each pixel into either one of the clusters.
3. Generate the binary mask by setting one cluster as the foreground and one as the background.
4. Remove small holes and objects in the binary mask by checking the size of the object if it is less than 10% of the overall size of the object.
5. Apply mask to image.

iii. **Fully Convolutional Network: Unet (FCN)**

The Unet framework has two main paths, one is the expansive path (right side) and the other is the contracting path (left side). The contracting path follows the typical architecture of a convolutional network. In this model, we applied two 3 × 3 convolutions, followed by a rectified linear unit (ReLU) and a 2 × 2 max pooling layer with stride 2 for down sampling. We doubled the number of feature channels at each down sampling step. In the expansive path, upsampling of the feature map was followed by a 2 × 2 convolution ("up-convolution") that divides the number of feature channels, a concatenation with the correspondingly cropped feature map from the contracting path, and two 3 × 3 convolutions, each followed by a ReLU. Because of the loss of border pixels in every convolution cropping is essential. This helps in maintaining the image content. A 1 × 1 convolution is used in the last layer to map each of the 64-component feature vectors to the desired number of classes. In all 23 convolutional layers are used in this network. It is suggested that the tile size be inputted in such a way that the max pooling operations can be applied successfully; in turn it will allow them to achieve the desired output, as in a segmented map.

3.1.3.3 Feature Extraction

i. **Geometric Features**

As discussed in Section 3.2.2 of the literature study of existing techniques, [13] and [10] proposed that the same equations be used to compute the geometric features of the input segmented image (from the ROI).

- A = the number of pixels of the skin lesion
- P = the number of edge pixels

- GD = the greatest diameter or the major axis length, i.e., the length of the largest line passing through the centroid and connecting two boundary points.
- SD = the smallest diameter or minor axis length, i.e., the length of the smallest line passing through the centroid and connecting two boundary points.

With this we have obtained all the ABCD geometric feature components from the input processed and segmented image.

ii. Color and Texture Features

We extract two types of color features; first is the covariance matrix1. The mean colors of the skin lesion and their covariance matrix are given in Equation 3.9:

$$\mu_X = \frac{1}{N}\sum_{i=1}^{N}X_i, \quad C_{XY} = \frac{1}{N}\left[\sum_{i=1}^{N}X_iY_i\right] - \mu_X\mu_y \tag{3.9}$$

$$\Sigma\begin{bmatrix} C_{RR} & C_{RG} & C_{RB} \\ C_{GR} & C_{GG} & C_{GB} \\ C_{BR} & C_{BG} & C_{BB} \end{bmatrix} \tag{3.10}$$

where X, Y are the R/G/B components, as given in Equation 3.10. Each color component is normalized by dividing it from the average of the color component from the same patient's healthy skin image.

For the next color feature, we check the change in the color from the interior of the lesion to the border area.

$$\text{ratio} = \frac{\text{mean color of region } A}{\text{mean color of region } B} \tag{3.11}$$

Using the formula given in Equation 3.11, as proposed by Ballerini et al. [14], two ratios are calculated by keeping the ratios of the regions (diameters) A to B as 9:1 and as 1:2. This is done for the RGB color space.

iii. A Feature Extraction Based on a Novel Bins Approach for Skin Cancer Detection

For our application, we used the eight-bins method having considered the input image in the RGB color model.

ALGORITHM

1. Separate the color image (ROI) into R, G, and B planes and then compute their histograms.
2. Find the CG (center of gravity) for each of the R, G, and B histograms; these mean values will be used as threshold values, e.g.:

r_threshold, b_threshold, and g_threshold.

3. Initialization and formation of eight bins: three planes in two partitions w.r.t. the mean threshold values leads to the generation of eight bin addresses ($2^3 = 8$ bins) from 000 to 111.

We can represent this by (Rp_i, Gp_i, Bp_i), which may range as

$$(0,0,0),(0,0,1),(0,1,0),(0,1,1),(1,0,0),(1,0,1),(1,1,0),(1,1,1).$$

4. Process: for each pixel p in the segmented region, we have to check its R, G, and B component (intensity):
   i. If the red component **is greater than** the r_threshold, then Rp_i will be 1; else 0.
   ii. If the green component **is greater than** the g_threshold, then Gp_i will be 1; else 0.
   iii. If the blue component **is greater than** the b_threshold, then value Bp_i will be 1; else 0.
   iv. Add the pixel to the bin corresponding to (Rp_i, Gp_i, Bp_i).

5. Computation of first three statistical moments for each bin contents is:
   i. Red, green, and blue – the mean for each bin.
   ii. Red, green, and blue – the standard deviation for each bin.
   iii. Red, green, and blue – the skewness for each bin. This generates a feature vector database for all three colors, where the size of each feature vector will be eight components as eight bins.

The above three techniques, that is geometric feature extraction, covariance based color and texture feature extraction, and the bins approach (color and texture features) generate the feature vector databases; these feature spaces will then be further forwarded to classifiers in order to identify the skin image which is either melonama or nevus.

3.1.3.4 Classification

All the above methods use feature extraction as an intermediary step, preceded by preprocessing and segmentation, which produces feature vectors further used for classifying by using multiple classifiers such as SVM, KNN, logistic regression, naive Bayes, and decision trees. The block diagram of the proposed system can be described as shown in Figure 3.6.

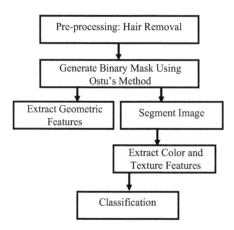

FIGURE 3.6 Classification along with feature extraction.

In this approach we first normalize the data and then test it using the following classifiers.

i. **Logistic Regression**
Logistic regression is a predictive analysis which can be used to perform regression analysis when the dependent variable has binary values. This helps us to analyze and describe the data and specifically the relationship between one dependent binary variable and one or more independent variables. Mathematically it estimates a multiple linear regression and can be defined as the function given in Equation 3.12.
logit(p) is given by:

$$\ln\left(\frac{p}{1-p}\right) = b_0 + b_1 x \qquad (3.12)$$

I. **Naive Bayes**
This classifier mainly deals with the probability of the events occurring and the probability of the events that have already happened. Bayes' theorem can be stated as given in Equation 3.13:

$$P(A \mid B) = P(B \mid A).P(A)P(B) \qquad (3.13)$$

where A and B are events and $P(B) > 0$.
- Probability of event A to be predicted, i.e., event B has already occurred and so can be used as a base or evidence if it is true.
- P(A) is the a priori probability of A, i.e., probability of A without having knowledge of prior events (already happened). We can say its feature value is of an unknown occurrence, i.e., event B.
- P(A|B) is the a posteriori probability of B, i.e., probability of the event after the occurrence is seen or evidence is verified.

Now, with regards to our dataset, we can apply Bayes' theorem as shown in Equation 3.14:

$$P(y \mid x1,\ldots,xn) = (x1 \mid y).P(x2 \mid y)\ldots.P(xn \mid y).P(y)P(x1).P(x2)\ldots.P(xn) \qquad (3.14)$$

II. **K-Nearest Neighbors**
K-nearest neighbors is the most popular classification algorithm in machine learning as discussed in detail in the literature section. It is a supervised learning algorithm.

ALGORITHM

Let **m** be the number of training data samples. Let **p** be an unknown point.

1. Take training data samples to create an array of data points arr[]. Each element of the array represents an entity or the record.
2. for i = 0 to m:
   i. Compute the Euclidian distance between the unknown point under consideration with and array elements.
3. In this step we create the set S of the K smallest distances obtained, where each of these distances corresponds to an already classified data point.
4. Based on the majority, decide on the class label for the data point under consideration.

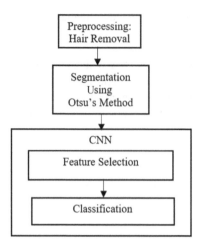

FIGURE 3.7 Feature extraction and classification using CNN.

In order to calculate the clear majority in the case of only two clusters for the data points to be classified correctly, K can be kept as an odd number. In our case two groups are possible (melanoma/nevus). With increasing K, we get more defined boundaries across different classifiers. Increasing the size of the data points in the training set increases the classification accuracy.

III. **SVM**

As explained in the literature section SVM is a supervised machine learning technique which can be used effectively for classification. Using SVM each data item is plotted as a point in an n-dimensional space of n feature vectors. By finding the hyper-plane, SVM spans the feature vectors into two classes very well by differentiating them.

Steps in SVM:

1. Identify the right hyper-plane;
2. Find the margin points;
3. Maximize the margin by changing the hyper-plane.

The second methodology follows preprocessing, segmentation to find the ROI, and uses a CNN for feature extraction and classification of the lesions. The block diagram of the proposed system can be described as shown in Figure 3.7.

As per the initial design plans, the resultant images from the segmentation step will be of size $600 \times 450 \times 3$. This serves as the input layer of the model which has the same size. Following which, the feature selection section of the CNN consists of about four convolution stack layers, each stack containing a convolution and one pooling layer. At the end of the four layers, feature maps are generated which can be flattened and placed as inputs to the classification section of the model. This section consists of a deep neural network consisting of two hidden layers. The output of this section would be a feature vector corresponding to a classification label. As these are preliminary design plans, alterations are to be expected during their implementation, in order to achieve a lower error rate.

3.1.4 RESULTS AND DISCUSSION

• **Comparing the Performance of Classifiers with an Entire Feature Vector Set**
We have experimented regarding the proposed system with extracted feature vectors and also with a CNN approach using a 70:30 train test split. Here the training data consisted of

TABLE 3.1

Results Obtained for the Entire Feature Vector (Train Test Split)

Classifier	Accuracy	Precision	Recall	F1 Score
Logistic Regression	91.03	89	93	91
Naive Bayes	74.68	74	72	73
Decision Tree	84.29	82	85	84
kNN	80.13	78	81	79
Linear SVM	89.42	89	89	89

TABLE 3.2

Results Obtained from Five-fold Cross-validation

Classifier	Accuracy	Precision	Recall	F1 Score
Logistic Regression	89.53	89.17	88.9	88.9
Naive Bayes	73.59	63.91	77.1	69.8
Decision Tree	85.25	83.90	85.5	84.6
kNN	80.50	78.30	80.7	79.4
Linear SVM	88.80	88.40	88.3	88.5

Notes: In Table 3.1 we can observe that among the tested classifiers (Logistic Regression, Naive Bayes, Decision Tree, kNN, and Linear SVM), Logistic Regression gives better results (Recall = 93%, Accuracy = 91.03%, F1 measure = 91%, and Precision = 89%). Even using cross-validation as seen in Table 3.2 we get better results using Logistic Regression (Recall = 99.8%, Accuracy = 89.5%, F1 measure = 88.9% and Precision = 89.17%).

726 images (melanoma: 350, nevus: 376) and the test data consisted of 312 images (melanoma: 147 and nevus: 165). The entire set of feature vectors are forwarded to all the classifiers to check and evaluate their performance with respect to the performance evaluation parameters: accuracy, precision, recall, and f1 measures as given in Equations (19), (20), (21), and (22).

"Recall" signifies the images have been correctly labeled by everyone who has had melanoma. "Precision" is a measure that answers the question: For everyone who has been classified as melanoma, how many actually have it?

In our application, the F1 score is an important performance measure as it takes both false positives and false negatives into account.

With this base performance of Logistic Regression, we have further tried checking the performance and contribution of each feature vector type individually and also with combinations of different feature vectors.

- **Individual Feature Vectors with Logistic Regression Classifier**
- **Performance of Combinations of Feature Vectors**
  Feature Extraction focuses on four main feature vectors, namely Geometric, Covariance, Ad hoc Features, and Eight-bins. As seen in Table 3.3, Geometric Features makes a high contribution to performance, and is used to extract shape information of the lesion. Three major color and texture feature vectors are extracted, i.e., Covariance, Ad hoc, and Bins. We have

TABLE 3.3
Comparison of Individual Feature Vectors

Feature Vector	Accuracy	Precision	Recall
Geometric Features	81.09	78	88
Covariance Matrix	62.82	61	58
Ad hoc Color Features	76.28	77	71
Eight-bins Approach	82.37	79	85

Notes: Comparing all the feature vector types we found that Geometric Features has Recall = 88%, Accuracy = 81.09%, and Precision = 78% and the Eight-bins Approach has Recall = 85%, Accuracy = 82.37%, and Precision = 79%.

TABLE 3.4
Comparison of Combinations of Feature Vectors

Combinations of Feature Vectors	Accuracy	Precision	Recall	F1 Score
Geometric + Covariance	89.10	87	90	89
Geometric + Ad hoc	85.26	80	91	85
Geometric + Eight-bins	90.06	87	93	90
Geometric + Covariance + Ad hoc	90.38	88	93	90
Geometric + Covariance + Eight-bins	90.71	89	92	90
Geometric + Ad hoc + Eight-bins	90.71	88	93	90

Notes: The best combination is Geometric + Ad hoc + Bins (Recall = 93, F1 score = 90, and Accuracy = 90.71); the combination of Geometric + Covariance + Bins gives similar results.

made various combinations of the color and texture features along with the geometric feature and compared their performance on a logistic regression classifier as well as the performance metrics.

This analysis further motivated us to evaluate the contribution of each feature component in each feature vector type.

- **Performance Using a Set of Individual Components of Feature Vectors**
  Another method for finding the most prominent features involves finding the contribution of each feature in their respective feature vectors. This is done by implementing a classifier (Logistic Regression) with only one individual feature at a time.
  We set a threshold of 60% accuracy to use the feature in the reduced feature set. The results are displayed in Tables 3.5 to 3.7.

TABLE 3.5
Individual Components in Geometric Features

crc	ira	irb	lrc	ird
70.83	52.88	**61.86**	55.77	**72.76**

TABLE 3.6

Individual Components in Covariance Matrix Features

c_rg	c_rb	c_bg	c_rr	c_gg	c_bb
54.81	52.88	51.28	52.88	52.88	56.41

TABLE 3.7

Individual Components in Ad hoc Color Features

adhocb1	adhocg1	adhocr1	adhocb2	adhocg2	adhocg3
75.64	75.64	63.46	68.27	71.47	63.14

TABLE 3.8

Individual Components in the First Moment (Mean) of Bins' Features

Bin number	Bin1	Bin2	Bin3	Bin4	Bin5	Bin6	Bin7	Bin8
Red	47.76	52.88	55.13	47.44	**60.58**	56.09	59.29	**60.13**
Blue	52.88	56.09	55.45	52.88	**61.22**	56.41	59.62	55.13
Green	53.21	52.88	55.77	47.44	**61.22**	56.09	59.94	57.69

TABLE 3.9

Individual Components in the Second Moment (Standard Deviation) of Bins' Features

Bin Number	Bin1	Bin2	Bin3	Bin4	Bin5	Bin6	Bin7	Bin8
Red	58.33	54.81	53.85	**62.50**	59.54	**61.29**	**60.90**	66.67
Blue	51.60	52.88	54.17	56.73	59.94	**66.99**	**61.22**	62.50
Green	52.88	52.88	53.53	**64.42**	61.54	**61.54**	60.26	63.78

TABLE 3.10

Individual Components in the Third Moment (Skewness) of Bins' Features

Bin Number	Bin1	Bin2	Bin3	Bin4	Bin5	Bin6	Bin7	Bin8
Red	52.88	**67.31**	53.85	55.13	60.58	**61.22**	53.85	**67.31**
Blue	**64.42**	57.05	51.28	53.53	55.77	**60.69**	58.01	52.88
Green	58.97	59.22	50.96	52.88	56.09	**61.54**	58.33	**68.27**

3.1.4.1   Performance of Eight-bins

From Table 3.5 we can identify that features crc, irb, ird have the best results among the components of the Geometric Features. There are no components in the Covariance Matrix which are above the threshold, as seen in Table 3.6. From Ad hoc Color Features we have maintained all the features as they are all above the threshold, as seen in Table 3.7. For Bins Features, from Tables 3.8 to 3.10 we selected the components 'rmean5', 'bmean5', 'gmean5', 'rmean8', 'rstd4', 'gstd4', 'rstd5',

TABLE 3.11
Performance of CNN

Data	Accuracy	Precision	Recall	F1 Score
Preprocessed Dataset	65.32	64.67	100	79.28
Preprocessed + Image Augmentation	63.95	62.50	100	76.93

'bstd5', 'gstd5', 'rstd6', 'bstd6', 'gstd6', 'rstd7', 'bstd7', 'gstd7', 'rstd8', 'bstd8', 'gstd8', 'bskew1', 'rskew2', 'bskew6', 'gskew6', 'rskew8', and 'gskew8' as they are above the threshold.

Combining the set of features whose individual accuracy is above 60% we get the feature set: { 'crc', 'ir b', 'ird', 'adhocb1', 'adhocg1', 'adhocr1', 'adhocb2', 'adhocg2', 'adhocg3', 'rmean5', 'bmean5', 'gmean5', 'rmean8', 'rstd4', 'gstd4', 'rstd5', 'bstd5', 'gstd5', 'rstd6', 'bstd6', 'gstd6', 'rstd7', 'bstd7', 'gstd7', 'rstd8', 'bstd8', 'gstd8', 'bskew1', 'rskew2', 'bskew6', 'gskew6', 'rskew8', 'gskew8'}.

For the above Feature set on training a logistic regression model we get an accuracy of 84.94%, precision of 82%, recall of 88%, and F1 score of 85%.

3.1.4.2   Performance of CNN

Comparing all our results obtained using different approaches and models in this chapter, we can see that Logistic Regression gives the best results (Table 3.11).

3.2   CONCLUSION, TAKE-AWAYS, AND FUTURE DIRECTIONS

In the course of our research, we have studied various approaches in the field of dermatology, such as hair removal, dermoscopic segmentation, and skin feature extraction for achieving our final goal of melanoma detection [19–21]. All approaches have been experimented with on a common dataset and evaluated using the same set of performance metrics, which are accuracy, precision, recall, and F1 score.

We found that preprocessing for hair removal can be done for a minimal amount of hair, as the hair increases hair removal results in the loss of texture features.

Otsu's segmentation gives better results as compared to Unet on most of the images; however, in some, when there is low contrast, Unet provides better results. Based on this we combined the two masks and kept the centrally located mask.

We completed the implementation of the proposed system with manual feature extraction of four feature vectors, which are Geometric Features, Covariance Matrix Features, Ad hoc Color Features, and Eight-bins Features.

We found that all feature vectors show significant contribution in the classification of melanoma and nevus, especially Geometric Features and Bins Features.

We tried various classifiers such as SVM, K-nearest Neighbours, Logistic Regression, Naive Bayes, and Decision Trees. From these we identified that Logistic Regression gives the best results on the entire set of feature vectors with the following performance scores: Recall = 93%, Accuracy = 91.03%, F1 measure = 91%, and Precision = 89%. This shows a good achievement in the medical domain, especially in skin cancer detection and classification.

REFERENCES

[1] T. Yamunarani, "Analysis of Skin Cancer using ABCD Technique", *International Research Journal of Engineering and Technology*, April 2018.

[2] Nabin K. Mishra and M. Emre Celebi, "An Overview of Melanoma Detection in Dermoscopy Images Using Image Processing and Machine Learning", arXiv.org, 2016.

[3] Azadeh Noori Hoshyar, Adel Al-Jumaily and Afsaneh Noori Hoshyar, "The Beneficial Techniques in Preprocessing Step of Skin Cancer Detection System Comparing", *ResearchGate*, 2013–2014.

[4] Abbas Hanon and Baidaa M. ALsafy, "Early Detection and Classification of Melanoma Skin Cancer", *ResearchGate*, November 2015.

[5] Gurkirat Kaur and Er Kirti Joshi, "Automatic Segmentation of Skin Melanoma Images Using Hybrid Method", *IJARCSSE*, February 2017.

[6] T. Lee, V. Ng, R. Gallagher, A. Coldman, and D. McLcan, "DullRazor software approach to hair removal from images Computers in Biology and Medicine", 199727533543 of SPIE Medical Imaging Image Processing, vol 6914462008 Medicine 199727533543

[7] Mohammad Taghi Bahreyni Toossi, Hamid Reza Pourreza, Hoda Zarel, Mohamad-Hoseyn Sigari, Pouran Layegh, and Abbas Azimi, *An effective hair removal algorithm for dermoscopy images*, Skin Research and Technology, Singapore, 2013.

[8] Scott E. Umbaugh, Randy H. Moss, and William V. Stoecker, Elsevier, "An Automatic Color Segmentation Algorithm with Application to Identification of Skin Tumor Borders", *Computerized Medical Imaging and Graphics*, 1992.

[9] Razl J. Alazani, Abbas Abdulaziz Abdulhameed, and Hussein Majeed Ahmed, "A Robustness Segmentation Approach for Skin Cancer Image Detection Based on an Adaptive Automatic Thresholding Technique", *American Journal of Intelligent Systems*, 2017.

[10] Shivangi Jain and Vandana Jagtap Nitin Pise, *Computer aided Melanoma skin cancer detection using Image Processing*, Elsevier, 2015.

[11] K. Saravanan and S. Sasithra, "Review on Classification Based on Artificial Neural Networks", *IJASA*, 2014.

[12] Amruta M. Gajbar and A. S. Deshpande, Detection and Analysis of Skin Cancer in Skin Lesions by using Segmentation", *International Journal of Advanced Research in Computer Science and Software Engineering*, April 2015.

[13] Amran Hossen Bhuiyan, Ibrahim Azad, and Kamal Uddin, "Image Processing for Skin Cancer Features Extraction", *International Journal of Scientific and Engineering Research*, 2013.

[14] L. Ballerini, R. B. Fisher, B. Aldridge, and J. Rees, "A color and texture based hierarchical K-NN approach to the classification of non-melanoma skin lesions," in *Color Medical Image Analysis*, M. E. Celebi and G. Schaefer, Eds., Netherlands, Springer, 2013.

[15] M. E. Celebi, H. A. Kingravi, B. Uddin, H. Lyatomi, Y. A. Aslandogan, W. V. Stoecker, and R. H. Moss, "A methodological approach to the classification of dermoscopy images," *Computerized Medical Imaging and Graphics*, 2007.

[16] Fikret Ercal, Anurag Chawla, William V. Stoecker, Hsi-Chieh Lee, and Randy H. Moss, *Neural Network Diagnosis of Malignant Melanoma From Color Images*, IEEE, September 1994.

[17] Jack V. Tu, *Advantages and Disadvantages of Using Artificial Neural Networks versus Logistic Regression for Predicting Medical Outcomes*, Elsevier Science, 1996.

[18] Arkadiusz Kwasigroch, Agnieszka Mikołajczyk, and Michał Grochowski, "Deep Neural Networks Approach To Skin Lesions Classification – a comparative analysis", *22nd International Conference on Methods and Models in Automation and Robotics (MMAR)*, 2017.

[19] P. Tschandl, C. Rosendahl, and H. Kittler, "A Large Collection of Multi-Source Dermatoscopic Images of Common Pigmented Skin Lesions", The HAM10000 dataset, *Science Data* 5, 180161 doi: 10.1038/sdata.2018.161, 2018.

[20] C. Noel F. Codella, David Gutman, M. Emre Celebi, Brian Helba, Michael A. Marchetti, Stephen W. Dusza, Aadi Kalloo, Konstantinos Liopyris, Nabin Mishra, Harald Kittler, and Allan Halpern "*Skin Lesion Analysis Toward Melanoma Detection: A Challenge at the 2017 International Symposium on Biomedical Imaging (ISBI), Hosted by the International Skin Imaging Collaboration (ISIC)*", arXiv.org, 2017.

[21] H. B. Kekre and Kavita Sonawane "Comparative study of color histogram-based bins approach in RGB, XYZ, Kekre's LXY and L′X′Y′ color spaces", *International Conference on Circuits, Systems, Communication and Information Technology Applications (CSCITA)*, IEEE 2014.

4 MentoCare
An Improved Mental Healthcare System for the Public

Anand Khandare, Apeksha Kamath, Shreya Kakade,
Yumna Khan, and Payal Kunwar
University of Mumbai, Mumbai, India

CONTENTS

4.1 INTRODUCTION

The World Health Organization (WHO) defines mental health as a "state of well-being in which the individual realizes his or her own abilities, can cope with the normal stresses of life, can work productively and fruitfully, and is able to make a contribution to his or her community" [1]. Therefore, mental health goes far beyond the mere absence of a mental health condition. It spans a wide complex spectrum and each person may experience it differently with variations in levels of distress, symptoms, and other social and cultural outcomes. Mental health conditions include mental disorders and psychological maladies as well as other mental states associated with significant distress, trauma, dysfunction, or risk of self-harm. People who are suffering from mental health issues are more likely to experience morbidity or lower levels of mental happiness. Exposure to unfavorable social, economic, political, and environmental conditions including poverty, violence, inequality, substance abuse, pollution and environmental deprivation can increase people's risk of experiencing mental health disorders [2].

Mental health risks can evince themselves at different stages of life, but those that occur during developmentally significant phases, especially early childhood, are particularly detrimental. For example, authoritarian parenting and physical punishments are known to undermine the health of children. Similarly, bullying can severely affect a child's mental health and lead them to lose their self-confidence. It is observed that symptoms related to emotional disorder are mostly seen in children [3]. This is also responsible for disability among adolescents as well as children. An important and critical stage of human life concerns the last years of childhood and adolescence, wherein changes pertaining to physique, cognition, and psychology take place. This is a matter of concern, and extreme care should be taken so that the complete development of the individual's personality takes place.

As per the 2011 census, about 2.21% of the population of India has certain disabilities, which indicates 26,800,000 people have some impairments. Out of a total of 623,200,000 Indian citizens, specifically the male gender, about 15,000,000 are disabled and out of a total of 587,600,000 who are females about 11,800,000 are disabled. Under the Rights of Persons with Disabilities (RPWD) Act passed in 2016, so far 21 types of disabilities have been identified, of which 19% of people are known to have disabilities related to eyesight and vision, about 19% have auditory impairments, 7% have impediments pertaining to speech, 20% have disabilities which affect mobility, 6% are known to be mentally retarded, 3% are living with some mental illnesses, 8% have multiple disabilities, and around 18% have other kinds of disabilities [4]. Surveys regarding mental health suggest that issues experienced by people with disabilities is five times higher than a normal adult [5]. According to one study, an estimated 17.4 million adults, that is, 32.9% of adults, who were physically disabled, experienced mental health issues frequently, for 14 or more days over the past 30. This is more than the expected use of mental health services, the presence of a chronic disease, or limitations due to their physical disability [6].

The data thus emphasize the need for professionals to provide mental health facilities and to attend to their emotional needs. Despite the urgency, there is a dearth of such programs and facilities that encourage well-being and optimistic emotions [7]. In this respect, modern technology and multimedia devices can be employed to considerably improve the quality of life of people with mental health issues and include them in society. The Internet offers various benefits for users and researchers alike, such as ease of use, greater transparency for individuals, and better access to people. However, existing technical solutions applied so far in such devices only partially fulfill the needs of people with disabilities. Some studies have been made on the usage of the Internet in school and colleges to support the screening, detection, and identification of mental disorders, suggesting that the Internet can play a significant role in this area with adolescents [8]. There has been a rise in the number of people with mental disorders, but there has also been a shortage of online screening or therapy programs that prevent such disorders and promote mental health in adolescents and people with disabilities. This stresses the need for the development of a system which involves routine check-ups for the prevention of mental distress and the promotion of psychological and emotional well-being in both adolescents and people with disabilities by providing a screening assessment that can be conducted by schools, the family, or pediatric physicians prior to consulting psychologists or psychiatrists [10]. Therefore, there is a requirement that such cases should be handled with an approach that is specifically designed for them.

Since, there is a dearth of online screening and mental health assessment tools, especially the ones that cater to the needs of adolescents, and a shortfall in making such tools easy to use for people with disability, we aim to create a web app that focusses on user friendliness and provides a one-stop destination that involves all activities, starting from early mental health screening to consultation with professionals.

This project has these purposes:

1. To implement an improved healthcare system using AI and machine learning (ML);
2. To provide a user-friendly system;
3. To provide the best mental health services available at the fingertips of users;
4. To create awareness among people about mental health through blogs and social forums;
5. To connect patients with experts for diagnosis.

4.2   RELATED WORK

Gathering related information in the form of research papers is an essential step that will help us to understand the perspectives of various authors and the research conducted by them. It helps in deriving insights and generating better ideas. Recently, there has been an increase in research in technology-based applications in the healthcare domain, ranging from physical to mental health conditions. Surveys suggest that consumers are increasingly opting for such applications or at least trying out new health apps. As per an international consumer survey of adults conducted in 2018, about 50% of the participants reported having previously utilized a health app. This percentage suggests an increase in the utilization of health apps by a factor of 3 since the year 2014 [17]. Surveys that particularly focus on mental health apps suggest that around 10% of total participants who come from diverse population groups use them [18, 19]. Health apps seem to be extensively consumer-driven, based on the fact that people discover such apps through social media, web searches, and word of mouth, rather than professional recommendations [20]. Though the current activity time on applications has been found to be high among users, efforts are still needed to increase the consistency of usage [35]. Consequently, mental health professionals are trying to gain insight as to how apps can be incorporated into clinical practice and its usage can be increased. In this respect, the gaps identified can help us to enhance their utilization.

In [9], the authors focus on secondary schools because they think this is a perfect situation for identifying young people undergoing psychological problems such as nervousness, misery, eating disorders, or sleeping disorders. According to their research, current methods for identifying mental health problems highly depend on textual valuations which are very prolonged, time consuming, and, for the school, very difficult for managing such data. So, they propose a prototype for a web app named Artemis-A which uses hi-tech adaptive testing skills that reduce the time of psychological health tests and provide universities with an achievable and easy way for assessing mental issues among students. The purpose of this research was to build a web app with the consultation of shareholders to boost the operators' experience, to conduct serviceability testing, and to confirm the app's strategy and functionalities, and also to check if it is suitable and acceptable in schools. The findings showed that early generation students considered the app to be visually appealing and easy to operate. However, school staff found it difficult to use, so they suggested that a few more functionalities should be added that would offer them more elasticity regarding the visualization of data obtained through assessments.

In [10], the authors propose a system for the detection of psychological health issues in children and teenagers. They focus on a bi-dimensional model which conceives psychological disorders and psychological well-being as two parts of mental health which provide a comprehensive grasp of individuals, unlike a uni-dimensional model that determines mental health based only on the existence or absence of psychological problems. They also proposed a DetectaWeb Project, a web-based assessment for the early detection of mental health issues in children and adolescents and which aims to provide a web-based platform for the screening of both psychological problems and personal strengths and for analyzing the key determinants of mental health issues. The paper focusses on developing a system based only on data samples collected from a region of Spain, hence its external validity is limited. Also, in this system, the assessments are conducted on a LimeSurvey platform which is a web-based platform for the creation and implementation of online surveys. The collected data is then transformed using statistical package for the social sciences (SPSS) software for further analysis. This indicates a lack of user friendliness and a systemic user interface of the application.

In [11], the authors discuss healthcare applications of big data, especially in analysis, future development, and management. The authors feel that if the study of big data supports good design and ease of use then society will benefit. They develop applications as well as software which is hi-tech and can make use of the rapid, low-cost, and up-scaled power of computation for such tasks. According to the authors, big data analytics help to remove slots within data sources which are structured, as well as the ones which are non-structured and available in huge volumes today. Gaps identified include possible healthcare growth and its revolutions. This can be achieved by grouping together three parts: first bioinformatics, which is a growing field for boosting health using IT and informatics; second health informatics; and third analytics, in order to promote treatments. This will help to personalize the treatment process and make it more efficient. In order to obtain useful information for boosting the development of healthcare, methods and technology need to be developed for understanding big data, as it is large by volume, is of different types and structures, and is complex.

In [12], the authors develop a web-based mental health detector to provide possible cures to the user. This solution is user-friendly and makes it easy to use for people of any and every age group. The method used for screening mental health issues makes it easy for the user to obtain possible cures for their mental health issues. It asks certain questions and is based on the algorithm and previous data on which they trained their model; possible cures are then suggested. It can be improved by focusing on people with disabilities. The scope of functionality can be increased so that users also access expert advice and other related benefits.

The ways of achieving pupil's welfare and applying numerous ML algorithms for the prediction of mental health issues based on the statistics of commercial capability among college students was explored in [13]. This paper investigates mental illness in college students admitted to various courses. Thirty of a hundred students testified to having mental disorders, which indicates that college students are more likely to experience depression, trauma, and anxiety as compared to adults [25, 26].

The authors utilized three analytical demonstrating techniques – decision trees (DTs), K-nearest neighbors (KNN), and support vector machine (SVM) – for predicting mental illness based on the structures in the dataset in [22]. The performance metrics indicated that DTs were the most appropriate algorithm for this prediction problem in the current dataset. The drawback was the size of data which was significantly trivial, consisting of 219 rows disturbing the performance of the analytical methods. However, this could be enhanced using the appropriate dataset. The results directed the major chosen by students, and gender as a feature had a noteworthy impact on a pupil's sense of comfort. Thus, DTs achieve better results than KNN and SVM, giving a correctness and F1-score of 0.640 and 0.610 respectively as shown in Table 4.1.

In [14], the authors proposed a web-based application on which people can express their emotional state of mind anonymously, without fear of being judged. The authors believe that Indian society has made it difficult for younger people to express their mental status by continuously neglecting mental health issues. The authors came up with an application which is suitable for all age groups and can be used by anyone. A questionnaire was used to collect data from users. All the collected data were added to the dataset. Further, the data collected help to determine the severity of the user's condition using technology like ML. Based on the severity of the user's condition, appropriate treatments are recommended. Overall, various ML algorithms were used for predicting the severity of the condition. In future, doctors can be recommended to use this application to better treat a user's mental health.

TABLE 4.1

Predictive Table with Evaluation Scores as Obtained from the Experiment

Model	Accuracy	Precision	Recall	F1-score	Area under the ROC curve (AUC)
DT	0.64	0.61	0.62	0.61	0.65
KNN	0.59	0.45	0.56	0.49	0.61
SVM	0.44	0.31	0.25	0.26	0.0

TABLE 4.2

Summary of the Research Conducted within the Domain of Mental Health

Paper Details	Findings	Gaps Identified
[9]	• Co-produced the core mechanisms of the Artemis-A app with shareholders to improve the user interface. • Discovered the satisfactoriness and possibility of using Artemis-A in schools or colleges.	• Visual representation of the results is needed. • Local and national helpline support can be included. • User interface should be user friendly.
[15]	• Survey results obtained from past health reports of the public indicate that people with disabilities are at a higher risk of facing mental health issues compared to people without any impairments. • Symptoms of mental conditions identified were depressive symptoms, frequent mental distress, suicidal tendencies, and substance abuse especially post COVID-19.	• The symptoms experienced by adults who are physically challenged are different as compared to those who are physically normal; this difference and uniqueness of the symptoms highlight the significance of the timely delivery of mental health screening and its treatment, more so considering the COVID-19 pandemic.
[11]	• The visualization and analysis of big data in a user-friendly way will be important for improvement of societal health. • Applications which are hi-tech, and which can make use of rapid and low-cost, up-scaled power of computation for such tasks were developed. • By using big data, the slot within the data sources (i.e. structure and the data which are not structured) can be removed.	• In order to induce a revolution in the field of healthcare there is a requirement to combine health informatics, analytics, and bioinformatics. This will promote personalized processes and efficient treatments. • In order to obtain useful information for boosting the development of healthcare, the methods and technology need to be developed for understanding big data, as this is large by volume, is of different types and structure, and is complex.
[27]	• Surveys provide strong evidence that digital interventions, including apps, can be effective in the mitigation of suicidal ideation. • In cases of depression, these apps have been proved to be moderately effective as compared to taking no action. These apps majorly incorporated cognitive behavioral therapy (CBT), mood monitoring, and mindfulness.	• The safety of personal digital data is a pivotal issue in both public and research contexts. The goal should be to ensure confidentiality, proper handling of personal data, and data security in general. • Studies based on usage of apps among the population suggest low engagement as another reason for the lack of awareness and resistance to acceptability of such apps.
[12]	• Web-based application to track the mental health of its users by suggesting tasks and keeping records of their progress. • Delivers mental health interventions through apps and has the potential to improve self-management, cognition skills training, social support, and symptoms on tracking.	• The system is limited to providing results based on simple mental health questionnaires. • There is no guarantee of the genuineness of the answers provided by respondents. • Consists of only a few features, though many more technologies can be added to increase performance.

4.3 PROPOSED METHODOLOGY

The documentation of measured mental health disorders is problematic due to significant symptom intersection between the disability and the mental health conditions, as well as the complications faced while differentiating between circumstances [21]. The review also highlighted how the research being conducted on app development has been insufficient. As per the studies conducted, the majority of mental health apps available for download are not supported by any evidence-based research and may not be following prescribed treatment guidelines.

Considering these issues, the project aimed to provide early screening, psychological support, mental well-being, and support from mental health experts in adolescents and PWDs by enabling detection and mediation prematurely and preventing future mental disorders, as well as promoting mental well-being.

After studying and gaining knowledge on our topic through the literature survey, we were able to design and think about the proposed methodology. This survey has helped us to go beyond our limits and come up with a solution that can eradicate the gaps identified by us.

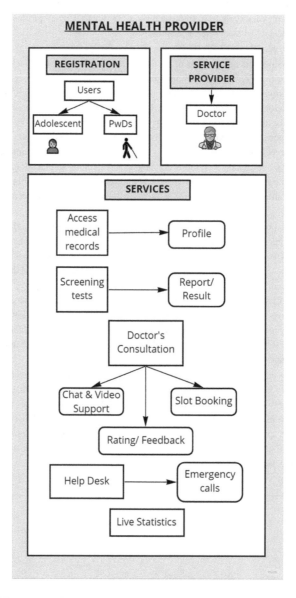

FIGURE 4.1   Flow of the proposed system.

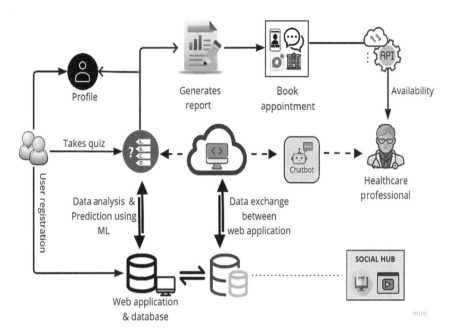

FIGURE 4.2   Architecture of the proposed system.

Our aim is to focus on ML or other AI technologies that could help address a number of challenges by: improving access to quality healthcare; particularly for adolescents and PWDs, keeping in mind low-income groups; addressing the scarcity or non-availability of skilled mental health professionals; improving the access and increasing awareness about various mental health conditions and mental well-being; and enabling the delivery of personalized healthcare at scale, also considering the recent pandemic situation.

Our idea is to design a platform that will provide early screening, psychological support, mental well-being, and support from mental health experts. The aim is to help people who are suffering from stress, anxiety, depression, panic attacks, post-traumatic stress disorders, substance abuse, suicidal ideation, pandemic-induced psychological issues, and other mental health emergencies. It will serve as a lifeline, providing adolescents and PWDs in need of assistance across the country with first-stage advice, counseling, and referrals in various languages as per their convenience.

A web-based portal will be designed using Python frameworks for a smooth user experience. The system will consist of various sections, each with its own importance regarding mental health.

The system will be implemented using HTML, CSS, Bootstrap, and JavaScript for the frontend, and Python Flask for the back-end. We will use application programming interfaces to provide audio–video calls. We also plan to design a chatbot for assistance using Microsoft Azure. We will collect mental health problems related to live data on which we will apply various ML algorithms and predict suggestive features as a precautionary measure to help youngsters. The entire system will be deployed on the cloud server Heroku for ease of access.

4.4   RESULTS AND DISCUSSION

There is a need for further research for developing the cogent and regulated actions of mental health issues among adolescents and PWDs. Concomitant mental health chaos is more prevalent in disabled people compared to normal people [31, 36]. Mental health issues result in reduced working and an urge for help in daily life, be it at a place of residence, at the academy, or at a workplace, including struggles due to the disability itself. These impediments are linked with a decreased quality of life for the person and the family. Consequently, careful evaluation of mental health should be a vital objective to benefit those with disability and should be incorporated into clinical practice.

MentoCare

FIGURE 4.3 User's registration page.

Though there are many apps that exist currently, the evidence base is scarce, especially for adolescents and PWDs. But a well-designed, appropriately tested, evidence-based system would prove to be very effective for the detection of mental health disorders.

Figma is a collaborative interface design tool which helps to brainstorm ideas into virtual reality. This gives a blueprint of the whole system before its execution. Below, we present the prototype of our system that has been designed using Figma.

1. **Users will have hassle-free access to the system**. On the login page, we provide an option for Google translate so that the user can login in their native language conveniently through one-time-password (OTP) verification.
2. **User friendly interface**. Our main focus is to build an application which has a user friendly interface. All age groups should be easily able to use the application.
3. **AI-based mental health predictions and statistics**. When any new user registers, their data will be added to the dataset. Further, we will use this dataset for making predictions and to display live statistics on the screen using ML.
4. **Chatbot**. The chatbot will be designed for basic help, i.e., the basic solution of the user's problem will be provided.
5. **Screening test quiz**. This section will contain various tests for depression, anxiety, etc. Each test will consist of nine questions. The user has to select one of the options and at the end will receive their report.
6. **Report generation**. Based on the test taken by the user, a report will be generated. This report will consist of the score, the test's name, the patient's basic details, and their reference number.
7. **Connect to doctors**. After receiving the auto-generated report, the user can book an appointment. This will be done using API. The user can consult a doctor by live chat, video, and audio call facility.
8. **Appointment booking**. Users can get in touch with doctors by submitting the required details as per their convenience.

9. **Social hub**. This section will consist of various blogs and videos related to mental health. Users can visit this section to get a broader idea about mental health and its symptoms.

10. **Discussion forum**. Feedback is a very important part of any system as it gives us a glimpse of the inside of our user's mind; we can then use the feedback to improve the user experience. In this section users and patients can give feedback on a doctor's consultation and the application's feedback.

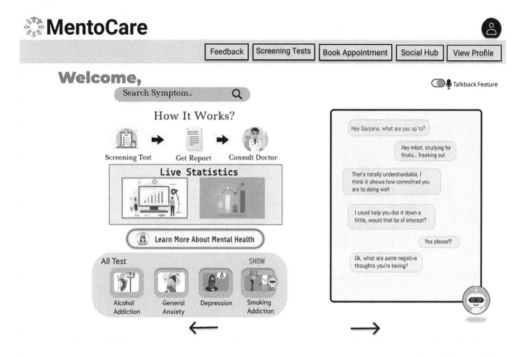

FIGURE 4.4   Home page.

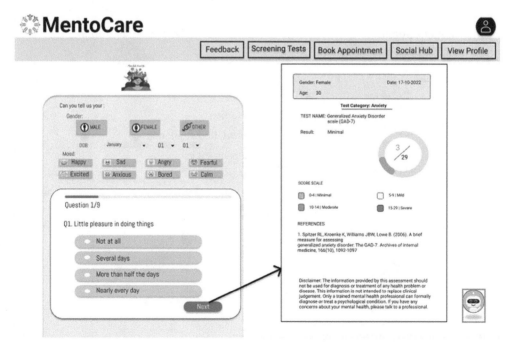

FIGURE 4.5   Screening test page.

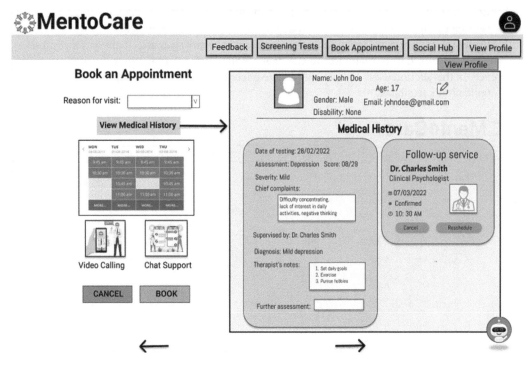

FIGURE 4.6 Appointment booking page.

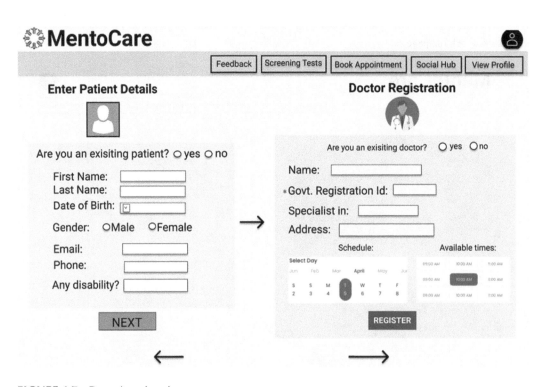

FIGURE 4.7 Doctor's registration page.

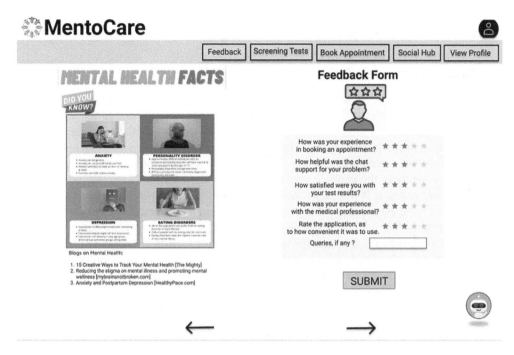

FIGURE 4.8 Social hub and feedback page.

TABLE 4.3

Comparison of Various Existing Apps with the Proposed System

App Name	MentoCare	Dr. Mind	MoodMission	Headspace
Supports (target audience)	PWDs, adolescents, and general public	All age groups	People dealing with stress, anxiety, or depression	For novice meditators and people new to the concept of mindfulness
Attractive features	Talkback feature for PWDs, social hub to learn more about symptoms, chatbot for solving basic queries	Get help from nearby centers, share test results with friends and family	In-app rewards, CBT-based activities in the form of missions	Progress tracking, guided meditation tracks, online forums
Doctor consultation facility	Yes	No	No	No
Cost structure	All the features are free, but doctor consultation is paid	Free	Paid	Paid (discount for students)
Offline features (if any)	Screening tests, emergency helpline	Read about different mental health problems	Missions can be used offline once downloaded	Sessions can be viewed offline once downloaded
Gaps	• No help from nearby centers	• Not very user friendly for adolescents and PWDs • Only available in standard languages	• Activities limited to missions • Time consuming activities • No professional help	• No mood assessment ratings • Exercises may feel repetitive • May not be very appropriate for clinical usage

Thus, we have also compared our proposed system with the existing ones and tried to finalize a solution that can overcome the problems with the existing apps.

4.5 CONCLUSION AND FUTURE SCOPE

Web apps have the potential to act as a safe and effective medium for the detection and treatment of a wide range of mental health conditions, provided the approaches followed for screening and treatment are evidence-based. Consequently, the use of virtual assessment tools lays out a variety of advantages such as cost reduction, increase in accessibility, evidence-based assessments, and counseling. Apart from this, due consideration is required of patients' data privacy and security, clinical approval, and the safety of the app's content [27]. Our proposed methodology will be useful for a wide range of communities. It will be an inclusive approach that will provide mental health facilities by keeping in mind the concerns of PWDs as well. Through our system we will try to provide a healthy environment which will give mental peace to users, where doctors can be easily connected to patients. Patients can easily approach the best mental health facilities using their fingertips. This platform can act as a tool for early screening to determine the symptoms and seriousness of an issue, to decide which professional must be referred to for treatment, and to learn more about mental health conditions and well-being in a more inclusive way than was conventionally followed. This will ensure less damage and more improvement at the earliest stage regarding the mental health of patients. Effort will be needed to improve the user friendliness of the application along with the incorporation of quality content of the data to increase the engagement of users to maximize the benefits of the application. Although proper integration of these online tools with the existing methods is important, technical implementations are never the largest barriers and digital healthcare tools already exist on the market [28]. Despite the extensive research and progress in the field of AI and ML, the implementation of the latter to solve real world problems is often perplexing. There is also a need to understand the risks and challenges involved in the incorporation of ML in healthcare and to try to bridge the gap between them. ML is already preforming miracles in healthcare systems [29]. Thus, we will try to incorporate this to help our users obtain better first aid results. The implementation of digital tools in enhancing patient care, reducing machine runtime, and minimizing care expenses have given an impetus to the growth of technology in the healthcare industry. When it comes to our healthcare industry, especially in the matter of life and death, the promise of technology to improve healthcare outcomes are very interesting and fascinating [30–36].

The usage of technology is associated with a number of moral and social issues pertaining to the lack of transparency and trustworthiness as perceived by the general population. Many issues here compound those raised by the use of data and healthcare technologies more broadly. A key challenge for the future governance of digital tools will be ensuring that they are developed and used in a way that is clear and suited to the public interest, whilst driving innovation in the sector. This match of demand and supply coupled with development will enable both fields to advance significantly in the foreseeable future, which will ultimately ameliorate the quality of life of people in society.

REFERENCES

1. World Health Organization. "Mental health: a state of well-being 2013". Report of the WHO Department of Mental Health. 2013 https://www.who.int/news-room/facts-in-pictures/detail/mental-health (accessed 10 Sep 2022).
2. "Mental health: strengthening our response," *Mental health: strengthening our response*, Jun. 17, 2022. https://www.who.int/news-room/fact-sheets/detail/mental-health-strengthening-our-response/ (accessed Sep. 10, 2022).
3. Susman, E. J., and Dorn, L. D. (2009). "Puberty: it's role in development," in *Handbook of Adolescent Psychology*, 3rd Edn., eds R. M. Lerner, and L. Steinberg (Hoboken, NJ: John Wiley and Sons), 116–151. doi: 10.1002/9780470479193.adlpsy001006

4. Kumar, L. "Disabled Population in India: Data and Facts," *WeCapable*, May 25, 2018. https://wecapable.com/disabled-population-india-data/ (accessed Sep. 10, 2022).

5. Centers for Disease Control and Prevention "Mental Health for All," Centers for Disease Control and Prevention, Nov. 30, 2020. https://www.cdc.gov/ncbddd/disabilityandhealth/features/mental-health-for-all/ (accessed Sep. 10, 2022).

6. Cree, R.A., Okoro, C.A., Zack, M.M., and Carbone, E. (2020). "Frequent Mental Distress Among Adults by Disability Status, Disability Type, and Selected Characteristics – United States 2018". Morbidity and Mortality Weekly Report (MMWR).

7. Vazquez, C., Hervas, G., Rahona, J.J., and Gomez, D. (2009). "Psychological well-being and health: Contributions from positive psychology". *Anuario de Psicologia Clinica y de la Salud/Annuary of Clinical and Health Psychology*, 5, 15–28.

8. Dekelver, Jan, Kultsova, Marina, Shabalina, Olga, Borblik, Julia, Pidoprigora, Alexander, and Romanenko, Roman (2015). "Design of Mobile Applications for People with Intellectual Disabilities". 535. 10.1007/978-3-319-23766-4

9. Burn, A.M., Ford, T.J., Stochl, J., Jones, P.B., Perez, J., and Anderson, J.K. (2022 Jan 10). "Developing a Web-Based App to Assess Mental Health Difficulties in Secondary School Pupils: Qualitative User-Centered Design Study". *JMIR form Research*, 6(1), e30565. doi: 10.2196/30565. PMID: 35006079; PMCID: PMC8787665.

10. Piqueras, J.A., Garcia-Olcina, M., Rivera-Riquelme, M., Martinez-Gonzalez, A.E., and Cuijpers, P. (2021). "DetectaWeb-Distress Scale: A Global and Multidimensional Web-Based Screener for Emotional Disorder Symptoms in Children and Adolescents". *Frontiers in Psychology*, 12, 627604. doi: 10.3389/fpsyg.2021.627604

11. Dash, S., Shakyawar, S.K., Sharma, M. et al. (2019). "Big Data in Healthcare: Management, Analysis and Future Prospects". *Journal of Big Data*, 6, 54.

12. Musale, Mukool, Desale, Disha, Jagadale, Harshal, Ravindravitnare, Yash, and Ospanova, A. (2022). "A Web-based Mental Health Detection and get Cure Application". *International Journal of Innovative Research in Science Engineering and Technology*. 11, 3504–3505. doi: 10.15680/IJIRSET.2022.1104054

13. Tate, A.E., McCabe, R.C., Larsson, H., Lundström, S., Lichtenstein, P., and Kuja-Halkola, R. (2020). "Predicting Mental Health Problems in Adolescence Using Machine Learning Techniques". *PLoS One*, 15(4), e0230389. https://journals.plos.org/plosone/article?id=10.1371/journal.pone.0230389

14. Saboo, S., Gupta, S., Nailwal, I., Gandhi, R., and Rana, S. (2021). "Diagnosing Mental Health Patient While Maintaining Anonymity," *IEEE Mysore Sub Section International Conference (MysuruCon)*, 2021, 244–248. doi: 10.1109/MysuruCon52639.2021.9641727

15. Okoro, C.A., Strine, T.W., McKnight-Eily, L., Verlenden, J., and Hollis, N.D. (2021). "Indicators of Poor Mental Health and Stressors during the COVID-19 Pandemic, by Disability Status: A Cross-Sectional Analysis". *Disability and Health Journal*, 14(4), 101110. doi: 10.1016/j.dhjo.2021.101110. Epub 2021 Apr 21. PMID: 33962896; PMCID: PMC8436151.

16. Koushik, C.S.N., Choubey, S.B., and Choubey, A. Chapter 7 – "Application of virtual reality systems to psychology and cognitive neuroscience research"; G.R. Sinha, J.S. Suri (Eds.), *Computer Modelling, and Cognitive Science JSBT-CI*, Academic Press (2020), pp. 133–147

17. Accenture, L.L.C. "Consumer survey on digital health results." (2018). https://www.accenture.com/t20180305t084516z__w__/us-en/_acnmedia/pdf-71/accenture-health-2018-consumer-survey-digital-health.pdf

18. Robbins, R., Krebs, P., Jagannathan, R., Jean-Louis, G., and Duncan, D.T. (2017 Dec 19). "Health App use among US Mobile Phone Users: Analysis of Trends by Chronic Disease Status." *JMIR mHealth and uHealth*, 5(12), e7832.

19. Torous, J., Wisniewski, H., Liu, G., and Keshavan, M. (2018 Nov 16) "Mental Health Mobile Phone App Usage, Concerns, and Benefits among Psychiatric Outpatients: Comparative Survey Study". *JMIR Mental Health*, 5(4), e11715.

20. Schueller, S.M., Neary, M., O'Loughlin, K., and Adkins, E.C. (2018 Jun 11). "Discovery of and Interest in Health Apps among Those with Mental Health Needs: Survey and Focus Group Study". *Journal of Medical Internet Research*, 20(6), e10141.

21. Halvorsen, M.B., Helverschou, S.B., Axelsdottir, B. et al. (2022). "General Measurement Tools for Assessing Mental Health Problems Among Children and Adolescents with an Intellectual Disability: A Systematic Review". *Journal of Autism and Developmental Disorders*. https://link.springer.com/article/10.1007/s10803-021-05419-5

22. "Prediction of Mental Health Among University Students" July 2021 *International Journal on Perceptive and Cognitive Computing* 7(1), 85–91.

23. Zhaorong, Y. and Yiwen, C. (2019). "Design and Application of Adolescent Mental Health Data Mining and Management System". *International Conference on Smart Grid and Electrical Automation (ICSGEA)*, 2019, 490–492, doi: 10.1109/ICSGEA.2019.00117

24. Chen, S. (2022). "Applicability Analysis of Data-driven Methods for Adolescents Mental Health Surveillance". *International Conference on Machine Learning and Knowledge Engineering (MLKE)*, 2022, 241–244, doi: 10.1109/MLKE55170.2022.00053

25. Chiang, Wen-Cheng, Cheng, Po-Husn, Mei-Ju, Su, Chen, Heng-Shuen, Wu, Ssu-Wei, and Lin, Jia-Kuan, "Socio-health with personal mental health records: Suicidal-tendency observation system on Facebook for Taiwanese adolescents and young adults," *2011 IEEE 13th International Conference on e-Health Networking, Applications and Services*, 2011, pp. 46–51, doi: 10.1109/HEALTH.2011.6026784

26. Grist, R., Porter, J., and Stallard, P. (2017). "Mental Health Mobile Apps for Preadolescents and Adolescents: A Systematic Review". *Journal of Medical Internet Research* May 25, 19(5), e176. doi: 10.2196/jmir.7332. PMID: 28546138; PMCID: PMC5465380.

27. Huckvale, Kit, Nicholas, Jennifer, and Torous, John Mark E Larsen, (2020). "Smartphone Apps for the Treatment of Mental Health Conditions: Status and Considerations". *Current Opinion in Psychology*, 36, 65–70, ISSN 2352-250X, https://doi.org/10.1016/j.copsyc.2020.04.008

28. Torous, J. and Hsin, H. (2018 May 16). "Empowering the Digital Therapeutic Relationship: Virtual Clinics for Digital Health Interventions". *NPJ Digital Medicine*, 1(1), 1–3.

29. Singh, A., Goyal, M., Vidhi, J. Nagpal, and Agarwal, A., "Cognitive Behaviour Analysis Of Adolescents," *2019 International Conference on contemporary Computing and Informatics (IC3I)*, 2019, pp. 44–48, doi: 10.1109/IC3I46837.2019.9055664

30. Subu, M. A. et al., "Social Media Use and Physical Activity among Junior High School Students in Indonesia," *2021 IEEE 45th Annual Computers, Software, and Applications Conference (COMPSAC)*, 2021, pp. 1394–1396, doi: 10.1109/COMPSAC51774.2021.00201

31. Mcmillan, Julie and Jarvis, Jane, (2013). "Mental Health and Students with Disabilities: A Review of Literature". *Australian Journal of Guidance and Counselling*, 23. doi: 10.1017/jgc.2013.14

32. Rivera-Riquelme, M., Piqueras, J. A., and Cuijpers, P. (2019). "The Revised Mental Health Inventory-5 (MHI-5) as an Ultra-brief Screening Measure of Bidimensional Mental Health in Children and Adolescents". *Psychiatry Research*, 274, 247–253. doi: 10.1016/j.psychres.2019.02.045

33. Gili, M., Castellví, P., Vives, M., de la Torre-Luque, A., Almenara, J., Blasco, M. J., et al. (2019). "Mental Disorders as Risk Factors for Suicidal Behavior in Young People: A Meta-analysis and Systematic Review of Longitudinal Studies". *Journal of Affective Disorders* 245, 152–162. doi: 10.1016/j.jad.2018.10.115

34. Francisco, R., Pedro, M., Delvecchio, E., Espada, J. P., Morales, A., Mazzeschi, C., et al. (2020). "Psychological Symptoms and Behavioral Changes in Children and Adolescents during the Early Phase of COVID-19 Quarantine in Three European Countries". *Frontiers in Psychiatry*, 11, 570164. doi: 10.3389/fpsyt.2020.570164

35. Baumel, A., Muench, F., Edan, S, and Kane, J.M. (2019 Sep 25). "Objective User Engagement with Mental Health Apps: Systematic Search and Panel-based Usage Analysis". *Journal of Medical Internet Research*, 21(9), e14567.

36. Westlake, F., Hassiotis, A., Unwin, G., and Totsika, V. (2021). "The Role of Behaviour Problems in Screening for Mental Ill-health in Adults with Intellectual Disability", *The European Journal of Psychiatry*, 35(2), 122–125, ISSN 0213-6163, doi: 10.1016/j.ejpsy.2020.11.002

5 An Employee Health Monitoring System Using Wireless Body Area Networks and Machine Learning

Yash U. Ringe, Pratik R. Sonar, Darshan V. Medhane, and Satish R. Devane
Savitribai Phule Pune University, MVPS's KBT College of Engineering, Nashik, India

CONTENTS

5.1 INTRODUCTION

Wireless body area networks (WBANs), one of the wireless communication technologies, are used as the basic network architecture for many types of sensors to minimise various medical and non-medical issues. The healthcare sector, sport, the military, and the defence sector are all affected. The sensors are utilised to acquire information on health status by successfully employing the WBAN design. To standardise WBANs, an Institute of Electrical and Electronics Engineers 802.15.6 working group was established. The next-generation smart healthcare system using WBANs is ushering in a new era.

Patients with chronic heart disease can benefit from this type of gadget. Those with these conditions run the risk of dying since their hearts could stop beating at any time. The main causes of the high prevalence of these diseases are genetic factors, obesity, stress, a diet heavy in salt and fat, and

DOI: 10.1201/9781003359456-5

lack of exercise. Additionally, increased risk factors like diabetes, hypertension, high blood fat levels, and weight gain brought on by menopause might lead women to experience a heart attack [21, 31].

According to studies on individuals with heart failure, 30% had been readmitted at least once in the previous 90 days. Readmission rates reach 25 to 54% within three to six months. Therefore, turning a passive healthcare mode into an active one is key to improving the healthcare performance of heart disease and lowering the death rate. Doctors and healthcare personnel should monitor patients' health status to help with their healthcare. This is where the WBAN-based Internet of Things (IoT) system comes in handy [30, 33].

Machine learning (ML) algorithms work with enormous amounts of data and are crucial to the decision-making process. To deploy an ML algorithm for analysis purposes the volume and the velocity of the data must be measured and known. ML models are being used in the healthcare sector for the analysis and prediction of data to provide patients with better, reliable, and much more affordable services. ML models combined with image processing and signal processing are used in the treatment of a variety of chronic diseases including cancer. ML models are also used in the detection of heart diseases like myocardial infarction (MI). They are covered in the literature review section. Most of these prediction models are based on general datasets and input from previous medical reports from patients. They do not include measuring and processing active data (in real time) through the model to obtain much more accurate and useful insights into a person's health [1, 29]

The objectives of the proposed work set out in this chapter are:

1. To design and develop wearable WBANs to monitor employees' health attributes and to transfer the data to a server for computing and analysis;
2. To display employees' health records to the employees, employer, and medical department of the organization;
3. To obtain insight and foresight into employees' health;
4. To analyse health attributes and produce predictions for employees;
5. To obtain predictions for MI and health dangers;
6. To provide an alert system in case of emergency.

5.2　LITERATURE SURVEY

Sarmah [1] presented an IoT-centred model to monitor patients with heart disease and focus on analysis and the prediction of threats using deep leaning and modified neural networks. The system implements a deep learning neural network algorithm and a cuttlefish optimisation algorithm to make informed predictions using patient's electronic health records. The final product is a web-based application that implements various technologies including a PDH-AES algorithm for encryption, and Guttman Scaling Algorithm (MHA) for data compression.

Parveen et al. [56] cover a brief overview of MI and its causes, as well as how ML is effective for its detection using different parameters. It focuses the habits and lifestyle of the subject and his or her cardiogram values.

Rashwand and Misic [2] present a brief study based on WBANs covering the uses, functionalities, architecture, and protocols. This provides a very clear idea for establishing WBANs and how to use them efficiently. It also targets the merits and demerits of different aspects of WBANs.

Parveen and Devane [4] present an ML model for the early detection of MI. This system provides an in-depth view on parameters that may cause MI. Algorithms like SVM, Naïve Bayes, and KNN were used to analyse the accuracy in prediction.

Di Franco [57] covers different aspects of using WBANs. The system provides a brief idea about how physical parameters like body shape and gender affect WBAN signals as well as the generated output.

Melillo et al. [58] focus on how heart diseases, MI, and congestive heart failures can be foreseen through the study of heart rate variability in a patient's cardiogram. This work describes the risk assessment as well as prediction for patients (Table 5.1).

TABLE 5.1

Survey on the Range of Parameters of Myocardial Infarction (MI)

	Angina	MI	Non-MI
Age [50, 54]	(1) >35 and average age 62 (2) <35 if diabetic, high bp, smoking, high cholesterol [56] (3) 45 to 60 By experts (India) [52]	(1) 30–39 age (15%) (2) 40–49 age M (17.5%) (3) 50–59 age M (22.5%) (4) 60 and above age (37.5%) (5) 61 and above age (7.5%) in F (6) 60+ more cases in F than M	(1) <35 should consider more [56] (2) 35–65 more MI (incidence rate of MI) [56] (3) Median age for MI is 53 [56] (4) 84–88% young age for non-MI [56] (5) 90–95% <40 age for non-MI [56]
Gender [37]	(1) 57.3 ± 18.72 M (2) 62.9 ± 23.84 F (3) >45 more in M (4) >35–54 more in F (5) More in F [34]	Mentioned above	Both men and women can be taken into account equally according to experts
ECG changes [38]	(1) 50% has normal ECG (2) Changes always result from expertise	Always yes, as per the professional judgement [22]	(1) Patients without MI may see ECG abnormalities due to another illness (2) No in opinion of experts
Cholesterol	The range of total cholesterol is 160–250 mg [40]	(1) More than 240 mg for MI (60+ age) [38] (2) 200–239 mg in M and F for MI (50–59) [56]	(1) For 30–39 is 185.5±41.9 mg (2) For 40–49 is 182.5±44.7 mg (3) For 50–59 is 172.2±47.6 mg (4) For 60–69 is 161.7±46.0 mg (5) For 70–79 is 156.7±45.8 mg
Trop-I [46, 48]	No changes	Increased troponin levels in MI indicate cardiac muscle cell death	(1) Numerous illnesses, such as abrupt pulmonary embolism, heart failure, myocarditis, and end-stage renal disease, are possible with troponin release [19] (2) No changes in Trop-I in non-MI patients as per observers [56]
Diabetic [23]	86% of angina patients have diabetes	(1) High risk factor (2) More in F then M [49]	
Systolic [45]	BP range is 130–180	BP is 139–180 or higher mmHg [56]	(1) For age 26–30 systolic bp is 113.5 (2) For age 31–35 systolic bp is 110.5 (3) For age 36–40 systolic value is 112.5 [55] (4) For age 41–45 systolic value is 115.5 [55] (5) For age 46–50 systolic bp is 199.5 (6) For age 51–55 systolic bp is 125.5 [55] (7) For age 56–60 systolic bp is 129.5 (8) For age 61–65 systolic bp is 143.5 (9) For 90 it is 170 Form available data

(Continued)

TABLE 5.1　(Continued)

	Angina	MI	Non-MI
Diastolic [41]	Diastolic blood pressure range is 80–120	Diastolic blood pressure range 90–120 or higher mmHg	(1) For 26–30 diastolic bp is 71.5 (2) For 31–35 diastolic bp is 72.5 (3) For 36–40 diastolic bp is 74.5 (4) For 41–45 diastolic bp is 78.5 (5) For 46–50 diastolic bp is 80.5 (6) For 51–55 diastolic bp is 80.5 (7) For 56–60 diastolic bp is 79.5 (8) For 61–65 diastolic bp is 76.5
Chest pain [42]	(1) Primarily chronic (2) Occasionally acute (3) Occasionally no pain By experts	(1) Mainly acute (2) At times persistent By experts	There is non-cardiac pain, which could be caused by acidity, reflex esophagitis, or muscular painBy experts
Left anterior descending (LAD) [39], left coronary artery (LCA), right coronary artery (RCA) [56]	(1) More than 70% blockages (2) It might be up to 100% say experts (3) Less than 50% multiple arteries	(1) LAD only (59.5%) (2) LAD and LCA (2.5%) (3) LAD and RCA (12.7%) (4) LAD, LCA, and RCA (10.1%) (5) Blockages 95 to 100% according to experts [56]	0–50% blockages in general
Creatine kinase-myoglobin binding [44]	No changes in CK-MB levels as per the experts [43, 56]	(1) 4–6 hours after the onset of symptoms, CK-MB first shows [56] (2) Expertise always suggests CK-MB changes [51]	(1) Elevated in non-cardiac conditions such as skeletal muscle injury, hypothyroidism, chronic renal failure, and severe exercise [56] (2) No changes in non-MI patients as per the experts [56]

5.3　MI THEORY

The coronary circulation is distinct in that, normally, it inhibits its own perfusion for the duration of the systolic portion of the cardiac cycle while concurrently producing the arterial tension required to perfuse the systemic circulation. Because coronary flow and oxygen delivery are closely related to myocardial contraction, oxygen supply and demand stability is a significant element in establishing the heart's usual beat behaviour. This link can be significantly disrupted by diseases that reduce coronary blood flow, and the imbalance that results may immediately start a new cycle that results in contractile failure from myocardial ischemia and hypotension from ischemia [10, 11, 44].

A myocardial MI happens when a coronary artery unexpectedly becomes blocked or has very sluggish blood flow. The formation of a blood clot shares the same primary cause of an immediate blockage in an artery [36].

Types of MI are:

1. ST-elevation myocardial infarction (STEMI);
2. Non-ST-elevation myocardial infarction (NSTEMI);
3. Angina.

5.3.1 STEMI

A STEMI is a serious type of cardiac tissue damage in which a substantial piece of the heart muscle (coronary) is deprived of blood due to blockages in an artery (it doesn't get enough blood). Figure 5.1 shows the shape of a normal ECG. Figure 5.2 shows the shape of a STEMI [12].

5.3.2 NSTEMI

A non-ST segment elevation MI is heart tissue damage (coronary) that causes far less injury to the patient's heart than an ST-segment elevation change would. However, such patients will need a positive blood test for a protein called troponin, which is produced when the heart muscle is injured. It is quite likely that any arterial obstructions in NSTEMI coronary heart failure are transient or fragmentary [47, 49].

5.3.3 ANGINA

Angina occurs as the artery wall thickens (plaque narrows down the artery), restricting the amount of blood that can travel through it. This can cause chest discomfort, pain, increased blood pressure, or even stop the blood flow entirely, damaging the heart [35]. Arterial constriction changes with time. Through imaging known as an angiogram, which is often done to examine capillaries for blockages, an arterial convulsion might not be seen since there might not be a build-up of plaque or a thrombus within the capillary [5, 10, 13].

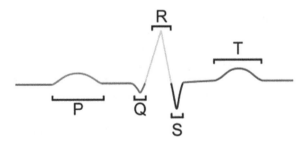

FIGURE 5.1 Normal ECG [4].

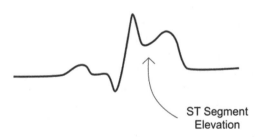

FIGURE 5.2 A STEMI [4].

5.4 PROPOSED METHODOLOGY

Today, the leading cause of mortality globally is heart disease. The method of heart attack prediction is exceedingly complex. Only a doctor with extensive expertise and knowledge of the condition can successfully do it. Especially when it come to MI, only a seasoned cardiologist can analyse the case and make a prediction. MI depends on a lot of statistical and Boolean data attributes like cholesterol, sugar history, family history, physical activity, and stress level. Hence, the effectiveness of an IoT-based health attribute measuring system and ML-based prediction and classification in models is at its peak [7]. WBANs are utilised to collect health attributes from the employee (patient) and upload it to the cloud as it gives high performance, consumes much less power, and is latency and noise free when used correctly. Patient privacy is at stake since this technology is not secure. To deal with this we can use the PDH-AES method which includes encryption while transferring data to the cloud and decryption from the cloud. After transmission the data can be pre-processed and fed to the ML model for further analysis [6, 16].

Figure 5.3 shows the working method.

5.4.1 DATA CREATION

Using different IoT sensors in WBANs is established over the employee's (patient's) body. We can then record the different health attributes of a person and create data packets. These data packets are then sent to the local antenna and then transferred to the cloud [8, 27, 28].

5.4.2 AUTHENTICATION

To confirm a user's identity, different systems require various forms of credentials. A secret password known only to the user and the system frequently serves as this credential.

Authentication utilises five steps: (I) register, (II) login service, (III) verification, (IV) uploading medical data, and (V) secure data transfer:

I. Register: This is the first step where all the users including the organisation (the super admin-owner), physicians (medical authorities), administration (management), and employees register for the system. After server utilisation, the username and passwords are handed out to all of the people connected with the organisation.

II. Login: This is the most crucial step. To maintain data integrity and to keep the data untampered restricted access is really important. By logging into their own account users will be able to access all the features suitable for their respective profile. Employees will only be able to see their own health attributes, whereas doctors can access the data of every employee as well as review predictions and data generated by models. Super admin and administration can access all the data and restricted features as well as being able to create and manage users and user access.

III. Verification: The system checks to see if the user is logged in or not. The health care application administrator checks the users by examining the user data. The username and password entered here are combined, and then used.

IV. Uploading medical data: The system will require the user to input all previous health records along with family medical history and routine habits. The user may need to upload previous cardiograms, ECGs, MRI scans, X-rays, blood-sugar reports, angiograms, CT scans, and other critical health reports for an accurate analysis and betterment of the model.

However, the employee's health records (EHR) include much data in a variety of sizes. To deal with this, before uploading the data to the server, the EHR is compressed and then saved to the server from where it can be accessed by authorised users and ML models [9]. For compression of the data, a modified Huffman algorithm (MHA) is used. Huffman cod-

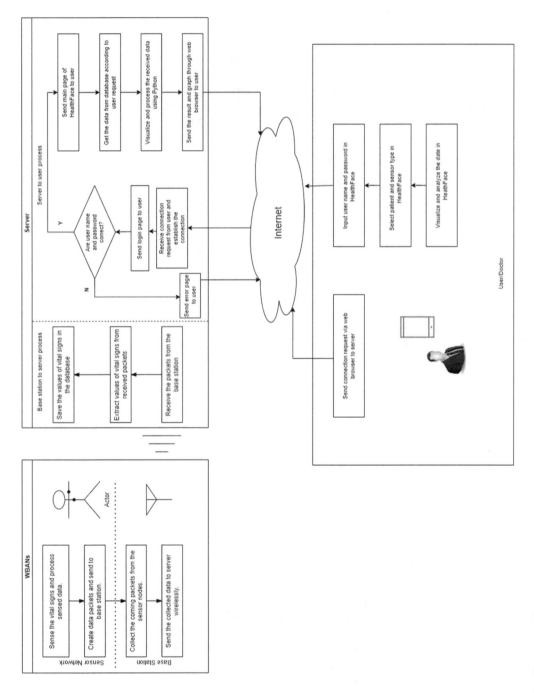

FIGURE 5.3 System architecture.

ing, also known as Huffman encoding, is an algorithm used for the lossless compression of files that is based on the frequency of the symbol's occurrence on the file, or in the course of compression. The least produced character receives a large code, whereas the character with the highest production rate receives a small code. The Huffman Tree (HT) is essentially a method for signifying each symbol.

V. Secure data transfer: As the employee's health records and observed data are very crucial, it is necessary to provide data security and maintain data integrity. To ensure secure data transfer Zigbee modules and Zigbee protocols are used for the mode of data transfer as well as the PDH-AES methods which are used for encryption and decryption of data during the transfer. The AES algorithm is essentially a symmetric-key block cypher that takes inputs of 128-bit data blocks and a key and outputs ciphertext [1]. The 128 bits in a data block are organised in "4" columns and "4" rows to be processed as a matrix; AES handles them as 16 bytes [1].

5.4.3 Disease Prediction System (DPS)

I. Data collection and management: The data transferred to the cloud is then saved in the database and pre-processing techniques are performed to remove the noise and make it more relevant to the analysis. The Irish HD dataset contains the classified results, which include both normal and aberrant results. For the proposed work, a total of 388 records or rows were taken from the dataset. There are various patients' health records in each row. The information found in these records, such as their blood pressure, heart rate, breathing rate, and pulse, is treated as a feature of the dataset. The system needs to be properly trained before disease classification in order to obtain an accurate result. The training set includes 72 attributes of HD patients from the Irish dataset. Data are initially obtained for this database's HD classification [14, 15, 20].

II. Pre-processing: Here we treat missing values, eliminate redundancy, and normalise the dataset. We treat missing values as the model is expected to be very sensitive and deal with critical healthcare aspects. Rather than replacing them with the attribute's mean, the maximum number of repeating attribute values is used to substitute these missing characteristics. The missing value of the particular attribute is restored when the age group, blood pressure, and cholesterol of all patients have been examined. When most of a patient's attribute values match, the value is switched around to the same position. In the end normalisation is performed [17, 18].

III. Prediction and classification: The dataset is then processed by the ML model to train a model that can generate insight and foresight of an employee's health as well as predictions for MI. Based on features like heart rate variety and resting heart rate the models classify the entry as normal or abnormal data [24].

   i. Classification of diseases: This is the crucial last stage in the disease prediction system process. Here, the pre-processed data is classified by the Deep Learning Neural Network. For deep learning, Artificial Neural Network's hidden layers are multiplied. Even the backpropagation process can be reduced with the additional use of algorithms like the cuttlefish optimisation algorithm (CFOA).

   ii. Using a neural network for classification (DLNN): The pre-processed data is used as the DLNN's input. The values that were randomly allocated and combined with each input are the weights. Nodes from this layer are designated as hidden nodes in the following layer, which is known as the hidden layer. These nodes perform the action of adding the weight vector of each input node that is connected to it as well as the product of the input value [1].

   iii. Real-time observed values along with the input values entered by the user are processed through the model to determine the health of the user, based on which predictions are made. These predictions are sent to physicians and healthcare personnel for evaluation and monitoring [3].

IV. Review and alerts: The generated predictions are then passed on to the physicians or medical personnel related to the organisation to review. All the emergency alerts are also shown and notified to authorised users and medical personnel who will be proven valuable in the case of emergency and risk management [25, 26].

5.5 ALGORITHM FOR DLNN

```
Input: Input from monitored data in input database.
Output: Optimised weight values for classification.
1.Procedure: (Input, Neurons, Repeat)
   Create input database
2. input in database with all the selected features from acquired
healthcare dataset
Train DLNNs
3. For Input 1 to End of input do        -> Change input on every run
   For N = 1 till 100 do                    -> Increase neurons
   on every run
4.       For N > 100 do                          -> Add/ Change Layer
5.       For repeat  1-100 do           -> Iterative run 100 times
6.          Train DLNN
7.          DLNN-datastore--- Save highest iteration R² in memory
8.       End For
 9.    End for
10.    Test on recorded data set from input
11.    DLNN-datastore--- Save best predictions done on actual data
12.    End for
13.    Return DLNN-datastore     -> Database with best predictions for
respective user
14. End procedure.
```

5.6 UML AND WORKING

Figure 5.4 represents the flow of our project abstractly. It provides a rough idea of the various processes that will be working behind the scenes to deliver the expected results. The diagram is divided into two sub-parts that involve two different parallel processes in the project (i.e. WBAN and Control Centre). The wireless body area network majorly deals with the IoT, data transmission, and pre-processing of data accumulated from the employee's compression wear covered with a sensor module to monitor vital signs, whereas the Control Centre will focus on the central logic of the project, predictions, and database management. The Control Centre delivers the essential tools for the efficient and reliable monitoring of vital health parameters and also provides essential insights into employees' health. Figure 5.5 shows the working methodology of the system.

The operational sequence unified modeling language diagram (see Figure 5.5) provides an in-depth view of the projects and their design specifications. It provides us with a glance of the interactions, structure, and behaviours of different elements in the project.

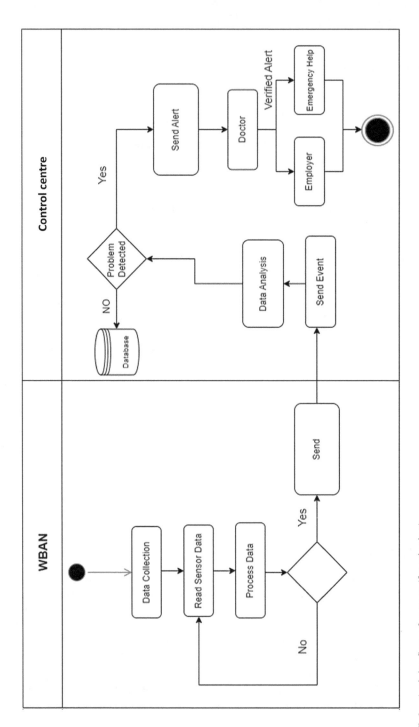

FIGURE 5.4   Activity flow of system (functioning).

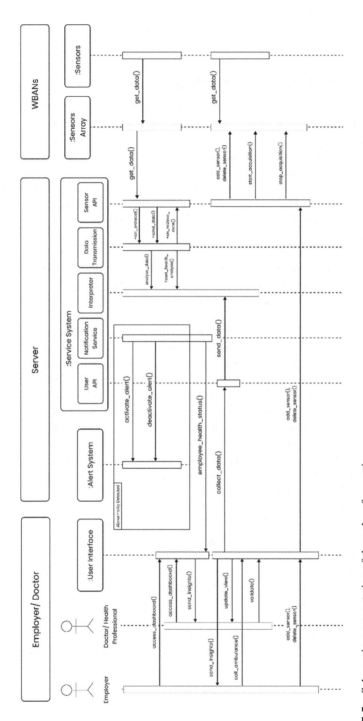

FIGURE 5.5 Schematic representation of the order of execution.

The essential components in the proposed project and the interaction between them are represented in the sequence diagram in Figure 5.5. The working of the project is based on three major elements containing WBANs – servers, and doctors/employers – which represent how the vital data from the sensors will be collected, processed, and analysed to provide valuable insights to medical professionals (doctors) and employers. By considering these insights the employer can take appropriate action to resolve employees' health issues.

5.7 WORKING ON THE PROPOSED PROJECT

Since a person's electronic health records contain sensitive information that is also vital, this system offers a way to manage them and draw valid conclusions from them. Given that we covered the project's operations above, here is an abstract illustration of how the system functions.

The solution we've suggested will combine hardware and software elements to offer an accurate employee health monitoring system. Wearable compression apparel with built-in sensors that gather and monitor employee health metrics is how WBAN technology is used in the project. These sensor modules are positioned so that they deliver the highest level of precision that the sensor is capable of. The ECG sensor, BP monitoring sensor, and SPO2 sensor are the main components of the currently planned system. The microcontroller will gather all the data from these sensors without imposing any limits on the employee wearing the compression clothing. Batteries will effectively power this system, and the equipment will reduce the module's overall heating issues. The microcontroller will first pre-process all of the sensor data before sending packets to the local antenna through the ZigBee module, which offers a stronger security channel, and then sending the data to the cloud server for further processing.

The enormous volume of real-time data that is gathered from the hardware after it has been received may be a concern since it will consume a lot of cloud resources. To solve this issue a modified form of Huffman coding (MHA) is used in order to meet the system's compression needs. After effective data management and compression, the data will be encrypted with the advanced encryption standard technique to protect its privacy before being saved in a cloud database.

The cloud-stored data is subsequently retrieved and subjected to analysis, but not before being carefully cleaned up and handled. This is a very important step to be done before working with the data in any way. After being cleaned, the data will be analysed to draw conclusions that are useful for the model's improvement while taking into account the prior electronic health attributes that were obtained from the employee, such as cardiograms, ECGs, MRI scans, X-rays, blood-sugar reports, angiograms, CT scans, and other crucial health reports.

After obtain insights from the data, the system will proceed to categorisation, where employees will be divided into categories to indicate those who may have health problems in the future, those who are physically fit, and those who have had previous health problems. Employers and medical professionals will be able to prioritise monitoring a certain group of people who are at risk of MI, possible cardiac issues, and may have a history of these issues. In addition to categorisation, the prediction model will also use the available data to improve forecast accuracy. It will be trained using individual health information.

Using DLNN, this model will be utilised to forecast employees' potential health issues in the future. An interactive graphical user interface will be used to provide all the data, insights, and foresight generated by the proposed system to the stakeholders. There will be three sections to this interface

5.7.1 ADMIN INTERFACE

The admin interface will provide various features to administration such as adding an employee to the available system and configuring the WBAN apparatus. Administration will play an important role in managing the application and providing proper access control to stakeholders.

5.7.2 MEDICAL PROFESSIONAL INTERFACE

The medical professional interface will be available for users with in-depth knowledge of the field of medicine, such as doctors. These doctors will provide valuable input to the system that will help us counter machine errors by adding an experienced view to the system. The medical professionals will be able to download data collected from the employee's WBAN system and by applying their knowledge they can trigger alerts for medical help for that employee.

5.7.3 EMPLOYER INTERFACE

Employers will have an insights-based interface that has complied and interpreted all the information gained from the analysis model, prediction model, and doctors' guidelines. The employer can utilise the information on employee welfare and provide emergency services to those who need help.

The proposed system seems very promising as it promotes employee wellbeing and provides security to them. This semi-automated system will help employers gain better insight into employees' health and provide appropriate emergency service on time.

5.8 CONCLUSION

Utilising this cutting-edge technology is about to revolutionise healthcare and change the way we live. WBANs allow us to closely monitor a user's health attributes and lets the user avoid and foresee the dangers of heart disease. The ML model helps employers and doctors to analyse the health of an organization's employees and provides trustworthy predictions with the help of DLNN, which utilises 24 different health attributes to predict MI and classify different heart diseases.

The system will work to favour the betterment of employee wellbeing and empower healthcare in organisations. It will be advantageous for both employers and employees to use it in the workplace.

APPENDIX A

Some frequently mentioned terms with their definitions.

1. Machine Learning (ML): This is a branch of artificial intelligence that focuses on learning from data by using specialised algorithms to imitate human learning.
2. Data Analysis: This is the process of investigating data for drawing possible conclusions.
3. Deep Learning: This is a subset of artificial intelligence that focuses on learning by exploring intricate structures in the data.
4. Wireless Body Area Networks (WBANs): This is a wireless technology that interconnects independent nodes that are situated on a person's body.
5. Deep Learning Neural Network (DLNN): This is a subset of Machine Learning that is used for learning and modelling the relationship between input and output data that are nonlinear and complex [56].
6. Healthcare Monitoring: This helps a system to actively monitor various health attributes.
7. Database: This is a structured set of data that is stored in a computational resource.
8. Myocardial Infarction (MI): This is a life-threatening condition when blood flow to the heart muscle is blocked.
9. Internet of Things (IOT): This is a technology that enables machines to interact with the physical world with the help of sensors, actuators, and computational devices.
10. Electrocardiogram (ECG): This is a record of the heart's electrical activity.
11. Huffman Encoding: This is a technique/algorithm used for data compression.
12. Advanced Encryption Standard (AES): This is a technique for electronic data encryption.

REFERENCES

[1] Sarmah, S. S. An efficient IoT-based patient monitoring and heart disease prediction system using deep learning modified neural network. *IEEE Access*, 2020; 8: 135784–135797, doi: 10.1109/ACCESS.2020.3007561

[2] Rashwand, Saeed and Misic, Jelena V., Bridging between IEEE 802.15.6 and IEEE 802.11e for wireless healthcare networks. *Ad Hoc & Sensor Wireless Networks*, 2015; 26: 303–337.

[3] Rafique, N. P. M., Devane, S. R., and Akhtar, S. Detection of myocardial infarction using ensemble algorithm and transfer learning. *2022 IEEE Region 10 Symposium (TENSYMP), Mumbai, India*, 2022, pp. 1–6, doi: 10.1109/TENSYMP54529.2022.9864399

[4] Parveen, N. and Devane, S.R., 2021. Efficient, Accurate and Early Detection of Myocardial Infarction Using Machine Learning. In *Disruptive Trends in Computer Aided Diagnosis* (pp. 115–153). Chapman and Hall/CRC.

[5] Bonaca, M. P., Gutierrez, J. A., Creager, M. A., Scirica, B. M., Olin, J., Murphy, S. A., Braunwald, E., and Morrow, D. A. Acute limb ischemia and outcomes with vorapaxar in patients with peripheral artery disease: Results from the trial to assess the effects of vorapaxar in preventing heart attack and stroke in patients with atherosclerosis–thrombolysis in myocardial infarction 50 (TRA2 P-TIMI 50). *Circulation*, 2016 Mar 8; 133(10): 997–1005.

[6] Thomas, J. and Princy, R. T. Human heart disease prediction system using data mining techniques. *2016 International Conference on Circuit, Power and Computing Technologies (ICCPCT)*, 2016 Mar 18, pp. 1–5, IEEE.

[7] Learning, M. Heart disease diagnosis and prediction using machine learning and data mining techniques: A review. *Advances in Computational Sciences and Technology*, 2017; 10(7): 2137–2159.

[8] Gowrishankar, S., Prachita, M. Y., and Prakash, A. IoT based heart attack detection, heart rate and temperature monitor. *International Journal of Computer Applications*, 2017 Jul; 170(5): 26–30.

[9] Westwood, J.D., Hoffman, H.M., Robb, R.A. and Stredney, D., Medicine meets virtual reality 02/10: digital upgrades: Applying Moore's Law to Health.

[10] Groennebaek, T., Sieljacks, P., Nielsen, R., Pryds, K., Jespersen, N. R., Wang, J., Carlsen, C. R., Schmidt, M. R., de Paoli, F. V., Miller, B. F., and Vissing, K. Effect of blood flow restricted resistance exercise and remote ischemic conditioning on functional capacity and myocellular adaptations in patients with heart failure. *Circulation: Heart Failure*, 2019 Dec; 12(12): e006427.

[11] www.youtube.com/watch?v=2kLlhlsesRQ

[12] Jessup, M. and Antman, E. Reducing the risk of heart attack and stroke: The American Heart Association/American College of Cardiology prevention guidelines. *Circulation*, 2014 Aug 5; 130(6): e48–e50.

[13] Revathi, J. and Anitha, J. A survey on analysis of ST-segment to diagnose coronary artery disease. *2017 International Conference on Signal Processing and Communication (ICSPC)*, 2017 Jul 28, pp. 211–216, IEEE.

[14] Ahmed, W. and Khalid, S. ECG signal processing for recognition of cardiovascular diseases: A survey. *2016 Sixth International Conference on Innovative Computing Technology (INTECH)*, 2016 Aug 24, pp. 677–682, IEEE.

[15] Haritha, C., Ganesan, M., and Sumesh, E. P. A survey on modern trends in ECG noise removal techniques. *2016 International Conference on Circuit, Power and Computing Technologies (ICCPCT)*, 2016 Mar 18, pp. 1–7, IEEE.

[16] Silverberg, J. I. Association between adult atopic dermatitis, cardiovascular disease, and increased heart attacks in three population-based studies. *Allergy*, 2015 Oct; 70(10): 1300–1308.

[17] Tikotikar, A. and Kodabagi, M. A survey on technique for prediction of disease in medical data. *2017 International Conference on Smart Technologies For Smart Nation (SmartTechCon)*, 2017 Aug 17, pp. 550–555, IEEE.

[18] Jabbar, M. A., Deekshatulu, B. L., and Chndra, P. Alternating decision trees for early diagnosis of heart disease. *International Conference on Circuits, Communication, Control and Computing*, 2014 Nov 21, pp. 322–328, IEEE.

[19] Bonow, R. O., Mann, D. L., Zipes, D. P., and Libby, P. *Braunwald's Heart Disease: A Textbook of Cardiovascular Medicine*, 9th ed. Philadelphia: Elsevier Science, 2011.

[20] Yusuf, S., Hawken, S., Ôunpuu, S., Dans, T., Avezum, A., Lanas, F., McQueen, M., Budaj, A., Pais, P., Varigos, J., and Lisheng, L. Effect of potentially modifiable risk factors associated with myocardial infarction in 52 countries (the INTERHEART study): Case-control study. *The Lancet*, 2004 Sep 11; 364(9438): 937–952.

[21] Egbe, A. C., Connolly, H. M., Miranda, W. R., Ammash, N. M., Hagler, D. J., Veldtman, G. R., and Borlaug, B. A. Hemodynamics of Fontan failure: The role of pulmonary vascular disease. *Circulation: Heart Failure*, 2017 Dec; 10(12): e004515.

[22] Uchihashi, M., Hoshino, A., Okawa, Y., Ariyoshi, M., Kaimoto, S., Tateishi, S., Ono, K., Yamanaka, R., Hato, D., Fushimura, Y., and Honda, S. Cardiac-specific Bdh1 overexpression ameliorates oxidative stress and cardiac remodeling in pressure overload–induced heart failure. *Circulation: Heart Failure*, 2017 Dec; 10(12): e004417.

[23] Khaw, K. T. and Barrett-Connor, E. Family history of heart attack: A modifiable risk factor? *Circulation*, 1986 Aug; 74(2): 239–244.

[24] Rafique, N. P., Devane, S. R., and Akhtar, S. Early detection of myocardial infarction using actual and synthetic datasets. *2021 IEEE Bombay Section Signature Conference (IBSSC)*, 2021 Nov 18, pp. 1–6, IEEE.

[25] Verma, P., Sood, S. K., and Kalra, S. Cloud-centric IoT based student healthcare monitoring framework. *Journal of Ambient Intelligence and Humanized Computing*, 2018 Oct; 9(5): 1293–1309.

[26] Subramaniyam, M., Singh, D., Jin Park, S., Eun Kim, S., Joon Kim, D., Nam Im, J., Lee, K.-S., and Nam Min, S. IoT based wake-up stroke prediction–recent trends and directions. *IOP Conference Series: Materials Science and Engineering*, 402, Oct. 2018, Art. no. 012045.

[27] Saheb, T. and Izadi, L. Paradigm of IoT big data analytics in the healthcare industry: A review of scientific literature and mapping of research trends. *Telematics Information*, 2019 Aug; 41: 70–85.

[28] Chui, K. T., Liu, R. W., Miltiadis Lytras, D., and Zhao, M. Big data and IoT solution for patient behaviour monitoring. *Behaviour & Information Technology*, 2019; 38, 940–949.

[29] Jagadeeswari, V., Subramaniyaswamy, V., Logesh, R., and Vijayakumar, V. A study on medical Internet of Things and big data in personalized healthcare system. *Health Information Science and Systems*, 2018 Dec; 6(1): 14.

[30] Ganesan, M. and Sivakumar, N. IoT based heart disease prediction and diagnosis model for healthcare using machine learning models. *Proceedings IEEE International Conference on System, Computation, Automation and Networking (ICSCAN)*, 2019 Mar, pp. 1–5.

[31] Kumar, P. M. and Devi Gandhi, U. A novel three-tier Internet of Things architecture with machine learning algorithm for early detection of heart diseases. *Computers & Electrical Engineering*, 2018 Jan; 65: 222–235.

[32] Kamble, A. and Bhutad, S. IOT based patient health monitoring system with nested cloud security. *Proceedings Fourth International Conference Computing, Communication Automation (ICCCA)*, Dec. 2018, pp. 1–5.

[33] Li, C., Hu, X., and Zhang, L. The IoT-based heart disease monitoring system for pervasive healthcare service. *Procedia Computer Science*, 2017 Jan 1; 112: 2328–2334.

[34] Amin, S. U., Agarwal, K., and Beg, R. Genetic neural network based data mining in prediction of heart disease using risk factors. *2013 IEEE Conference on Information & Communication Technologies*, 2013 Apr 11, pp. 1227–1231, IEEE.

[35] https://www.mhealth.org/blog/2017/february-2017/five-things-to-know-about-angina

[36] https://www.mayoclinic.org/diseases-conditions/angina/symptoms-causes/syc-20369373

[37] Sharma, A. K., Dar, M. I., Iqbal, M., and Tramboo, N. A. Gender-based differences in coronary artery disease: A prospective observational study from a North Indian state. *Heart India*, 2020 Apr 1; 8(2): 85.

[38] https://www.medscape.com/answers/150215-69325/what-is-the-role-of-ecg-in-the-workup-of-angina-pectoris

[39] https://www.google.co.in/search?q=lad+blockages+in+percentage+initially+in+angina%

[40] https://www.cdc.gov/bloodpressure/about.htm

[41] https://www.healthline.com/health/heart-disease/can-you-die-from-angina#treatment

[42] Junghans, C., Sekhri, N., Zaman, M. J., Hemingway, H., Feder, G. S., and Timmis, A. Atypical chest pain in diabetic patients with suspected stable angina: Impact on diagnosis and coronary outcomes. *European Heart Journal–Quality of Care and Clinical Outcomes*, 2015 Jul 1; 1(1): 37–43.

[43] Channamma, G. Age and Gender distribution in patients with acute Myocardial Infarction. *Medica Innovatica (Original Article)*, 2016 Jul; 5: 29–31.

[44] https://en.ecgpedia.org/wiki/Myocardial_Infarction#:~:text=In%20a%20myocardial%20infarction%20transmuralfinally%20pathologic%20Q%20waves%20develop

[45] https://patient.info/doctor/cardiac-enzymes-and-markers-for-myocardial-infarction

[46] Ohtsuki, S. Morimoto Tropnin-I. In *Encyclopedia of Biological Chemistry* (Second Edition), ScienceDirect 2013.

[47] Soyemi, S.S., Faduyile, F.A. and Osuolale, F.I., 2018. Fatal Myocardial Infarction: A Retrospective Autopsy Study. *Journal of Clinical & Diagnostic Research*, *12*(1).

[48] https://timesofindia.indiatimes.com/life-style/health-fitness/health-news/when-should-you-start-worrying-about-your-blood-pressure/articleshow/67643278.cms

[49] Leon, B. M. and Maddox, T. M. Diabetes and cardiovascular disease: Epidemiology, biological mechanisms, treatment recommendations and future research. *World Journal of Diabetes*, 2015 Oct 10; 6(13): 1246.

[50] Gupta, R., Rao, R. S., Misra, A., and Sharma, S. K. Recent trends in epidemiology of dyslipidemias in India. *Indian Heart Journal*, 2017 May 1; 69(3): 382–392.

[51] https://my.clevelandclinic.org/health/articles/17385-heart-disease-prevention-and-reversal

[52] Sharma, M. and Ganguly, N. K. Premature coronary artery disease in Indians and its associated risk factors. *Vascular Health and Risk Management*, 2005 Sep; 1(3): 217.

[53] https://www.medscape.com/answers/150215-69325/what-is-the-role-of-ecg-in-the-workup-of-angina-pectoris

[54] Bookshelf, N. C. *A Service of the National Library of Medicine, National Institutes of Health. StatPearls [Internet]*. Treasure Island (FL): StatPearls Publishing, 2021.

[55] Korff, S., Katus, H. A., and Giannitsis, E. Differential diagnosis of elevated troponins. *Heart*, 2006 Jul 1; 92(7): 987–993.

[56] Parveen, Nusrat, Devane, S. R., and Akthar, Shamim Synthetic datasets for myocardial infarction based on actual datasets. *International Journal of Application or Innovation in Engineering & Management (IJAIEM)*, 2021 May; 10(5): 093–101, ISSN 2319 - 4847.

[57] Di Franco, F. et al. The effect of body shape and gender on wireless Body Area Network on-body channels. *IEEE Middle East Conference on Antennas and Propagation (MECAP 2010)*, Cairo, Egypt, 2010, pp. 1–3, doi: 10.1109/MECAP.2010.5724195

[58] Melillo, P., De Luca, N., Bracale, M., and Pecchia, L. Classification tree for risk assessment in patients suffering from congestive heart failure via long-term heart rate variability. *IEEE Journal of Biomedical and Health Informatics*, 2013 May; 17(3): 727–733, doi: 10.1109/jbhi.2013.2244902. PMID: 24592473.

6 Monitoring Operational Parameters in the Manufacturing Industry Using Web Analytical Dashboards

Masood Ismail Tamboli, Tejas Patil, Niraj Patil, Ankita Shinde, and Leena Deshpande
Vishwakarma Institute of Information Technology, Pune, India

CONTENTS

6.1 INTRODUCTION

A dashboard is a visual representation of the most crucial data needed to accomplish one or more goals, presented on a single screen for quick viewing [3]. Few [2005, p. 1] defines a dashboard as "a visual display of the most important information required to accomplish one or more objectives". He also states that dashboards are intended to communicate. In order to communicate effectively, it is important to eliminate any ambiguity, which is one of the challenges of dashboard design [3, 4]. Dashboards for web analytics are used to analyze and enhance company performance as it relates to website usage. A dashboard should be user-friendly, adaptable, interactive, and actionable, and it should be a component of the business intelligence strategy, according to Saifee [2005, p. 3].

This chapter also focuses on customizable, interactive, and actionable parts to increase productivity in the manufacturing industry. This web-based application is intended to perform data cleaning, to transform input data provided in Excel format, and later to use this cleaned data to create

DOI: 10.1201/9781003359456-6

dashboards with various visualizations such as bar charts, pie charts, and line charts. For each separate Excel file, all these visuals are interactive, responsive in size, and simple to understand.

This web application supports a limited number of Excel sheets, such as the static format of an Excel sheet generated by software in the manufacturing industry. This sheet of data is converted into JSON format to enable easy working on cleaned data for finding inferences, performing data analytics, and many more tasks.

Data visualization tools available on the market include Power BI by Microsoft, Tableau by Salesforce, and Google Charts by Google. They provide a very good set of tools and techniques for data visualization, data transformation, data loading, and other tasks, but they have the drawback of requiring repetitive use.

For example, if the data provided has the same structure every time, such as in MIS Production or Daily Production Report datasets (mentioned in Section 6.5), then the data analyst has to perform operations like data extraction, data transformation, data loading, data visualization, and data analyzing to create a dashboard for a single sheet. When a new sheet arrives on another day, with new data and new values, the structure is the same, but the analyst has to perform all the operations again for this new data, which is time consuming and a repetitive task.

This problem of repetitive data cleaning, data extraction, preprocessing, finding inferences, creating visuals, and creating dashboards can be avoided by using scripting. This chapter will help the manufacturing industry to create dashboards automatically without any human intervention using Python and JavaScript libraries. We used Python for data extraction from Excel sheets, data cleaning, preprocessing, finding inferences from the data, and converting it to JSON format before sending it to the front-end for use as input for creating visuals and dashboards. JavaScript frameworks like Apex JS and Next JS are used to create the dashboards and the front-end of a website.

6.2 CHALLENGES

Every day, businesses face the never-ending challenge of analyzing massive amounts of data. The volume of data created is predicted to grow steadily from 90 zettabytes in 2022 to double this by 2025 [2].

Data analytics often enables companies to make better decisions, increase efficiency, and acquire a competitive edge. But accomplishing these objectives can be difficult given the rapidly increasing volume of data and the corresponding obstacles (storage, management, and analysis).

Businesses (especially analysts) should be aware of the potential hurdles in order to manage them and collect the insights needed to guide company choices and procedures [7, 9].

Below are some challenges faced during the development of our project:

1. Extracting meaningful data: It is challenging to extract meaningful data from the large amount available. Data generated by a production department should be considered important for each part. Retrieving the important and meaningful data was a big challenge [9].
2. Proper visualization of data: It is important to present data in a manner that facilitates understanding. Usually, this visualization is presented using charts, graphs, infographics, and other means. Using proper visuals and colors to visualize dashboards was another challenging task [9].
3. Raw data: The analysis of raw data is one of the most challenging aspects of this work. The raw data is generally not preprocessed and contains all the values which may or may not be useful for the visualization and analytics. The data provided by the manufacturing industry was software generated and it also contained some null values and integer plus string values combined, e.g. 12 hr, 50 sec, and 10 kg [10].
4. Complex data structure: As the data was from the production department we had no knowledge about which fields were important or which field was dependent upon which other field; the values and their units were not clearly defined [12].

6.3   LITERATURE REVIEW

Tools for gathering and processing a large amount of data that is structured from internal and external systems, books, emails, files, employee records, and other business sources are known as business intelligence (BI) tools [27].

To overcome the various challenges, power BI tools are available on the market, such as:

1. Power BI: With this, raw data is analyzed and visualized through the use of technology to present actionable information. Combining business analytics, data visualization, and best practices may assist a company to make data-driven choices, which can benefit the firm [22, 27].
2. Tableau: This is a potent and quickly expanding data visualization application used by the business intelligence sector. It transforms complex raw data into a format that is simple to grasp. Professionals at all levels of a business can understand the data thanks in part to Tableau. Additionally, it enables non-technical users to design unique dashboards. With the help of the Tableau application, data analysis can be completed extremely quickly, and dashboards and worksheets are used to produce the visuals [22, 31].
3. Rubiscape: This is a revolutionary platform that makes open source, algorithms, computation, and business people work together harmoniously. Rubiscape extensions (which connect to any data) and Rubiscape apps (which are industry specific) provide unmatched value. At the core of the Rubiscape backbone is: a very powerful data science workbench; a design and analysis studio; natural language processors; a library of statistical and machine learning functions; and the ability to create, test, and maintain basic and advanced analysis and models [31].
4. Google Charts: This is a charting library built entirely on JavaScript that is intended to improve online applications by enabling interactive charting. It accommodates a variety of charts. In common browsers like Chrome, Firefox, Safari, and Internet Explorer, charts are drawn using SVG (IE). The graphics in IE 6 are drawn using VML [22].

For data analytics, three major steps have to be performed to avoid further problems related to the data and its visualization. The software processes that facilitate the original loading and periodic refreshment of the data warehouse contents are commonly known as extraction–transformation–loading (ETL) processes [5].

ETL processes are responsible for [5, 6]:

1. The extraction of the appropriate data from the sources.
2. Their transportation to a special purpose area of the data warehouse where they will be processed.
3. The transformation of the source data and the computation of new values (and possibly records) in order that they obey the structure of the data warehouse relation to which they are targeted.
4. The isolation and cleansing of problematic tuples, in order to guarantee that business rules and database constraints are respected.
5. The loading of the cleansed, transformed data to the appropriate relation in the warehouse, along with the refreshment of its accompanying indexes and materialized views.

6.4   METHODOLOGY

Our methodology is a web-based model which uses data analytics techniques for effective decision making from the manager's perspective.

The objectives of our project are:

1. Understanding the production environment and interpreting operational data;
2. Performing extraction, preprocessing, and transformation on the provided data;

3. To perform analysis of the extracted data and create a web-based dashboard with partial interactions;
4. To generate a performance analysis report.

The web application consists of four major modules, which makes it user friendly and more efficient:

1. Module 1 was to understand the operational data provided by the company and to understand how the actual production happens and how this data is usually generated.
2. Module 2 of our task was to obtain these Excel files so as to understand their structure and extract all the data and convert it to JSON; for that process we used Python pandas. This was one of the complex tasks we performed, as the data was software generated and was horizontally added. After extracting the data we cleaned it up and performed its transformation.
3. In Module 3, our task was to find out the inference and measures between each column. These relations and measures were further used by the front-end team to generate dashboards, which were interactive as they display more information when mouse hovering, mouse clicking, etc.
4. After the dashboards were created we analyzed them and produced inferences for each one, which represents statistical data; a small summary was generated for each dashboard.

6.5   DATASETS

The datasets used in this web application were provided by the manufacturing department, were in Excel format, and were software generated. These files are related to the production department; one is the Daily Production report and the other is MIS Production; they have a previously defined structure as they were generated by software. These datasets are in horizontal format.

All the data provided in Excel is technical and concerns production; there are multiple sheets in each Excel file. The MIS Production file has two sub-sheets: one is FC-Machine Shop and the other is FC-Operation-In House Prod. The other file is the Daily Production Report which also has multiple sub-sheets for Day 1, Day 2, and so on.

Figures 6.1 and 6.2 display screenshots of the dataset.

TABLE 6.1
Daily Production Dataset Description

Number of sheets	2
Number of columns	22
Number of records	48
Number of null fields	0
Numeric columns count	11
String values column count	5
Size of dataset	270 KB

TABLE 6.2
MIS Production (FC-Machine Shop) Dataset Description

Number of sheets	2
Number of columns	89
Number of records	22
Number of null fields	204 cells
Numeric column count	68
String values column count	3
Size of dataset	47.7 KB

FLUID CONTROLS OPERATIONS : MONTHLY MIS : IN-HOUSE PRODUCTION / ASSEMBLY

Month: JULY-2021

Sr	Detail	Unit	Apr-21 Fittings	Valves	Clamp	Total	May-21 Fittings	Valves	Clamp	Total	Jun-21 Fittings	Valves	Clamp	Total	Jul-21 Fittings	Valves	Clamp	Total
	Needle Valve Bodies	Nos		351		351		1311		1,311		990		990		1,200		1,200
	Ball Valves Bodies/ECS	Nos		881.5		882		454		454		750		750		670		670
	Check Valve Bodies	Nos		30		30		140		140		130		130		60		60
3	In House Production : Clamps/Flanges																	
	Weld Plates		0	0	0	0				0				0			0	0
	Top Plates		0	0	0	0				0				0			0	0
	Intermediate Plates		0	0	0	0				0				0			0	0
	Intermediate Bolt		0	0	0	0				0				0			0	0
	Drilling / boring - PP and Alum Clamps		0	0	0	0				0				0			2,340	2,340
	Flanges / Sleeves		0	0	0	0				0				0			0	0
4	Assembly Monitoring																	
	Total Assemblies	Nos	1,17,626	3,569	28,087	1,49,282	2,32,402	1,935	52,684	2,87,021	1,33,956	5,004	30,057	1,69,017	2,33,499	8,249	40,683	2,82,431
	Domestic	Nos	6,909	1,106	1,540	9,557	6,474	631	21,105	28,210	5541	1,656	16,139	23,336	11,292	1,472	19,240	32,004
	Railways	Nos	77,582	527	19,223	97,332	1,20,791	925	14,089	1,35,805	1,20,969	1,765	12,857	1,35,591	1,25,739	3,913	3,998	1,33,650
	Exports	Nos	33135	1,934	7,324	42,393	105137	379	17,490	1,23,006	7446	1,583	1,061	10,090	96,468	2,864	17,445	1,16,777

FC - Machine Shop   FC - Operations - In House Prod   +

FIGURE 6.1 MIS Production sheet 1 (FC-Machine Shop).

DAILY PRODUCTIVITY REPORT

01-07-2021

	JOB ORDER NO	Part Name	opration	Cy.time with loading/ unloading	Part running time	Operator	Actual production time	production per hour	Qty. Req.	Qty. Achived	Loss Qty	Loss m/c hrs.	S-T	PROGRAMMER BUSY	NO OPERATOR	NO POWER	FINISH. CHATTERING & THREADING PROBLEM	JAW/TOOL/ DRILL/INSERT NOT AVB & INSERT CHANGE
CNC-01	J2207-0557	BiCM 12-6 NL Body	1ST	223.00	11.00	AHAJI KAD	9.35	16.14	150.94	119.00	31.94	1.98	1.98	0.00				
	J2207-0557	BiCM 12-6 NL Body	1ST	223.00	3.00	VI SHEGOH	2.55	16.14	41.17	34.00	7.17	0.44	0.44	0.00				
	J2207-0556	G-4 HN-Rx	1ST	180.00	4.00	VI SHEGOH	3.40	20.00	68.00	62.00	6.00	0.30	0.30	0.00				
	J2207-0561	G-4 RAF-RX	1ST	220.00	4.00	VI SHEGOH	3.40	16.36	55.64	51.00	4.64	0.28	0.28	0.00				
	J2207-0609	6 SCB AN-1	1ST	247.00	7.00	MESH DHO	5.95	14.57	86.72	60.00	26.72	1.83	1.83	0.00				
CNC-02	J2207-0562	8-SCF M16X1.5	FINISH	345.00	4.00	MESH DHO	3.40	10.43	35.48	30.00	5.48	0.53	0.53	0.00				
	J2207-0562	8-SCF M16X1.5	1ST	345.00	4.00	JKESH KUM	3.40	10.43	35.48	30.00	5.48	0.53	0.53	0.00				
	J2206-2049	SCFB-8-8 N	FINISH	556.00	7.00	KESH KUM	5.95	6.47	38.53	30.00	8.53	1.32	1.32	0.00				
CNC-04	J2206-2645	STBR-28-28-22	2ND	440.00	11.00	VVIND OVH	9.35	8.18	76.50	41.00	35.50	4.34	2.00	2.34				
	J2206-2644	STBR-28-28-18	3rd	390.00	11.00	SHNA KUM	9.35	9.23	86.31	58.00	28.31	3.07	2.00	1.00				
CNC-05	J2207-0533	BT-6 BPED-RP-SPL	1ST	185.00	11.00	ILESH MOH	9.35	19.46	181.95	170.00	11.95	0.61	0.61	0.00				
	J2207-0533	BT-6 BPED-RP-SPL	1ST	185.00	11.00	AMIT SINGH	9.35	19.46	181.95	142.00	39.95	2.05	2.00	0.89				
CNC-06	J2207-0367	8.8-SCB	1ST	342.00	11.00	HIKANT G	9.35	10.53	98.42	68.00	30.42	2.89	2.00	0.89				
	J2207-0367	8.8-SCB	1ST	342.00	4.00	HIAV PANC	3.40	10.53	35.79	35.00	0.79	0.08	0.08	0.00				
	J2207-0367	8.8-SCB	FINISH	279.00	7.00	HIAV PANC	5.95	12.90	76.77	60.00	16.77	1.30	1.30	0.00				
CNC-07	J2206-2640	SEM-22-12 RP	FINISH	469.00	11.00	HIKANT G	9.35	7.68	71.77	71.00	0.77	0.10	0.10	0.00				
	J2206-2141	SEM-22-M26X1.5	FINISH	378.00	11.00	HIAV PANC	9.35	9.52	89.05	77.00	12.05	1.27	1.27	0.00				
CNC-13	J2206-2097	SPL-NDMO 6L	1ST	340.00	11.00	NARAYAN	9.35	10.59	99.00	90.00	9.00	0.85	0.85	0.00				
	J2206-2097	SPL-NDMO 6L	1ST	340.00	11.00	AMBHAJI C	9.35	10.59	99.00	80.00	19.00	1.79	1.79	0.00				
CNC-15	J2207-0562	8 SCF M16X1.5	1ST	300.00	8.00	MESH DHO	6.80	12.00	81.60	50.00	31.60	2.63	1.12	0.00				
	J2206-2049	SCFB-8-8 N	1ST	426.00	3.00	MESH DHO	2.55	9.45	21.55	16.00	5.55	0.66	0.66	0.00				
	J2206-2049	SCFB-8-8 N	1ST	410.00	11.00	KESH KUM	9.35	8.78	82.10	72.00	10.10	1.15	1.15	0.00				
CNC-16	J2206-1250	6MM OD INSERT	FINISH	240.00	11.00	AHAJI KAD	9.35	15.00	140.25	134.00	6.25	0.42	0.42	0.00				
	J2206-1250	6MM OD INSERT	FINISH	240.00	11.00	MESH DHO	9.35	15.00	140.25	140.00	0.25	0.02	0.02	0.00				
CNC-17	J2207-0268	6 FON	1ST	212.00	11.00	VIN URUN	9.35	16.98	158.77	144.00	14.77	0.87	0.87	0.00				
	J2207-0268	6 FON	FINISH	70.00	8.00	AY AMBHIC	6.80	51.43	349.71	400.00	-50.29	-0.98	0.00	0.00				
	J2207-0260	4 FON	FINISH	150.00	3.00	AY AMBHIC	2.55	24.00	61.20	50.00	11.20	0.47	0.47	0.00				
CNC-18	J2207-0622	12/16 BLV-LP/RLV-2.5S	1ST	286.00	3.00	VIN URUN	2.55	12.59	32.10	28.00	4.10	0.33	0.33	0.00				
	J2207-0622	12/16 BLV-LP/RLV-2.5S	2ND	120.00	6.00	VIN URUN	5.10	30.00	153.00	150.00	3.00	0.10	0.10	0.00				
	J2206-2092	B6C 10L Body	1ST	200.00	2.00	VIN URUN	1.70	18.00	30.60	30.00	0.60	0.03	0.00	0.00				
CNC-19	J2206-2092	B6C 10L Body	1ST	150.00	11.00	AY AMBHIC	9.35	24.00	224.40	245.00	-20.60	-0.86	0.00	0.00				
	J2206-2238	INTERMEDIATE FLANGE	1ST	280.00	3.00	JKESH KUM	2.55	12.86	32.79	12.00	20.79	1.62	1.62	0.00				
	J2206-2238	INTERMEDIATE FLANGE	2ND	240.00	8.00	JKESH KUM	6.80	15.00	102.00	50.00	52.00	3.47	2.00	1.47				
	J2206-2240	4 SN	FINISH	60.00	6.00	HESH DUC	5.10	60.00	306.00	300.00	6.00	0.10	0.10	0.00				
	J2206-2023	6 SN	FINISH	80.00	5.00	HESH DUC	4.25	45.00	191.25	160.00	31.25	0.69	0.69	0.00				
CNC-20	J2207-0595	12-12-6 TRP Body	2ND	600.00	11.00	JKESH KUM	9.35	6.00	56.10	59.00	-2.90	-0.48	0.00	0.00				
	J2206-0579	12-12-4 TRP	2ND	602.00	11.00	JKESH KUM	9.35	5.98	55.91	51.00	4.91	0.82	0.82	0.00				
	J2206-2414	ST 28	1ST	460.00	0.00	HJAV SUTAR	0.00	7.83	0.00	0.00	0.00	0.00	0.00	0.00				

FIGURE 6.2 Daily Production report, day 1.

6.6 EXPERIMENTAL INVESTIGATION

Individuals and businesses can make sense of data with the aid of data analytics. For insights and patterns, data analysts often study raw data. To assist businesses in making decisions and succeeding, analysts employ a variety of tools and strategies [16].

6.6.1 NEED OF DATA ANALYTICS

Data analytics is significant since it aids in the performance optimization of enterprises. Companies can help to cut costs by locating more effective ways to do business by incorporating analytics into their business strategy. Additionally, a corporation can use data analytics to improve business decisions and track consumer preferences and trends to develop fresh, improved goods and services [14].

6.6.1.1 Steps of Data Analytics

Data analytics involves several different steps [16–18]:

1. Identifying the data needs or how the data is grouped is the first stage. Data might be divided based on gender, income, age, or other factors. Data values could be categorical or numerical.
2. The second stage is the data collection procedure. To do this, a variety of resources may be employed, including computers, the internet, cameras, environmental sources, and human workers.
3. Data must first be arranged so that it may be studied after it has been gathered. A spreadsheet or other piece of software that can handle statistical data may be used for this.
4. The data is cleaned up and double-checked to make sure there are no duplicates, errors, or missing information. Before the data is sent to a data analyst for analysis, this stage aids in the correction of any inaccuracies.

6.6.1.2 Types of Data Analytics

Data analytics is broken down into four basic types [18–20]:

1. Descriptive analytics: This provides a description of what has happened over a period of time. Has the number of posts increased? Is there a significant increase in sales this month compared to last month?
2. Diagnostic analytics: This focuses more on the reasons why something happened rather than what happened. As a result, there is a need for more diverse data inputs as well as speculation. Are beer sales affected by the weather? What effect did that recent marketing campaign have on sales for your company?
3. Predictive analytics: This concerns what is likely to be happening in the near future. Did the last hot summer affect sales in the same way as the last time we had a hot summer? Approximately how many weather models have predicted a hot summer for this year?
4. Prescriptive analytics: This suggests a course of action that needs to be taken. If the average of these five weather forecasts predicts a hot summer and it is over 58%, we should hire a second tank and add an evening shift to the brewery to improve production.

6.6.1.3   Benefits of Data Analytics [23–29]

1. Data analytics helps an organization make better decisions: Organizational decisions are frequently based more on intuition than on facts and figures. Lack of access to high-quality data that can aid in better decision-making may be one cause of this. Analytics may assist in converting the available data into useful information for executives to enable them to make better decisions.
2. Increase the efficiency of the work: To assist in achieving certain business goals, analytics can swiftly evaluate vast amounts of data and provide it in a defined way. By enabling management to communicate to staff the insights from the analytics results, it promotes an environment of efficiency and cooperation.
3. Identification of potential risks: Today's high-risk environments are ideal for business growth, but they also call for crucial risk management procedures, which have been made possible by the wealth of data used in their creation. Data analytics can increase the efficiency of crucial simulations used to forecast risk in the future and improve planning.
4. Reduces data size: When the data analyst performs data analysis and data visualization on inputted raw data it reduces its size; size in the context of rows and columns can be converted into visuals which reduces the complexity and enables and understanding of the data.
5. Removes unwanted data: The data which is important from the view of company growth is only used to show insights in the data and unwanted data is not used.

In the production department, the manager needs to evaluate the production cost of each item they produce, the delivery details of each item (e.g. its delivery date/time), the type of item, and other parameters of the item related to delivery. The manager also needs to evaluate the quality of the items, productivity of items per unit of time, cost of each particular item or cost of a set of items, production time of each item, total cost involved in production based on business, the quantity of raw material wastage, and various other parameters [25].

To analyze these parameters a daily monitoring system is required which uses graphical representations. To find inferences and perform analysis on data a statistical model based on various statistical parameters like standard deviation, mean, mode, correlation, and skewness can be applied [8, 28, 30]:

1. Standard deviation: This refers to a measurement of the data's dispersion from the mean. A low standard deviation implies that the data are grouped around the mean, whereas a large standard deviation shows that the data are more dispersed.
2. Mean: The ratio between the sum of all observations and the total number of observations in a data collection.
3. Mode: In statistics, a mode is described as the value that appears most frequently in a group of data.
4. Correlation: A statistical concept which describes how closely two variables are linearly connected, or change at the same pace.
5. Skewness: The direction of outliers is revealed by skewness. A distribution curve's tail is longer on the right side when there is a positive skew. As a result, the distribution curve's outliers are more extreme to the right and closer to the mean to the left.

6.7 TOOLS AND TECHNOLOGIES USED

Tools:

1. Visual Studio Code, also known as VS Code, is a source code editor with features like debugging in any language, auto-completion, syntax highlighting, and code refactoring; users can also add vs code extensions to make it more user friendly.
2. Git is a version control tool that enables you to manage and monitor the history of your source code. You may control Git repositories using the cloud-based hosting service GitHub.
3. Postman is software to test or to use your APIs; you can use it to design, build, and test APIs.
4. The XAMPP server is one of the most popular cross-platform web servers, which enables programmers to construct and test their applications on a local web server.

Technologies:

1. React JS V18.2.0: This is a front-end JavaScript library that is open-source, free, and used to construct user interfaces using UI components.
2. Next JS V13.0.2: This is an additional React framework that makes it possible to generate static and dynamic web pages and perform server-side rendering.
3. ApexCharts V3.36.0: This is a contemporary charting framework that aids developers in producing attractive and interactive visualizations for websites. It is free and open-source.
4. Python 3.0: This is an interpreted, object-oriented, high-level programming language created by Guido van Rossum that has dynamic semantics.
5. MySQL: This is a relational database management system that is open source; data is stored in the form of rows and columns.
6. Pandas: This is a dataset manipulation Python library. It offers tools for data exploration, cleaning, analysis, and manipulation.
7. Flask server: This is described as server software that consists of one or more computers that are packaged together and specifically used for operating the software program on the World Wide Web. It is capable of performing HTTP requests on the public World Wide Web, private LANs, and private WANs.
8. JSON stands for JavaScript Object Notation. It is a lightweight format for storing and transporting data.

6.8 RESULTS AND DISCUSSION

- Module 1: Registration Page. A responsive registration page designed to register users with mandatory fields such as first name, last name, username, password, and email.
- Module 2: Login Page. When a user is registered he or she is now authorized to access this web analytics service and can access it by logging in using valid credentials.
- Module 3: File Uploading Page. In this module the user can upload a specified structured Excel sheet using an upload file API and can convert it to JSON to visualize dashboards.
- Module 4: Data Analytics and Visualization Page. In this page the uploaded sheets can be used as input to generate dashboards, which are dynamic and generate a short inference about what a chart is actually representing; at the top of the dashboard is a summary of the Excel sheet that was auto-generated.

6.9 RESULTS

6.9.1 DAILY PRODUCTION REPORT DASHBOARD

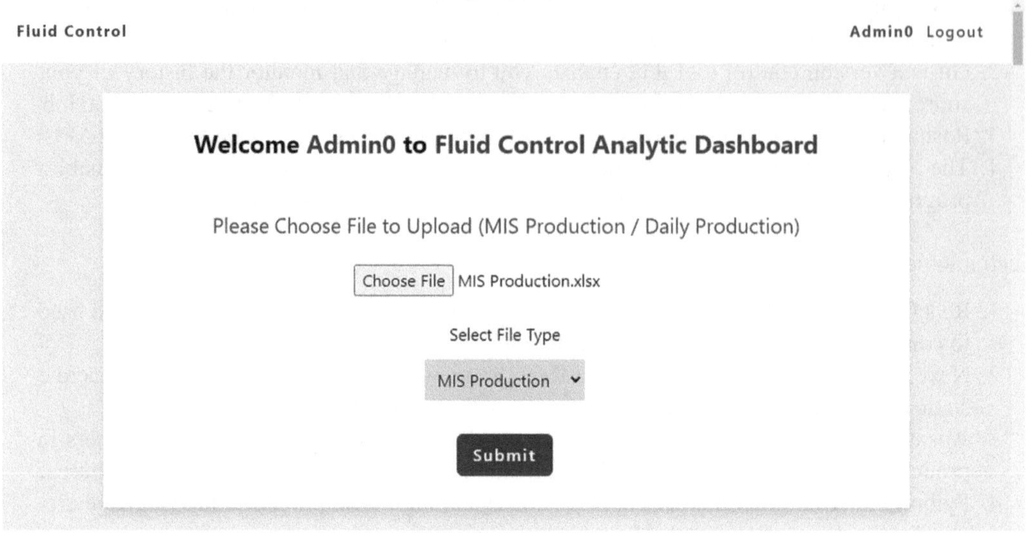

FIGURE 6.3   Landing page to upload Excel files to server and convert it to JSON.

FIGURE 6.4   A short summary of the Daily Production Report.

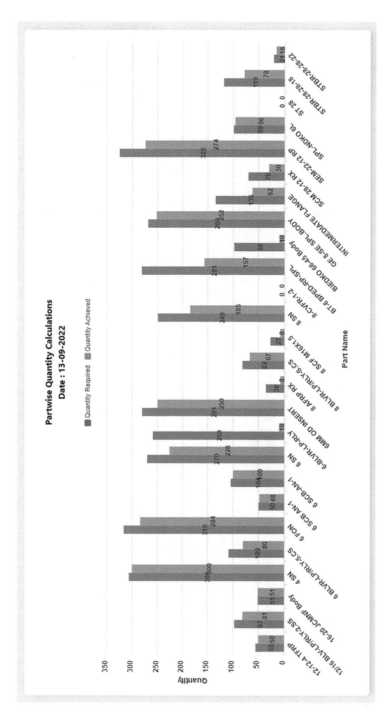

FIGURE 6.5 A joint bar graph to show the quantity required and quantity achieved of each part.

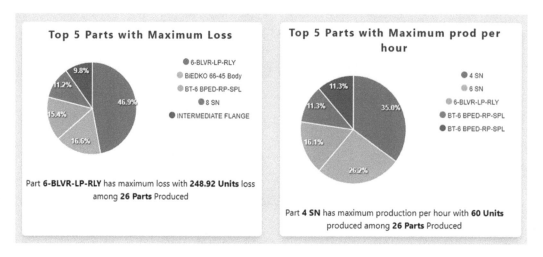

FIGURE 6.6   Top five parts with maximum loss and top five parts with maximum production per hour.

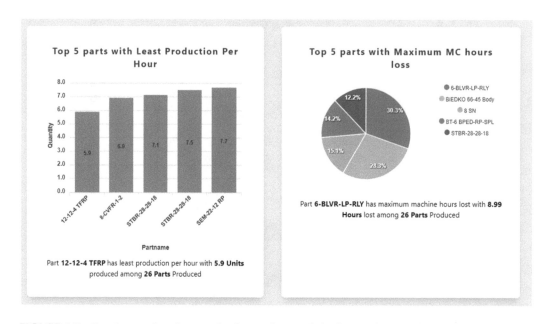

FIGURE 6.7   Bar chart to show least production per hour and pie chart to show maximum MC hour loss.

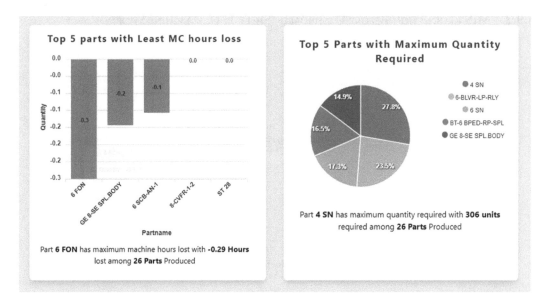

FIGURE 6.8 Negative bar graph to show least MC hour loss and pie chart to show maximum quantity required.

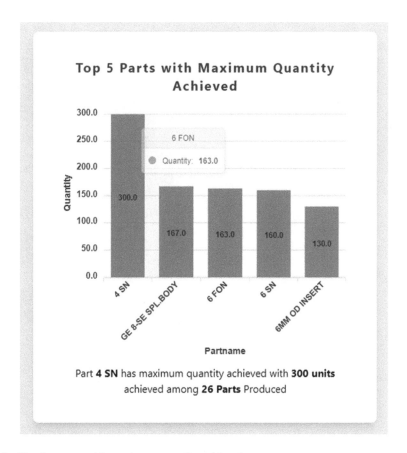

FIGURE 6.9 Top five parts with maximum quantity achieved.

6.9.2   MIS PRODUCTION REPORT DASHBOARD (SHEET 1: FC-MACHINE SHOP)

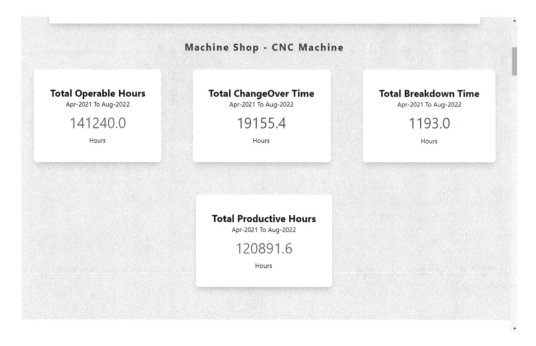

FIGURE 6.10   A short summary of CNC machine data.

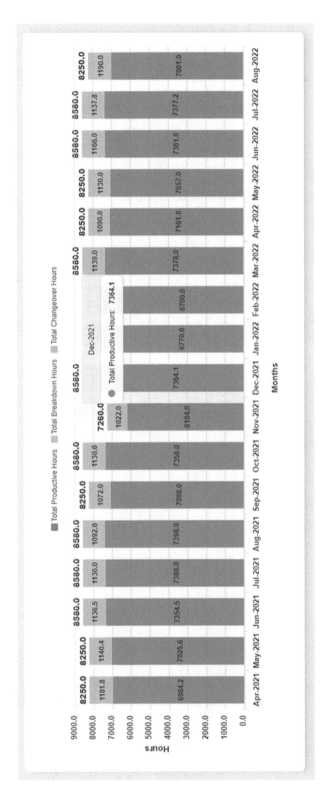

FIGURE 6.11 Multi-variable bar chart showing total production hours, total breakdown hours, and total changeover hours of CNC machine for each month.

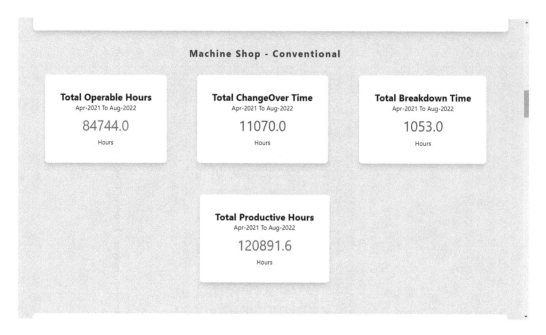

FIGURE 6.12   A short summary of conventional machine data.

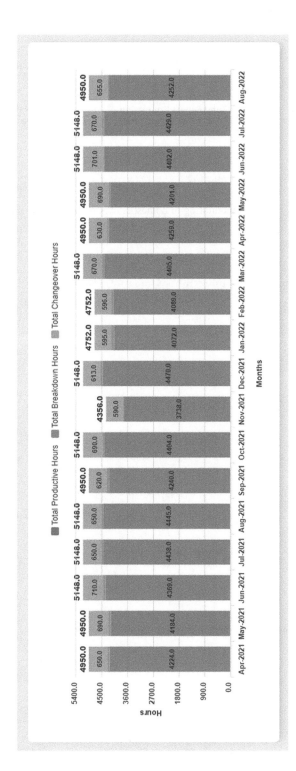

FIGURE 6.13 Multi-variable bar chart showing total production hours, total breakdown hours, and total changeover hours of conventional machine for each month.

6.9.3 MIS PRODUCTION REPORT DASHBOARD (SHEET 2: FC-OPERATIONS IN HOUSE PRODUCTION)

FIGURE 6.14 A summary of assembly monitoring in domestic, export, and railway production from April –21 to August 22.

FIGURE 6.15 Summary of total number of each part from April –21 to August –22.

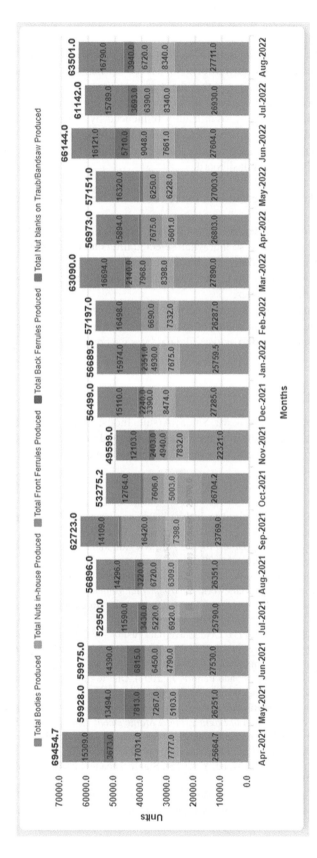

FIGURE 6.16 Multi-variable bar chart showing total bodies, nuts in-house complete, front ferrules, back ferrules, nut blanks on Traub/bandsaw produced from April –21 to August –22.

6.10   FUTURE DIRECTIONS

The massive data analytics market in India is anticipated to reach USD 118.7 billion by 2026, expanding steadily as a result of the government's push for digitalization and the construction of new data centers. By 2026, it is anticipated that the data analytics sector will have produced over 11 million new jobs and increased investment in AI and machine learning by 33.49% in 2022. The future of Industry 4.0 is expected to be significantly influenced by India's data analytics sectors, which will also likely lead to major job growth and improved living conditions. Future paradigm shifts will be brought about by this industry, which will be disruptive [11, 13].

Future work on our web analytics dashboard:

1. The work that will be implemented with future editions of the software is described in the following section.
2. Allow users to have more access to charts allowing them to interact with dashboards.
3. Apply filters on each dashboard so that when selected filters all other charts or dashboards should dynamically change and display dynamic data.
4. This web app is now valid for up to two Excel sheets; later other APIs could be used to extract data for other Excel sheets.
5. This web app is valid only for a single department, i.e. the manufacturing department; later we could generate as many dashboards as there are departments, based on their data.
6. This web application is limited to statistical data; later we could work on operational data.

ACKNOWLEDGMENT

We would like to express our gratitude to Mr. Sanjay Arsule, Industry Mentor, Fluid Control Chakan Pune, for providing us with information on their manufacturing department, assisting us in understanding it, and offering appropriate guidance up to the completion of this project.

REFERENCES

[1] Hemlata, C. and Gulia, P. (2016). Big data analytics. *Research Journal of Computer and Information Technology Sciences*, 4(2), pp. 1–4.
[2] Axryd, S. (2019). *Why 85% of Big Data Projects Fail*, www.digitalnewsasia.com/insights/why-85-big-data-projects-fail [Accessed 10 September 2019].
[3] Grainger, S., Mao, F., and Buytaert, W. (2016). Environmental data visualization for non-scientific contexts: Literature review and design framework. *Environmental Modelling and Software*, 85, pp. 299–318.
[4] Wolfe, J. (2015). Teaching students to focus on the data in data visualization. *Journal of Business and Technical Communication*, 29(3), pp. 344–359.
[5] Bleiholder, J. and Naumann, F. (2005). Declarative data fusion - syntax, semantics, and implementation. *9th East European Conference on Advances in Databases and Information Systems (ADBIS 2005)*, pp. 58–73, Tallinn, Estonia, September 12–15, 2005.
[6] Carreira, P., Galhardas, H., Lopes, A., and Pereira, J. (2007). One-to-many data transformations through data mappers. *Data Knowledge Engineering*, 62(3), pp. 483–503.
[7] Kakhani, M. K., Kakhani, S., and Biradar, S. R. (2015). Research issues in big data analytics. *International Journal of Application or Innovation in Engineering & Management*, 2(8), pp. 228–232.
[8] Li, X. et al. (2015). Advanced aggregate computation for large data visualization. *Proceedings of IEEE Symposium on Large Data Analysis and Visualization*, pp. 137, 138.
[9] Jin, X., Wah, B. W., Cheng, X., and Wang, Y. (2015). Significance and challenges of big data research. *Big Data Research*, 2(2), pp. 59–64.
[10] Kuo, M. H., Sahama, T., Kushniruk, A. W., Borycki, E. M., and Grunwell, D. K. (2014). Health big data analytics: Current perspectives, challenges and potential solutions, *International Journal of Big Data Intelligence*, 1, pp. 114–126.

[11] https://www.inventiva.co.in/trends/top-10-best-data-analytics-institutes-in-india-in-2023/

[12] Das, T. K. and Kumar, P. M. (2013). Big data analytics: A framework for unstructured data analysis. *International Journal of Engineering and Technology*, 5(1), pp. 153–156.

[13] Park, Y.-E. (2021). A data-driven approach for discovery of the latest research trends in higher education for business by leveraging advanced technology and big data. *The Journal of Education for Business*, 96(5), pp. 291–298.

[14] Zhu, H., Xu, Z., and Huang, Y. (2015). Research on the security technology of big data information. *International Conference on Information Technology and Management Innovation*, pp. 1041–1044.

[15] Valaskova, K., Ward, P., and Svabova, L. (2021). Deep learning-assisted smart process planning, cognitive automation, and industrial big data analytics in sustainable cyber-physical production systems. *Journal of Self-Governance and Management Economics*, 9(2), pp. 9–20.

[16] Cohen, J., Dolan, B., Dunlap, M., Hellerstein, J. M., and Welton, C. (2009). MAD skills: New analysis practices for big data. *Proceedings of the ACM VLDB Endowment*, 2(2), pp. 1481–1492.

[17] Ary, D., Jacobs, L. C., Irvine, C. K. S., and Walker, D. (2018). *Introduction to research in education*. Cengage Learning.

[18] Al Sakka, F. A. (2014). *Human capital development in special economic zones: The case of Dubai*. University of Salford (United Kingdom).

[19] Collis, J. and Hussey, R. (2013). *Business research: A practical guide for undergraduate and postgraduate students*. Macmillan International Higher Education.

[20] Erickson, F. (2006). Definition and analysis of data from videotape: Some research procedures and their rationales. *Handbook of Complementary Methods in Education Research*, 3, pp. 177–192.

[21] https://www.techtarget.com/searchbusinessanalytics/definition/business-intelligence-BI

[22] https://www.selecthub.com/business-intelligence/key-types-business-intelligence-tools/

[23] Farrokhi, F. and Mahmoudi-Hamidabad, A. (2012). Rethinking convenience sampling: Defining quality criteria. *Theory & Practice in Language Studies*, 2(4).

[24] Jebb, A. T., Parrigon, S., and Woo, S. E. (2017). Exploratory data analysis as a foundation of inductive research. *Human Resource Management Review*, 27(2), pp. 265–276.

[25] Administration Industrially General Purveyance Organization -Commandment, Coordination Controlee, Paris Dunned, 196.

[26] Vocationa Business: Training, Developing and Motivating People by Richard Barrett - Business & Economics, 2003.

[27] https://www.simplilearn.com/tutorials/power-bi-tutorial/what-is-power-bi

[28] Wilder, R. T., Flick, R. P., Sprung, J., Katusic, S. K., Barbaresi, W. J., Mickelson, C., et al. (2009). Early exposure to anesthesia and learning disabilities in a population-based birth cohort. *Anesthesiology*, 110, pp. 796–804. [PMC free article] [PubMed] [Google Scholar]

[29] https://www.teradata.com/Blogs/Benefits-of-Data-and-Analytics

[30] Sprent, P. (2003). Statistics in medical research. *Swiss Medical Weekly*, 133, pp. 522–529. [PubMed] [Google Scholar]

[31] https://www.simplilearn.com/data-visualization-tools-article

7 Concurrent Line Perpendicular Distance Functions for Contour Point Analysis

Ratnesh Kumar and Kalyani Mali
University of Kalyani, Nadia, India

CONTENTS

7.1 INTRODUCTION

The system of natural intelligence known as human vision has the ability to conveniently, effectively, and efficiently recognize the shape of an object from a set of objects by using the presence of humour. Similar tasks are very critical in analytical work for a system of artificial intelligence called machine vision. Due to the absence of natural intelligence, machine vision is unable to perform shape classification tasks in the area of pattern recognition and image processing problems. Analytically, the geometrically invariant feature in shape classification and matching is a very crucial problem in computer vision. It is widely used in many applications such as object recognition [1, 2, 16–18, 23–25], part structure and articulation [3], character recognition [4], robot navigation [5], shape evolution [6], topology analysis in sensor networks [7], and medical image and protein analysis [8]. It is a very difficult task to recognize and classify a similar object from an object database which looks similar to human vision. Therefore, geometrically invariant and shape-preserving boundary point analysis into an object has been one of the key problems in computer vision for binary shape classification. The structural problem of geometrically invariant (translation, rotation, scaling, etc.) shape-preserving boundary point analysis for the classification of objects has to be intuitively defined and solved by rich shape descriptors, which should be more informative, discriminative, and efficient for the contour matching process. An excellent shape descriptor should not only tolerate the geometric differences of objects from the same category but, at the same time, it should allow the discriminating of objects from different shape classes. The aim of this work is to extend the elegant analysis of features extracted from shape boundary points [1, 18]. The purpose of the proposed methodology is to overcome the problem of the oversampling and undersampling of shape boundary points. The result of the oversampling of an object's boundary points becomes information loss, and it might deviate from the exact characteristics of the shape boundary points. On the another hand, the result of the undersampling of boundary points can be selected as a combination of shape feature vectors of a larger number of non-discriminating object contour points, and it may have a lesser number of discriminating object contour points from one shape to another shape. The problem of the oversampling and undersampling of shape boundary points in binary object classification and recognition can be overcome by a concurrent line perpendicular distance function (CLPDF) base shape descriptor. The proposed CLPDF methodology has incurring the boundary point's perpendicular distance on sampling of line passing through object centroid. During a study of the literature [19], we analysed the methodology of the shape classification approaches developed by renowned researchers based on outer and inner pixels. There are mainly two types of shape descriptors: contour-based shape descriptors and region-based shape descriptors. In the study stage [11], we can see that local or global features alone are not excellent features for shape classification. The global feature vectors are overwhelmed by local feature vectors, or local feature vectors are overwhelmed by global feature vectors. In addition, many expensive computational feature vectors having large dimensions overwhelm the small dimension feature vectors, even though the small feature vectors may contain large discriminating information. Therefore, we need an effective feature selection algorithm that reduces expensive computational feature vectors into small dimensions and combines large and small dimension feature vectors into a single feature vector. In this chapter, we develop two-dimensional (2D) feature vectors for binary object silhouettes, CLPDFs. We have effectively computed the new features from the object contour points by using the traditional concept of coordinate geometry known as concurrent lines for shape features and produce a compact feature vector for object classification. Figure 7.1 shows the proposed methodology as a flow diagram. The eigenvalue of the moment generating functions has used for dimensions reduction and

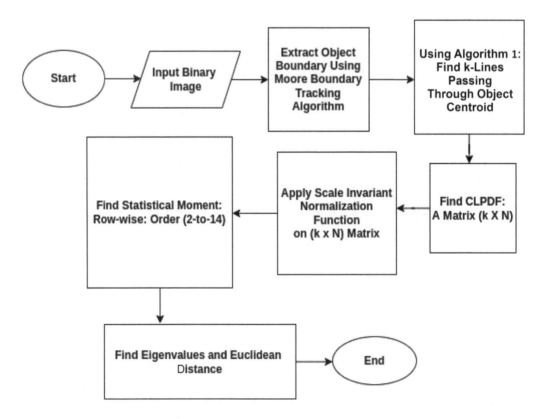

FIGURE 7.1   Flow diagram of our approach.

selection tools of statistical moments on the normalized multi-lines perpendicular distance functions. Its ability of decorrelation serves to decorrelate redundant features, and its energy packing property serves to compact useful information into new dominant features.

During our literature survey [1–3, 16, 17, 23, 24], we analysed the steps required for obtaining the scale invariant features. Mainly, two steps are required for scale invariant data normalization: the first is at the features level and the second concerns the number of pixels that contribute to feature selection. In [1–3], the authors normalize the data of the second level by sampling the contour points of an object. The sampling produces lossy information. So, we required a data-driven lossless information methodology for a scale invariant shape classification approach that discriminates inter-class objects.

Now, we have been reported on the work related to our proposed methodology. The ability to find the shape-preserving contour-based features from object contour points is one of the well-known kinds of descriptors. The object contour describes the road map of shape that has been reported by several image processing researchers. In [1], shape matching and classification using height functions formulate the problems of shape-preserving object classification by using height functions. The authors first sample the contour points of an object and then compute the perpendicular distances called height functions from the object contour points to the tangent lines. They describe the very high accuracy in experimental results on shape databases. In [9], learning context-sensitive similarity by shortest path propagation developed the shape/object classification methodology based on shortest path propagation. In [13], "Finding Salient Points of Shape Contour for Object Recognition", the authors proposed an adaptive contour points evolution algorithm to capture the salient points from the boundary of an object for feature extraction. In [12], "Binary Plankton Image Classification", the authors developed several new shape preserving descriptors and selected the best set of features by using a normalized multilevel dominant eigenvector for binary plankton object recognition. In [10], "A Bioinformatics Approach to 2D Shape Classification", the authors incorporate the bioinformatics/biological tools with well-known chain coding for 2D shape analysis. In [2], "Farthest Point Distance: A New Shape Signature for Fourier Descriptors", the authors find the farthest point distance between two contour points and incorporate the Fourier descriptors for shape classification.

The rest of this chapter is organized as follows. Section 7.2 represents the basic background of shape-preserving features in detail. Section 7.3 discusses shape descriptors using the multi-line perpendicular distance function. Section 7.4 develops the methodology for shape scale invariant features. Section 7.5 presents the experimental results. Finally, Section 7.6 draws some conclusions.

7.2 BACKGROUND

One key problem in contour-based object classification and recognition in computer vision is a sampling of the boundary points that produces the low power of discriminative features between inter-class shapes and that has fewer informatic feature vectors. In this case, shape feature vectors depend on some selected points of a contour of an object that has not yielded a discriminative power. We have developed contour-based strong discriminating power features for shape-preserving object classification by considering all contour points of an object. The other key problem of a binary object is boundary extraction that can be solved by the Moore boundary tracking algorithm, following Moore (1968). This algorithm produces N number of points on a binary object contour that renders the structure of a shape.

Let $X = X_i$; $i = 1, ..., N$ denote the N number of points on the outer contour of an object, extracted by the Moore boundary tracking algorithm, where index i is the points along the outer contour of a given shape. To compute the perpendicular distance on the given concurrent straight lines is the most important step in our algorithm. The method which computes the CLPDF from each point of an object contour to the given concurrent straight line passes through the centre of gravity of an object. Here, the key observation is the projection line that provides an excellent reference line for perpendicular distance functions. For each point X_i on the contour and centre of gravity (X_c, Y_c) of a shape formed reference line for perpendicular distance functions. The concept of the centre of gravity (X_c, Y_c) of an object for point $(x(i), y(i))$ on a contour is defined as:

$$X_c = \frac{1}{N}\sum_{i=1}^{N}x(i), \quad Y_c = \frac{1}{N}\sum_{i=1}^{N}y(i) \tag{7.1}$$

The other most critical concept in our algorithm is the equation of concurrent straight lines passing through the centre of gravity of an object boundary. Therefore, the equation of the concurrent straight lines whose slope is $m(0 \le m \le 2\pi)$ and which passes through the point (X_c, Y_c) is given as:

$$(Y - Y_c) = m(X - X_c) \tag{7.2}$$

Now, the perpendicular distance P from an object's contour points to the concurrent straight lines is:

$$|P| = \frac{|m\alpha - \beta + Y_c - mX_c|}{\sqrt{m^2 + 1}} \tag{7.3}$$

Here we consider (α, β) are the contour points of an object for computing the perpendicular distance on the family of lines defined in Equation 7.2. We have been choosing the slope of the initial line $m(0 \le m \le 2\pi)$ by using Algorithm 7.1 and computing subsequent multi-lines for finding the perpendicular distance from an object's contour points.

Theorem 7.1: *A straight line is such that the algebraic sum of the perpendiculars drawn upon it from any number of fixed points on the curve is zero. Show that the line always passes through a fixed point called the centre of gravity of a curve.*

Corollary 7.1: *The algebraic sum of the perpendicular distance from a set of points on the line passing through a centre of gravity of points is zero.*

7.3   SHAPE DESCRIPTOR

Our main objective is to develop an optimal mathematical data analysis approach to get most information from finite object contour points. So, our next task is to represent the characteristics of our proposed methodology, the CLPDF for shape classification and recognition. Mathematically, the concurrent lines' perpendicular distance functions have been implemented by selecting k-lines in an anticlockwise direction from the initial line by using Equation 7.2 and Algorithm 7.1: for different values of slope $m(0 \le m \le 2\pi)$ and having equal distance between two slopes. The perpendicular distance on the ith$(i = 1, ..., k)$ line from the jth$(j = 1, ..., N)$ point of an object contour is defined by the distance value $d_{i,j}$. Specifically, the perpendicular distance value $d_{i,j}$ is positive, negative or zero when the jth points on contour X_j is to the left of, to the right of or just on the line l_i. Obviously, the positive or negative symbol of the distance value makes a more precise representation for the relative location of the point x_j to the line l_i. We know not only the distance, but also which side it stands on. Note that the line l_i passes through the centre of gravity (X_c, Y_c) of the shape X, which divides the shape contour into two or more parts. Figure 7.2, selected from the Kimia-99 dataset, represents the structural view of the shape boundary and the centroid. The centroid of the closed boundary can be found by using Equation 7.1. Figure 7.2(a) shows the contour of an object that has been extracted by using the Moore boundary tracking algorithm, and Figure 7.2(b) shows their centre of gravity that has been used for constructing the initial line.

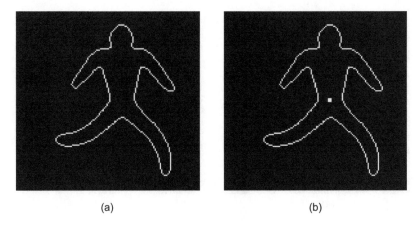

(a)   (b)

FIGURE 7.2   Shape selected from the Kimia-99 dataset: (a) contour of a shape; (b) their centre of gravity.

ALGORITHM 7.1:   Selecting k-lines randomly using Equation 7.2.

Require: $N > 0$ *is the number of object contour points.*
Ensure: $p = (i, j)$ *and* $q = (s, t)$ *are two points lying on the object's contour.* $i \leftarrow 0$, $j \leftarrow 0$, $s \leftarrow 0$, $t \leftarrow 0$, $r \leftarrow 0$, $K \leftarrow 0$, $r^t \leftarrow 0$, m, n, x, y;
  while $i \leq N - 1$ **do**
    while $j \leq N - 1$ **do**
      while $s \leq N - 1$ **do**
        while $t \leq N - 1$ **do**

$$r_{p,q} = \sqrt{\left(s-i\right)^2 + \left(t-j\right)^2}$$

        if $r \leq r_{p,q}$ **then**
          $r \leftarrow r_{p,q}$, $m \leftarrow s$, $n \leftarrow t$;
        end if
      end while end while
     if $r^t \leq r$ **then**
      $r^t \leftarrow r$, $x \leftarrow i$, $y \leftarrow j$;
     end if
    end while end
  while
Generate 1st line for our CLPDF:
p=(x,y) and q= (m,n)
Shift the line(p,q) on the centroid;
Generate 2-to-k line for our CLPDF:
Slope (m)=(360/k); k= Number of lines.

  while $K \leq k$ **do**
    Rotate the line(p,q) clockwise;
    New slope(p,q) = slope(p,q)+slope(m);
  end while

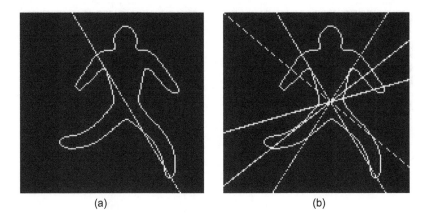

FIGURE 7.3　The ith line passing through the centre of gravity: (a) the single line; (b) the multiple line.

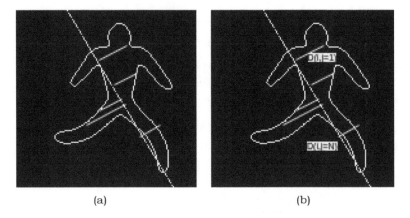

FIGURE 7.4　Representation of the ith line shape descriptor using a perpendicular distance function: (a) the perpendicular distance from contour points; (b) the distance descriptor $D_{1,j} = D_{1,j=1}, D_{1,j=2}, ..., D_{1,j=N}$.

The furthest point distance signature has been explained and is used in [2] for binary shape classification. In our proposed algorithm, we have used the concept of the farthest point distance for finding the initial line. Here, we select these two points on the object's boundary that have maximum distance from any other combinations of two points and are collinear with the object's boundary centroid. The above scenario is shown in Figure 7.3(a), which represents the most distant collinear points. Here, we have included three points for computing the furthest distance, two points on the object boundary and another point at their centroid. The most distant collinear points are used for constructing the initial line in our proposed algorithm, which is used for the purpose of extracting an enhanced and powerful shape feature for discriminating the objects of one class from another.

The family of concurrent lines passing through the centre of gravity is shown in Figure 7.3(b) and which is used for computing the perpendicular distance from an object's boundary points. Here, we have to select only k-concurrent lines that have started from initial lines in an anticlockwise direction. These k-lines should be of equal slope distance. Figure 7.4(a) shows the perpendicular distances on the ith line that has passed through concurrent points. Figure 7.4(b) represents the overall design of our proposed model CLPDF. Here, we calculate the perpendicular distance values of every contour point to the line l_i. Now, the shape descriptor of the object contour points X_j with respect to the shape X is defined as:

$$L = l_i; \text{ where } i = 1, 2, \ldots, k.$$

Here, k is an experimental parameter and its value depends on the shape database.

$$l_i = D_{i,j} = \left(D_{i,1}, D_{i,2}, \ldots, D_{i,N} \right); Where, \ j = 1, \ldots, N \tag{7.4}$$

· Here, N is the number of boundary points of an object which have been extracted using the Moore boundary tracking algorithm. $D_{i,j}$ denotes the perpendicular distance value between the ith line and the jth point on the contour of a given shape. Here, we have observed that L is a 1D vector that consists of slopes corresponding to k-lines. The first element in a 1D vector L corresponds to the slope of the furthest collinear points. The remaining $(k−1)$ slopes of the corresponding lines can be generated by subdividing the slope of the closed boundary in the anti clockwise fashion. We have been considering the line l_i corresponding to ith slope in L. The perpendicular distance on the line l_i generates a row vector corresponding to the ith slope in L. Therefore, $D_{i,j}$ generates a 2D matrix corresponding to each slope in L. The proposed descriptor L depends not only on the direction of line l_i, but also on the location of the contour point X_j of a shape X. In Figure 7.4(a), the perpendicular distance descriptors are represented on a black background and a white foreground, and in Figure 7.4(b), the distance descriptors for the three points $D_{i,j=1}$, $D_{i,j=2}$, and $D_{i,j=N}$ are given. It is obvious that our descriptor may be totally different because the reference line l_i has totally different properties. This leads to a strong discriminative power to find the correct correspondence between the points from two shapes.

Since the reference line and perpendicular distance values are defined directly on the contour points, the proposed descriptor explicitly contains the information of the geometric relationship of the contour points. This makes CLPDF, translations, and rotations invariant features. As all the contour points will translate and rotate synchronously, the geometric relationship between them will remain unchanged. However, the descriptor defined above consists of the relative location for every single contour point to the reference line. Such a precise description may be too sensitive to local boundary deformations. One solution to this problem is to extract the boundary by using the Moore boundary tracking algorithm.

7.4   SCALE INVARIANT FEATURES

The CLPDFs discussed in Section 7.3 are invariant to the translations and rotations. The descriptor $L = l_i = D_{i,j}$ defined in Equation 7.4 generates a k x N 2D feature matrix. In order to make our own such matrix invariant to the shape scale, we introduced a normalization approach based on standard deviation. The 2D feature matrix corresponding to the randomly chosen slope that produced k-concurrent lines is represented in Equation 7.2. The row-wise feature matrix for the contour points of an object is represented by $L = D_{i,j}$, which is derived in Equation 7.4. The computational value of the perpendicular distances on the lines $l_i(i = 1, 2, \ldots, k)$ partition into two categories based on the sign of their magnitude. The upper part of a line is called the set of positive values, and the lower part of a line is called the set of negative values. Hence, our intuition that the sign of the shortest distance on each line in the CLPDF matrix classifies the object contour points into two sets, $d_{i,j}^+$ and $d_{i,j}^-$. $d_{i,j}^+$ represents the set of positive magnitudes and $d_{i,j}^-$ represents the set of negative magnitudes. Therefore, the shape scale invariant normalization function for the matrix $D_{i,j}$ is represented by Equation 7.6. To make our method geometrically scale invariant, we have developed a row-wise normalization function for $D_{i,j}$ using the standard deviation $\left| \sigma_i^+ \right| + \left| \sigma_i^- \right|$ corresponding to each subdivision of a CLPDF matrix row into $d_{i,j}^+$ and $d_{i,j}^-$.

$$D_{i,j}^{(norm)} = \frac{D_{(i,j)} - \bar{D}_{(i,j)}}{\left|\sigma_i^+\right| + \left|\sigma_i^-\right|} \tag{7.5}$$

From corollary, Since, mean $\bar{D}_{(i,j)} = 0$. Therefore, $D_{i,j}^{(norm)}$, the normalized CLPDF, may be deduced as:

$$D_{i,j}^{(norm)} = \frac{D_{(i,j)}}{\left|\sigma_i^+\right| + \left|\sigma_i^-\right|} \tag{7.6}$$

If m^i denotes the rth central moment of the ith row of a k × N matrix $D(i,j)$. Now, we consider a matrix $A(4,4)$ which has some special characteristics that can be used for the reduction of data-driven knowledge into a more compact form, as is derived in Equation 7.7.

$$A_{(4,4)} = \begin{bmatrix} m_2^i & m_4^i & m_6^i & m_8^i \\ m_4^i & m_6^i & m_8^i & m_{10}^i \\ m_6^i & m_8^i & m_{10}^i & m_{12}^i \\ m_8^i & m_{10}^i & m_{12}^i & m_{14}^i \end{bmatrix} \tag{7.7}$$

Further, we analyse the largest eigenvalue corresponding to the moment generating matrix given in Equation 7.7 and remove the other smallest eigenvalues that have only a small discriminating power. Therefore, CLPDF $D(i,j)$ generates a 1D feature vector of the largest eigenvalue corresponding to a moment generating matrix for each row in $D(i,j)$ having dimension k × N. Hence the row-wise data in $D(i,j)$ is represented by the largest eigenvalue, and which reduced a k × N matrix into a k × 1 matrix. For the task of shape recognition, usually a shape similarity or dissimilarity is computed by finding the optimal correspondence of contour points, which is used to rank the dataset of shapes for shape retrieval. In this chapter, we have used a well-known distance measure function between two shapes called the Euclidean distance. Then the shape similarity or dissimilarity between two shapes X and Y is the sum of the Euclidean distances of the corresponding k eigenvalues. For the two given shapes the k largest eigenvalues, extracted by using Equation 7.7, corresponding to each row of the $D(i,j)$ matrix, are described as follows. The shape features for objects $X = (x_i)$ and $Y = (y_j)$ for $i = 1, ..., k$ and $j = 1, ..., k$ represent the eigenvalue feature vector. Now, the discriminating functions are the two eigenvalue feature vectors that computed the dissimilarity between two shapes:

$$Dissimilarity(X,Y) = \sqrt{\sum_{i=1}^{i=k} (x_i - y_i)^2} \tag{7.8}$$

where x_i and y_i for $i = 1, 2, ..., k$ are the two feature vectors corresponding to the largest eigenvalue for shapes X and Y.

7.5   EXPERIMENTS AND ANALYSIS

The experimental results on popular benchmark datasets using our proposed algorithm achieve encouraging results. We used the Kimias 99 [14] and MPEG-7 CE- Shape-1 [15] dataset for the experiments. All the experiments in this chapter were conducted using a Python programming tool and tested on an Intel CORE-i5 CPU with 3GB RAM on a Linux Mint Operating System. The experimental setup for different databases for extracting data-driven knowledge for shape-preserving object recognition and classification is based on their number of contour points. We take $k = 20$ for Kimia's datasets and $k = 50$ for MPEG-7 CE-Shape-1 datasets.

7.5.1 KIMIA'S DATASET

Kimia's dataset has recently been widely used for testing the performances of shape preserving descriptors for shape matching and classification. It contains 99 images from 9 categories, each category containing 11 images (as shown in Figure 7.5). In the experiment, every binary object in the dataset is considered a query, and the retrieval result is summarized as the number of tops 1 to top 10 closest matches in the same class (excluding the query object). Therefore, the best possible result for each of the rankings is 99. Table 7.1 lists the results of the perpendicular distance functions and some other recent methods. Our method performance is comparably better than recent approaches.

7.5.2 MPEG-7 DATASET

The other widely tested dataset is MPEG-7 CE-Shape-1, which consists of 1400 silhouette images from 70 classes. Each class has 20 different binary objects; some typical objects are shown in Figure 7.6. The recognition rate is measured by the bullseye test used by several authors in the literature [20–22].

FIGURE 7.5 Kimia's 99 dataset.

TABLE 7.1
Retrieval Results from Kimia's 99 Dataset

Algorithms	1st	2nd	3rd	4th	5th	6th	7th	8th	9th	10th
Salient points [13]	99	99	98	96	95	93	93	90	84	77
IDSC [3]	99	99	99	98	98	97	97	98	94	79
Height function [1]	99	99	99	99	98	99	99	96	95	88
CLPDF Model	**99**	**99**	**99**	**99**	**98**	**99**	**99**	**97**	**96**	**90**

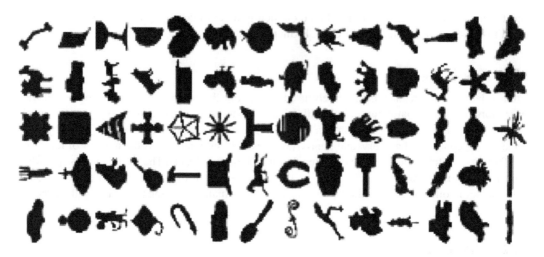

FIGURE 7.6   The MPEG-7 CE-Shape-I dataset.

TABLE 7.2

Retrieval Rate (Bullseye Score) of Different Algorithms for the MPEG-7 CE-Shape-1 Dataset

Algorithms	Score (%)
IDSC+DP [3]	85.40
Salient points [13]	87.54
Bioinformatics approach [10]	77.24
Height functions [1]	89.66
Height functions + shape complexity [1]	90.35
Our method (CLPDF)	**91.86**

The bullseye score for every queried image in the dataset is matched with all other images and the top 40 most similar images are counted. Of these 40 images, at most 20 are from the queried image class of those correctly hit. The score of the test is the ratio of the number of correct hits of all images to the highest possible number of hits. In this case, the highest possible number of hits is 20×1400 = 28,000. Table 7.2 lists the results in terms of bullseye score (%) for perpendicular distance functions and some other recent methods. Our method's performance is comparably better than recent approaches.

7.6   CONCLUSIONS

We have presented a new shape-preserving feature vector based on CLPDFs. In this developed model, we compute the shortest distance from each point of the object contour to the family of lines which pass through the centre of gravity of an object contour. The multi-line perpendicular distance function with respect to the reference line parallel to the furthest points on the object contour and which pass through the centre of gravity of an object computed the shortest distance (perpendicular distance) of all the points on the contour. The proposed descriptors are more compact and reveal loss-less information from an object. The model has achieved excellent retrieval results, making it attractive for adoption in different applications. The experimental results on popular benchmark datasets show that the proposed method is effective under geometrically variant object transformations. Here, perpendicular distance functions are only used for binary images in order to analyse the outer closed contours of objects. It is possible to extend this work to combine the inner and outer contours of an object in addition to several known small features such as boundary roughness and the B-shapiness of an object.

REFERENCES

[1] J. Wang, X. Bai, X. You, W. Liu, L. J. Latecki, Shape matching and classification using height functions, *Pattern Recognition Letters* 33, 134–143 (2012).

[2] A. El-Ghazal, O. Basir, S. Belkasim, Farthest point distance: A new shape signature for Fourier descriptors, *Signal processing: Image Communication* 24, 572–586 (2009).

[3] H. Ling, D. W. Jacobs, Shape classification using the inner-distance, *IEEE Transactions on Pattern Analysis and Machine Intelligence* 29(2), 286–299 (February 2007).

[4] G. Amayeh, S. Kasaei, G. Bebis, A. Tavakkoli, K. Veropoulos, Improvement of Zernike moment descriptors on affine transformed shapes, *IEEE Conference*, 1-4244-0779-6/07-2007.

[5] D. Wolter, L. J. Latecki, Shape matching for robot mapping, *PRICAL: Pacific Rim International Conference on Artificial Intelligence* (2004).

[6] S. Lewin, X. Jiang, A. Clausing, Perceptually motivated shape evolution with shape-preserving property, *Pattern Recognition Letters* 31(6), 447–453 (2010).

[7] H. Jiang, W. Liu, D. Wang, C. Tian, X. Bai, X. Liu, Y. Wu, W. Liu, CASE: Connectivity-based skeleton extraction in wireless sensor networks, *INFOCOM: IEEE International Conference on Computer Communications* 2916–2920 (2009).

[8] Z. Wang, M. Liang, Locally affine invariant descriptors for shape matching and retrieval, *IEEE Signal Processing Letters* 17(9), 803–806 (2010).

[9] J. Wang, Y. Li, X. Bai, Y. Zhang, C. Wang, N. Tang, Learning context sensetive similarity by shortest path propagation, *Pattern Recognition* 44(10–11), 367–2374 (2011).

[10] M. Bicego, P. Lovato, A bioinformatics approach to 2D shape classification, *Computer Vision and Image Understanding* 145, 59–69 (2016).

[11] N. Alajlan, I. E. Rube, M. S. Kamel, G. Freeman, Shape retrieval using triangle- area representation and dynamic space warping, *Pattern Recognition* 40, 1911–1920 (2007).

[12] X. Tang, F. Lin, S. Samson, A. Remsen, Binary plankton image classification, *IEEE Journal of Oceanic Engineering* 31(3), 728–735 (July 2006).

[13] Y. Shen, J. Yang, Y. Li, Finding Salient Points of Shape Contour for Object Recognition, *Proceedings of the 2015 IEEE Conference on Robotics and Biomimetics Zhuhai*, China, December 6–9, 2015.

[14] T. B. Sebastian, P. N. Klein, B. B. Kimia, Recognition of shapes by editing their shock graphs, *IEEE Transactions on Patterns Analysis Machine Intelligence* 25, 116–125 (2004).

[15] L. J. Latecki, R. Lakamper, U. Eckhardt, Shape descriptors for non-rigid shape with a single closed contour. *CVPR International Conference on Computer Vision and Pattern Recognition*, 424–429, 2000.

[16] R. Kumar, K. Mali, Local binary pattern for binary object classification using coordination number (CN)* and Hu's moments. *2021 9th International Conference on Reliability, Infocom Technologies and Optimization (Trends and Future Directions) (ICRITO)*, 1–7, 2021, doi: 380 10.1109/ICRIT051393. 2021.9596458

[17] R. Kumar, K. Mali, Fragment of binary object contour points on the basis of energy level for shape classification. *2021 8th International Conference on Signal Processing and Integrated Networks (SPIN)*, 609–615, 2021, doi: 10.1109/SPIN52536.2021.9566080

[18] R. Kumar, K. Mali, Shape classification via contour matching using the perpendicular distance functions, *International Journal of Engineering and Applied Physics* 1(2), 192198 (May 2021).

[19] S. Loncaric, A survey of shape analysis techniques, *Pattern Recognition*, 31(8), 983–1001 (1998). ISSN 0031-3203, https://doi.org/10.1016/S0031-2023 (97)00122-2.

[20] R. Kumar, K. Mali, Concurrent lines perpendicular distance functions for contour points analysis. Available at SSRN: https://ssrn.com/abstract=3998737 or https://doi.org/10.2139/ssrn.3998737

[21] R. Kumar, K. Mali, Local binary patterns of segments of a binary object for shape analysis, *Journal of Mathematical Imaging and Vision* (2022). https://doi.org/10.1007/s10851-022-01130-x

[22] R. Kumar, K. Mali, Bond dissociation energy and pattern spectrum for shape classification. *2021 5th International Conference on Electrical, Electronics, Communication, Computer Technologies and Optimization Techniques (ICEECCOT)*, Mysuru, India, 2021, 788–793, 2021. https://doi.org/10.1109/ICEEC-COT52851.2021.9707936

[23] R. Kumar, K. Mali, A novel approach to edge detection and performance measure based on the theory of "Range" and "Bowley's Measure of Skewness" in a Noisy environment, *Journal of Image Processing and Pattern Recognition Progress* 8(1), 31–38 (2021).

[24] R. Kumar, K. Mali. Binary shape segmentation and classification using coordination number (CN)*, *Research and Reviews: Discrete Mathematical Structures* 8(1), 22–30 (2021).

[25] P. C. Mali, On morphological shape classification of discrete binary images using bivariate pattern spectrum, *Journal of the Calcutta Mathematical Society* 12(2), 113–136 (2016).

8 A Resemblance of Convolutional Neural Network Architectures for Classifying Ferrograph Images

Sangita M. Jaybhaye and Vedmani A. Vaidya
Vishwakarma Institute of Technology, Pune, India

Maheshwar D. Jaybhaye
COEP Technological University, Pune, India

Sandeep R. Shinde
Vishwakarma Institute of Technology, Pune, India

CONTENTS

8.1 INTRODUCTION

Wear and tear of machine elements during continuous operation are frequently the root cause of machine failures. Wear particle analysis is a powerful tool for understanding the underlying causes of wear and tear in mechanical components. Wear particles produced by mating pairs of elements give useful information about the condition of the mechanism, its wear rate, and its severity. As a result, analysis of wear debris is acknowledged as an efficient method for the wear monitoring of a machine and its condition. This also helps in fault detection (Fan et al., 2017; Cao et al., 2018). Ferrographic image analysis is treated as a highly effective method for information gathering of wear particles.

Condition monitoring of a machine can be performed using ferrography, which provides health information of a machine through wear particles, including particle concentration and wear type.

Ferrographic analysis involves collecting and analyzing oil samples to monitor the condition of lubricated systems, and is a well-established technique. By examining the properties, chemical composition, wear particle presence, and contamination in the lubricating oil, it is possible to determine the mode, source, and severity of wear in a system. Ferrographic images can be particularly useful in this process, as they allow for detailed analysis of wear particles (Cao et al., 2014; Wu et al., 2014; Henneberg et al., 2015; Fan et al., 2018). Many approaches have been reported based on particle feature extraction for developing relationships between particle types and wear mechanisms.

Historically, the analysis of ferrographic images has involved manually examining them through visual inspection, a process that can be time-consuming and requires specialized expertise. Particle feature extraction is the foundation of wear particle classification and is used as input for categorizing wear debris. The process of manually extracting features from ferrographic images typically involves four steps:

- Collecting a sample of particles;
- Extracting features from the images;
- Establishing a database;
- Processing the feature information.

Convolutional neural networks (CNNs) are used as a promising method for automating the analysis of wear particles, allowing for faster and more accurate analysis.

Initiatives to automate the study of wear debris have been undertaken over the years. Thomas et al. (1991) attempted to automate the classification of wear particles by calculating various features, such as skewness, aspect ratio, area, roundness, and dispersion. Kirk et al. (1995) also developed numerical parameters, including area, convex area, perimeter, convexity, and fiber length, to describe the morphology of wear particles.

Grey system theory was used by Peng and Kirk (1999) for classifying wear particles into six types using 3D images and applying a fuzzy logic approach. Myshkin et al. (1997) introduced the possibility of the application of neural networks with Fourier descriptors for the classification of wear debris. A BP neural network with a two-level strategy and a CNN model with six layers are used for classifying wear particles into five types (Wang et al., 2019). Other conventional methods of identifying wear debris helps to classify particles that are stuck together. Peng and Wang (2019b) addressed this issue by developing a CNN model with InceptionV3 using fully connected layers that can effectively classify overlapping particles.

An automatic process for detecting and classifying wear was developed by Peng et al. (2020) using a cascade of two CNNs and a classifier using a support vector machine (SVM). This decreases the computing time and increases accuracy when compared to R-CNN and Faster R-CNN. A hybrid CNN with transfer learning was used by Peng et al. (2019) to reduce the dependency on sample numbers utilized and which uses an SVM to enhance the accuracy of automatic wear particle classification.

CNN used for ferrography termed FECNN was proposed by Peng and Wang (2019a) for wear particle identification. The proposed CNN model includes dropout operations to prevent overfitting. A 1D convolutional operation is also included to reduce the number of parameters used in the model.

A small dataset and different wear particle sizes make it difficult to classify ferrographic images. To cope with the problem of insufficient samples, a data augmentation algorithm based on the permutation of image patches was developed by Peng and Wang (2020) along with a custom feature loss function to extract more abundant features and to reduce redundant representations.

Fan et al. (2020) proposed a method for recognizing the wear particles in a small sample through ferrographic images that leverage CNN and transfer learning using a virtual ferrographic image dataset. The AlexNet framework is used to study parameters such as activation function, network structure, learning rate, L2 regularization, and optimization mode. Xie and Wei (2022) addressed challenges related to fuzzy edges of wear particle images and the complex surface texture that hindered the accuracy of computer models and feature extraction and proposed a multichannel image encoder to mitigate these issues. This encoder enhanced the image's visible edge and surface charac-teristics, and the resulting model (called MCECNN) was created by linking the encoder with a CNN.

The blurred ferrographic images are due to contamination of the lubricant and limited optical field depth. Wu et al. (2019) developed a restoration method to address this issue. The degradation model was created using larger convolutional kernels to capture the blurring process accurately, and a pixel-by-pixel regression procedure was used to perform the final restoration using a trained network. This proposed method is more efficient than conventional deblurring techniques, which makes it suitable for online applications.

Wang et al. (2021) utilized 3D topographical information of wear particles to create a knowledge-embedded double CNN model to classify fatigue and severe sliding wear particles. A height map was constructed using 2D and 3D wear particles. The performance was improved by utilizing a knowledge base of particle properties for identifying wear mechanisms through four effective kernels. Feature maps are used to build a second CNN network of these kernels with six layers of parallel convolution.

More and Jaybhaye (2022) used a teachable machine to create a model that evaluates the condi-tion monitoring and health of a lubricated system. The developed CNN recognized five types of wear particles with 95.4% accuracy. Jia et al. (2020) conducted a study to evaluate the potential of deep CNN architectures for identifying wear particles in condition monitoring systems. In this study, the researchers employed five different CNN models – InceptionV3, AlexNet, VGG16, ResNet50, and DenseNet121 – and evaluated their performance on a dataset containing seven types of wear particles. The results obtained show that DenseNet121 achieved the highest accuracy (88.39%), indicating that DCNNs can be effectively used for wear particle classification.

This study investigates the compatibility of several CNN architectures for identifying wear par-ticles. Popular CNNs are focused and employ transfer learning with a fine-tuning approach. The training of CNN models on the ImageNet dataset was done by Deng et al. (2009), which is one of the most extensive and commonly used datasets for image classification. In particular, we focused on popular DCNN models, such as VGG, ResNet, InceptionV3, MobileNet, MobileNetV2, Xception, DenseNet, EfficientNet, and ConvNext. In order to tailor these architectures to the task of wear par-ticle classification, we fine-tuned them on a specific dataset of wear particles. The dataset used for tuning is the same dataset described in More and Jaybhaye (2022). The results shows that the pre-trained CNN models are effectively used for wear particle classification, providing further evidence of the potential of CNNs in condition monitoring applications. Overall, our study builds upon the work of Jia et al. (2020) and More and Jaybhaye (2022), providing additional support for using CNN architectures for wear particle classification.

8.2   DATASET

The dataset consists of 979 images of five types of wear particle images obtained through ferrography, including, normal rubbing, rubbing and cutting wear, cutting wear, red oxide, and severe sliding wear. The dataset is divided into three categories: training, validation, and testing. Out of the 979 images, 100 are designated as test data, 175 (20% of the total) are randomly chosen for the validation set, and the remaining 704 are used to train the CNN model. Table 8.1 shows the distribution of images in the dataset.

TABLE 8.1
Class Representation in the Dataset

Type of Wear Particle	Training Data	Validation Data	Testing Data
Cutting wear	81	27	12
Normal rubbing wear	68	12	10
Rubbing and cutting wear	230	54	33
Red oxide	46	14	9
Severe sliding wear	279	68	36

8.3 TRANSFER LEARNING AND FINE TUNING

Transfer learning (TL) involves adapting a model trained on one task to a new, related task. TL with fine-tuning is used to enhance and improve the performance of the models for the classification of wear particles and monitoring the condition of the systems. TL is beneficial when the dataset for the new task is small or limited, as is often the case in these systems. TL reduces the data and number of computations required by using a pre-trained model as the starting point for training a new model on a different dataset. It improves the performance of the new model. In the pre-trained model, a deep neural network can be transferred to the new task. The pre-trained model with a large dataset is more effective than training a new model from scratch. All the models were pre-trained on the ImageNet dataset (Deng et al., 2009). The fine-tuning approach allows a pre-trained model to be used on a different but related task. In the case of wear particle classification, which typically has a small dataset, TL with fine-tuning can be used to adapt a pre-trained CNN model for the classification of wear particles. A pre-trained model is used as a starting point for training a new model on the target dataset; the weights of the pre-trained model can be adjusted through fine-tuning to fit the new data better. This process, known as transfer learning with fine-tuning, can improve the generalizability of machine learning models. TL can help ensure that the new model can handle a wide range of data and is manageable for a specific dataset by using pre-trained models which are trained on large and diverse datasets. This can improve the model's performance and make it more applicable to real-world situations.

The output layers of all architectures are modified to match the number of classes in the dataset. This adapts the pre-trained model for the classification of wear particles. The weights for the layer are randomly initialized; the output layer is replaced with a dense layer with five units matching the number of classes in the dataset. The rest of the model is then frozen, and just the output layer is trained on the training dataset by retraining the model on the training data, using a lower learning rate to prevent the pre-trained model from forgetting the features it has already learned.

8.4 HARDWARE AND CONVOLUTIONAL NEURAL NETWORK ARCHITECTURES

For experimentation, an NVIDIA Tesla T4 GPU with 15,109 MB of memory and a high-performance Intel(R) Xeon(R) CPU @ 2.00 GHz with two cores and two threads per core are used. This section will concentrate on the various deep learning network architectures that have been used in this research and are significant in the field of computer vision, including VGG, ResNet, InceptionV3, Xception, MobileNet, DenseNet, MobileNetV2, EfficientNet, and ConvNeXt. The details of each architecture, including its underlying principles and key features, are as follows.

8.4.1 VGG

The VGG architecture developed by Simonyan and Zisserman (2014) achieved high accuracy on ImageNet Large Scale Visual Recognition Challenge (ILSVRC) localization and classification tasks. VGG architecture is a straightforward and uniform CNN architecture. It consists of multiple convolutional layers with pooling layers followed by a few layers which are connected. When processing an input image of size 224×224 in RGB format, the VGG architecture subtracts the RGB mean value. The image is then passed over a series of convolutional layers that utilize 3×3 filters for feature extraction. The filters, having a small receptive field, extract detailed features from the input image. Spatial pooling is performed using five max-pooling layers. Spatial padding is applied after each convolution operation to preserve spatial resolution. Throughout the network, the VGG architecture employs the same convolutional layer configuration, including the same number and size of filters. There are multiple versions of the VGG architecture: VGG16 and VGG19 architectures are focused and have 16 and 19 weight layers, respectively.

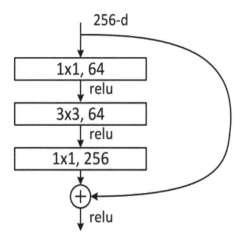

FIGURE 8.1   "Bottleneck" building block for ResNet.

8.4.2 ResNet

He et al. (2016) proposed the ResNet CNN architecture, winning first place in the ILSVRC 2015 classification task. When deep neural networks begin to converge, a problem is observed: as network depth increases, accuracy gets saturated and degrades rapidly. The addition of more layers leads to more training errors. ResNet architecture addresses this issue by introducing a deep residual learning framework. The bottleneck, as shown in Figure 8.1, introduced in ResNet, is a type of residual block that lowers filters in the layer. It reduces the network's computational complexity without sacrificing accuracy. This is achieved by using a 1 × 1 convolutional layer to reduce the number of filters, followed by a 3 × 3 convolutional layer, and then another 1 × 1 convolutional layer to restore the original number of filters. Batch normalization (BN), and a rectified linear unit (ReLU) activation function are all present in each residual block. The output of the block is then combined with its input using a shortcut or skip connection. Instead of attempting to model the entire mapping from input to output, this enables the network to learn residual functions, or the differences between the input and the desired output.

Figure 8.1 depicts a bottleneck building block of ResNet architecture, which is a convolutional neural network (CNN) layer made up of three separate layers. The first layer is a 1 × 1 convolutional layer with 64 filters and a ReLU activation function. The second layer is a 3 × 3 convolutional layer with 64 filters, which also has a ReLU activation function. The final layer consists of 256 1 × 1 convolutional filters, restoring the original number of channels in the feature map. The output of the previous block is concatenated with the output of the final layer of this block and a ReLU activation function is applied.

The ResNet architecture has several variants, including ResNet50, ResNet101, ResNet152, and ResNet169. We took into account ResNet50, ResNet101, and ResNet152 for this study. The number in the name indicates the network's weight layers. ResNet50, for instance, has 50 layers of weight, whereas ResNet152 has 152 layers.

8.4.3 InceptionV3

InceptionV3 architecture was proposed by Szegedy et al. (2016) as an upgrade to the original Inception (GoogleNet) architecture. InceptionV3 incorporates several improvements over the previous version, including improvements proposed in InceptionV2. InceptionV3 replaces 5 × 5 convolutions used in Inception architecture with two 3 × 3 convolutions (Figure 8.2(a)). Although there are fewer parameters, the receptive field stays the same.

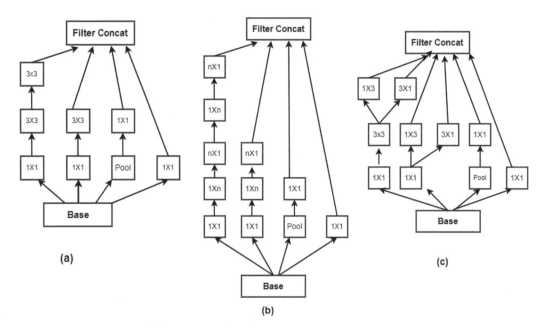

FIGURE 8.2 InceptionV3 building blocks: (a) 5 × 5 convolution from original inception architecture is replaced by two 3 × 3 convolutions.; (b) Principal of replacing n × n convolution with 1 × n convolution and n × 1 convolution.; (c) Expanded filter banks in IncpetionV3.

Figure 8.2 consists of three sub figures a,b,c. In Figure a 5 × 5 convolution from original inception architecture is replaced by two 3 × 3 convolution. Figure b represents the principal of replacing n × n convolution with 1 × n convolution and n × 1 convolution. Figure c shows the inception module with expanded filter banks using the principles showed in figure a and figure b

The InceptionV3 architecture combines 1 × n and n × 1 convolutions (Figure 8.2(b)) to factorize more extensive convolutions and reduce the model's computational complexity. Additionally, to avoid the "representational bottleneck" that can happen when using deep neural networks, the filter banks in the InceptionV3 architecture have been expanded (made broader rather than deeper) (see Figure 8.2(c)). InceptionV3 incorporates all the discussed improvements using an RMSProp optimizer, factorized by BN, 7 × 7 convolutions, and label smoothing.

8.4.4 Xception

Xception is a CNN developed by Chollet (2017). It is based entirely on layers of depth-separable convolution. It is a type of Inception architecture designed to improve Inception's performance. Figure 8.3 illustrates how the Xception architecture uses 1 × 1 first for mapping the cross-channel correlations of each output channel. The networks in the Xception architecture extracts the features using 36 convolutional layers. All 14 modules that make up the 36 convolutional layers, except the first and last, have linear residual connections. The Xception architecture can be described as a series of depthwise convolution layers with residual connections arranged in a linear stack.

Figure 8.3 comprises three sub-figures labeled a, b, and c. Sub-figure a depicts the replacement of a 5 × 5 convolution from the original Inception architecture with two consecutive 3 × 3 convolutions. Sub-figure b illustrates the concept of replacing an n × n convolution with a 1 × n convolution and an n × 1 convolution. Sub-figure c shows an inception module with an expanded filter bank using the principles illustrated in sub-figures a and b.

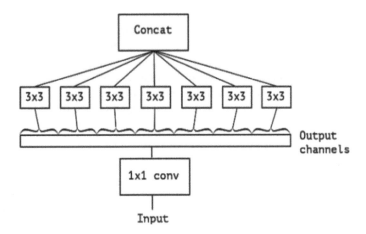

FIGURE 8.3   Xception module (Chollet, 2017).

8.4.5   MOBILENET

MobileNet is a CNN architecture developed by Howard et al. (2017) and designed for efficient use on mobile and embedded devices. MobileNet architecture is based on the use of depthwise separable convolutions. With MobileNet, each input channel is subjected to a single filter as part of a depthwise convolution, which is followed by pointwise convolution, which combines the results of depthwise convolution using a 1×1 convolution, drastically reducing model size and computation. MobileNet consists of a series of 3×3 depthwise separable convolutional layers, followed by BN, and a ReLU nonlinearity, followed by a 1×1 convolution (pointwise convolution) with BN and ReLU. Two new global hyperparameters were introduced by MobileNet that let the model builder trade-off between accuracy and latency. This makes it possible to adapt the model to the particular constraints of the current problem. While pointwise and depthwise convolutions are counted as separate layers, MobileNet has 28 layers. Two hyperparameters, Width Multiplier and Resolution Multiplier, are left at their default values of 1.0 and 1.0 for this study.

8.4.6   DENSENET

One of the main concepts behind DenseNet is the incorporation of dense connections between layers. In a traditional CNN, each layer only receives input from the preceding layer. Each layer in DenseNet connects to other layers that utilize the feature maps of preceding layers. These layers act as the input and their feature maps act as output to subsequent layers. This allows the network to learn features at various scales, which can enhance the model's performance (Huang et al., 2017). A DenseNet block implements a non-linear transformation using BN, ReLUs, pooling, or convolution (Conv). Layers between two dense blocks are called transition layers, which perform BN, a 1×1 convolutional operation, and a 2×2 average pooling operation. DenseNet introduces a hyperparameter called the growth rate (k). This refers to the number of filters added to the output of a convolutional layer each time a new such layer is added. For this study, DenseNet121, DensNet169, and DenseNet201 are used, with a growth rate of 32. The number of layers and filters per layer varies between these versions.

8.4.7   MOBILENETV2

MobileNetV2 (Sandler et al., 2018) expands on the concepts proposed in MobileNetV1 architecture. Similar to MobileNet, MobileNetV2 uses depthwise separable convolution. It is an efficient building block that has two new features: (1) linear bottlenecks and (2) shortcut connections. The foundation of MobileNetV2 is an inverted residual structure. In this the connections between the bottleneck layers are the residual connections. The residual connections in MobileNetV2's inverted residual structure are those between the bottleneck layers. The MobileNetV2 architecture consists of 32 filters in an initial fully convolution layer with 19 additional bottleneck layers. Kernels of 3 × 3 size are used, as is the standard for CNN. MobileNetV2 significantly improves on MobileNetV1 and advances mobile visual recognition, including classification, object detection, and semantic segmentation.

8.4.8 EFFICIENTNET

The key idea behind EfficientNet is the concept of model scaling, which involves scaling up the size of a neural network in a systematic and principled way. This is in contrast to traditional approaches, which often involve simply increasing the number of layers or filters in each layer without considering the overall architecture of the network (Tan & Le, 2019). One of the ways that EfficientNet achieves better performance is by using a compound scaling method, which involves simultaneously scaling up the dimensions of the network (such as the width and depth) and the resolution of the input images. This allows the network to maintain a similar level of complexity while handling higher-resolution images, which can improve performance on tasks such as image classification. If more computational power is available, then network depth is increased by width and image size, which are determined by a small grid search on the original model. Another critical aspect of EfficientNet is its use of a novel building block called an MBConv block, which stands for mobile inverted bottleneck convolution. This uses depthwise separable convolutions like MobileNet, which can reduce the number of parameters and computations required by the network. It also includes an inverted bottleneck structure similar to MobileNetV2, which can further improve the efficiency of the network. Squeeze-and-excitation optimization with MBConv block is used to create a baseline model EfficientNetB0, which is further scaled according to requirements using the compound scaling method (Tan & Le, 2019).

8.4.9 CONVNEXT

ConvNeXt is a family of CNN architectures designed to compete with vision transformers (ViTs) in terms of accuracy and scalability (Liu et al., 2022). Facebook AI researchers and University of California, Berkeley researchers Liu, Mao, Wu, Feichtenhofe, Darrell, and Xie proposed the ConvNext convolutional network architecture. Training Techniques, Macro Design, ResNeXt-ify, Inverted Bottleneck, Large Kernel, and Micro Design are just a few of the crucial components that the authors found to be essential in "modernizing" a standard ResNet toward the Vision Transformer architecture and explaining the performance difference. For model training, authors used the AdamW optimizer, regularization techniques like Stochastic Depth and Label Smoothing, and data augmentation methods like Mixup, Cutmix, RandAugment, and Random Erasing. In the Macro Design of ConvNext architecture, following the Swin Transformer design, the number of blocks in ResNet50 at each stage was modified to (3, 3, 9, 3). In the modified ResNet model, the stem cell has been replaced with a "patchify" layer, which is implemented using a 4 × 4 convolutional layer with stride 4. The width of the network has also been increased to match the number of channels in Swin-Transformers (96), following the strategy proposed in ResNeXt. The original stem cell consisted of a 7 × 7 convolution layer with stride two, followed by a max pool. ConvNext, like the MobileNetV2 architecture, utilizes inverted bottlenecks. ConvNext makes use of 7 × 7 convolutions and employs Gaussian error linear unit (GELU) activation, which is used in advanced transformers like BERT, GPT-2, and ViT. Other differences from ordinary convNexts include layer normalization and independent downsampling layers. ConvNext-T version was trained on the ImageNet-1K dataset used for this study.

8.5 MODEL CONFIGURATION AND TRAINING

This section discusses the overall network architecture used to fine-tune the CNN architectures discussed for wear particle classification and training configuration.

Figure 8.4 displays a flowchart for the process of fine-tuning a pre-trained model for image classification tasks, consisting of six steps: input image, Resize and Rescale layer, pre-trained model, global average pooling layer, dropout layer, and classification layer.

The image is first passed through a resize and rescale layer, reshaped to a $224 \times 224 \times 3$ shape, and normalized by dividing every pixel value by 255. As a result, the pixels' values are changed from having a range of 0 to 255 to 0 to 1. The normalized image is then passed to the base model architecture with the top classification layer removed. A global average pooling layer receives the output of the base model instead of fully connected layers. A dense classification layer (output layer), which assigns the image to one of the dataset's classes, receives the output from the average pooling layer after passing it through a dropout layer.

Multiple deep learning architectures are used as pre-trained models, including VGG16, VGG19, ResNet50, ResNet101, ResNet152, InceptionV3, DenseNet121, DenseNet169, DenseNet201, Xception, MobileNet, MobileNetV2, EfficientNetB0, and ConvNext-T, and fine-tuned by the process shown in Figure 8.4.

Global average pooling is a technique used in CNNs to reduce the dimensionality of the data (Lin et al., 2013). This method uses feature maps produced by convolutional layers instead of fully connected layers on top of these feature maps, allowing the model to retain important features learned by the convolutional layers while also reducing the number of required parameters and computational resources. This replaces the need for fully connected layers, allowing for a more efficient and effective model. Global average pooling has several advantages over fully connected layers, including improved interpretability of the feature maps and reduced risk of overfitting. Output from the global average pooling layer is fed directly into the dropout layer.

Dropout is a method of regularization in neural networks that helps to prevent overfitting (Srivastava et al., 2014). It randomly drops units (and their connections) from the network during training, preventing them from becoming too co-adapted. The dropout rate is the fraction of randomly dropped units during training. In our experiment, we used a dropout rate of 0.2. The dropout layer helps improve the model's generalizability by preventing the units from becoming too specialized for the training data.

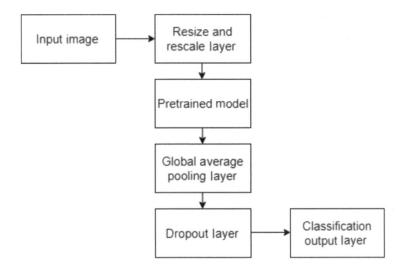

FIGURE 8.4 Process flow of overall model architecture for fine-tuning.

Following the dropout layer, the output is passed into a dense layer with five neurons with a softmax activation. The dense layer uses the output from the dropout layer to classify the image into one of the five classes of the dataset. The softmax activation is commonly used in the output layer of a classification model because it ensures that the predicted probabilities for each class sum to 1, allowing the model to make a probabilistic prediction for each class. In our experiment, we used a softmax activation in the final dense layer to enable the model to make probabilistic predictions for each of the five classes in the dataset.

To track the progress of our experiments and model versions during training, we utilized the Weights & Biases (wandb) library (Biewald, 2020). This allows easy login, visualizing of the training process, and keeping track of the different versions of the models. Fine-tuned models are compared, based on various performance metrics, including training accuracy, validation accuracy, F1 score, precision, recall, number of parameters, and floating-point operations (FLOPs).

8.6   RESULTS

We demonstrate the effectiveness of the previously discussed CNN architectures for the wear particle classification task in this section. We compared the performance of VGG16, VGG19, ResNet50, ResNet101, ResNet152, InceptionV3, DenseNet121, DenseNet169, DenseNet201, Xception, MobileNet, MobileNetV2, EfficientNetB0, and ConvNeXt-T based on different parameters like training accuracy, validation accuracy, number of parameters, and FLOPs.

The EfficientNetB0 architecture showed the best performance with a validation accuracy of 99.43%, followed by the DenseNet201 architecture with a 99.32% validation accuracy. ResNet architectures ResNet152, ResNet50, and ResNet101 achieved the least validation accuracies of 56.57, 57.71, and 64.57% respectively. Validation accuracy and training accuracy for the discussed CNN architecture are listed in Table 8.2.

The validation accuracy reflects the model's performance on a holdout dataset that was not used for training, while the training accuracy reflects the model's performance on the training data. The variation of training accuracy over 40 epochs can be observed in Figure 8.5.

Figure 8.5 shows a line plot of the progress of fine-tuning pre-trained models for image classification over 40 epochs. The plot displays the training accuracy on the y-axis and the number of epochs

TABLE 8.2
Training and Validation Accuracy

Name	Training Accuracy	Validation Accuracy
EfficientNetB0	0.995739	0.994286
DenseNet201	1	0.993243
DenseNet121	0.997159	0.988571
DenseNet169	1	0.986486
MobileNet	1	0.982857
MobileNetV2	1	0.977143
InceptionV3	1	0.971429
ConvNeXt- T	0.992898	0.971429
Xception	0.99858	0.971429
VGG19	0.923295	0.902857
VGG16	0.9375	0.897143
ResNet101	0.646307	0.645714
ResNet50	0.643466	0.577143
ResNet152	0.639205	0.565714

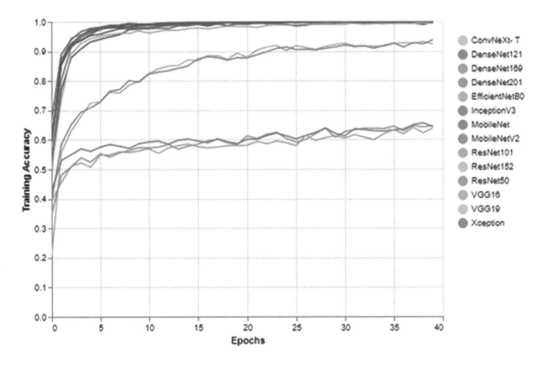

FIGURE 8.5   Training accuracy vs number of epochs.

on the x-axis. The EfficientNet model achieved the highest training accuracy, while ResNet152 exhibited the lowest accuracy.

EfficientNetB0, DenseNet201, DenseNet121, DenseNet169, MobileNet, MobileNetV2, InceptionV3, and Xception models have low training loss and validation loss, indicating that they are making accurate predictions on both the training data and the validation data. The VGG16, VGG19, ResNet50, ResNet101, and ResNet152 models, on the other hand, have higher training loss and validation loss, indicating that they may be struggling to make accurate predictions.

Table 8.3 lists the training loss and validation loss for CNN architectures. The validation loss represents the model's error on a holdout dataset that wasn't used for training, whereas the training loss represents the model's error on the training data.

The variation of training loss over 40 epochs of training can be observed in Figure 8.6.

Figure 8.6 shows a line plot of the progress of fine-tuning pre-trained models for image classification over 40 epochs. The plot displays the training loss on the y-axis and the number of epochs on the x-axis. The EfficientNet model achieved the lowest training loss, while ResNet152 exhibited the highest loss.

FLOPs is a measure of the computational complexity of a model and is often used to compare the performance of different models on the same hardware. A model with a higher number of GFLOPs will generally be more computationally expensive to train and may require more powerful hardware to run efficiently. Table 8.4 lists the number of GFLOPs for all the architectures.

The EfficientNetB0 model has the lowest number of GFLOPs, at 0.06. The MobileNetV2 and MobileNet models also have relatively low numbers of GFLOPs, at 0.3 and 0.57, respectively. It can be replaced with: DenseNet121 has a slightly higher number at around 2.8, while InceptionV3, ResNet, DenseNet201, ConvNeXt-T, Xception, and VGG models have increasing GFLOPs values.

TABLE 8.3

Cross-Entropy Training and Validation Loss

Name	Training Loss	Validation Loss
EfficientNetB0	0.027881	0.05973
DenseNet201	0.015449	0.061714
DenseNet121	0.039728	0.058115
DenseNet169	0.0165	0.064547
MobileNet	0.013799	0.049526
MobileNetV2	0.00648	0.057727
InceptionV3	0.007701	0.06866
ConvNeXt- T	0.060722	0.105909
Xception	0.025288	0.083657
VGG19	0.292491	0.292816
VGG16	0.281643	0.342128
ResNet101	0.963095	0.974254
ResNet50	0.907582	0.952705
ResNet152	0.987763	1.030513

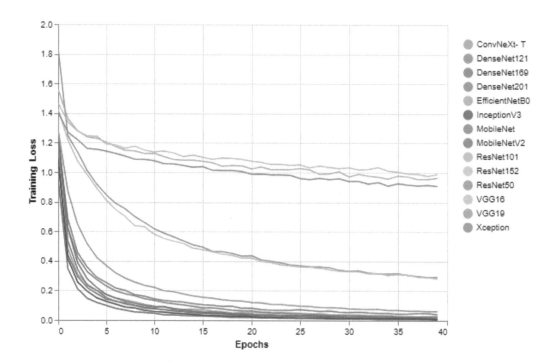

FIGURE 8.6   Training loss vs number of epochs.

Table 8.5 lists the number of parameters for CNN architectures. The number of parameters reflects the amount of memory required to store the models' weights and biases.

The MobileNetV2 model has the lowest number of parameters, at 2.2 million. The MobileNetV2 and EfficientNetB0 models also have relatively low numbers of parameters, at 3.2 million and 4.1 million, respectively. The VGG16 and VGG19 models have a higher number of parameters, with

TABLE 8.4
GFLOPs

Name	GFLOPs
EfficientNetB0	0.06387
MobileNetV2	0.364
MobileNet	0.5678
DenseNet121	2.834
InceptionV3	2.842
DenseNet169	3.359
ResNet50	3.862257679
DenseNet201	4.290869839
ConvNeXt- T	4.487
Xception	4.554
ResNet101	7.577037839
ResNet152	11.29242011
VGG16	15.357
VGG19	19.519

TABLE 8.5
Parameters for Convolutional Neural Networks

Name	Parameters
MobileNetV2	2,264,389
MobileNet	3,233,989
EfficientNetB0	4,055,976
DenseNet121	7,042,629
DenseNet169	12,651,205
VGG16	14,717,253
DenseNet201	18,331,589
VGG19	20026949
Xception	20,871,725
InceptionV3	21,813,029
ResNet50	23,597,957
ConvNeXt- T	27,823,973
ResNet101	42,668,421
ResNet152	58,381,189

42.7 million and 58.4 million, respectively. The ResNet152 model has the highest number of parameters with 58.4 million.

Table 8.6 presents the results of the evaluation of CNN architectures on a test dataset of 100 images. The columns of the table provide various metrics of model performance, including the loss (cross-entropy loss), accuracy (the percentage of correct predictions), precision (the percentage of true positive predictions), recall (the percentage of true positive cases that the model correctly identified), and F-score (a measure of the balance between precision and recall).

The architectures with the highest F-score are EfficientNetB0, DenseNet121, MobileNet, and ConvNeXt-T with 0.9942. These architectures performed particularly well on test data with high

TABLE 8.6

Evaluation of Architectures on Test Data

Name	Loss	Accuracy	Precision	Recall	F-score (macro)
EfficientNet	0.0739	0.99	0.9946	0.9939	0.9942
DenseNet121	0.1085	0.99	0.9946	0.9939	0.9942
MobileNet	0.0886	0.99	0.9946	0.9939	0.9942
ConvNeXt-T	0.1023	0.99	0.9946	0.9939	0.9942
InceptionV3	0.0659	0.98	0.9791	0.9883	0.9834
Xception	0.1091	0.98	0.9895	0.9773	0.9828
MobileNetV2	0.0804	0.97	0.9834	0.955	0.9681
DenseNet169	0.1469	0.95	0.9735	0.9429	0.9565
VGG19	0.2666	0.95	0.9576	0.93	0.9424
DenseNet201	0.1683	0.94	0.9065	0.9636	0.9267
VGG16	0.3068	0.94	0.9541	0.8962	0.9212
ResNet101	1.0494	0.61	0.4147	0.4409	0.4183
ResNet152	1.1318	0.61	0.4424	0.4303	0.4167
ResNet50	0.9738	0.59	0.44	0.3646	0.3319

accuracy, precision, and recall scores. Conversely, the models with the lowest F-scores were ResNet50, ResNet101, and ResNet152. These models had higher loss values and lower accuracy, precision, and recall, indicating that they made more errors and were less accurate in their predictions.

Upon comparing the validation accuracy and test accuracy of different CNN architectures, it was observed that the DenseNet201 and DenseNet169 models appeared to be overfitting on the validation data, as their performance on the test data was relatively poor compared to their validation accuracy. On the other hand, the EfficientNetB0 and DenseNet121 models demonstrated a good ability to generalize to unseen data, as they achieved a relatively high level of accuracy on the test set as well.

8.7   CONCLUSION

This study was aimed at identifying the most effective CNN architectures for the classification of wear particles and evaluating TL effectiveness with fine-tuning for this task. A total of 14 CNN architectures, namely EfficientNetB0, VGG16, VGG19, ResNet50, ResNet101, ResNet152, InceptionV3, MobileNet, MobileNetV2, Xception, DenseNet121, DenseNet169, DenseNet201, and ConvNeXt, were fine-tuned on a small dataset of wear particle images.

The results show that the EfficientNetB0, DenseNet121, and MobileNet architectures achieved the best performance in terms of accuracy, precision, and recall, while the ResNet architectures performed poorly. Based on these findings, it can be concluded that the EfficientNet, DenseNet121, and MobileNet architectures are the most effective CNN architectures for wear particle classification, while the ResNet architectures are not suitable for TL with a fine tuning approach for wear particle classification. The fine-tuning methodology used in this study is not suitable for ResNet architectures for wear particle classification.

After evaluating various factors, including accuracy, precision, recall, and computational efficiency, it was found that the EfficientNetB0 architecture demonstrated the best overall performance for wear particle classification. This architecture achieved a validation accuracy of 99.42% and an F-score of 0.99 on a small test dataset and was also computationally efficient with the least number of FLOPs among the CNN architectures studied. The results suggest that these architectures could be used for efficient and accurate wear particle classification. Overall, this study has contributed to the development of more effective and efficient methods for wear particle classification, which could have significant implications for various fields such as predictive maintenance and online machine condition monitoring.

REFERENCES

Biewald, L. (2020). Experiment Tracking with Weights and Biases. https://www.wandb.com/

Cao, W., Chen, W., Dong, G., Wu, J., & Xie, Y. (2014). Wear condition monitoring and working pattern recognition of piston rings and cylinder liners using on-line visual ferrograph. *Tribology Transactions*, *57*(4), 690–699.

Cao, W., Dong, G., Xie, Y.-B., & Peng, Z. (2018). Prediction of wear trend of engines via on-line wear debris monitoring. *Tribology International*, *120*, 510–519.

Chollet, F. (2017). Xception: Deep learning with depthwise separable convolutions. *Proceedings of the IEEE Conference on Computer Vision and Pattern Recognition*, 1251–1258.

Deng, J., Dong, W., Socher, R., Li, L.-J., Li, K., & Fei-Fei, L. (2009). Imagenet: A large-scale hierarchical image database. *2009 IEEE Conference on Computer Vision and Pattern Recognition*, 248–255.

Fan, B., Feng, S., Che, Y., Mao, J., & Xie, Y. (2018). An oil monitoring method of wear evaluation for engine hot tests. *The International Journal of Advanced Manufacturing Technology*, *94*(9), 3199–3207.

Fan, B., Li, B., Feng, S., Mao, J., & Xie, Y.-B. (2017). Modeling and experimental investigations on the relationship between wear debris concentration and wear rate in lubrication systems. *Tribology International*, *109*, 114–123.

Fan, H., Gao, S., Zhang, X., Cao, X., Ma, H., & Liu, Q. (2020). Intelligent recognition of ferrographic images combining optimal CNN with transfer learning introducing virtual images. *IEEE Access*, *8*, 137074–137093.

He, K., Zhang, X., Ren, S., & Sun, J. (2016). Deep residual learning for image recognition. *Proceedings of the IEEE Conference on Computer Vision and Pattern Recognition*, 770–778.

Henneberg, M., Eriksen, R. L., Jørgensen, B., & Fich, J. (2015). A quasi-stationary approach to particle concentration and distribution in gear oil for wear mode estimation. *Wear*, *324*, 140–146.

Howard, A. G., Zhu, M., Chen, B., Kalenichenko, D., Wang, W., Weyand, T., Andreetto, M., & Adam, H. (2017). Mobilenets: Efficient convolutional neural networks for mobile vision applications. *ArXiv Preprint ArXiv:1704.04861*.

Huang, G., Liu, Z., van der Maaten, L., & Weinberger, K. Q. (2017). Densely connected convolutional networks. *Proceedings of the IEEE Conference on Computer Vision and Pattern Recognition*, 4700–4708.

Jia, F., Yu, F., Song, L., Zhang, S., & Sun, H. (2020). Intelligent classification of wear particles based on deep convolutional neural network. *Journal of Physics: Conference Series*, *1519*(1), 012012.

Kirk, T. B., Panzera, D., Anamalay, R. V., & Xu, Z. L. (1995). Computer image analysis of wear debris for machine condition monitoring and fault diagnosis. *Wear*, *181*, 717–722.

Lin, M., Chen, Q., & Yan, S. (2013). Network in network. *ArXiv Preprint ArXiv:1312.4400*.

Liu, Z., Mao, H., Wu, C.-Y., Feichtenhofer, C., Darrell, T., & Xie, S. (2022). A convnet for the 2020s. *Proceedings of the IEEE/CVF Conference on Computer Vision and Pattern Recognition*, 11976–11986.

Masters, D., & Luschi, C. (2018). Revisiting small batch training for deep neural networks. *ArXiv Preprint ArXiv:1804.07612*.

More, P. P., & Jaybhaye, M. D. (2022). Wear particles recognition through teachable machine. *Industrial Lubrication and Tribology*. 74(2), 274–281.

Myshkin, N. K., Kwon, O. K., Grigoriev, A. Y., Ahn, H.-S., & Kong, H. (1997). Classification of wear debris using a neural network. *Wear*, *203*, 658–662.

Peng, P., & Wang, J. (2019a). FECNN: A promising model for wear particle recognition. *Wear*, *432*, 202968.

Peng, P., & Wang, J. (2019b). Wear particle classification considering particle overlapping. *Wear*, *422*, 119–127.

Peng, P., & Wang, J. (2020). Ferrograph image classification. *ArXiv Preprint ArXiv:2010.06777*.

Peng, Y., Cai, J., Wu, T., Cao, G., Kwok, N., & Peng, Z. (2020). WP-DRnet: A novel wear particle detection and recognition network for automatic ferrograph image analysis. *Tribology International*, *151*, 106379.

Peng, Y., Cai, J., Wu, T., Cao, G., Kwok, N., Zhou, S., & Peng, Z. (2019). A hybrid convolutional neural network for intelligent wear particle classification. *Tribology International*, *138*, 166–173.

Peng, Z., & Kirk, T. B. (1999). Wear particle classification in a fuzzy grey system. *Wear*, *225*, 1238–1247.

Sandler, M., Howard, A., Zhu, M., Zhmoginov, A., & Chen, L.-C. (2018). Mobilenetv2: Inverted residuals and linear bottlenecks. *Proceedings of the IEEE Conference on Computer Vision and Pattern Recognition*, 4510–4520.

Simonyan, K., & Zisserman, A. (2014). Very deep convolutional networks for large-scale image recognition. *ArXiv Preprint ArXiv:1409.1556.*

Srivastava, N., Hinton, G., Krizhevsky, A., Sutskever, I., & Salakhutdinov, R. (2014). Dropout: a simple way to prevent neural networks from overfitting. *The Journal of Machine Learning Research, 15*(1), 1929–1958.

Szegedy, C., Vanhoucke, V., Ioffe, S., Shlens, J., & Wojna, Z. (2016). Rethinking the inception architecture for computer vision. *Proceedings of the IEEE Conference on Computer Vision and Pattern Recognition,* 2818–2826.

Tan, M., & Le, Q. (2019). Efficientnet: Rethinking model scaling for convolutional neural networks. *International Conference on Machine Learning,* 6105–6114.

Thomas, A. D. H., Davies, T., & Luxmoore, A. R. (1991). Computer image analysis for identification of wear particles. *Wear, 142*(2), 213–226.

Wang, S., Wu, T. H., Shao, T., & Peng, Z. X. (2019). Integrated model of BP neural network and CNN algorithm for automatic wear debris classification. *Wear, 426,* 1761–1770.

Wang, S., Wu, T., & Wang, K. (2021). Automated 3D ferrograph image analysis for similar particle identification with the knowledge-embedded double-CNN model. *Wear, 476,* 203696.

Wu, H., Kwok, N. M., Liu, S., Li, R., Wu, T., & Peng, Z. (2019). Restoration of defocused ferrograph images using a large kernel convolutional neural network. *Wear, 426,* 1740–1747.

Wu, T., Peng, Y., Wu, H., Zhang, X., & Wang, J. (2014). Full-life dynamic identification of wear state based on on-line wear debris image features. *Mechanical Systems and Signal Processing, 42*(1–2), 404–414.

Xie, F., & Wei, H. (2022). Research on controllable deep learning of multi-channel image coding technology in Ferrographic Image fault classification. *Tribology International, 173,* 107656.

9 The Role of Artificial Intelligence and the Internet of Things in Smart Agriculture towards Green Engineering

*Sonali Kadam, Amruta Sudhakar Shinde,
and Anjali Manish Bari*
Bharati Vidyapeeth's College of Engineering for Women, Pune, India

J. G. Gujar
Sinhgad College of Engineering, Pune, India

CONTENTS

DOI: 10.1201/9781003359456-9

9.1   INTRODUCTION

Agriculture was the beginning of civilization, and is still highly essential today, despite the changes in humanity. Even today, it is regarded as one of the most important industries around the world. Despite the growing population, rising food demand, lack of infrastructure, and other factors, most people continue to use traditional agricultural farming practices. Agriculture is the second-largest producer of greenhouse gases because of factors like fertilizers that are based on fossils, biomass, as well as technology. The agriculture industry forms the backbone of the economy in some developed and developing countries. This field makes a significant contribution to the expansion of developing countries' gross domestic products (GDP), such as India, Nepal, and Myanmar.

To meet the rising demand for food around the world, traditional crop management techniques are no longer adequate. This issue is exacerbated by poor agricultural practices, climate change, and exponential population growth. According to a new United Nations estimate released, the current global population of 7.6 billion people will increase to 8.6 billion in 2030, 9.8 billion in 2050, and 11.2 billion in 2100. Even if fertility rates continue to drop, the growing trend in population size is expected to continue, with about 83 million people added to the world's population each year [1].

Additionally, farmers' improper crop management practices and soil degradation, including acidification of the soil, are frequently brought on by large-scale resource extraction, heavy metal pollution, and a host of other issues. Farmers must utilize a variety of resources like nutrients, water, and fertilizers in a highly optimal manner in order to produce food that is sustainable. Because of this, they have a great opportunity to address agricultural challenges while simultaneously preserving the environment thanks to smart farming [1]. "Smart agriculture" is a commonly used term that refers to a revolution in the agriculture business that can address a variety of local and global challenges. The agriculture industry has progressed from low-tech to high-tech standards in the last two decades. Processes are increasingly being automated to conserve physical and human resources while also increasing economic viability. Agriculture is now a $5 trillion worldwide business that is trying to feed a growing global population.

One essential characteristic that sets humans apart from other species is intelligence. Artificial intelligence (AI) is a method that enables a machine or computer to mimic people and carry out activities.

The Internet of Things (IoT), big data, and conventional agricultural practices may be combined in the future of agriculture [2]. Utilizing modern technology in agriculture aims to boost profits by reducing crop failure risks and enhancing the overall quality of the produce.

Information and communication technologies that are used in machinery, equipment, and sensors as part of high-tech, network-based farm administration cycles have been the main focus of the development of smart farming. The IoT, cloud computing, and cutting-edge technologies are predicted to foster growth and expand the use of robotics and AI in agriculture. Such ground-breaking innovations have an impact on traditional agricultural methods and present a number of challenges. This chapter examines the methods and tools used in wireless sensor applications in IoT agriculture, as well as the potential issues that might develop when technology is incorporated into conventional farming methods.

Crop and soil monitoring, precision farming, harvesting, and product commercialization are all improved by automation in agriculture. AI and IoT-based smart technologies, along with image processing, have made a significant contribution to disease detection at the initial stage, hence increasing agricultural output. Computer vision is used to program agricultural robots and drones to execute tasks such as weeding, seed sowing, disease diagnosis, and watering. Farmers in the 21st century have smartphones, allowing them to use GPS, AI, and IoT-enabled tools for remote monitoring, soil scanning, disease detection and treatment, and adequate watering and harvesting. AI and the IoT have replaced traditional farming methods, allowing the world to become a better place. Table 9.1 provides summary details concerning soil management.

TABLE 9.1
Summary of Soil Management

Technique	Strength	Limitation	References
ANN	Predicts the activity of soil enzymes, accurately classifies soil structure.	Measures a small number of soil enzymes; more classification is taken into account than soil performance enhancement.	[3]
ANN	Can forecast the average monthly soil temperature	Focuses mainly on temperature when determining how well soil will function.	[4]
ANN	Forecasts soil structure	A large amount of data is necessary for training; has limitations regarding application regions.	[5]
ANN	Capable of forecasting soil moisture	The forecast will eventually be wrong because weather conditions are so difficult to predict.	[6]
ANN	Reports soil texture effectively	It does not provide a solution for improving poor soil texture.	[7]
ANN	Cost-efficient, time-saving, and 92% accurate	Big data is required.	[8]
ANN	Can calculate the nutrients in soil after erosion	The largest erosion estimates were not correctly predicted by the ANN-derived framework.	[9]

9.2 ARTIFICIAL INTELLIGENCE IN AGRICULTURE

With the growing population and need for efficient farming, AI in agriculture has been a topic of discussion. The principal goal of AI is to help farmers improve the overall harvest quality by making precise and accurate predictions. It enables farmers to produce more output with minimum input. By using AI tools, farmers are able to monitor soil health, crop deficiencies, as well as weather conditions. These tools make it easier to analyze the market and sell products at high prices by establishing a strong connection to the global market. To achieve this, a variety of technologies are proposed from time to time in various sectors of agriculture and which are discussed below.

Water conservation and irrigation have been inextricably intertwined throughout the process of the evolution of the agricultural sector and precision farming. However, it is a delicate task to make use of natural water resources efficiently with effective cost management for technology and infrastructure. Since agriculture accounts for approximately 70% or more of the use of global water, minimizing its consumption is important. As food demand is taken to new heights, water consumption is estimated to rise to an additional 15% [10]. By implementing smart irrigation systems, AI tools propose algorithms for managing the irrigation process with minimal and efficient use of water resources. These technologies are developed to lessen human efforts across time by increasing the ability to detect water levels, temperature, the nutritious content of the soil, and forecasting the weather. A microcontroller is used to perform this operation, which it does by switching the irrigator pump on or off. Technology has also been developed to facilitate communication, including the sharing of data between nodes in the agricultural field and to the server via the main network.

The formation of an automated robotic model for temperature and moisture content detection uses Arduino and Raspberry Pi [10]. The data is gathered in this case on a regular basis and transferred to the microcontroller, Arduino, which transforms the matching input into a digital signal [2]. The signal is then transmitted to Raspberry Pi 3 (which incorporates the KNN (K-nearest neighbor) algorithm), which sends it once more to Arduino to initiate irrigation. The water is supplied on the basis of demand by the resource, and it also updates and stores the sensor values. Another technique used to improve the irrigation process is the use of various sensors, such as the molecular sensor which is used to enhance crop growth, and the temperature, soil moisture, pressure regulator, and pressure sensors which are used for measuring these qualities of the soil [11].

9.3 PRECISION AGRICULTURE ARTIFICIAL INTELLIGENCE

In the context of digitization, the concept of precision agriculture is widely mentioned. Observing, quantifying, and adapting to crop variability both within and between fields are the foundation of this farming management concept. The foundation of this idea is the computerized processing of certain facts to assist in decision-making [12]. A decision support system (DSS) for overall farm management that maximizes input returns while conserving resources is the goal of precision agriculture research. Systems that aid in decision-making like agricultural DSSs are simply informational resources that help farmers make decisions based on their understanding of different crop-growth characteristics [13]. DSS entails gathering, organizing, and analyzing data to make short- or long-term decisions. DSS can, for example, create a list of fertilizers that might be used for pest or weed control or even suggest, depending on the crop species, growth stage, and other factors, a combination of chemical and non-chemical approaches to be studied [14].

9.3.1 GEOGRAPHIC INFORMATION SYSTEM (GIS)

GIS is used in several areas of agriculture, including crop management, disease, weed control, land degradation forecasting, irrigation control, automation farming, livestock monitoring, erosion forecasting, vegetation mapping, and yield estimation [15]. As a result, the use of GIS is appropriate for precision farming, generating public awareness, and making significant contributions to meeting the needs of increasing food demands [15].

9.3.2 AUTOSTEER

This is the latest technology that has numerous applications in the agricultural sectors, especially in precision agriculture. It is used to automate vehicles which in turn reduces costs associated with fuels and the overuse of chemicals, and reduces human error [16].

The objectives of precision agriculture are:

1. Profitability: Identify crops, market them strategically, and compute the return on investment (ROI) depending on cost and profit-making [17].
2. Efficiency: Incorporating a precision algorithm, farmers will be able to take advantage of improved, quick, and low-cost farming opportunities. This allows for efficient resource utilization overall.
3. Sustainability: Improved socioeconomic and environmental operations ensure additive improvements in all performance indicators, season after season.

9.4 AGRICULTURAL ROBOTICS AND DRONES

Agricultural robots are specialized techniques that can be used to perform numerous tasks to ease the burden on farmers. They can analyze, consider, and carry out a wide range of tasks, and they can be programmed to grow and evolve to meet the demands of complex jobs.

9.4.1 HARVEST CROO ROBOTICS

Crop harvesting is a very important component of any kind of farming. Leafy vegetables are prone to rips, whereas fruits are known for bruising. The need for exceptional accuracy and thorough study is necessary since each variety of produce has certain issues. At the same time, this is a very tiring and long procedure, including lots of human effort due to its repetitive nature. Because of the nature of this job, robots need to take over. That is why, Harvest CROO Robotics developed a prototype for a fully autonomous strawberry harvester that aids farmers in the field in identifying, selecting, and picking only ripe strawberries while leaving unripe berries and plants unharmed, resulting in reduced labor costs. The company believes that by implementing this technology, it will be able to improve the quality of the berries picked, reduce energy consumption, and increase strawberry yields [18].

9.4.2 ROBOT DRONE TRACTORS

In this technology, robots have the authority to make decisions such as when to harvest and how to choose the best route for crisscrossing the farmland. They also help minimize the unwanted usage of pesticides, herbicides, fertilizers, and water [19]. In this case, the cabin is equipped with a small industrial computer that uses electronics to control the tractor and connect it to external equipment such as planters and grain bins. The system has directional awareness thanks to an inertial measurement unit. The tractor and the farmer communicate via wireless and cellular networks. The use of an agricultural camera allows a human supervisor to monitor operations from a distance [19].

9.4.3 FARM BOTS

Precision farming was boosted by FarmBot, a company established in 2011, by allowing environmentally conscious people to grow crops on their land using precision farming technology. FarmBot is a $4000 product that enables the owner to handle all aspects of farming independently. This physical bot manages everything using an open-source software system, including seeding, weeding detection, soil testing, and plant watering [18].

9.4.4 AUTONOMOUS TRACTORS

Similar to the robot drone tractor, these self-driving tractors have been developed so that they can freely identify their furrowing position in the field, choose their speed, and keep themselves away from any kind of impediments such as water system items, people, and creatures [15].

9.4.5 UNMANNED AERIAL VEHICLES (UAVs)

A UAV is an agricultural drone that can be used for the entire crop management process, beginning with soil treatment, progressing on to sowing, plant treatment, physiological control and observation, and finally determining harvest time. A drone's aerial view can aid in monitoring crop growth in real-time stages, crop health, and soil variations, allowing for any necessary mitigation. UAVs' multispectral sensors can take pictures in the electromagnetic spectrum's visible and near-infrared ranges. Alongside this, the advancement in its technology has now enabled drones to deliver water, fertilizers, herbicides, and pesticides as well as generate maps of the field to assist farmers in making management decisions [19]. There are two illustrations of maps that can be created using this kind of agricultural drone:

1. Red green blue (RGB) maps: A precise perspective of the field can be obtained from an RBG map. These maps help with crop monitoring over time, enabling us to make modifications from season to season. They give a centimeter-by-centimeter breakdown of how much land you have to work with [20].
2. Normalized difference vegetation index (NDVI) maps: An RGB map provides information, but NDVI adds more detail. The map depicts how much infrared light is reflected in a given area, which is considered a sign of malnutrition and drought. The information gathered by this map is essential because it can be used to spot crops that are unhealthy one to two weeks before any outward symptoms appear [20].

Examples of drones are:

1. The Agras T30 (or T20 or T10): These are optimal for spraying large fields, with a capacity to cover up to 40 acres per hour.

2. Phantom 4 RTK: This is a real-time kinematic (RTK)-integrated drone, specifically designed to generate precise maps. It is an ideal tool for surveillance purposes.

3. P4 Multispectral: This is integrated with a spectral sunlight sensor and RTK module, designed primarily for agricultural purposes. This tool uses multispectral imaging to provide instant insight into the health of plants [20].

9.5 IMAGE-BASED INSIGHT GENERATION

Images captured by drones can help in the analysis of the farm, monitoring crops, scanning the field, and other tasks. A combination of technologies like computer vision, the IoT, as well as drone data can be used to ensure prompt action [13].

The following are some examples of applications for computer vision technology.

1. Plant Disease Detection: Cloud-based AI algorithms for image processing enabled real-time diagnosis and assisted experts in analyzing the seriousness of a disease with the help of geographic visualization. High-resolution images are captured using UAVs and deep convolutional neural networks (DCNNs) to detect if the crop is affected by any kind of disease. DCNNs which are used in visual imagery techniques are currently the most widely used method for diagnosing plant diseases because they support the efficient tracking of pests and diseases. Because this technique is not very labor intensive, it is a realistic approach for the computational analysis of plant diseases [19]. Table 9.2 gives details about disease management using (AI [21].

TABLE 9.2
Disease Management Using AI

Technique	Strength	Limitations	References
Computer vision system (CVS), genetic algorithm (GA), ANN	Performs at a rapid pace; able to multitask	Dimension-based detection that could harm beneficial species	[22]
Rule-basedexpert, database (DB)	Specific outcomes in the testing set	DB is inefficient when used on a large scale	[23]
Fuzzy logic (FL), web geographic information system (GIS)	Cheap and environmentally friendly	Distributional inefficiency brought on by dispersion; takes time to find and distribute data; mobile browser determines the data's location	[24]
FL web-based,web-Basedintelligent disease diagnosis system (WIDDS)	Better precision; promptly reacts to the type of crop ailment	Restricted use because it needs an internet connection; since only four seed crops were taken into consideration, their efficacy cannot be determined	[25]
FL and text to speech (TTS) converter	Quickly solves plant pathological issues	Requires a fast internet connection; utilizes voice services as the interface for its multi-media components	[26]
Disease detection expert system employing rule-based technology	Quicker diagnosis of illnesses, leading to quicker treatmentConsidering its preventive strategy, it is cost-effective	Takes a lot of time; requires ongoing observation to see if the pest has developed resistance to the preventive measure	[27]
ANN, GIS	95% accuracy	Internet-based; some farmers in rural areas won't have access	[28]

2. Plantix App: PEAT GmbH, a Berlin-based AI startup, developed the Plantix application, which is a deep-learning application that detects potential soil defects and nutrient deficiencies. The analysis is carried out using software algorithms that link specific foliage patterns to soil defects, plant pests, and diseases. This app uses images captured by a camera to generate an insight into the possible defects in the plants and provides appropriate suggestions for treatment as well.

3. Soil Health Monitor: Soil health is an essential aspect of agriculture as it can improve or deteriorate the quality of the yield produced. Hence, the implementation of the right technology to ensure the proper quality of soil is imperative. The fusion of the image recognition technique and deep learning models has opened the doors for distributed soil health monitoring. Data signals received from remote satellites and local images captured of the farms, aid farmers to take immediate possible action to restore soil health. To achieve this, Soilsens technology was introduced. This is a soil monitoring system embedded with soil moisture, soil temperature, humidity, and ambient temperature sensors. Using all these sensors and considering various other parameters, Soilsens advises the farmer about optimum irrigation using a mobile app [19].

9.6 ARTIFICIAL INTELLIGENCE IN MANAGEMENT ACCOUNTING

A fundamental process is currently underway to divide digital and exponential economies that have emerged from the post-industrial economy. Exponential economies mean gaining access or sharing works better than ownership. It's what allows them to scale faster than we're used to with traditional linear growth models. AI, cloud computing, quantum computing, robotics, distributed ledgers, and other technologies are used in exponential economics to enable increasing the effectiveness of corporate operations. AI has the potential to be used in management accounting because of:

- Its end-to-end nature for implementing AI-based applied technological solutions;
- The impact of AI-based technological solutions regarding the efficiency of management accounting;
- A variety of instruments for the creation of AI-based accounting management technology;
- The requirement for processing huge quantities of data which are produced by both employees and technical devices in the organization [29].

Apart from the applications stated above, AI still has a wide range of scope in the agricultural sector. This never-ending technology can be used in:

1. Crop health monitoring;
2. Checking the quality of fruits and vegetables;
3. Weather forecasting;
4. Predictive analysis;
5. Crop classification;
6. Crop maintenance;
7. Price forecasting and market direction;
8. Services for crop loans and insurance.

Challenges:

1. AI is a data-driven technology. Without sufficient quantity and quality of datasets, AI applications are useless. This means that it's critical to collect and store relevant data in a structured manner; otherwise, AI and machine learning models won't be able to produce anything useful [30]. To develop a reliable ML model, a sufficient amount of span is required as it takes time for the data infrastructure to mature. Because of this, AI seems to be more beneficial for agronomic products than for precision solutions [13].

2. In most parts of the world, there is still illiteracy regarding the use of high-tech machine-learning solutions. Farming is highly exposed to numerous external factors like weather, soil conditions, and pest exposure. As a result, what appears to work well as a starting harvesting option may not be the best option due to changes in external parameters [18].

3. Even though the food industry has spread across the globe, farmers' income continues to be a source of concern. With low income, the affordability of high-tech solutions to ease farming techniques is difficult.

4. Interoperability issues: The incompatibility of various standards makes the operation of an agricultural IoT and other platforms difficult [31].

5. The capability of an intelligent or expert system to carry out tasks precisely and quickly is a vital aspect. In general nearly all systems have temporal or precision limitations, or even both. A user's choice of task procedure is a result of a system delay. The following three methodologies are available to people who want to reduce effort while increasing precision: performance, pacing, and monitoring, which are all automated.

6. Scheduled machines and software must be updated regularly. Farmers must update their systems as technology advances to obtain more accurate and current data. With the old version, some systems will not function properly.

7. The application of AI methods in agriculture necessitates a different set of skills. These technologies are made up of hardware, software, sensors, and a variety of tools that require training to use properly [32].

8. With technological unity comes vulnerability. If one component of the system fails, it can have a result that affects the entire system. This necessitates that proper education should be implemented at all levels to ensure proper monitoring of the system [16].

Benefits:

1. Predictive analytics, which has the power to completely alter industries. The best times to plant and harvest crops can be determined by analyzing market demand, forecasting prices, and using AI.

2. Data collection and forecasting of current weather conditions, particularly humidity, high temperature, precipitation, and solar energy. When this data is combined with AI, the developed solution can decrease the loss of crops and increase the yield.

3. AI can also monitor the weather, track the state of the soil, recommend fertilizer, and determine when the product is ready. All this information aids farmers in making wiser choices throughout the entire crop-growing process.

4. This technology can be useful in developing a monitoring system for livestock which can thereby increase productivity.

5. It also allows farmers to improve their learning, manage farm activities, and properly maintain supply chain processes. As a result of various AI applications, such as machine learning and deep learning, farmers can benefit more from increased farming productivity and less resource use, resulting in higher income levels and improved social and economic well-being [33].

9.7 AGRICULTURE AND THE INTERNET OF THINGS

Principal monitoring in the agricultural sector involves the use of the IoT, along with control and actuation. By keeping track of the agricultural supply chain, reducing losses, and ensuring food safety, the IoT can facilitate real-time information sharing on agri-food products. Furthermore, by combining technology, including big data, AI, and the IoT, smart agriculture can achieve several important farming goals like increasing productivity and reducing the use of pesticides. Using various sensors and network technologies, IoT technologies have been deployed to many specialized agricultural activities during the last few decades. Farmers may deploy IoT-based agriculture that is of high-efficiency and low-cost by choosing the right sensors and networks for their farm settings and working surroundings [34].

The conventional agricultural era 1.0, as it is known historically, was characterized by agricultural methods which centered on human survival and the production of food in cultivated fields and the raising of animals [33]. Mostly, this involved using laborers and animals. Shovels and sickles were among the basic implements used in farming. Because manual labor constituted the majority of the work, productivity remained low (Figure 9.1).

The agricultural sectors saw the introduction of new machinery during the 19th century in the shape of the steam engine. The widespread utilizing of agricultural equipment and the glut of chemicals that farmers used heralded the beginning of agricultural period 2.0 and significantly increased the efficiency of farms and farmers. However, at the same time, extremely negative effects including chemical pollution, environmental destruction, resource waste, and excessive energy use emerged. Due to the explosive rise of electronics and computation during the 20th century, agricultural era 3.0 was born. Robotic methods, agricultural machinery that is programmed, and other technologies effectively improved agricultural processes. Agricultural period 2.0-related problems were resolved, and the policies were updated to reflect the new agricultural era. By distributing the work, using targeted irrigation and fewer chemicals, applying nutrients specifically to a place, and using effective insect management methods, among other things, the latest agricultural iteration, known as agricultural era 4.0, incorporates modern technology. The next agricultural era will be characterized by technologies such as the IoT, big data analysis, AI, cloud computing, and remote sensing.

A network of intelligent, connected objects that can communicate with one another and provide pertinent environmental knowledge in which they operate is known as the IoT [35]. The primary benefit of incorporating the IoT into farming is to increase precision and proficiency while reducing human intervention. IoT modernization aids in the collection of data on variables such as weather

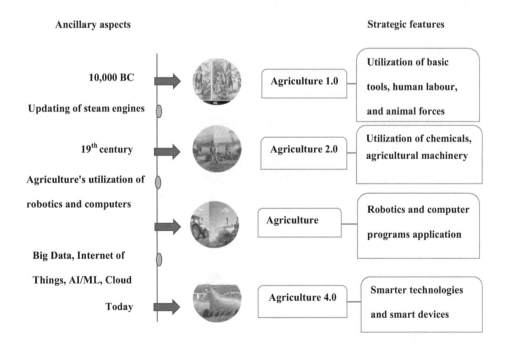

FIGURE 9.1 Agricultural decision support system framework [35].

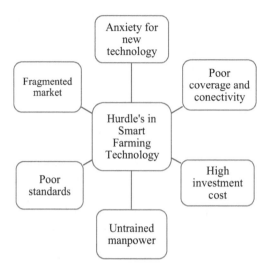

FIGURE 9.2 Barriers in the implementation of smart agriculture technology [35].

and dampness [36]. It has started a new era in agriculture, with applications in farm monitoring, irrigation control, greenhouse environmental control, and agricultural drones, all of which contribute to agricultural automation.

This new technology of the IoT essentially allows remote connections between devices to enable smart farming [36]. Improvements in the efficiency and performance of the IoT have already begun to have an impact on a variety of businesses, including biomedical applications, communications, energy, and agriculture across all sectors [37–39]. Information on the effects of the IoT and its as-yet-unrecognized behaviors is available from current applications. IoT technologies, however, are expected to play a significant role in many farming activities, including using communication infrastructure, data collection, intelligent cloud-based information, mobile devices, smart objects, sensors, decision-making, and the automation of agricultural activities (Figure 9.2). IoT technology uses mobile phones and other devices to remotely access data from mobile devices and monitor plants and animals. Farmers can predict production levels and evaluate the weather thanks to sensors and devices. More than ever, the IoT is involved in water collection, monitoring and regulating the flow rate, determining the water needs of crops, the timing of supply, and water conservation [40].

9.8 THE PRECISION FARMING INTERNET OF THINGS (IoT)

Precision farming is a method that improves the accuracy and management of the farming process for cultivating crops and raising livestock with the use of sensors, computerized hardware, robotics, control systems, and many others. A decision support system for overall farm management that ensures profitability, sustainability, and environmental protection is what precision agriculture research aims to create. One of the most well-known IoT initiatives in the agricultural sector in recent years is precision agriculture, and many organizations have started using it globally [37].

To maximize agricultural production, precision farming uses a variety of technologies, including GPS systems, sensors, and big data. Information on all elements of farming might be provided through a decision support system based on information and communication technology (ICT) with real-time data to back it up [35].

Similar to smart cities, smart farming is a management idea that focuses on giving agricultural businesses the framework to use cutting-edge technology, like big data, IoT, and the cloud, to detect, monitor, and evaluate activities [37]. Automated irrigation techniques eliminate the need for human intervention. To sense the various aspects of the soil, a variety of sensors are used, including temperature, humidity, and soil moisture, and judgments are made on whether or not to irrigate depending on sensor results [39]. Smart sensors (e.g. dielectric soil moisture, electrochemical, and location sensors) play a critical role in the agriculture and pharmaceutical industries, where not only is production increased, but also long-term growth is realized. For example, soil moisture sensors detect the amount of water in the soil with great precision and they help in irrigation efficiency. Correct irrigation control produces healthier seeds and increases profitability. It can help the irrigators figure out the status of the crop's root zone, which can result in reduced use of water [40].

9.8.1 Agriculture Sensors

1. pH sensors: These are to maximize a plant's growth potential and produce highly productive harvests. Understanding soil conditions in greater depth is essential. pH sensors give crucial information about soil nutrient deficits and the presence of undesirable substances. Smart agriculture uses these sensors to track daily, weekly, monthly, and annually changes in soil pH and nutrient levels to continue to inform the agricultural business [41].
2. Location sensors: By looking at their plot from different angles and unlocking more value with location-based sensors, farmers may better comprehend the potential of their cultivable land. The land and soil composition in the planted zone can be analyzed in three dimensions using GPS and GIS-based sensors, as well as human and unmanned aerial systems like drones and satellite photos [42].
3. Asset monitoring: Temperature sensing is also important in asset monitoring, which is another use in smart agriculture. Temperature sensors monitor the machinery that gathers the plants in addition to the plants that are already harvested. When an equipment system requires minor maintenance, is underperforming, or is critically malfunctioning, temperature sensors give out signals. To prevent overheating and catastrophic failure, they're found in practically every predictive and reactive maintenance system [41].
4. Optical sensors: In agriculture, optical sensors are used to measure the amount of reflected light on the growing regions of the crop in real-time to understand the qualities of the soil and crop. Optical sensors instruct analytical tools to boost nitrogen dosage for weaker and unhealthy plants while regulating it for good plants. Optical sensors are also used to study crop vigor by using characteristics such as soil biomass and the ratio of nitrogen to other gases in the soil. This aids farmers in controlling moisture levels in the air and soil, as well as avoiding damp conditions [42].

Fertilization in smart agriculture also helps to properly predict the required amount of nutrients, according to the findings. Using the IoT will help agriculture become smarter. The following are some of its key roles:

1. Soil management includes determining several soil properties, e.g. pH and moisture content. These parameters can be easily assessed with IoT sensors, and farmers can subsequently take action like fertilization and irrigation [43].
2. Water management may be done very efficiently using various IoT sensors. This reduces water waste while also increasing agricultural output. This aids in the detection of diseases caused by water in ponds and agricultural areas.
3. IoT sensors like the DHT11 temperature sensor and radio frequency identification system (RFID) chips can be used to identify plant and crop diseases. The reader can extract information from RFID tags and share it over the internet. The farmer can study this data remotely and take appropriate action based on it. Pathogens will be kept away from the crops as a result of this [43].
4. Agricultural drones, often known as UAVs, are used to collect agricultural data in smart farming. Aside from monitoring capabilities, drones may be used to do jobs that formerly required human labor, such as crop planting, pest management, infection control, and crop tracking [39].

5. IoT agriculture sensors, like those for other applications, can be mounted for monitoring the health and performance of farm animals. Tracking and monitoring of livestock collects information on the cattle's location, condition, and state of health. Cattle monitoring sensors can detect sick or injured animals, allowing farmers to separate them from the herd and stay away from further infection. Additionally, drones for cattle tracking enable farmers to reduce labor costs [39].

9.8.2 Communication in Agriculture

The backbone of precision agriculture is timely reporting and communication of information. A firm, trustworthy, and secure link between numerous participating items are required to achieve this goal. Operators of telecommunications can play a critical part in the agriculture industry to ensure communication reliability. If we want to widely implement the IoT in agriculture, we will need a sufficiently vast architecture [44]. The farm's automated equipment can network information to a central management hub on-site, giving operators the most recent data on herd health, environmental conditions, and other things.

9.9 THE INTERNET OF THINGS CLOUD

The IoT cloud is critical for delivering data and transmitting it between devices. Predictive big data analysis, item identification, plant diseases, and sensor output all have their storage. A farmer can also acquire knowledge about smart agriculture or future predictions from agro-professionals over the internet. Experts can advise on field crop planting, pesticide control, and agricultural land management. The traditional farmer may have these services available in the agricultural sector. This would have excellent usability and IoT devices would power the primary server [45].

9.9.1 Climate Change

Climate change has a huge impact on agriculture. And having erroneous climate knowledge can severely reduce the quantity and quality of the produce. IoT solutions, on the other hand, allow us to learn about current weather conditions in real-time and make decisions based on that information. Agricultural areas have sensors installed both inside and outside of them. The entire IoT environment is comprised of sensors that can precisely locate current weather conditions, including temperature, precipitation, and humidity. There are several sensors that are available to detect many of these aspects and adjust them to match our smart farming requirements [37].

9.9.2 Smart Greenhouses

Greenhouse farming boosts agricultural, vegetable, and fruit yields, among other things, in the soil. Greenhouses use two methods to regulate environmental parameters: a proportional control mechanism in addition to manual intervention. There are different sensors that are employed in these techniques [46]. IoT-enabled smart greenhouse embedded structures intelligently monitor and regulate the climate. As a result, any need for human intervention is eliminated [37].

9.9.3 Internet of Things-based Tractors

An average-sized tractor can work traditional agricultural labor and can be completed 40 times faster and for a small fraction of the expense. To meet the growing demand, producers of agricultural machinery like John Deere, Case IH, and Hello Tractors have begun to create better solutions centered on the needs of the producer. Most of these manufacturers now offer tractors with auto-driven as well as cloud-computing capabilities, due to technological advancements. Self-driving tractors can avoid reassessment of the same area or same row by decreasing the overlapping to a fraction of an inch, which is one of its key advantages. Moreover, they can also execute highly precise turns without the presence of a driver. This facility allows for greater precision with minimum errors, particularly when insecticide is sprayed, which is almost inescapable when the machines are controlled by a human [44].

9.10   CHALLENGES WITH THE INTERNET OF THINGS

Despite the IoT's rapid growth, there are still some conceptual, fundamental, and developmental difficulties lingering on from previous decades:

1. Many researchers are still struggling with creating a model which is cost-efficient. They concentrate on forming systems that are affordable by lowering the hardware and software requirements for IoT implementation. Farmers find it challenging to install equipment and technology due to economic variations between countries. As a result, it's critical to create certain economic models [47].
2. Each device has its own set of operations and servicing requirements. Because most agricultural models rely on heterogeneous equipment, it's critical to establish a connection between these wireless communication innovations and heterogeneous modules. The network's complexity rises as a result of heterogeneity, and faked results may occur.
3. The need for current hardware and software to be accessible anywhere and anytime is necessary when developing any farming DSS utilizing IoT technology or any other devices. These issues must be addressed to ensure that services are available at all times. If the essential equipment is not available, the services may be disrupted and delayed [47].
4. The most pressing problem with a wireless sensor network (WSN), IoT systems, and other communication devices is energy. Until now, conventional energy sources have been used to support the development and operation of models. However, as the number of devices grows, traditional energy use is no longer a viable option. Although they haven't had much success so far, non-conventional ideas for energy collecting from solar, water, and wind sources should be examined, and new approaches to exploit them for model development should be devised.
5. Reliability is a key issue for IoT devices for successful and seamless functioning in terms of data transmission. Since decisions are made based on the information that has been received and assessed, the devices must gather and send accurate data. Due to node and system failures, battery problems, and other considerations, reliability is still an issue [47].
6. The developed systems or models are typically stagnant. Mobility is crucial for the seamless deployment of the framework because the majority of devices and apps are portable. Still, a difficult task is dealing with the connectivity issue in mobile models.

9.10.1   FUTURE SCOPE OF THE INTERNET OF THINGS IN AGRICULTURE

Data sharing should be encouraged in practically all IoT-based precision farming models, as well as integration and system design mapping. This could pave the way for the creation of an international interactive model. This characteristic can also aid in the worldwide awareness of topographic and demographic difficulties faced by diverse locations. As a result, those working in resource-constrained contexts could create appropriate solutions.

The communication sector is undergoing a gradual and dynamic transformation. Because IoT models are placed remotely, improved connectivity is required. As a result, high-speed connection techniques like 5G must be considered to make gadgets more accessible with fewer delays [47].

Farmers can benefit from the IoT focused on agriculture employing geospatial technology because everyone can readily grasp the information with the help of maps. This methodology aids the government in a variety of ways, including evaluating the rate of agricultural and vegetable production in a given state or region. Agriculture, as we all know, plays a critical part in the growth of our country's economy. Sensors and sensor tractors, which were previously employed in farming, were quite expensive and took a long time to analyze the output of the given data [48].

9.11 INTEGRATING ARTIFICIAL INTELLIGENCE AND THE INTERNET OF THINGS IN AGRICULTURE

With the adoption of the IoT comes a rapid change in the economy. It is useful to gather a huge quantity of information from numerous sources. Understanding this avalanche of data gathered from countless sources makes data collection, processing, and analysis difficult. The convergence of intelligent machines and the IoT has the capability of reshaping the way that economies, corporations, and industries function today. AI-powered IoT produces intelligent robots that imitate intelligent behavior and provide decision-support without any need for human intervention. The combination of these two benefits both ordinary people as well as experts. The IoT along with supply chain management systems powered by AI provide revolutionary insights and control over agricultural processes. The IoT and AI significantly affect agriculture and trade as the agricultural tech revolution gets underway. A high-tech, expensive technology called "smart farming" helps farmers produce food sustainably and cleanly. IoT tools utilized in intelligent farming include smart greenhouses, animal monitoring systems, and agricultural drones.

In order to meet the growing demand for more food and higher crop quality, smart farming uses the IoT and AI. This helps farmers in the following ways to boost yield:

1. It monitors crop-specific growth, the quality of the soil, temperature, and humidity conditions so that it yields healthier crops. Crop wastage is reduced thanks to real-time updates based on continuous observation.
2. Trends can also be investigated using the information gathered. The effectiveness of the food supply chain and the improvement of agribusiness returns are both facilitated by data-driven forecasts.
3. Cost management is aided by smart IoT applications as they effectively use resources like water and electricity. They can guarantee prompt irrigation and pest control from anywhere using connected devices and automated systems.

9.12 APPLICATIONS OF ARTIFICIAL INTELLIGENCE AND THE INTERNET OF THINGS IN AGRICULTURE

Some of the IoT and AI applications in agriculture for green engineering are:

1. Precision farming systems: There are numerous uses of AI and the IoT to enhance the goal of precision farming. To achieve this, numerous sensors, autonomous machinery, and internet connectivity are required. Among the services offered are soil moisture probing, cloud-based centralized water management, and variable rate irrigation (VRI) optimization.
2. Livestock monitoring and tracking solutions: Advanced video analytics have enabled people to guard their animals and fields. For a large-scale agricultural operation, video surveillance systems are as reliable as for small-scale farms. Surveillance systems based on machine learning can be trained to distinguish between humans and vehicles. For monitoring cattle on the farm IoT networks and connected devices can cut labor costs. This is an efficient way to track animals and monitor their health using IoT sensors. In huge areas or farms, farmers can easily spot animals from a distance and can even stop the spread of disease by removing sick animals from the herd, safeguarding the produce, and reducing livestock expenses [49].

3. Smart greenhouse: IoT-enabled smart greenhouses use a proportional control system to increase yield. To maintain crops in a controlled environment, they use sensors. Data is processed on cloud servers, and the system is remotely monitored. The smart greenhouse monitors sun light, temperature, and humidity levels with minimal manual intervention.

4. Weather trackers: Smart sensors based on the IoT provide real-time weather and climate updates. The comprehensive forecast can be used by farmers to determine what crops they will require. Some systems also have alarms to help farmers preserve their harvest in the event of a blizzard.

5. Spray hose: Drones with AI can track the vegetation index of crops and their health. Insect infestations and diseases are monitored by their sensors. Only infected plants are sprayed with pesticides by these devices. This reduces the use of chemicals on otherwise healthy crops and stops the infection from spreading at the same time [50].

6. Crop price forecasting and yield forecasting applications: Machine learning is an ideal technology for combining large datasets and providing constraint-based crop yield optimization suggestions. AI and big data are being combined to assist farmers in predicting crop yield. Price fluctuations are studied using historical data, and it is possible to predict prices at harvest. The precise yield per hectare can be calculated with the help of farm mapping. A number is calculated by farmers based on a number of variables, including rainfall, the use of pesticides, pH levels, temperature, and other environmental variables [49].

9.13 CONCLUSION

In light of the ever-dwindling amount of arable land, a focus on better, more effective, and more intelligent crop-growing methods is necessary. Farmers are being compelled to yield more to provide for the rising need for food as the global population rises. Some of the factors that affect the volume and standardization of agricultural products include a lack of information about soil management, irrigation, crop monitoring, plant diseases, and pesticide use. Recent developments in the IoT and AI have made it possible to overcome these issues. Precision farming is a concept that is aimed at improving agricultural society and agricultural progress appears to be attainable. Furthermore, many industries are expressing their inclination towards the digital phase of this new and modern agriculture to correctly incorporate the competence of old traditional practices and discoveries. There are a lot of innovative trends that may improve the application of agricultural inefficiency technology. In that context, this chapter provides a thorough knowledge of the features and technologies necessary, as well as the opportunities and limitations of making sustainable smart agriculture a reality.

REFERENCES

1. A. Faid, M. Sadik, E. Sabir 2022. An agile AI and IoT-augmented smart farming: A cost-effective cognitive weather station. *Agriculture* 12, 35. https://doi.org/10.3390/agriculture12010035

2. S. Katiyar, A. Farhana 2021. Smart agriculture: The future of agriculture using AI and IoT. *Journal of Computer Science*, 17 10, 984–999. https://doi.org/10.3844/jcssp.2021.984.999

3. S. Tajik, S. Ayoubi, F. Nourbakhsh 2012. Prediction of soil enzymes activity by digital terrain analysis: Comparing artificial neural network and multiple linear regression models. *Environmental Engineering Science*, 29 8, 798–806.

4. E. R. Levine, D. S. Kimes, V. G. Sigillito 1996. Classifying soil structure using neural networks. *Ecological Modelling*, 92 1, 101–108, https://doi.org/10.1007/978-1-4615-5289-5_2

5. M. Bilgili 2011. The use of artificial neural network for forecasting the monthly mean soil temperature in Adana, Turkey. *Turkish Journal of Agriculture and Forestry*, 35 1, 83–93. https://doi.org/10.48084/etasr.2756

6. Z. Zhao, T. L. Chow, H. W. Rees, Q. Yang, Z. Xing, F. R. Meng 2009. Predict soil texture distributions using an artificial neural network model. *Computers and Electronics in Agriculture*, 65 1, 36–48. https://doi.org/10.1016/j.compag.2008.07.008

7. A. Elshorbagy, K. Parasuraman 2008. On the relevance of using artificial neural networks for estimating soil moisture content. *Journal of Hydrology*, 362 1–2, 1–18. https://doi.org/10.1016/j.jhydrol.2008.08.012

8. D. H. Chang, S. Islam 2000. Estimation of soil physical properties using remote sensing and artificial neural network. *Remote Sensing of Environment*, 74 3, 534–544. https://doi.org/10.1016/S1002-0160(12)60025-3

9. T. Behrens, H. Forster, T. Scholten, U. Steinrucken, E. D. Spies, M. Goldschmitt 2005. Digital soil mapping using artificial neural networks. *Journal of Plant Nutrition and Soil Science*, 168 1, 21–33. https://doi.org/10.1002/jpln.200421414

10. Yuanyuan Zhou, Qing Xia, Zichen Zhang, Mengqi Quan, Haoran Li, 2022. Artificial intelligence and machine learning for the green development of agriculture in the emerging manufacturing industry in the IoT platform. *Acta Agriculturae Scandinavica, Section B — Soil & Plant Science*, 72 1, 284–299. https://doi.org/10.1080/09064710.2021.2008482

11. Tanha Talaviya, Dhara Shah, Nivedita Patel, Hiteshri Yagnik, Manan Shah, 2020. Implementation of artificial intelligence in agriculture for optimization of irrigation and application of pesticides and herbicides. *Artificial Intelligence in Agriculture*, 4, 58–73 https://doi.org/10.1016/j.aiia.2020.04.002

12. V. Martos, A. Ahmad, P. Cartujo, J. Ordoñez 2021. Ensuring agricultural sustainability through remote sensing in the era of agriculture 5.0. *Applied Sciences*, 11, 5911. https://doi.org/10.3390/app11135911

13. N. Navatha, D.A.R. Devi 2020. Artificial intelligence- a new era in agriculture. *Vigyan Varta*, 1 3, 52–55. https://www.vigyanvarta.com/adminpanel/upload_doc/VV_0720_15a.pdf

14. Rayda Ben Ayed, Mohsen Hanana 2021. Artificial intelligence to improve the food and agriculture sector. *Journal of Food Quality*, 7. https://doi.org/10.1155/2021/5584754

15. I. A. Magomedov, M. S.-U. Khaliev, L. V. Ibragimova 2020. The need for introducing new technology in agriculture to ensure a sustainable future. *IOP Conference Series: Earth and Environmental Science*, 548, 032026. https://doi.org/10.1088/1755-1315/548/3/032026

16. Akshaya Gambhire, Shaikh Mohammad, N. Bilal 2020. Use of artificial intelligence in agriculture (2020). *Proceedings of the 3rd International Conference on Advances in Science & Technology (ICAST)*. https://doi.org/10.2139/ssrn.3571733

17. Deepak G. Panpatte 2018. Artificial Intelligence in Agriculture: An Emerging Era of Research, *Conference: Intuitional Science*, Canada. https://www.researchgate.net/publication/328555978_Artificial_Intelligence_in_Agriculture_An_Emerging_Era_of_Research

18. Rahul Kumar, Shipra Yadav, Mukesh Kumar, Jitendra Kumar, Monu Kumar 2020. Artificial Intelligence: new technology to improve Indian agriculture. *International Journal of Chemical Studies* 8 2, 2999–3005. https://doi.org/10.22271/chemi.2020.v8.i2at.9208

19. I. Kumar, J. Rawat, N. Mohd, S. Husain 2021. Opportunities of artificial intelligence and machine learning in the food industry. *Journal of Food Quality*, 1–9. https://doi.org/10.1155/2021/4535567

20. K. S. Sidhu, A. S. Gill, A. Arora, R. Singh, G. Singh, M. K. Verma, B. Kaur 2021. Advancements in farming and related activities with the help of artificial intelligence: A review. *ECJ*, 22, 55–62. https://doi.org/10.36953/ECJ.2021.SE.2206

21. N. C. Eli-Chukwu 2019. Applications of artificial intelligence in agriculture: A review. *Engineering, Technology & Applied Science Research*, 9 4, 4377–4383. https://doi.org/10.48084/etasr.2756

22. K. Balleda, D. Satyanvesh, N. V. S. S. P. Sampath, K. T. N. Varma, P. K. Baruah 2014. Agpest: An Efficient Rule-Based Expert System to Prevent Pest Diseases of Rice & Wheat Crops. *8th International Conference on Intelligent Systems and Control*, Coimbatore, India, January 10–11.

23. J. Jesus, T. Panagopoulos, A. Neves 2008. Fuzzy Logic and Geographic Information Systems for Pest Control in Olive Culture. *4th IASME/WSEAS International Conference on Energy, Environment, Ecosystems & Sustainable Development*, Algarve, Portugal, June 11–13.

24. S. Kolhe, R. Kamal, H. S. Saini, G. K. Gupta 2011. A web-based intelligent disease-diagnosis system using a new fuzzy-logic based approach for drawing the interferences in crops. *Computers and Electronics in Agriculture*, 76 1, 16–27.

25. S. Kolhe, R. Kamal, H. S. Saini, G. K. Gupta 2011. An intelligent multimedia interface for fuzzy-logic based inference in crops. *Expert Systems with Applications*, 38 12, 14592–14601.

26. M. Y. Munirah, M. Rozlini, Y. M. Siti 2013. An Expert System Development: Its Application on Diagnosing Oyster Mushroom Diseases. *13th International Conference on Control, Automation and Systems*, Gwangju, South Korea, October 20–23, https://docplayer.net/158761216-Applications-of-artificial-intelligence-in-agriculture-a-review.html

27. G. Liu, X. Yang, Y. Ge, Y. Miao 2006. An Artificial Neural Network–Based Expert System for Fruit Tree Disease and Insect Pest Diagnosis. *International Conference on Networking, Sensing and Control*, Lauderdale, USA, April 23–25, https://doi.org/10.48084/etasr.2756

28. F. Siraj, N. Arbaiy 2006. Integrated Pest Management System Using Fuzzy Expert System. *Knowledge Management International Conference & Exhibition*, Kuala Lumpur, Malaysia, June 6–8.

29. Carl Johan Casten Carlberg & Elsa Jerhamre Uppsala, 2021. *Artificial Intelligence in Agriculture Opportunities and Challenges, UPTEC STS 21018*. https://media.jordbruksteknniskaforeningen.se/2022/05/Artificial-Intelligence-in-Agriculture_final_thesis-1.pdf

30. Anu Jose, S. Nandagopalan, Chandra Mouli Venkata, Srinivas Akana, 2021. Artificial Intelligence Techniques for Agriculture Revolution: A Survey. Annals of R.S.C.B., ISSN: 1583-6258, 25 4, 2580–2597.

31. Yogesh Awasthi 2020. Press "A" for artificial intelligence in agriculture: A review. *JOIV*, 4 3, 112–116.

32. Sanjiv Sharma, Jashandeep Singh 2020. A review on usage and expected benefits of artificial intelligence in agriculture sector. *International Journal of Advanced Science and Technology*, 29, 1078–1085. https://www.academia.edu/43357425/A_Review_on_Usage_and_Expected_Benefits_of_Artificial_Intelligence_in_Agriculture_Sector

33. W. S. Kim, W. S. Lee, Y. J. Kim 2020. A review of the applications of the Internet of Things (IoT) for agricultural automation. *Journal of Biosystems Engineering*, 45, 385–400. https://doi.org/10.1007/s42853-020-00078-3

34. Lalit Kumar, Prasant Ahlawat, Pradeep Rajput, R. I. Navsare, Pradeep Kumar Singh 2021. Internet of things (IoT) for smart precision farming and agricultural systems productivity: A review. *International Journal of Engineering Applied Sciences and Technology*, 5 9, ISSN No. 2455-2143, 141–146. https://doi.org/10.33564/IJEAST.2021.v05i09.022

35. Muthumanickam Dhanaraju, Poongodi Chenniappan, Kumaraperumal Ramalingam, Sellaperumal Pazhanivelan, Ragunath Kaliaperumal 2022. Smart farming: Internet of Things (IoT)-based sustainable agriculture. *Agriculture* 12, 1745. https://doi.org/10.3390/agriculture12101745

36. Rakesh Kumar Saini & Chandra Prakash, 2020. Internet of Things (IoT) for agriculture growth using wireless sensor networks. *Global Journal of Computer Science and Technology: E Network, Web & Security*, 20 2. https://globaljournals.org/GJCST_Volume20/4-Internet-of-Things-IoT-for-Agriculture.pdf

37. A. Sagheer, M. Mohammed, K. Riad, M. Alhajhoj 2021. A cloud-based IoT Platform for precision control of soilless greenhouse cultivation. *Sensors*, 21 1, 223. https://doi.org/10.3390/s21010223

38. J. G. Gujar, Sonali Kadam, Ujwal D. Patil, 2022. *Recent Advances of Artificial Intelligence (AI) for Nanobiomedical Applications*, ed. Swati V. Shinde, Parikshit N. Mahalle, Varsha Bendre, Oscar Castillo, 1–14. 1st pub, CRC Press.

39. Raja Venkatesh Gurugubelli, Dilleswararao Nettimi, Vidya Sagar Gorle, Sairam Panda, Anil Kumar Navuluri, Rosepreet Kaur Bhogal, 2021. Internet of Things based smart agricultural system for farmers. *International Journal of Scientific Research in Computer Science, Engineering and Information Technology*, 7 3, 535–540. https://doi.org/10.32628/CSEIT2172142

40. Meghna Raj, Shashank Gupta, Vinay Chamola, et al. 2021. A survey on the role of Internet of Things for adopting and promoting Agriculture 4.0. *Journal of Network and Computer Applications*, 187 11. https://doi.org/10.1016/j.jnca.2021.103107

41. P. K. R. Maddikunta, S. Hakak, M. Alazab, S. Bhattacharya, T. R. Gadekallu, W. Z. Khan, Q. V. Pham 2021. Unmanned aerial vehicles in smart agriculture: Applications, requirements, and challenges. *IEEE Sensors Journal*, 21 16, 17608–17619. https://doi.org/10.1109/JSEN.2021.3049471

42. Monu Bhagat, Deobrata Kumar, Dilip Kumar 2019. Role of Internet of Things (IoT) in Smart Farming: A Brief Survey. https://doi.org/10.1109/DEVIC.2019.8783800

43. Muhammad Ayaz, Mohammad Ammad-Uddin, Zubair Sharif, Ali Mansour, El-Hadi M. Aggoune 2019. IoT-based smart agriculture: Toward making the fields talk. *IEEE Accesss*, 7, 129551–129583. https://ieeexplore.ieee.org/stamp/stamp.jsp?tp=&arnumber=8784034

44. V. Suma 2021. Internet of Things (IoT) based smart agriculture in India: An overview, *Journal of ISMAC*, 3 1, 1–15. https://doi.org/10.36548/jismac.2021.1.001

45. V. B. Kirubanand, V. Rohini, V. Laxmankumar 2021. Internet of Things in agriculture to revolutionize traditional agricultural industry. *ITM Web Conference*, 37, 01018. https://doi.org/10.1051/itmconf/20213701018

46. Vippon Preet Kour, Sakshi Arora 2020. Recent developments of the Internet of Things in agriculture: A survey. *IEEE Access*, 8, 129924–129957. https://doi.org/10.1109/ACCESS.2020.3009298

47. Lalit Kumar, S. Srinivasan, M. Varsha, Prachi Gupta, Tipu Sultan, Rudra Mohan 2021. Future of the internet of things (IoT): agriculture using geospatial technology. *Turkish Journal of Physiotherapy and Rehabilitation*, 32 3, 11725–11734.

48. Nawab Khan, Ram L. Ray, Ghulam Raza Sargani, Sohaib Ismail 2021. Current progress and future prospects of agriculture technology: Gateway to sustainable agriculture, *Sustainability*, 3 9. https://doi.org/10.3390/su13094883

49. Eissa Alreshidi 2019. Smart Sustainable Agriculture (SSA) solution underpinned by Internet of Things (IoT) and Artificial Intelligence (AI). *International Journal of Advanced Computer Science and Applications*, 10 5. https://doi.org/10.14569/IJACSA.2019.0100513

50. I. M. Nasir, A. Bibi, J. H. Shah, M. A. Khan, M. Sharif, K. Iqbal, Y. Nam, S. Kadry 2021. Deep learning-based classification of fruit diseases: An application for precision agriculture. *CMC-Computers Materials & Continua*, 66 2, 1949–1962. https://doi.org/10.32604/cmc.2020.012945

10 Intuitionistic Fuzzy Hypergraphs and Their Operations

N. Yogeesh

Government First Grade College, Tumkur, India

CONTENTS

10.1 INTRODUCTION

Sometimes, abstract equational representations have a lot going on that makes them difficult to understand. That's why it's important to figure out more realistic methods to portray them. Graphical representations of fuzziness are an effective learning tool because they provide a visual representation of the visual set of data equations [6]. Real-world systems of varying complexity may often be represented by networks. Standard practice dictates that the definition of a graph be communicated to computers in a matrix representation due to the former's superiority in numerical manipulation over visual and graphical recognition [18, 19]. A wide variety of applications may be found for matrices along with the graphical representations in the area of engineering and also in the research field. However, the area of an uncertain setting, the solutions provided by the conventional abstract theory, are not always adequate. It may seem more natural to define vague or nebulous beliefs in terms of their graphs from a set's membership functions. While Kauffmann [1] first proposed the notion of fuzzy graphs in 1973, it wasn't until 1975 that Rosenfeld [3] elaborated on it.

In the year 1965, the mathematician Zadeh [12] introduced the new idea of "fuzzy sets" as a way to display regular uncertainty, since science and technology don't always have all the relevant information. So, we need mathematical formulas to deal with different kinds of systems with uncertain parts. Rosenfeld then came up with fuzzy graphs. Fuzzy graphs can be used to show relationships that involve uncertainty. They are very different from traditional graphs and can be used to solve problems in many different fields, such as computer and electrical science engineering, operational research,

DOI: 10.1201/9781003359456-10

areas of economics, network management, and the routing and management of transportation. Nagoor Gani and Shajitha Begum [2, 13] introduced fuzzy graphs along with regular fuzzy graphs.

Rosenfeld also investigated the fuzzy interactions between different fuzzy sets. He also created a framework for fuzzy structural graphs, finding analogues of different types of ideas from the theory of graphs. On the basis of fuzzy relations given by Zadeh [12] in 1965, Kaufman [1] initially defined a fuzzy graph in 1975. Intuitionistic fuzzy (IF) relationships as well as the fuzziness of intuitionistic graphs (IFGs) were first proposed by Atanassov [4, 5]. The idea of the IFG was first suggested and its components analysed by Karunambigai and Parvathi [11]. Index matrices as a representation of the fuzziness of intuitionistic graphs were first developed and their various operations studied in detail by Atanassov [9, 10]. The use of index matrices for operations over intuitionistic properties of fuzzy graphs was described by Parvathi et al. [14, 15, 16].

Problems involving decision-making, clustering algorithms, pattern matching, medical diagnosis, and networks all benefit greatly from the use of intuitive fuzzy hypergraphs [8]. When there is room for guesswork in a situation, intuitive fuzzy matrices come in handy along with fuzzy hypergraphs. My interest in and discussion of intuitionistic fuzzy hypergraphs and their characteristics was prompted by their potential use in a variety of contexts. This chapter will start with the terminology used to describe graphs with intuitionistic fuzziness and then develop the topic of intuitionistic fuzzy hyper-graphs and explore their properties. Furthermore, the chapter will establish the connections among different operations of intuitionistic fuzzy graphs, thereby enhancing the understanding of their functioning.

Rosenfeld came up with the conceptual idea of the fuzziness of graphs in 1975 and established other connecting notions in FGs at the same time he defined the operations on IFGs. As a result, operations on intuitionistic fuzzy hypergraphs (IFHGs) are considered. The definition of an IFHG's complement is presented in this chapter, as well as certain features of self-complementary IFHGs. Isomorphism between two IFHGs has also been shown. In addition, operations, such as union–intersection and the join of two IFHGs, the Cartesian product of two graphs, and compositions, are defined and explained with a number of examples, and it is shown that the complementation of two IFHGs equals the complementation of union. It is also demonstrated that the combination of two different powerful IFHGs are equally very strong. On self-complementary IFHGs, further findings have been obtained.

We assume that i, j, and $\nu_{i,j}$ are reflexive throughout this chapter and that loops are unnecessary. In all instances, it is assumed that the fundamental set V is finite, and ij may be selected in any way to meet the definition of an IFHG [17]. The multiplication operation is denoted by the symbol "•".

10.2   THE LITERATURE REVIEW

The increasing popularity of intuitionistic fuzzy sets makes it all the more important to comprehend their applications in areas like analysis, processing, and decision-making. Knowledge-handling systems that can deal with and distinguish between various forms of imprecision require accurate and structured characteristics of the equations used in mathematics that reflect such types of analyses, and this is where the fuzziness of hypergraphs and fuzzier directed hypergraphs with intuitionistic properties come in [20].

10.3   PRELIMINARIES

A number of fundamental axioms and concepts along with definitions and examples are presented here for assistance in proving the subsequent findings.

Definition 10.1

Each edge in a walk connects two nodes in the graph, and the nodes at either end of an edge are the vertices immediately before and after it. You can't walk the same route again, therefore we call it a path. A walk (or trail, or route) is said to be "u-v" if it starts at some point "u" and "ends" at some point "v". If a walk starts and finishes at the same vertex, then it is said to be closed [7].

Definition 10.2

The shortest route between a pair of two vertices, say ν_i & ν_j, are, in a given graph $\mathbb{G}^*$, symbolically represented by the path of a distance in between them, which is represented as $dG^*(\nu_i, \nu_j)$ [7].

Definition 10.3

Take the intuitive graph with fuzziness "$G = (V, E)$" for example. Intuitively, we determine a path of distance/route "P" in that fuzzy graph "G" is to be a set with "n" number of vertices $\nu_1, \nu_2, \ldots, \nu_n$ where one of these two requirements holds true [11]:

(1) If $\mu_{ij} > 0$ & $\nu_{ij} = 0$ there exist some $i\&j$. (2) If $\mu_{ij} > 0$ & $\nu_{ij} > 0$ there exist some $i\&j$.

Definition 10.4

Let IFHG, $G = \langle V, E \rangle$ be termed semi-μ stronger IFHG if $\mu_{i,j} = \mu_i \cdot \mu_j$ for every i and j.

Definition 10.5

Let IFHG, $G = \langle V, E \rangle$ be termed semi-ν stronger IFHG if $\mathcal{V}_{i,j} = \mathcal{V}_i \cdot \mathcal{V}_j$ for every i and j.

Definition 10.6

Let IFHG, $G = \langle V, E \rangle$ be termed stronger IFHG if $\mathcal{M}_{i,j} = \mathcal{M}_i \cdot \mathcal{M}_j$ and $\mathcal{V}_{i,j} = \mathcal{V}_i \cdot \mathcal{V}_j$ for all $\left(\mathcal{V}_i, \mathcal{V}_j\right)$.

Definition 10.7

An IFHG, $G = \langle V, E \rangle$, if each hyper-edge has size k, E_i is said to be k-uniform IFHG. The entire k-uniform IFHG on n vertices, in particular, contains all k-subsets of $\{1, 2, \ldots, n\}$ as edges.

Definition 10.8

An IFHG, $G = \langle V, E \rangle$ is called a complete k–uniform -$\mathcal{M}$ stronger IFHG if $\mathcal{M}_{i,j} = \left(\mathcal{M}_i \cdot \mathcal{M}_j\right)$ and $\mathcal{V}_{i,j} < \left(\mathcal{V}_i \cdot \mathcal{V}_j\right)$ for every i & j.

Definition 10.9

Let IFHG, $G = \langle V, E \rangle$ be termed complete k–uniform -$\mathcal{V}$ stronger IFHG if $\mathcal{M}_{i,j} < \left(\mathcal{M}_i \cdot \mathcal{M}_j\right)$ and $\mathcal{V}_{i,j} = \left(\mathcal{V}_i \cdot \mathcal{V}_j\right)$ for every i & j.

Definition 10.10

Let IFHG, $G = hV, E_i$ be termed complete k-uniform IFHG if $\mathcal{M}_{i,j} = \mathcal{M}_i \cdot \mathcal{M}_j$ and $\mathcal{V}_{i,j} = \mathcal{V}_i \cdot \mathcal{V}_j$ for every $\mathcal{V}_i, \mathcal{V}_j \in V$. As shown in Figure 10.1.

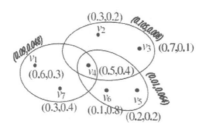

FIGURE 10.1 Complete 3-uniform IFHG.

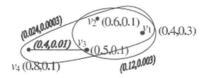

FIGURE 10.2 Strong IFHG but not complete k–uniform.

Property: Every IFHG with a full k-uniform is powerful. The inverse, on the other hand, does not have to be the case. This may be seen in the example below.

Example 10.1: The IFHG shown in Figure 10.2 is a powerful one. It is not, however, a full k-uniform IFHG.

10.4 DIFFERENT TYPES OF OPERATIONS WITH RESPECT TO IFHGs

10.4.1 COMPLEMENT OF AN IFHG

Definition 10.11 The representation of a graph-complementation of a given IFHG, $\mathbb{G} = \langle V, E \rangle$ is given by $\bar{\mathbb{G}} = \langle \bar{V}, \bar{E} \rangle$, hence when

$$\bar{V} = V$$

$\bar{\mathcal{M}_i} = \mathcal{M}_i$ again, $\bar{V_i} = V_i$, for all $i = \{1, 2, 3, ..., n\}$.
$\bar{\mathcal{M}}_{i,j} = \left(\mathcal{M}_i \cdot \mathcal{M}_j \right) - \mathcal{M}_{i,j}$ again, $\bar{V}_{i,j} = \left(V_i . V_j \right) - V_{i,j}$
for all $i, j = \{1, 2, 3, ..., n\}$.

Example 10.2: Now consider $\mathbb{G} = \langle V, E \rangle$ as a given IFHG, where $V = \{v_1, v_2, v_3, v_4\}$ and $E = \{e_1$ and $e_2\}$. Its complement $\bar{\mathbb{G}}$ is represented in Figure 10.3.

Note: Everyone can verify $\bar{\bar{G}} \equiv G$.
Proposition

(i) A complete k-uniform IFHG is the complement of a full k-uniform μ-stronger IFHG.
(ii) A total k-uniform v-stronger IFHG has a complete k-uniform IFHG as its complement.

Proof

(i) Here, let $G = \langle v, E \rangle E_i$ be the completeness of a k-uniform μ-stronger IFHG.
Hence, therefore, $\mu_{ij} = \mu_i \cdot \mu_j$ and $v_{ij} < v_i \cdot v_j$ for all i and j.
Prove that either (a) $\bar{\mu}_{ij} > 0$ or $\bar{v}_{ij} > 0$ or (b) $\bar{\mu}_{ij} = 0$ or $\bar{v}_{ij} > 0$. That is,

$$\bar{\mu}_{ij} = \mu_i \cdot \mu_j - \mu_{ij}$$
$$= 0 \ if \ \mu_{ij} > 0$$
$$= \mu_i \ if \ \mu_{ij} > 0 \ and$$
$$\bar{v}_{ij} = v_i \cdot v_j - v_{ij} > 0$$

for every i and j, since G is a representation of a complete k-uniform μ-stronger IFHG.
(ii) Proof of evidence for (ii) is equivalent to proof of evidence for (i).

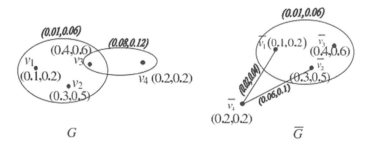

FIGURE 10.3 Fuzziness of an intuitionistic H-graph and its complement.

Definition 10.12

Let an IFHG be a self-complement, hence the graph G is isomorphic. This can be represented in symbolic form as given by $\overline{G} \cong G$.

Theorem 10.1

Let the IFHG given by $G = \langle \vee, E \rangle$ be a self-complement. Now, there exists an isomorphic of $\hbar : v \to \overline{v}$ such that $\overline{\mu_i(\mathcal{V}_i)} = \mu_i; \overline{\mathcal{V}_i(\mathcal{V}_i)} = \mathcal{V}_i$, for every $\mathcal{V}_i \in V$ and $\overline{\mu_{i,j}}\left[\hbar(\mathcal{V}_i) \text{ and } \hbar(\mathcal{V}_j)\right] = \mu_{i,j}; \overline{\mathcal{V}_{i,j}}\left[\hbar(\mathcal{V}_i) \text{ and } \hbar(\mathcal{V}_j)\right] = \mathcal{V}_{i,j}$ for every $\mathcal{V}_i$ and $\mathcal{V}_j \in V$.

Proof By Definition 10.11, we know that

$$\overline{\mu_{i,j}}\big(h(\upsilon_i), h(\upsilon_j)\big) = \mu_i\big(h(\upsilon_i)\big) \cdot \mu_i\big(h(\upsilon_j)\big) - \mu_{i,j}$$

$$\Rightarrow \mu_{i,j}\big(\upsilon_i, \upsilon_j\big) = \mu_i \cdot \mu_j - \mu_{i,j}$$

$$\Rightarrow \sum_{i \neq j} \mu_{i,j} = \sum_{i \neq j}\big(\mu_i \cdot \mu_j\big) - \sum_{i \neq j}\mu_{i,j}$$

$$\Rightarrow 2\sum_{i \neq j} \mu_{i,j} = \sum_{i \neq j}\big(\mu_i \cdot \mu_j\big)$$

$$\Rightarrow \sum_{i \neq j} \mu_{i,j} = \frac{1}{2}\sum_{i \neq j}\big(\mu_i \cdot \mu_j\big)$$

and $\overline{\mathcal{V}_{i,j}}\left[\hbar(\mathcal{V}_i) \text{ and } \hbar(\mathcal{V}_j)\right] = \mathcal{V}_i\left[\hbar(v_i)\right] \cdot \mathcal{V}_i\left[\hbar(\mathcal{V}_j)\right] - \left[\mathcal{V}_{i,j}\right]$

$$\Rightarrow v_{i,j} = v_i \cdot v_j - v_{i,j}$$

$$\Rightarrow \sum_{i \neq j} v_{i,j} = \sum_{i \neq j}\big(v_i \cdot v_j\big) - \sum_{i \neq j}v_{i,j}$$

$$\Rightarrow 2\sum_{i \neq j} v_{i,j} = \sum_{i \neq j}\big(v_i \cdot v_j\big)$$

$$\Rightarrow \sum_{i \neq j} v_{i,j} = \frac{1}{2}\sum_{i \neq j}\big(v_i \cdot v_j\big).$$

Important remark The condition of Theorem 10.1 is insufficient.

Theorem 10.2

Now, if graph G is a stronger IFHG, then the given graph G is also stronger.

Proof Let us consider, $\mathcal{UV} \in E$. Now we have

$$\overline{\mathcal{M}_{i,j}}(\mathcal{UV}) = \left[\mathcal{M}_i(\mathcal{U}) \cdot \mathcal{M}_i(\mathcal{V})\right] - \left[\mathcal{M}_{i,j}(\mathcal{UV})\right]$$

$$= \left[\mathcal{M}_i(\mathcal{U}) \cdot \mathcal{M}_j(\mathcal{V})\right] - \left[\mathcal{M}_i(\mathcal{U}) \cdot \mathcal{M}_i(\mathcal{V})\right], \text{ since G is stronger}$$

$$= 0; \text{ and again}$$

Let us again consider, $\mathcal{UV} \in E$. Then we have

$$\overline{\mathcal{M}_{i,j}}(\mathcal{UV}) = \left[\mathcal{M}_i(\mathcal{U}) \cdot \mathcal{M}_i(\mathcal{V})\right] - \left[\mathcal{M}_{i,j}(\mathcal{UV})\right]$$

$$= 0; \text{ and also}$$

$$\overline{\mathcal{V}_{i,j}}(\mathcal{UV}) = \left[\mathcal{V}_i(\mathcal{U}) \cdot \mathcal{V}_i(\mathcal{V})\right] - \left[\mathcal{V}_{i,j}(\mathcal{UV})\right]$$

$$= \mathcal{V}_i(\mathcal{U}) \cdot \mathcal{V}_i(\mathcal{V}).$$

10.4.2   UNION OF TWO IFHGs

Definition 10.13

Let $\mathbb{G}_1 = \langle \mathcal{V}_1, E_1 \rangle$ & $\mathbb{G}_2 = \langle \mathcal{V}_2, E_2 \rangle$ be two IFHGs along with $(\mathcal{V}_1 \cap \mathcal{V}_2) = \phi$ and let $\mathbb{G} = (\mathbb{G}_1 \cup \mathbb{G}_2) = \langle \mathcal{V}_1 \cup \mathcal{V}_2$ & $E_1 \cup E_2 \rangle$ be the union of two graphs (IFHG) $\mathbb{G}_1$ & $\mathbb{G}_2$. Hence then the union of IFHGs $\mathbb{G}_1$ and $\mathbb{G}_2$, $\mathbb{G} = (\mathbb{G}_1 \cup \mathbb{G}_2) = \langle \mathcal{V}_1 \cup \mathcal{V}_2,$ and $E_1 \cup E_2 \rangle$ is an IFHG and is defined by

$$\left(\mu_i \cup \mu'_i\right)(\upsilon) = \begin{cases} \mu_i(\upsilon) & \text{if } \upsilon \in V_1 - V_2 \\ \mu'_i(\upsilon) & \text{if } \upsilon \in V_2 - V_1 \end{cases}$$

$$\left(v_i \cup v'_i\right)(\upsilon) = \begin{cases} v_i(\upsilon) & \text{if } \upsilon \in V_1 - V_2 \\ v'_i(\upsilon) & \text{if } \upsilon \in V_2 - V_1 \end{cases}$$

$$\left(\mu_{i,j} \cup \mu'_{i,j}\right)(\upsilon_i \upsilon_j) = \begin{cases} \mu_{i,j} & \text{if } e_{i,j} \in E_1 - E_2 \\ \mu'_{i,j} & \text{if } e_{i,j} \in E_2 - E_1 \end{cases}$$

$$\text{and} \left(v_{i,j} \cup v'_{i,j}\right)(\upsilon_i \upsilon_j) = \begin{cases} v_{i,j} & \text{if } e_{i,j} \in E_1 - E_2 \\ v'_{i,j} & \text{if } e_{i,j} \in E_2 - E_1 \end{cases}$$

where (μ_i, v_i) & $\left(\mu'_i, v'_i\right)$ refer to graph $\mathbb{G}_1$ and $\mathbb{G}_2$'s vertex membership and non-membership, respectively; and (μ_{ij}, v_{ij}) and $\left(\mu'_{ij}, v'_{ij}\right)$ with reference to $\mathbb{G}_1$ and $\mathbb{G}_2$, respectively.

10.4.3   INTERSECTION OF TWO IFHGs

Definition 10.14

Here, consider $\mathbb{G}_1 = \langle \mathcal{V}_1, E_1 \rangle$ and $\mathbb{G}_2 = \langle \mathcal{V}_2, E_2 \rangle$ as two IFHGs. Then the intersection of two IFHGs $\mathbb{G}_1$ and $\mathbb{G}_2$, $\mathbb{G} = \mathbb{G}_1 \cap \mathbb{G}_2 = \langle \mathcal{V}_1 \cap \mathcal{V}_2, E_1 \cap E_2 \rangle$ is an IFHG and is defined by

$$\left(\mu_i \cap \mu'_i\right)(\upsilon) = \begin{cases} \mu_i(\upsilon) & \text{if } \upsilon \in V_1 \text{ and } V_2 \\ \mu'_i(\upsilon) & \text{if } \upsilon \in V_1 \text{ and } V_2 \end{cases}$$

$$\left(\nu_i \cap \nu'_1\right)(\upsilon) = \begin{cases} \nu_i(\upsilon) & \text{if } \upsilon \in V_1 \text{ and } V_2 \\ \nu'_i(\upsilon) & \text{if } \upsilon \in V_1 \text{ and } V_2 \end{cases}$$

$$\left(\mu_{i,j} \cap \mu'_{i,j}\right)(\upsilon_i \upsilon_j) = \begin{cases} \mu_{i,j} & \text{if } e_{i,j} \in E_1 \text{ and } E_2 \\ \mu'_{i,j} & \text{if } e_{i,j} \in E_1 \text{ and } E_2 \end{cases}$$

$$\text{and } \left(\nu_{i,j} \cap \nu'_{i,j}\right)(\upsilon_i \upsilon_j) = \begin{cases} \nu_{i,j} & \text{if } e_{i,j} \in E_1 \text{ and } E_2 \\ \nu'_{i,j} & \text{if } e_{i,j} \in E_1 \text{ and } E_2 \end{cases}$$

where (μ_i, ν_i) and (μ'_i, ν'_i) correspond to $\mathbb{G}_1$ and $\mathbb{G}_2$'s vertex membership and non-membership, respectively; and (μ_{ij}, ν_{ij}) and (μ_{ij}, ν'_{ij}) $\mathbb{G}_1$ and $\mathbb{G}_2$ have edges with membership and without membership, respectively.

10.4.4   RING SUM OF TWO IFHGs

Definition 10.15

Here, consider $\mathbb{G}_1 = \langle \mathcal{V}_1, E_1 \rangle$ and $\mathbb{G}_2 = \langle \mathcal{V}_2, E_2 \rangle$ as any two IFHGs. Then the ring sum of IFHGs $\mathbb{G}_1$ and $\mathbb{G}_2$, $\mathbb{G}_1 \oplus \mathbb{G}_2$ is an IFHG defined by $\mathbb{G}_1 \oplus \mathbb{G}_2 \equiv \mathbb{G}_1 \cup \mathbb{G}_2 - \mathbb{G}_1 \cap \mathbb{G}_2$.
That is $\mathcal{V} = \mathcal{V}_1 \cup \mathcal{V}_2$ & $E \notin (E_1 \cap E_2)$.

10.4.5   JOIN OF TWO IFHGs

Definition 10.16

The join of any two IFHGs $\mathbb{G}_1$ & $\mathbb{G}_2$, $\left(\mathbb{G}_1 + \mathbb{G}_2\right)$, is an IFHG
$\mathbb{G} = \left(\mathbb{G}_1 + \mathbb{G}_2\right) = \langle \mathcal{V}_1 \cup \mathcal{V}_2, \ E_1 \cup E_2 \cup E' \rangle$ derived by

$$\left(\mu_i + \mu'_i\right)(\mathcal{V}) = \left(\mu_i \cup \mu'_i\right)(\mathcal{V}) \qquad \textit{if } \mathcal{V} \in V_1 \cup V_2$$

$$\left(\mathcal{V}_i + \mathcal{V}'_i\right)(\mathcal{V}) = \left(\mathcal{V}_i \cup \mathcal{V}'_i\right)(\mathcal{V}) \qquad \textit{if } \mathcal{V} \in V_1 \cup V_2$$

$$\left(\mu_{i,j} + \mu'_{i,j}\right)(\upsilon_i \upsilon_j) = \begin{cases} \left(\mu_{i,j} \cup \mu'_{i,j}\right)(\upsilon_i \upsilon_j) & \text{if } \upsilon_i \upsilon_j \in E_1 \cup E_2 \\ \mu_i(\upsilon_i).\mu'_i(\upsilon_j) & \text{if } \upsilon_i \upsilon_j \in E' \end{cases}$$

$$\text{and } \left(\nu_{i,j} + \nu'_{i,j}\right)(\upsilon_i \upsilon_j) = \begin{cases} \left(\nu_{i,j} \cup \nu'_{i,j}\right)(\upsilon_i \upsilon_j) & \text{if } \upsilon_i \upsilon_j \in E_1 \cup E_2 \\ \nu_i(\upsilon_i).\nu'_i(\upsilon_j) & \text{if } \upsilon_i \upsilon_j \in E'. \end{cases}$$

where $E' =$ the set of edges used to join two vertices called $\mathcal{V}_1$ and $\mathcal{V}_2$.

Example 10.3: Let us consider $\vee_1 = \{\nu_1, \nu_2, \nu_3, \nu_4\}$ and $\vee_2 = \{u_1, u_2\}$ such that $\vee_1 \cap \vee_2 = \phi$.

For the operations of intersection and ring sum, consider $\vee_1 = \{\nu_1, \nu_2, \nu_3\}$ and $\vee_2 = \{\nu_1, \nu_2, \nu_3\}$ such that $\vee_1 \cap \vee_2 \neq \phi$.

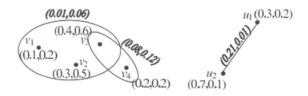

FIGURE 10.4 G_1 and G_2.

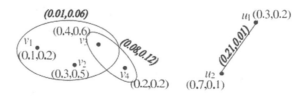

FIGURE 10.5 $G_1 \cup G_2$.

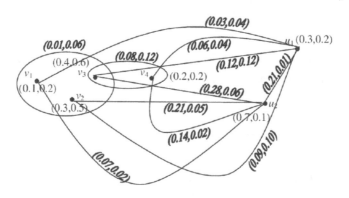

FIGURE 10.6 $G_1 + G_2$.

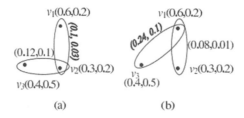

FIGURE 10.7   (a) G_1; (b) G_2.

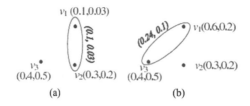

FIGURE 10.8   (a) $G_1 \cap G2$; (b) $G_1 \oplus G_2$.

10.4.6 CARTESIAN PRODUCT OF TWO IFHGs

Definition 10.17

Here, consider $\mathbb{G} = (\mathbb{G}_1 \times \mathbb{G}_2) = \langle \vee, E'' \rangle$ represents the Cartesian product from any two relevant graphs $\mathbb{G}_1$ & $\mathbb{G}_2$, respectively, with $\vee = \vee_1 \times \vee_2$ & here

$$E'' = \left\{ (u, u_2)(u, v_2) : u \in \vee_1, u_2 v_2 \in E_2 \right\} \cup \left\{ (u_1, \omega)(v_1, \omega) : \omega \in \vee_2, u_1 v_1 \in E_1 \right\}.$$

The Cartesian product of IFHGs $\mathbb{G}_1$ and $\mathbb{G}_2$ is thus derived as an IFHG. $\mathbb{G} = \mathbb{G}_1 \times \mathbb{G}_2 = \langle \vee, E'' \rangle$ where

(i) $\left(\mu_i \times \mu_i' \right)(u_1, u_2) \equiv \mu_i(u_1) \cdot \mu_i'(u_2)$ for every $(u_1$ and $u_2) \in V$ and

$\left(v_i \times v_i' \right)(u_1, u_2) \equiv v_i(u_1) \cdot v_i'(u_2)$ for every $(u_1$ and $u_2) \in V$

(ii) $\left(\mu_{i,j} \times \mu_{i,j}' \right)(u, u_2)(u, v_2) \equiv \mu_i(u) \cdot \mu_{i,j}(u_2 v_2)$ for every $u \in V_1$ and $u_2 v_2 \in E_2$.

$\left(v_{i,j} \times v_{i,j}' \right)(u, u_2)(u, v_2) \equiv v_i(u) \cdot v_{i,j}(u_2 v_2)$ for every $u \in V_1$ and $u_2 v_2 \in E_2$.

$\left(\mu_{i,j} \times \mu_{i,j}' \right)(u_1, \omega)(v_1, \omega) \equiv \mu_i(\omega) \cdot \mu_{i,j}(u_1 v_1)$ for every $\omega \in V_2$ and $u_1 v_1 \in E_1$.

$\left(v_{i,j} \times v_{i,j}' \right)(u_1, \omega)(v_1, \omega) \equiv v_i(\omega) \cdot v_{i,j}(u_1 v_1)$ for every $\omega \in V_2$ and $u_1 v_1 \in E_1$.

Example 10.4 Let $V_1 = \{v_1, v_2, v_3, v_4\}$ and $V_2 = \{u_1, u_2, u_3, u_4\}$

such that $V_1 \cap V_2 = \phi$.

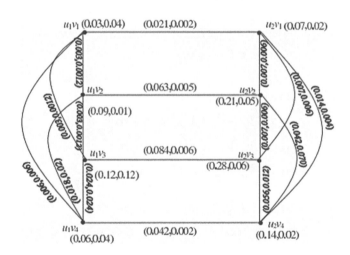

FIGURE 10.9 $G_1 \otimes G_2$.

10.4.7 COMPOSITION OF TWO IFHGs

Definition 10.18

The nature of the composition of any two IFHGs $\mathbb{G}_1$ & $\mathbb{G}_2$, denoted by $\mathbb{G} = \mathbb{G}_1 \circ \mathbb{G}_2$, is an IFHG explained by

(i) $\left(\mu_i \circ \mu_i' \right)[u_1, u_2] = \mu_i(u_1) \cdot \mu_i'(u_2)$ for every $(u_1$ and $u_2)$ which belongs to $V_1 \times V_2$ and

$\left(v_i \circ v_i' \right)[u_1, u_2] = v_i(u_1) \cdot v_i'(u_2)$ for every $(u_1$ and $u_2) \in V_1 \times V_2$

(ii) $\left(\mu_{i,j} \circ \mu'_{i,j}\right)\left[(u,u_2)(u,v_2)\right] = \mu_i(u) \cdot \mu_{i,j}(u_2 v_2)$ for every $u \in V_1$ and $u_2 v_2 \in E_2$

$\left(v_{i,j} \circ v'_{i,j}\right)\left[(u,u_2)(u,v_2)\right] = v_i(u) \cdot v_{i,j}(u_2 v_2)$ for every $u \in V_1$ and $u_2 v_2 \in E_2$

$\left(\mu_{i,j} \circ \mu'_{i,j}\right)\left[(u_1,\omega)(v_1,\omega)\right] = \mu_i(\omega) \cdot \mu_{i,j}(u_1 v_1)$ for every $\omega \in V_2$ and $u_1 v_1 \in E_1$

$\left(v_{i,j} \circ v'_{i,j}\right)\left[(u_1,\omega)(v_1,\omega)\right] = v_i(\omega) \cdot v_{i,j}(u_1 v_1)$ for every $\omega \in V_2$ and $u_1 v_1 \in E_1$

$\left(\mu_{i,j} \circ \mu'_{i,j}\right)\left[(\mu_1,\mu_2)(v_1,v_2)\right] = \mu'_i(u_2) \cdot \mu'_i(v_2) \cdot \mu_{i,j}(u_1,v_1)$

for every $(u_1, u_2)(\nu_1, \nu_2) \in E - E''$ and

$$\left(v_{i,j} \circ v'_{i,j}\right)(u_1,u_2)(v_1,v_2) = v'_i(u_2) \cdot v'_i(v_2) \cdot v_{i,j}(u_1,v_1)$$

for every $(u_1, u_2)(\nu_1, \nu_2) \in (E - E'')$ and
hence it becomes Where as

$$E'' = \left\{(u,u_2)(u,v_2) : u \in V_1, \ \forall \ u_2 v_2 \in E_2\right\} \cup \left\{(u_1,\omega)(v_1,\omega) : \omega \in V_2, \forall u_1 v_1 \in E_1\right\}$$

Theorem 10.3

Now consider $\mathbb{G}_1 = \langle V_1, E_1 \rangle$ and again $\mathbb{G}_2 = \langle V_2, E_2 \rangle$ as any two strong IFHGs. Hence, $\mathbb{G}_1 \,^\circ \mathbb{G}_2$ is a strong IFHG. This is graphically visualized in Figure 10.10.

Proof Let $\mathbb{G}_1 \circ \mathbb{G}_2 = \mathbb{G} = \langle \vee, E \rangle$, $\vee_1 \times \vee_2$, and therefore

$$E = \left\{(u,u_2)(u,v_2) : u \in \vee_1, u_2 v_2 \in E_2\right\} \cup \left\{(u_1,\omega)(v_1,\omega) : \omega \in \vee_2, u_1 v_1 \in E_1\right\} \cup$$
$$\left\{(u_1,u_2)(v_1,v_2) : u_1 v_1 \in E_1, u_2 \neq v_2\right\}$$

(i) $\mu_{i,j}(u,u_2)(u,\upsilon_2) = \mu_i(u) \cdot \mu_{i,j}(u_2 \upsilon_2)$

$\qquad = \mu_i(u) \cdot \left(\mu'_i(u_2) \cdot \mu'_i(\upsilon_2)\right)$, since G_2 is strong

$\qquad = \left(\mu_i(u) \cdot \mu'_i(u_2)\right) \cdot \left(\mu_i(u) \cdot \mu'_i(\upsilon_2)\right)$

$\qquad = \left(\mu_i \circ \mu'_i\right)(u,u_2) \cdot \left(\mu_i \circ \mu'_i\right)(u,\upsilon_2).$

$v_{i,j}(u,u_2)(u,\upsilon_2) = v_i(u) \cdot v_{i,j}(u_2 \upsilon_2)$

$\qquad = v_i(u) \cdot \left(v'_i(u_2) \cdot v'_i(\upsilon_2)\right)$, since G_2 is strong

$\qquad = \left(v_i(u) \cdot v'_i(u_2)\right) \cdot \left(v_i(u), v'_i(\upsilon_2)\right)$

$\qquad = \left(v_i \circ v'_i\right)(u,u_2) \cdot \left(v_i \circ v'_i\right)(u,\upsilon_2).$

(ii) $\quad \mu_{i,j}\big((u_1,w)(v_1,w)\big) = \mu'_i(w)\cdot\mu_{i,j}(u_1,v_1)$

$$= \mu'_i(w)\cdot\big(\mu_i(u_1)\cdot\mu_i(v_1)\big), \text{ since } G_1 \text{ is strong}$$

$$= \big(\mu'_i(w)\cdot\mu_i(u_1)\big)\cdot\big(\mu'_i(w)\cdot\mu_i(v_1)\big)$$

$$= \big(\mu_i\circ\mu'_i\big)(u_1,w)\cdot\big(\mu_i\circ\mu'_i\big)(v_1,w).$$

$\quad v_{i,j}\big((u_1,w)(v_1,w)\big) = v'_i(w)\cdot v_{i,j}(u_1,v_1)$

$$= v'_i(w)\cdot\big(v_i(u_1)\cdot v_i(v_1)\big), \text{ since } G_1 \text{ is strong}$$

$$= \big(v'_i(w)\cdot v_i(u_1)\big)\cdot\big(v'_i(w)\cdot v_i(v_1)\big)$$

$$= \big(v_i\circ v'_i\big)(u_1,w)\cdot\big(v_i\circ v'_i\big)(v_1,w).$$

$$= \big(v_i\circ v'_i\big)(u_1,w)\cdot\big(v_i\circ v'_i\big)(v_1,w).$$

(iii) $\quad \mu_{i,j}(u_1,u_2)(v_1,v_2) = (\mu_{i,j}(u_1,v_1)\cdot\mu'_i(u_2)\cdot\mu'_i(v_2))$

$$= \big(\mu_i(u_1)\cdot\mu_i(v_1)\big)\cdot\mu'_i(u_2)\cdot\mu'_i(v_2)),$$

$$\text{since } G_1 \text{ is strong}$$

$$= \big(\mu_i(u_1)\cdot\mu'_i(u_2)\big)\cdot\big(\mu_i(v_1)\cdot\mu'_i(v_2)\big)$$

$$= \big((\mu_i\circ\mu'_i)(u_1,u_2)\cdot(\mu_i\circ\mu'_i)(v_1,v_2)\big).$$

$\quad v_{i,j}(u_1,u_2)(v_1,v_2) = (v_{i,j}(u_1,v_1)\cdot v'_i(u_2)\cdot v'_i(v_2))$

$$= \big((v_i(u_1)\cdot v_i(v_1))\cdot v'_i(u_2)\cdot v'_i(v_2)\big),$$

$$\text{since } G_1 \text{ is strong}$$

$$= \big((v_i(u_1)\cdot v'_i(u_2))\cdot(v_i(v_1)\cdot v'_i(v_2))\big)$$

$$= \big(v_i\circ v'_i\big)(u_1,u_2)\cdot\big(v_i\circ v'_i\big)(v_1,v_2).$$

From proof (i) and (ii) along with (iii), the graph G is a stronger IFHG.

Example 10.5: Consider any two vertices, $V_1 = \{u_1,\ u_2,\ u_3,\ u_4\}$ and $V_2 = \{v_1,\ v_2,\ v_3,\ v_4\}$ such that $V_1 \cap V_2 = \phi$.

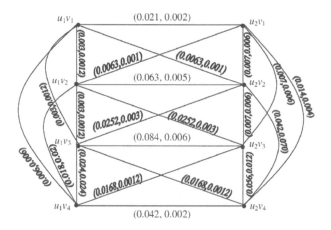

FIGURE 10.10 $G_1 \degree G_2$.

10.5   SUMMARY

The operations described on IFDGs and the usage of index matrices are very thrilling and used to investigate the structural behaviour of IFDGs. As a result, operations on IFHGs are considered. The definition of an IFHG's supplement has been offered in this chapter, in addition to certain functions of self-complementary IFHGs. Isomorphism among IFHGs has additionally been proven. In addition, operations together with the union, Cartesian product, and composition of IFHGs have been described, as well as the proof that the supplement of an IFHGs is a part that equals the union of their complements. We have additionally proven that the mixture of effective IFHGs is similarly strong. On self-complementary IFHGs, additional findings were obtained.

Computer science makes extensive use of the theoretical ideas behind graphs and hypergraphs, especially in study areas in computational/computer science, such as the mining of data, various segmentation techniques, networking, image capturing, and cluster analysis. Intuitionistic fuzziness frameworks are so much better than the classic as well as fuzzy models because they are more precise, flexible, and compatible. Here, in this chapter, we have focused on the fuzziness of intuitionistic graphs. Fuzzy hypergraphs and their various operations are less flexible than the fuzziness of intuitionistic hypergraphs and their operations. The relevant idea of IFDHGs and how they work can be used in various different fields of study in computer and data science and also engineering.

This idea of the fuzzy directed hypergraph with intuitionistic properties was produced in a variety of scenarios, including the union–intersection and join of two IFHGs, the Cartesian product of two graphs, and compositions, which have been defined and explained with a number of examples. This chapter has verified the various properties of the types of intuitionistic fuzzy graphs and their operations using graphical examples. Axioms involved in proving the future relevant results were also mentioned.

LIST OF ABBREVIATIONS

IFDG	Intuitionistic Fuzzy Directed Graph
IFDHG	Intuitionistic-Fuzzy Directed Hypergraph
IFG	Intuitionistic-Fuzzy Graph
IFHG	Intuitionistic-Fuzzy Hypergraph

REFERENCES

[1] A. Kaufmann, *An introduction to theory of fuzzy sub sets*, vol. 1, Academic Press, New York, 1975.

[2] A. Nagoor Gani and S. Shajitha Begum, Order and size in intuitionistic fuzzy graphs. *International Journal of Algorithms, Computing and Mathematics*, 33, 2010, 137–149.

[3] A. Rosenfeld, Fuzzy graph, in: L.A. Zadeh, K.S. Fu, and M. Shimura (Eds.), *Fuzzy sets and their applications to cognitive and decision process*, Academic Press, New York, 1975, pp. 77–95.

[4] K. Atanassov, On index matrix interpretations of intuitionistic fuzzy graphs. *Notes on Intuitionistic Fuzzy Sets*, 8(4), 2002, 73–78.

[5] K.T. Atanassov *On intuitionistic fuzzy sets theory*, Springer, Berlin, 2012.

[6] C. Berge, *Graphs and hyper-graphs*, North-Holland, Amsterdam, 1976.

[7] J.A. Bondy and U.S.R. Murthy *Graph theory with applications*, American Elseiver Publishing Co., New York, 1976.

[8] H. Bustine and P. Burillo, Vague sets are intuitionistic fuzzy-sets. *Fuzzy-Sets and Systems*, 79 (3), 1996, 403–405.

[9] K.T. Atanassov, Intuitionistic fuzzy-sets. *Fuzzy-Sets and Systems*, 20 (1), 1986, 87–96.

[10] K. T. Atanassov, New operations defined over the intuitionistic fuzzy-sets. *Fuzzy-Sets and Systems*, 61 (2), 1994, 137–142.

[11] M.G. Karunambigai and R. Parvathi, "Intuitionistic Fuzzy Graphs", *Proceedings of 9th Fuzzy Days International Conference on Computational Intelligence*, Springer-Verlag, 20 2006, 139–150.

[12] L.A. Zadeh, Fuzzy sets. *Information and Control* 8, 1965, 338–353.

[13] A. Nagoor Gani and S. Shajitha Begum, Degree, order and size in intuitionistic fuzzy graphs. *International Journal of Algorithm, Computing and Mathematics*, 33 August 2011, 312–321.

[14] R. Parvathi, S. Thilagavathi M. G. Karunambigai Operations on intuitionistic fuzzy hypergraphs. *International Journal of Computer Applications*, 51(5), 2012 46–54.

[15] R. Parvathi, M. G. Karunambigai and K. Atanassov, "Operations on Intuitionistic Fuzzy Graphs", *Proceedings if IEEE International Conference on Fuzzy Systems (FUZZ-IEEE)*, August 2009, 1396–1401.

[16] R. Parvathi and M. G. Karunambigai, "Operations on Intuitionistic Fuzzy Graphs", *Proceedings of FUZZ-IEEE 2009*, South Korea, 2009, 1396–1401.

[17] N. Yogeesh, A conceptual discussion about an intuitionistic fuzzy-sets and its applications. *International Journal of Advanced Research in IT and Engineering* 1(6) 2012, 45–56. (ISSN: 2278-6244).

[18] N. Yogeesh, Illustrative study on intuitionistic fuzzy hyper-graphs and dual-intuitionistic fuzzy hyper-graphs. *International Journal of Engineering, Science and Mathematics*, 2(1) 2013, 255–264.

[19] N. Yogeesh, Operations on intuitionistic fuzzy directed graphs. *Journal of Advances and Scholarly Researches in Allied Education(JASRAE)*, 3(6) 2012, 1–4, www.ignited.in/p/305246

[20] N. Yogeesh, Study on hypergraphs and directed hypergraphs. *Journal of Advances and Scholarly Researches in Allied Education(JASRAE)*, 5(10) 2013, 1–5(5), www.ignited.in/p/305247

11 Spammer Detection Based on a Heterogeneous Multiple-mini-graph Neural Network

Kavita Jatwar, Rishabh Dadsena, Sajal Ranjan Chakravarty, and K. Jairam Naik
National Institute of Technology Raipur, Raipur, India

CONTENTS

11.1 INTRODUCTION

Today online social networks are the cheapest mode of communication across the globe and are extensively used by groups of communities to share data or information through their posts. This information is shared among friends and other connections in the form of photos, files, videos, or comments and these are used as features which help to find the nature of the user.

The internet can be used as a communicating platform or for promotional purposes like encouraging genuine users to review their products. Social networking sites like Twitter, Facebook, Weibo, and other online social networks (OSNs) allow users to share a wide range of information, including news, opinions, and even their moods.

DOI: 10.1201/9781003359456-11

Spammerscan be categorized based on:

1. *False opinions*: Popular social media platforms (such as Facebook and Twitter) are used to store and share a vast amount of information in the form of likes, comments, tags, and hashtags, among other things. With thousands of communicating users, there is also a concentration of malicious users. They take advantage of interactions based on user trust to achieve their malicious goals. This fake content is generally posted from fake accounts. So, basically detection of fake accounts is a major concern.
2. *Brand based reviews*: Many companies provide discounts, coupons, or membership cards to encourage users to promote their products. Also, after buying some products, customers go to review the product on a review site if they like the product. Further, customers intend to buy the product based on positive reviews of them. Here lies the role of spammers who try to mislead customers for their business purpose. This fraudulent behavior may affect genuine buyers and the seller company.

In this chapter, we focus more on detecting spammers on social media platforms. Generally, spammers on social media networks pretend to be genuine users. So, recognizing them in the group of genuine users is a challenging task.

To distinguish one user from another, two sets of attributes are considered: *review content attributes* and *user abnormal behavior attributes*. The tweets posted by users can be used as features known as content attributes. User behavior attributes, on the other hand, collect specific characteristics of user behavior in terms of posting frequency (i.e., number of frequent posts made by user on social media), interaction (connection with their followers), and impact on social media platforms.

The categorization is based on a variety of factors, including fake content or posts, trending topics, and identifying fake users. The proposed method combines textual content characteristics with social network information.

In all previous work, model training has taken lots more time and made models vulnerable for real-time use, along with the fact that they have an accuracy of around 84%, which could be improved if we used a better focus on feature selection. This would train the model with more different patterns and hence use different mini-graphs for training, which would increase our model's reliability for real-time usage. It also would give a decent accuracy of around 90% (±3% based on different hardware). So, the main objectives of this chapter are:

- To provide knowledge to users about fake profiles, posts, or comments on social media;
- To promote high-quality products and enhance the user experience, especially focusing on social media platforms;
- To ensure that genuine users are treated fairly, and that their trust is maintained.

Spam detection is important because it ensures that genuine users are treated fairly, and that their trust is maintained. The algorithms that have been developed so far are ineffective at determining the best parameters for supervised learning. As a result, the complete automation of spam detection systems with maximum efficiency is made possible. The number of spammers is rapidly increasing as social media platforms such as Twitter, Facebook, and LinkedIngain in popularity and use. As a result, several spam detection techniques need to be developed which:

- Provide sensitivity to the client and users to adapt well to future spam techniques;
- Increase security and control;
- to other social media services;
- Develop more features which cannot be fabricated.

The present way of spammer detection by existing methodologies is not an option in such a large network, so it is necessary to develop a learning model that uses the latest technology. However, it has been discovered that even existing learning techniques have flaws, and that no method is completely effective enough in and of itself. As a result, we've proposed a model based on deep learning. The main motivation for us to develop the model is:

- Spam content is constantly cluttering inboxes;
- It is cmmonly removed using rule-based filters;
- Spam often has similar properties, which allows detection to be easier using machine learning methodologies.

11.2 LITERATURE REVIEW

11.2.1 EXISTING WORK

Most of the existing work only depends on detecting spam and spammers and is focused less on feature extraction. Several traditional machine-learning techniques have been of interest to researchers for spammer detection. So, in this section we will be discussing the different techniques used for and how it has evolved.

A support vector machine was used Wu et al. (2021) where a summarized recurrent graph neural network (GNN) + convolutional GNN + spatial temporal GNN model was developed. The advantages of that model were analyzing different GNNs and their performances, but it doesn't propose any new method; it just generalizes the comparison. A graph convolutional network (GCN) + DeG model (deep graph) (Zhiwei Guo et al. 2021) was developed which very accurate and very efficient, but due to the usage of GCN it makes feature selection very poor, which might lead to failure for big datasets.

Network embedding + a support vector machine (SVM) model (Li Kuang et al., 2020) was developed;the advantages were a simple way of implementation, but it doesn't work for large networks because they don't use graphs. A collaborative neural-network-based model (Co-Spam) (Guo et al., 2020) was also developedwhich works on the Internet of Things (IOT) cyberspace to detect spammers. But the F1 score is approximately 70%. An aspect-rating local outlier factor model (AR-LOF) model (You et al., 2020) was developedwhich was highly effective and intelligent but works on a brute force approach and hence runtime is high for big networks.

Reversible privacy-preserving clustering, based on a k-means algorithm model (Lin, 2020) was developed which was based on simple K-means clustering that makes it easy to be used by programmers, though it uses a protection method in which inputted data can't be recovered for future uses. A logistic regression model (Hussain et al., 2020) was developed; its advantage is that it works on linguistic and spammer behavioral methods, but it does not specify a specific method for modeling. A cuckoo search + Fermat Spiral (clustering method) model (Pandey and Rajpoot, 2019) was developed where experimental results and statistical analysis validation out run other methods, though it only compares other models to generate a comparison table.

A graph classification approach model was developed by Liu et al. (2019) and its advantages capture certain statistical characteristics of datasets, though graph classification is implemented on the whole network as a single graph, which makes it complex for feature engineering. A graph convolution network model (Li et al., 2019) was developed, and its advantage is that the information from reviews, the features of users, and items being reviewed is utilized, but the model is the same as graph classification and has poorer feature engineering than our method which leads to an increase in run time of approximately three seconds in each iteration.

Users can communicate directly with the device, and anomalous entities can be identified via queries, using feature engineering and the SVM model (Ranjbar et al., 2019), which is quite like ours, though its detecting is based on queries. It could be further optimized if we use homogeneous and heterogeneous concept-based classification. Using feature engineering, an SVM model (Herzallah et al., 2018) was developed and its advantages are that it describes how a model can be built using features, but it requires more access time as compared to a Bayesian network. A Bayesian network + intelligent decision system (Rathore et al., 2018) model was developed, and its advantages are that it works for small networks only and gives an accuracy of 87%. But it does not work for large networks because they don't use graphs. Table 11.1 summarizes the below.

Most approaches use SVM, decision trees, naive Bayesian, Random Forest, and k-nearest neighbors (KNN). In all these approaches some specific type of social network is used for spammer detection, which is ineffective in the situation where a person has accounts on multiple social networks. So, a better approach needs to be developed, keeping in mind the flaws of the previous approaches.

TABLE 11.1
List of Existing Techniques

Authors and Year of Publication	Technology Used	Description
Wu et al. (2021)	Summarized recurrent GNN + convolutional GNN + spatial temporal GNN	Analyzes different GNNs and their performances. It doesn't propose any new method it just generalizes the comparison.
Zhiwei Guo et al. (2021)	GCN + DeG model	Combination of GCN and deep graph makes it very accurate and very efficient. Due to usage of GCN it makes feature selection very poor which might lead to failure for big datasets.
Li Kuang et al. (2020)	Network embedding + SVM	Simple way of implementation. Does not work for large networks because they don't use graphs.
Guo et al. (2020)	Collaborative neural network-based model (Co-Spam)	Works on IOT cyberspace to detect spammers. The F1 score is approximately 70% which is much less and can be improved.
You et al. (2020)	Aspect-rating local outlier factor model (AR-LOF)	High effectiveness and intelligence of model. Works on brute force approach and hence runtime is high for big networks.
Lin et al. (2020)	Reversible privacy-preserving clustering, based on k-means algorithm	Based on simple K-means clustering which makes it easy to use for programmers. It uses protection method in which inputted data can't be recovered for future uses.
Hussain et al. (2020)	Logistic regression	Works on linguistic and spammer behavioral methods. It does not specify a specific method for modeling.
A.C. Pandey and D.S. Rajpoot. (2019)	Cuckoo search + Fermat spiral (clustering method)	Experimental results and statistical analysis validation outruns other methods. It just compares other models for which it generates a comparison table.
Liu et al. (2019)	Graph classification approach	States capture certain statistical characteristics of the datasets. Graph classification is implemented on the whole network as a single graph which makes it complex for feature engineering which will increase the model's run time.
Li et al. (2019)	Graph convolution network	Information of review features of users and items being reviewed are utilized. GCN is the same as graph classification and has poorer feature engineering than our method which leads to an increase in run time of approximately three seconds in each iteration.

(Continued)

TABLE 11.1   (Continued)

Authors and Year of Publication	Technology Used	Description
Ranjbar et al. (2019)	QANet: tensor decomposition approach and clustering methods	Users interact directly with the system and anomalous entities can be detected through queries. This model is quite similar to the one proposed, but detecting is based on queries and can be further optimized if we use homogeneous and heterogeneous concept-based classification.
Herzallah et al. (2018)	Feature engineering, SVM	This paper describes how a model can be built using features. It requires more access time when compared to a Bayesian network.
Rathore et al. (2018)	Modelling (Bayesian network + intelligent decision system)	For small networks it gives an accuracy of 87%. It does not work for large networks because they don't use graphs.

11.2.2   SUMMARY OF THE LITERATURE

Traditional methods suffer from high computational costs and excessive memory requirements, but graph analytics may lead to better understanding and control of complex networks. Graph embedding techniques can convert high-dimensional sparse graphs into low-dimensional, dense, and continuous vector spaces while preserving the graph's structural properties. GCN is one of the most well-known advancements, in which node features are aggregated from nearby neighbors. So, when it comes to spam detection, we mostly focus on:

- Improving the security of the network and working according to the sentiments of the user;
- Reducing the malware activities on social media and therefore maintaining the user's trust;
- A reliable system is to be developed that ensures the system performs nominally under extreme circumstances.

In the next section, we will be discussing the major graph terminologies before moving on to the methodology section.

11.3   GRAPH TERMINOLOGIES

Graph methods have been applied in many domains such as recommendation systems, in healthcare, and for detecting malicious activities. Therefore, it is important to study the graph and its features.

11.3.1   GRAPH NEURAL NETWORKS

A graph can represent many things including social media networks where people tend to form connections with others. This relationship forms a network of graphs where the nodes of the graph can be thought of as users while the edges represent connections. Each edge can connect different nodes together that have similar features which could be used for spam detection. A social media graph of any social media network would look like that shown in Figure 11.1.

We can add an edge property called "weight" by assigning a value to the edges; we can also assign "value" to each node in a similar way. Each node has a set of features defining it. These

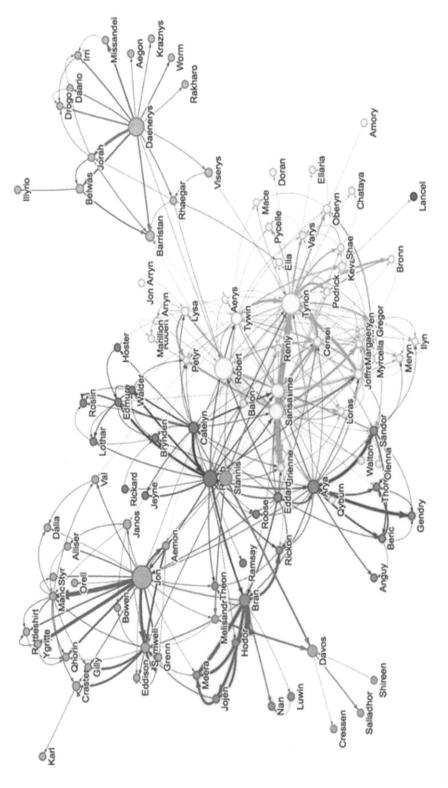

FIGURE 11.1 Basic illustration of graph networks and their connections. Source: Wu et al. (2021).

Personal Attributes	Interactive Attributes
Authentication Status	Vector of Social Relations
Location	Originality of Speeches
Age	Frequency of Comments
Registration Time	Forwarding frequency
Personal Tags	Sequential Relevance of Speeches

FIGURE 11.2   Types of attributes.

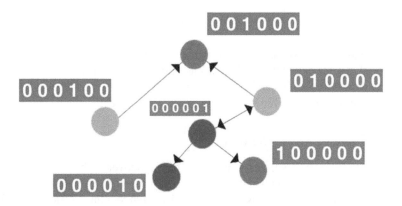

FIGURE 11.3   Message passing in the network along edges.

features are also referred to as attributes, which are normally the details of the users; in this way we can represent personal attributes (which hold the personal details of the user) and interactive attributes (which hold the actions of users like speeches, posts, and comments). This is shown in Figure 11.2.

Now these attributes are added to as values of each node and thereby the graph can be represented in the vector form. Vector representation of graphs could be as shown in Figure 11.3.

Adding neural networks to the network changes the graph. After all the nodes and edges have been converted, the graph performs message passing between nodes, for all nodes, n times. This gives the entire graph an even more accurate representation.

Messages are associated with edges. Edges and messages are linked. Each message takes a value from the edge's source node and delivers it to the edge's destination's "mailbox". Reduce functions empty the mailboxes, perform a computation, and change a node's property. The reduced function adds up all the in-degrees after the messages are sent to each node's mailbox.

The embedding vectors of all nodes are then added together to produce the graph representation H, which represents the entire graph. H is then passed to the higher layers. This is illustrated in Figure 11.4.

The general idea behind a graph neural network is that it constantly exchanges information (message) with its neighbors until it reaches a stable equilibrium.

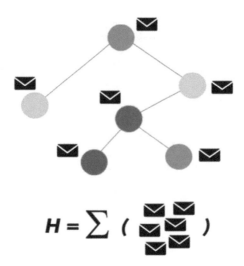

$$H = \sum \left(\begin{array}{c} \text{✉} \\ \text{✉} \end{array} \right)$$

FIGURE 11.4   Evaluation of aggregate result of whole graph.

GNNs can be divided into several categories, but we will be discussing its two important categories that are particularly relevant to the work presented in this chapter. The GCN is good at handling
structured graphs with information carried by their nodes, while heterogeneous GNNs are good at
handling heterogeneous graph structures.

11.3.2   GRAPH CONVOLUTIONAL NETWORKS

The center of this model is a CNN which is a type of neural network. The graph convolution layer
acts as a filter and extracts features from graphs. The graph input is computed using GCN to filter
and produce a compressed graph. In convolution, we take neighbors into account by defining some
filters that slide over nearby pixels. Similarly, we consider two nodes in a graph as neighbors if they
have an edge in common. As illustrated in Figure 11.5, to extract hidden features of a red node, the
GCN may take the average of node features of itself along with its neighbors.

Graph convolution (GC) is a technique for learning graph properties as well as input features. We
feed the adjacency matrix **A'** along with the input features. A non-linear operation is applied after

FIGURE 11.5   Graph convolutional network.

Source: Wu et al. (2021).

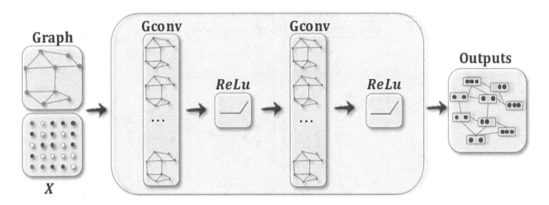

FIGURE 11.6 GCN architecture.

Source: Wu et al. (2021).

several GCs are applied sequentially. A feature matrix is the output of a GCN. Between the GCN layers, we use a rectified linear unit (ReLU) activation function. We divide the nodes into a training set and a test set to train the network by creating a Boolean vector that is True when the node is in the test set and False when it is not. Figure 11.6 shows the architecture of a GCN layer.

We consider the graph in the proposed system to be directed and weighted. Let us consider $G = (V, E)$ to represent the graph network, where V is the vertices set and E is the edges set linked to the vertices.

We can define the equation for the output adjacency matrix of a graph with node features as:

$$Z = \sigma\left(A'F\,W + b \right) \tag{11.1}$$

In Equation (11.1) we have:

Z = output matrix; σ = non-linearity function (ReLU);
A' = graph structure (adjacency matrix); F = node feature (feature matrix);
W, b = trainable weights (variable weights).

The graph structure is represented as an adjacency matrix which represents which node is connected to which other node or whether there is any connection between any two nodes in that graph. The contribution of each neighboring node accords with how it is connected to other nodes in the graph when **A'** is normalized.

The non-linear function, i.e., **ReLU** is applied to (**A'FW + b**) for completing the layer definition. This layer's output matrix **Z** can be fed into another GCN layer to allow deep neural operation to learn the hierarchy of the complex node features.

11.3.3 HETEROGENEOUS GNNs

In homogeneous graphs, there is only one type of node and one type of edge. The nodes represent individuals, and an edge represents their connections. Heterogeneous graphs, on the other hand, have two or more forms of nodes and/or edges. A heterogeneous network is a social network with edges of various types, such as "friendship" and "co-worker", connecting nodes of the "person" type. This is illustrated in Figure 11.7. In this figure, the node in a different color depicts different types of users and similarly the different colored edges show connections with different nodes or users. Therefore, the figure illustrates the difference between homogeneous and heterogeneous graphs.

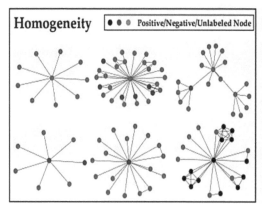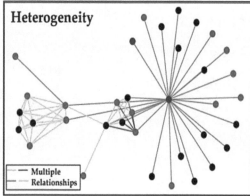

FIGURE 11.7 Homogeneous and heterogeneous GCNs.

Source: Wu et al. (2021).

The approach is to deal with the heterogeneous graphs individually and predict the output by combining the output from each graph.

Unfortunately, graphs typically contain a wide variety of vertices and edges called multipartite graphs. They also complicate the process of calculating embeddings, such as for a customer product graph where we have Customer, Product, Purchase, Web Visit, Web Search, Product Review, Product Return, Product Complaint, Promotion Response, Coupon Use, Survey Response, and so on, which are all possible types in a customer graph. Setting up and tuning machine learning algorithms to create embeddings from complex data sets can take a long time.

11.3.4 Vanilla Feature Embedding

Traditional methods suffer from high computational costs and excessive memory requirements, but graph analytics can lead to better quantitative understanding and control of complex networks. Graph embedding techniques can convert high-dimensional sparse graphs into low-dimensional, dense, and continuous vector spaces while preserving the graph structure properties to the greatest extent possible.

The primary goal of graph embedding methods is to compress each node's properties into a smaller vector. The generated graph embeddings can be used to solve a variety of graph analytics tasks in the future (e.g., node classification, link prediction, community detection, visualization).

We present some basic concepts in graph analytics and graph embedding methods in this review, focusing on random walk-based and neural-network-based methods. Also, we highlight the various advantages of graph embedding methods in different applications and provide implementation details.

11.3.5 Random Walk

These algorithms tend to be based on natural language processing. They operate by traversing all nodes at random, beginning with a target node. The walks effectively create sentences about the target vertex, which are then used in the same way that NLP algorithms are used. In a random walk, we start from a node and then keep on moving randomly through nodes that come along in its path and process them to maintain the list of paths obtained. In other words, we try to cover the maximum of the graph network from that node. Graph embeddings are stored as a vector of numbers that are associated with a vertex or subgraph, as shown in Figure 11.8.

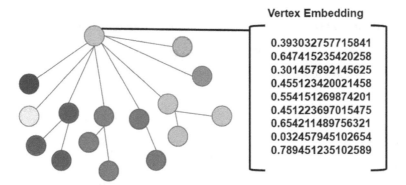

Vertex Embedding

$$
\begin{bmatrix}
0.393032757715841 \\
0.647415235420258 \\
0.301457892145625 \\
0.455123420021458 \\
0.554151269874201 \\
0.451223697015475 \\
0.654211489756321 \\
0.032457945102654 \\
0.789451235102589
\end{bmatrix}
$$

FIGURE 11.8   Vertex embedding of sub-graph of a graph.

In the next section we propose our model that is built on multiple mini heterogeneous graph networks and that helps to build the model precisely. Additional information on the applications of artificial neural networks (ANNs) is found in Jairam Naik et al. (2021a, 2021b) and Jairam Naik and Mishra (2020).

11.4   PROPOSED SPAMMER DETECTION METHODOLOGY

The proposed model uses a GCN to detect spammers. It is a deep learning method where hypergraphs are first generated by concatenating mini-graphs. Then a heterogeneous GCN is used with vanilla embedding for feature extraction, Finally we present the model training and analysis. Some key points of the workflow of the model are:

- Our purpose is to modify a Graph Convolutional Network (GCN) model to get optimized results.
- We are basically dividing our graph into small sub-graphs or networks based on KNN (K-nearest neighbors). Here we will use the BFS method to find similar kinds of nodes in a graph so that it will be easy to build features.
- Afterwards we will use vanilla feature embedding to get an enhanced and better predicted tuple of features.
- Using this methodology our model will be trained using more training sets and finally the model will be presented with the training and analyzing the output predicted.

11.4.1   HYPERGRAPH GENERATION

A normal graph is represented by an adjacency matrix with each edge connecting only two nodes. But a hypergraph can be expanded to form a multi-modal one. A hypergraph is the combination of the hyper-nodes and normal nodes of a graph network. Algorithm 11.1 gives the pseudo-code for hypergraph generation, which can be explained as follows. First the nodes with different features are loaded. The feature of N data object is represented as $X = \{ x_1, x_2, \ldots\ldots, x_n \}$. Then multiple hyper-edge structure groups are constructed according to the distance between two features, that is (x_i, x_j).

Next, each hyper-edge is constructed by combining one vertex and its k-nearest neighbors, and we get the adjacency matrix $\mathbf{A}_{N \times N}$ with N hyper-edges that connects $(k + 1)$ vertices. So, for every ith data, a hypergraph adjacency matrix $\mathbf{H}_i$ is constructed. After all the hypergraphs from the different features have been generated, the adjacent matrix $\mathbf{H}_i$ is concatenated to build a multi-modal hypergraph adjacency matrix $\mathbf{H}$. Further this adjacency matrix is fed into a GCN with some activation function to generate output.

ALGORITHM 11.1:   The pseudo-code of hypergraph generation.

`Input:` graph G = (V, E), feature matrix X

`Output:` *H* as hypergraph incidence matrix

1: feature nodes are loaded
2: `for` each ith node **do**
3.   Calculate Euclidean distance d(xi, xj)

3:      Generate hyper-graph adjacency matrix H_i
4: end for
5: Concatenate all H_i to build H (multi-modal hypergraph
incidence matrix)

11.4.2 HETEROGENEOUS GRAPH CONVOLUTION

Next, graph convolution operates on the output incidence matrix along with the input node feature matrix to give output which is further fed as input to the next set of graphs. We convert the vanilla graph to the sub-graph and find the adjacency matrix of each graph. Here activation function ReLU is used at the output of the last layer. And this process is repeated for different epochs to give the final output as a binary array.

To begin, we divide the graph G = (V, E) into sub-graphs, each of which retains all of G's vertices. Each layer's vanilla feature embedding is shared among the different sub-graphs.

A hypergraph is denoted by $G = (V, E, W_e)$, where edge $e \in E$ connects vertices V and is assigned weight $w \in W_e$. The incidence adjacency matrix of the hypergraph is represented by H:

$$H_{v \, X \, e} = \begin{cases} 1, & \text{if } v \in e \\ 0, & \text{if } v \notin e \end{cases} \tag{11.2}$$

Graph convolution processes the high order interaction between the nodes and generates node embeddings. All these steps are bound together in the pseudo-code as shown in Algorithm 11.2. Some of the important notation used in this algorithm is:

$V = \{v_1, v_2, \ldots v_n\}$ is the set of vertices; $E = \{E^1, E^2, \ldots E^{|D|}\}$ is the set of edges;

X denotes the feature matrix of the nodes; x_v represents the feature vector of node v;

H^l denotes the hidden state in the lth layer; σ is the activation function (sigmoid and ReLU function); $X^{(l+1)}$ is the output from the *n*th layer of the convolution.

ALGORITHM 11.2:   The pseudo-code of the Heterogeneous
Multiple-mini-graph Neural Network (HMGNN)

`Input:` vanilla graph G = (V, E), feature matrix X, T, epochs

`Output:` $X^{(l+1)}$
1: **for** i = 1, · · · n, epoch do
2:    $H^l \leftarrow X_v$
3:       **for** l = 1, ….., T layers do
4:             calculate hidden representation in each layer
5:          end **for**
6: σ (ReLU) activation function is added in output layer
7: Optimize the model
8: end **for**
9: Output predictions $X^{(l+1)}$

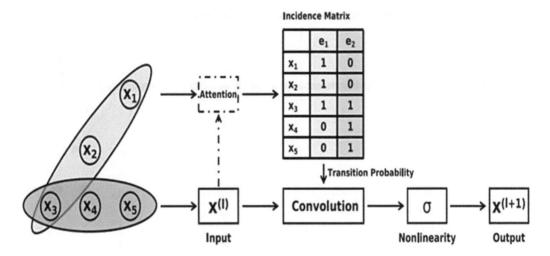

FIGURE 11.9 Hypergraph convolution with five vertices and two hyper-edges.

The overall hypergraph convolution process is illustrated in Figure 11.9.

11.4.3 MODEL TRAINING AND ANALYSIS

11.4.3.1 Model Training

We use 60% of the dataset for training purposes and 40% for testing purposes.

11.4.3.2 Model Analysis

Figure 11.10 shows the architecture diagram of the proposed model. The left section of the architecture shows the generation of hypergraphs (which is the combination of hyper-node features and normal node features). This is then fed into the convolution layers where the output feature matrix of the hypergraph is combined with the feature matrix generated by the set of mini-graphs. Here vanilla embedding is used where the output of one layer is fed as input to the next layer. Then at the

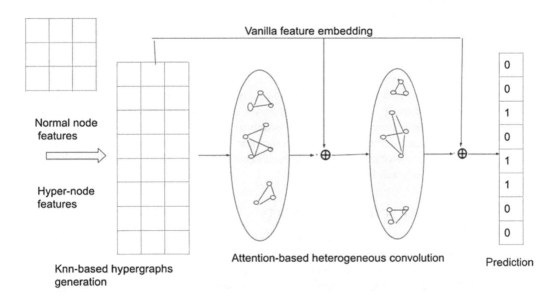

FIGURE 11.10 Architecture of model being used (vanilla embedding architecture).

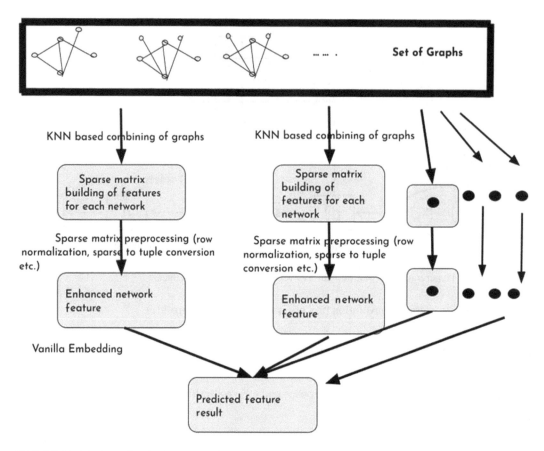

FIGURE 11.11 Data flow in the proposed system.

final output layer, an activation function is added which gives the predicted output as a binary array. This binary array represents 1 as the spammer and 0 as the genuine user.

This architecture is essentially based on semi-supervised learning. On one side it is using features extracted from mini-graphs and on other side from vanilla embedded architecture using small networks of multiple mini-graphs.

Figure 11.11 shows the data flow diagram of the proposed model. In the figure, it can be seen that the raw set of small graphs are taken as input and then small graphs are combined using KNN and a sparse matrix is built for every set of graphs, which is also called a feature matrix. But this feature matrix cannot be used directly, so we must preprocess it using transformations like "row transformation"; furthermore the feature matrix must be combined with the other features of a different set of graphs. So, the feature matrix is converted into a tuple using "matrix to tuple transformation". Finally, the resultant tuple is obtained as an enhanced network feature. And after vanilla embedding the predicted feature result will be output.

11.5 EXPERIMENTAL SETUP AND RESULTS

In this section, we report all the experimental results obtained during model design and evaluation. We will define all the experimental analytical results along with the description of the dataset being used and the parameter settings for building the model; furthermore, with the use of the analytical results, you will be able to see the suitability of the model designed for the classification of a dataset.

Analytical skill is one of the most important key features which helps to build an understanding of the context and to analyze the growth of the evaluation of the model, that is, visualization. So here we use visualization techniques for showing the experimental results. We will use graphs to demonstrate the understanding of validation accuracy and loss and show how it grows as the number of epochs increases.

The dataset is divided into the training and testing of parts during the experimentation process. The model is trained using training data, and their performance is evaluated using testing data in terms of the metrics.

11.5.1 Parameters Defined

The parameters are defined in "hparam.py". The major parameters used here are defined and described in Table 11.2. The parameter definition in one file helps us to reduce data redundancy. Parameters like "feature dimension" represent the number of users and "label kinds" represents the types of output classes. Our model does not reweight the adjacency matrix and is based on attention-based modeling for which we are using vanilla embedding.

All the above parameters are defined in a separate file to eliminate the redundancy of code for future uses; otherwise our code would be bulky and runtime high.

11.5.2 Experimental Setting

11.5.2.1 Preprocessing Input

The dataset for this chapter has been taken from Cora. The Cora dataset consists of 2708 scientific publications that have been saved as ".npy in dir./data".

As shown in Table 11.3, datasets are classified into three folders named "label.npy", "features. py", and "edges_mat.npy". The label and features folder are used for training purposes and the edges folder is for testing purposes. Therefore, we use 60% of the data for training and 40% for testing.

From the graph shown in Figure 11.12, we can see that as the number of the epoch value increases, so the loss percentage decreases for both training and validation. Also, both the curves are very close to each other, from which it can be concluded that the model is a "GOOD FIT" and hence is going in the right direction.

TABLE 11.2
Description of Parameters Defined

Parameters	Values Defined
Feature dimensions: feature dim	1433
Label kinds	7
Train ratio	0.6
Validation ratio	0.4
Whether or not to reweight adjacency matrix	FALSE
Dropout rate (1 - keep probability)	0.2
Epochs	2000
Learning rate	0.0005
Whether or not using attention: attention	TRUE
Whether or not using vanilla features: residual	TRUE
Hyper nodes K-nearest neighbors	5

TABLE 11.3
Description of Dataset

Name of Dataset File	Shape of File, i.e., (M, N)	Type of File	Description and Usage
label.npy	(2708,7)	NumPy	Each publication falls into one of seven categories. There are 2708 users, each of whom is assigned to one of seven categories.
features.py	−2,70,81,433	NumPy	A 0/1-valued word vector which describes each publication. There are 1433 words in the dictionary.
edges_mat.npy	(2, 10556)	NumPy	Each element in edges_mat.npy represents a node-id in the graph, which has 10,556 links.

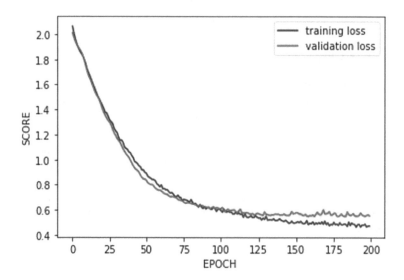

FIGURE 11.12   Training loss vs. validation loss.

11.5.3 PERFORMANCE ANALYSIS

From the graph shown in Figure 11.13, we can see that as the number of the epoch value increases, so the accuracy percentage also increases for both training and validation. Also, as both the curves are very close to each other, we can conclude that the model is a "GOOD FIT" and hence is going in the right direction.

The proposed method still achieves the best results across all evaluation metrics, demonstrating the robustness and efficiency of our approach. The evaluation of the performance (comparison of the values) of the proposed model using the F1-score, area under the ROC curve (AUC), and epoch training time based on the number of values (k) is shown in Table 11.4.

Figures 11.14–11.16 depict how the model output changes as the k value changes. These graphs have been constructed using labeled data from the coding during the training and testing period. The k represents the number of nearest neighbors used for hypergraph generation. From the graphs it is noted that when the value of k is very small, then the output is poor as the created hyper-nodes make

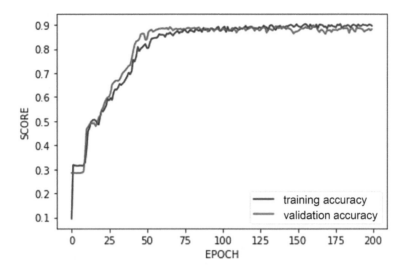

FIGURE 11.13   Training accuracy vs. validation accuracy.

TABLE 11.4
Comparison Table of F1-Score, AUC, and Epoch Training Time vs. k

k	F1-score	AUC	Epoch Training Time (sec)
1	0.89	0.952	4.5
10	0.895	0.955	4.7
20	0.8935	0.954	5
50	0.8925	0.953	5.5
200	0.89	0.95	6.9
1000	0.8875	0.949	7.5

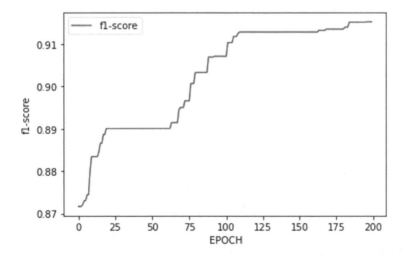

FIGURE 11.14   F1-score vs epoch (k).

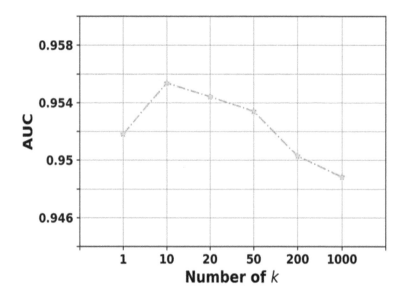

FIGURE 11.15   AUC performance.

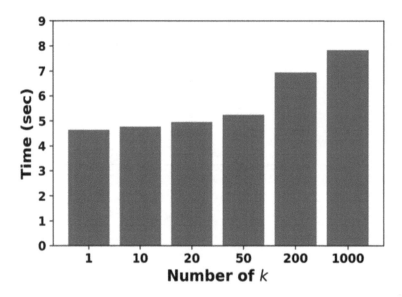

FIGURE 11.16   Epoch training time.

accurate modeling difficult. This will result in poor performance and possible increase of training costs. Now, if we increase the value of k, we don't find much variation in the F1-score and AUC.

This graph in Figure 11.17 shows how the validation runtime of each epoch varies with respect to the increase in epoch. Here the runtime is even less than 0.05 seconds, and even constant as time increases, which shows that this model can be run on big networks.

Figure 11.18 demonstrates the precision and recall that are used for evaluating the model's precision, which gives a true positive ratio with the summation of true positives and false positives. Model behavior can partially be represented by the precision value, which here is approximately 0.65.

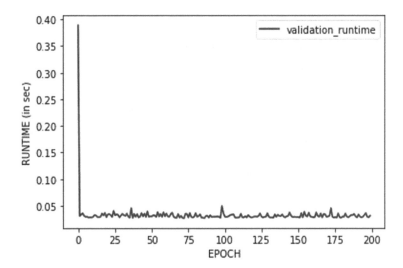

FIGURE 11.17   Epoch vs. runtime.

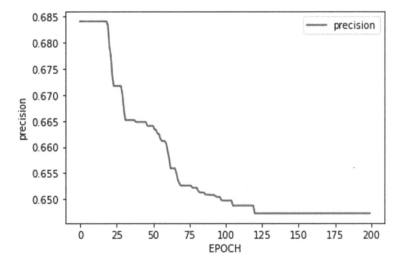

FIGURE 11.18   Epoch vs. precision.

11.5.4   PERFORMANCE COMPARISON

Table 11.5 provides the comparison drawn between the existing models and the proposed model on the basis of the epoch and F1-score graph shown in Figure 11.14. The comparison between the algorithms of the existing models and the proposed models is shown in Figure 11.19. Therefore, we can clearly see that the algorithms used, such as LDA + K-mean, LSTM + LR, SVM, CNN, and DeG-Spam, have lower F1-scores than the proposed HMGNN model. In Table 11.5, the best results are boldened.

In the previous work, the F1-scores of models were around 0.82 to 0.87, which is improved to 0.9074 in the latest research and which was based on DeG-Spam (deep graph) as shown in Table 11.5. From Figure 11.19 we can clearly see that, with the use of heterogeneous multiple mini-graph neural networks we obtained an F1-score equal to 0.9152, which is achieved because

TABLE 11.5
Comparison of Previous Algorithms

Algorithms	Maximum F1-score
LDA + K-mean	0.8261
LSTM + LR	0.8354
SVM	0.8479
CNN	0.8761
DeG-Spam	0.9074
HMGNN (Proposed)	**0.9152**

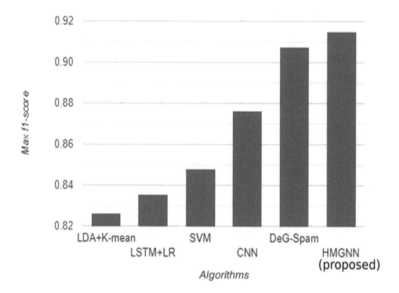

FIGURE 11.19 Comparison chart of proposed HMGNN algorithm and existing algorithms.

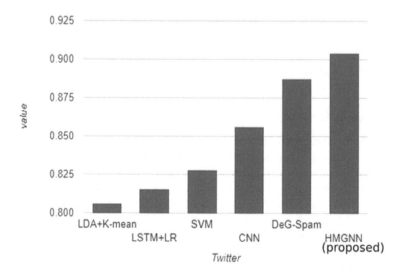

FIGURE 11.20 Proportion of training data: 50%.

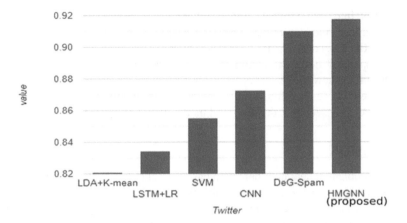

FIGURE 11.21 Proportion of training data: 60%.

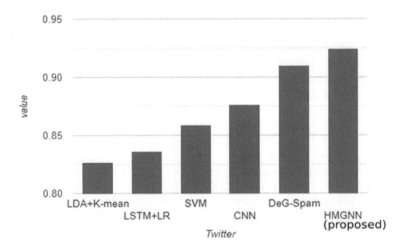

FIGURE 11.22 Proportion of training data: 70%.

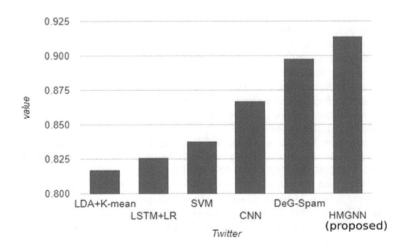

FIGURE 11.23 Proportion of training data: 80%.

we divided the graph into smaller ones: a divide and conquer approach; hence feature engineering is done to a very good level and so provides a good F1-score.

Importance of the F1-score. The F1-score is calculated using both precision and recall; in other words, the performance of model evaluation can be an F1-score.

Figures 11.20–11.23 show the results of the dataset are generated by taking different proportions of training data. Here we can see four training data proportions that have been taken: 50, 60, 70, and 80%. It can be clearly seen that the proposed model performs better than the other algorithms.

11.6 CONCLUSION

A solution for the problem of spammer detection has been suggested in this chapter. Although many approaches have been proposed to solve this problem in the past, every approach has its own limitations and benefits. We have proposed a new methodology using deep graph neural networks to detect spammers and distinguish them from normal users. The proposed model deals with network homogeneity and heterogeneity at the same time. Therefore, the proposed model can predict spammers with an accuracy of 91.4%, which is pretty good. Using the Cora dataset, a hypergraph network was generated from the normal graph network, followed by vanilla feature embedding and a convolution network to predict the output. The proposed model works on mini-graphs, which give more accurate predictions than any other method.

We would like to extend our methodology to more practical applications, particularly in more dynamic real-time graph scenarios with more data, where the existence of edges and nodes keeps changing over time in the future.

REFERENCES

Z. Guo, Y. Shen, A.K. Bashir, M. Imran, N. Kumar, D. Zhang, and K. Yu "Robust spammer detection using collaborative neural network in internet of thing applications," *IEEE Internet Things Journal IEEE* 19 June 2020. https://doi.org/10.1109/JIOT.2020.3003802 (2020).

W. Herzallah, H. Faris, and O. Adwan "Feature engineering for detecting spammers on Twitter: Modelling and analysis," *Journal of Information Science*, 4230–4247. First Published Jan. 9, 2017 Research Article. https://doi.org/10.1177/0165551516684296 (2018).

N. Hussain, H. Turab Mirza, I. Hussain, F. Iqbal, and I. Memon "Spam review detection using the linguistic and spammer behavioral methods," *IEEE Access*, vol. 8, pp. 53801–53816. https://doi.org/10.1109/ACCESS.2020.2979226 (2020).

K. Jairam Naik, Siddharth Chandra, and Paras Agarwal "Dynamic workflow scheduling in the cloud using a neural network-based multi-objective evolutionary algorithm," *International Journal of Communication Networks and Distributed Systems*, vol. 27, no. 4, pp. 424–451. https://doi.org/10.1504/IJCNDS.2021.10040231 (2021b).

K. Jairam Naik and Avani Mishra "Filter Selection for Speaker Diarization using Homomorphism: Speaker Diarization", *Artificial Neural Network Applications in Business and Engineering* (300919-093756), Chapter https://doi.org/10.4018/978-1-7998-3238-6.ch005, IGI Global Publishers, (2020).

K. Jairam Naik, Mounish Pedagandham, and Amrita Mishra "Workflow scheduling optimization for distributed environment using artificial neural networks and reinforcement learning (WfSo_ANRL)", *International Journal of Computational Science and Engineering (IJCSE)*, vol. 24, no. 6, pp. 653–670. https://doi.org/10.1504/IJCSE.2021.10041146 (2021a).

Li Kuang, Huan Zhang, Ruyi Shi, Zhifang Liao, and Xiaoxian Yang "A spam worker detection approach based on heterogeneous network embedding in crowd sourcing platforms," *Computer Networks Volume*, vol. 183, no. 24, p. 107587Dec. 2020. https://doi.org/10.1016/j.comnet.2020.107587 (2020).

A. Li, Z. Qin, R. Liu, Y. Yang, and D. Li "Spam review detection with graph convolutional networks," in *Proceedings of the 28th ACM International Conference on Information and Knowledge Management*, Beijing, China, ACM, pp. 2703–2711. https://dl.acm.org/doi/abs/10.1145/3357384.3357820 (2019).

C.Y. Lin "A reversible privacy-preserving clustering technique based on k-means algorithm," *Applied Soft Computing*, vol. 87, p. 105995 Feb. 2020. https://doi.org/10.1016/j.asoc.2019.105995 (2020).

Y. Liu, B. Pang, and X. Wang "Opinion spam detection by incorporating multimodal embedded representation into a probabilistic review graph," *Neurocomputing*, vol. 366, no. 2019, pp. 276–283 (2019).

A.C. Pandey and D.S. Rajpoot. "Spam review detection using spiral cuckoo search clustering method," *Evolutionary Intelligence*, vol. 12 (2) IEEE, pp. 147–164 (2019).

V. Ranjbar, M. Salehi, P. Jandaghi, and M. Jalili "QANet: Tensor decomposition approach for query-based anomaly detection in heterogeneous information networks," in *IEEE Transactions on Knowledge and Data Engineering*, vol. 31, no. 11, pp. 2178–2189, 1 Nov. 2019. https://doi.org/10.1109/TKDE.2018.2873391 (2019).

S. Rathore, V. Loia, and J. H. Park "SpamSpotter: An efficient spammer detection framework based on intelligent decision support system on Facebook," *Applied Soft Computing*, vol. 67, pp. 920–932. Volume 67, June 2018, Page 920–932. https://doi.org/10.1016/j.asoc.2017.09.032 (2018).

Z. Wu, S. Pan, F. Chen, G. Long, C. Zhang and P. S. Yu, "A Comprehensive Survey on Graph Neural Networks," in *IEEE Transactions on Neural Networks and Learning Systems*, vol. 32, no. 1, pp. 4–24 Jan. 2021, https://doi.org/10.1109/TNNLS.2020.2978386 (2021).

L. You, Q. Peng, Z. Xiong, D. He, M. Qiu, and X. Zhang "Integrating aspect analysis and local outlier factor for intelligent review spam detection," *Future Generation Computer Systems*, vol. 102, pp. 163–172. https://doi.org/10.1016/j.future.2019.07.044 (2020).

LiangguiTang ZhiweiGuo, Keping Yu TanGuo, Mamoun Alazab and Andrii Shalaginov, "Deep Graph neural network-based spammer detection under the perspective of heterogeneous cyberspace," *Future Generation Computer Systems*, vol. 117, pp. 205–218 April 2021, https://doi.org/10.1016/j.future.2020.11.028 (2021).

12 Spam Email Classification Using Meta-heuristic Algorithms

Ulligaddala Srinivasarao, R. Karthikeyan, and B. Vasavi
Vardhaman College of Engineering Hyderabad, Hyderabad, India

CONTENTS

12.1 INTRODUCTION

Email communications include spam, junk, and promotional and non-commercial emails. In this investigation, all of the contacts were classified as spam emails, despite the fact that they differed somewhat. "Spam" is a term used to describe communications that are sent to a large number of people and do not include helpful information. It's possible to send spam in various formats and platforms, including social media content, forum spam, instant messages, and emails, even though numerous internet-based platforms may be efficiently utilized (Méndez et al., 2019). Srinivasarao et al. 2021) proposed the use of data science and different issues in the field of big data analytics, which is reviewed in this chapter. It also explains the advantages and disadvantages of developing new computer technology.

Marketers who want to push their products and fraudsters who want to trick people may benefit from email as a communication medium. But it can turn into tragedy. It is estimated that spam emails cost organizations and people millions of dollars each year in lost productivity time and resources, not only because of the waste they cause but also because they raise the burden of communication and cybercrime on enterprises and individuals worldwide. Besides draining resources like bandwidth and requiring a significant amount of time and effort to remove, spam emails may also put your computer and data at risk (Batra et al., 2021). In order to acquire access to a victim's personal information, attackers use a wide range of techniques. Recently some researchers have developed sentiment-based email classification using a sentiment lexicon library (Srinivasarao and Sharaff, 2021).

Users must manually identify fraudulent emails to stop attackers from using them to spread their ideas. Users who notice the features of suspicious emails should act immediately to prevent the spread of spam (Guo and Chen, 2014) to make recognizing suspicious emails easier. However, creating effective systems that instantly recognize unwanted emails is crucial. The process of automatically detecting spam emails is difficult, and various techniques have been created and launched. However, not all of them exhibit 100% accuracy. Email spam identification has been one of the most popular uses of machine learning in recent years (Srinivasan et al., 2021), as different natural language processing approaches have been used to improve classification accuracy (Sharaff and Srinivasarao, 2020).

Developing spam detection systems may be made more accessible with optimization techniques (Naik et al., 2021). The optimization methods provide the best solutions to big and low-dimensional problems. In this chapter, our aim is to present a novel spam email detection technique based on the horse herd optimization approach. Previously this technique was used to solve multi-objective problems. By identifying the significant properties of spam emails, this new multi-objective binary horse herd optimization approach can accurately classify spam emails received and determine whether they are spam or non-spam. Then, the two categories are compared. The horse herd optimization technique was used in this work because of its excellent performance in different high-dimensional spam identification tasks, rapidly identifying the best solution while minimizing both cost and complexity. Researchers are developing several new optimization algorithms, such as the moth-flame optimization (Mirjalili, 2016) and the dragonfly approach (Mirjalili, 2016), which are outperformed by other models in terms of accuracy. Examples of these algorithms include the grasshopper (Seremi et al., 2017), sine cosine (Wang and Lu, 2021), and multi-verse (Mirjalili et al., 2016) optimization algorithms.

The main contributions of this chapter are:

- A herd optimization technique, a new optimization model for high investigation and rapid convergence, is applied. This technique has yet to be used to find spam email classification.
- A multi-objective algorithm based on a discretized horse herd optimization algorithm (HOA) is developed in this work. Binary opposition-based algorithms were developed from the initial high-speed search HOA.
- An innovative spam email detection system is suggested that uses HOA for feature selection.
- To categorize a large collection of spam emails, the support vector machine (SVM) classification approach is utilized.
- The results show that the suggested approach is better than well-known methods in precision, accuracy, kappa statistics, and root mean square errors.

12.2 RELATED WORK

Spam emails sent by marketers to promote their goods are considered bothersome since they take up a lot of server space (Mostafa et al., 2010). Furthermore, phishing emails can potentially deceive unsuspecting individuals (Hu and Wang, 2018). In order to steal money, scammers send these emails to get access to their victim's bank account information. Attackers and hackers use spam emails to disseminate viruses and other harmful software, and these emails often conceal their links beneath enticing offers (Karim et al., 2019). Spam emails need to be dealt with swiftly, and appropriate steps must be taken to manage this issue. In the United States, endeavors have been made to limit spam messages, including advancing further developed screening frameworks hostile to spam (Batra et al., 2021).

Academics have developed multiple methods for detecting spam in email over the years. Machine learning and deep learning methods have been used to identify and categorize spam, as discussed in the following section. To solve this issue, Naive Bayes (NB) (Saab et al., 2014; Shajideen and Bindu, 2018) is a popular method. There are several methods for identifying spam, but our primary emphasis will be on meta-heuristic algorithms.

Optimization strategies have been discussed in the literature, as feature selection is a procedure that seeks to identify the most relevant characteristics based on predetermined criteria. In Sankhwar et al. (2019), the radial basis function neural network (RBFNN), which contains counerfeit neurons called units, was utilized because of its simplicity and quick learning ability. Hidden neurons in the RBFNN were discovered using particle swarm optimization (PSO). They enabled better convergence and precision.

Papa et al. (2018) also suggested binary brain storm optimization in the framework of meta-heuristic optimization as a method for selecting features. They were able to provide outcomes that were comparable to those achieved using the most advanced techniques. Saleh et al. (2019) proposed a unique mixture of a regulated learning system with a changed AI method motivated by human invulnerability. This company's algorithm evaluates emails using a scale that measures the likelihood that an email contains spammy words. Emails were screened using a blocked-IP address database and a database of spam-confirmed keywords and phrases that were commonly used. In their efforts, they were able to boost detection rates by 5%.

Indeed, even while metaheuristic ideas were proposed to improve local search heuristics in order to find better solutions and extensive model-building time, looking through the element space to pick out specific elements for a given AI model costs a great deal of time. When phishers send mass messages with URLs and inserted joins, they are trying to entice the target user to visit their bogus websites and give them their personal information. Sankhwar et al. (2019) developed an enhanced malicious URL detection (EMUD) model. Their approach relied on 14 criteria to determine whether an email is spam or non-spam or a phishing email. A two-step process was involved (El Aassal et al., 2020). Fourteen heuristic URLs may help to identify phishing emails in the initial part of this process, applying the EMUD model to the URLs. A support vector machine was used to classify data in the next step. Their algorithm outperforms other competing models with an accuracy rate of 93.01%. They only looked at malicious URLs and the attributes that rely on URLs for discrimination; the email body properties were not considered.

Srinivasarao and Sharaff (2022) proposed email thread sentiment identification using different similarity methods. They set out to study the benchmark framework using a variety of reliable and scalable detection techniques. The authors found that the phishing classifier's performance suffers when the dataset's imbalance percentages are varied in this way. They also looked at how the preparation time varies depending on the size of the dataset and the AI innovation used.

12.3 PROPOSED SYSTEM ARCHITECTURE

In the first place, the HOA is changed, and afterward, its altered rendition is utilized for highlight determination for spam email identification. Since this is a discrete issue, the original continuous HOA technique must be converted to a binary one before being used for feature selection. Oppositional inputs are then used to create the final algorithmic output. The binary opposition-based HOA is updated to a multi-objective one to solve multiple issues. Lastly, the multi-objective-based HOA is used to identify spam messages.

Spam often comes from unknown senders with unusual email addresses, which is the norm. This doesn't infer, however, that each email received from a mysterious source is consequently classified as spam. Accordingly, it is crucial to utilize appropriate strategies to recognize spam messages from genuine messages that convey basic data. This approach requires that every email sent from the server be followed by a sequence of processes before it can be classified as spam or legitimate. After receiving an email from the server, pre-processing is the first stage. Feature selection, the following

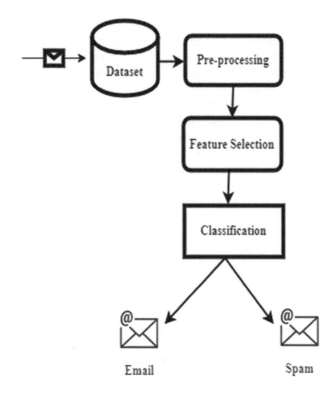

FIGURE 12.1 Proposed methodology.

step, involves identifying and removing characteristics that are irrelevant or duplicate. The last stage is categorization: to determine if an email is spam. Figure 12.1 shows a flowchart of the new spam email detection technique, which illustrates this approach's general structure. In the following sections, we will cover each stage of changing the HOA algorithm in greater detail.

12.3.1 Pre-processing

Unstructured email data is common. As a result, pre-processing is critical in order to obtain the relevant data and, subsequently, to employ improved emails in trials. Pre-processing in text mining includes tokenization, stemming, and removing stop words. There is a problem with noisy data, such as quotes and headers, that may be filtered out of the email. The pre-processing we used is: symbols, phrases, and words that are broken down into tokens during tokenization. Stemmed words are those that have had their roots identified by their root words. It is uncommon for people to use stop words in conversation. The significance of deleting stop word removal is one of the most commonly used preprocessing steps across different NLP related applications. Space dimensionality will be reduced as a result of this. The double hunt space's streamlining system impressively differs from the enhancement cycle in constant pursuit space.

12.3.2 Horse Herd Optimization Algorithm

A stage length might be added to the position vector of a pony search specialist to refresh its area in the non-stop pursuit space. It is preposterous to expect to restore the hunt specialist's area by adding a stage length to the inquiry specialist's position vector since the pursuit specialist position vector must be 0 or 1. So, we had to make a two-way version of the HOA to give people a choice, which is a straightforward job.

The HOA calculation's paired form is relatively easy to make. Run the method after adjusting the variables' lowest and maximum values to a range of 0 to 1. Although the factors tend to stay constant, they may become paired when they arrive at the expense capability, where the most significant integer function will represent them. As a result of this distinction, algorithms see the issue as either continuous or discrete. One of the functions creates the correspondence language between the double expense capability and the constant calculation during this time. There are two successive integers in Equation (12.1), and the actual value x lies between these two numbers. The biggest integer function is applied to it, and the result is k. This method may employ a continuous algorithm to tackle discrete issues.

$$k = \lfloor x \rfloor \tag{12.1}$$

12.3.3 Multi-objective Opposition-based Binary HOA

These models are called single-objective models when they are employed to solve issues with just one goal. Our goal is to discover the best possible solution to a single-objective problem. More than one goal function is standard in designing and engineering complex systems. This kind of issue is called multi-objective optimization. Multi-objective opposition-based binary (MOBHOA) issues are often characterized by established conflicting objective functions (Mirjalili, 2016). That suggests that the goals are different from one another. A multi-objective approach is required to identify spam messages successfully. These objectives are the number of highlights and their characterization precision, where the number of elements should be as few as possible. At the same time, the arrangement exactness should be as high as possible. Order exactness shows that most messages are put in the appropriate groupings with more than one characterization, and the grouping mistake rate is low. As a result, to avoid over-complicating the classification process, the newly modified HOA meta-heuristic algorithm recommends keeping the number of characteristics as common as possible. Using a multi-objective optimization strategy is essential since several goals must be satisfied. Engineers and system designers benefit significantly from these techniques since there is more than one method for tackling the issue. These techniques show the best way to accomplish a decent harmony between the various objectives. A multi-objective improvement issue might be expressed numerically by utilizing Equation (12.2).

$$Minimize: f_m(x), m = 1, 2, \ldots, M$$

$$Subject\ to: g_i(x) \geq 0, J = 1, 2, \ldots, J \tag{12.2}$$

$$H_k(x) = 0, k = 1, 2, \ldots, K$$

$$L_i < x_i < U_i, n\ i = 1, 2, \ldots, n$$

In Equation (12.2), M represents the number of objectives, J the number of imbalance limitations, and K the number of uniformity requirements. Numerical operators would not be used to compare the outcomes of a multi-objective problem. Several single-objective meta-heuristic approaches have been turned into multi-objective ones (Zhang et al., 2020). Our conversion from a single-objective HOA to one with multiple objectives is explained here. Using Equation (12.3) as the basis for a weight vector, the multi-objective HOA method seeks to determine the connection between the horses in a multi-objective search space. Using this Equation (12.3), M merges the goals of each horse into a single plan.

$$F\left(xi\right) = \frac{1}{M}\sum_{j=1}^{M} fi\left(xi\right) \tag{12.3}$$

The procedure by which the goals in a single-objective HOA are updated differs significantly from that in a multi-objective HOA. It would be possible to quickly narrow down the search space to only one goal by picking the best solution found. However, the goal must be chosen from a collection of optimum solutions in a multi-objective HOA. One of the stored ideal solutions would be the final goal. The goal here is to discover a way to increase the spread of the stored solutions. An objective's probability of selection is determined by Equation (12.4).

As a result, these locations are better spread across the search space. When running a multi-objective HOA, it's important to keep the archive as compact as possible and to keep it updated often. It can be challenging to tell the difference between the two methods. In order to improve the archive, the multi-objective HOA must be able to handle these situations. Discarding it immediately is the only option in this situation. Other times, the archive is completely occupied by new answers. It is necessary to include a non-dominant solution in order for the archive to have the dominant ones. It is important to note that if a solution dominates the archive, it should be replaced with a new one. When deciding which features to include, a multi-objective optimization issue needs to be considered in spam detection. Greater classification accuracy and a smaller number of chosen characteristics are achieved in multi-objective tasks. Consequently, a classification method is necessary to describe the feature selection algorithm (Hosseinalipour et al., 2021).

The fewer features, the better the solution; nevertheless, a decreased number of components may sometimes increase classification error rates. Furthermore, the lower the classification error, the better the solution; however, increasing the number of characteristics may be required. More factors are not necessarily better, as a reduced number of features may degrade classification accuracy beyond a specific limit. However, a lower classification error rate may result in more features being picked. As with other thresholds, the threshold for each issue is different. This is why Equation (12.4) is used as a multi-objective function for choosing characteristics to strike a compromise between the two. A near-optimal answer is found by balancing the two competing goals in this equation.

$$\text{Fitness} = \propto \gamma_R + \beta \frac{|R|}{|N|} \tag{12.4}$$

At the same time, $|R|$ reflects the multi-linearity of the chosen subset in Equation (12.4), while the total number of features in the dataset is given by $|N|$ and represents the relative weights assigned to classification quality and subset size, respectively. Based on values from Emary et al. (2016), we've used (0, 1) and = ((1 − 1)/(1 − 1)). Because the starting point is 0.99 in this research, the corresponding value is determined as 0.01. The number of optimization methods is developed in the area of spam email detection (Abualigah et al., 2018; Rajamohana and Umamaheswari, 2018). A benchmark for all algorithms is provided by SVM, which enables us to assess the chosen feature using the proposed approach and other comparable methods properly.

12.3.4 Spam Detection Using MOBHOA

Following a pre-processing step and the extraction of characteristics, the dataset used in this research was used in the present investigation. Spam emails are distinguished from legitimate ones by several distinct features. Here are some of the natural mechanisms used by HOA to make this happen.

For example, the feature selection method is a four-step process that begins with developing and assessing feature subsets, then criterion verification, and ends with validating the findings. Various

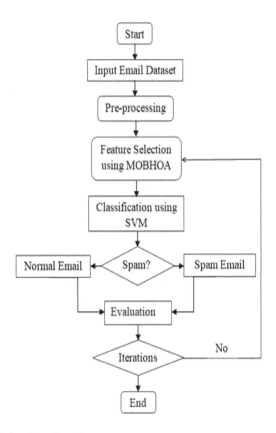

FIGURE 12.2   Proposed algorithm flowchart.

subsets of the dataset are used to construct the feature subset. Candidate features are sought for using HOA's search technique in this subgroup. Subsets of candidates are compared to the best value of an evaluation characteristic that has previously been used. If a better subset is found, the prior best one is discarded, and the new one is used instead. The creation and assessment of subsets continue until the HOA's termination requirement is met.

Prior to reaching the optimal global solution, HOA is performed numerous times. Fitness functions are used to determine how well a classifier performs in each cycle. Candidates are generated, fitness levels are calculated, and the assessment process is repeated until all requirements have been completed and the selection is complete. The rate of error and the total number of iterations are the most commonly used criteria for determining whether a process is finished. For the sake of spam email detection, we aimed to suggest a new optimization strategy for selecting features. The recommended strategy's flowchart may be seen in Figure 12.2.

12.4   RESULTS ANALYSIS

Implementation and simulation of the new approach were done on the 64-bit i5 CPU and using 8GB of RAM Python software. Spam Base was used as a model for the simulation; 80% of the data was used for testing, while 20% was used for training. Tests using the Spam Base dataset from the unique client identifier (UCI) data repository were done to see how well the algorithm detected spam. Table 12.1 shows that of the 4601 emails utilized, 1789 were spam emails, and 2812 were non-spam emails. Each entry in this database has 58 characteristics, the most recent of which indicates whether or not an email is spam (0). The first 48 characteristics show the frequency of keywords. This is the

TABLE 12.1
Dataset Details

Dataset Name	Total Emails	Spam Emails	Non-spam Emails
Enron Email Dataset	4601	1789	2812
Spam Assassin	3252	501	2751

proportion of words and phrases in the email that match a given term or phrase. The characters' frequency is shown by the following six features, while the following three features reveal the dataset's characters.

Measuring the appropriate number of classified email messages is insufficient due to the high cost of unsolicited bulk email (UBE) misclassification. New measurements developed from information retrieval and decision theory may therefore help to produce better results. Effective communication could be lost if a legitimate email is unintentionally removed as spam or phishing. When phishing emails are mistakenly categorized as honest communications, privacy is violated.

Accuracy: Similar to Equation (12.5), this statistic calculates the average proportion of correctly classified emails throughout the entire email database.

$$\text{Accuracy} = \frac{TP + TN}{TP + FP + FN + TN} \tag{12.5}$$

A true positive (TP) is supported by evidence, whereas a false positive (FP) is not.

Percentage of true positives to total positives: This statistic measures the filter's dependability by comparing genuine positive discoveries to the total number of positive results in the dataset. The formula is:

$$\text{Precision} = \frac{TP}{TP + FP} \tag{12.6}$$

The kappa statistic measures the degree to which the instances perceived by the AI classifier match the information named as the ground truth.

$$\text{Kappa statistics} = \frac{p(a) - p(e)}{1 - p(e)} \tag{12.7}$$

In this case, it stands for the expected value, the total number of observations, and the actual value.

$$\text{RMSE} = \sqrt{\sum_{i=1}^{n} \frac{(\hat{x}_i - x_i)^2}{n}} \tag{12.8}$$

Here, we compare the suggested method's spam detection accuracy to alternative optimization techniques. Table 12.2 shows the results of SVN, the proposed approaches, and how accurate they are at classifying using different methods.

As seen in Table 12.2, SVN techniques outperformed PSO in terms of spam detection, as seen in the Enron email dataset. SVN was performed in essentially the same way as the next two calculations in the underlying cycles, though it proved superior as the number of emphases increased. Using an opposition-based technique, we found options in the opposite search area.

TABLE 12.2
Enron Email Dataset

Methods	Accuracy	Precision	Kappa Statistics	RMSE
Proposed	0.954	0.941	0.891	0.25
SVM	0.910	0.897	0.791	0.69
MSFO	0.892	0.875	0.787	0.12
PSO	0.925	0.917	0.896	0.71
NB	0.794	0.783	0.748	0.58

TABLE 12.3
Spam Assassin Dataset

Methods	Accuracy	Precision	Kappa Statistics	RMSE
Proposed	0.914	0.925	0.878	0.46
SVM	0.890	0.864	0.789	0.54
MFO	0.875	0.779	0.757	0.19
PSO	0.901	0.815	0.871	0.79
NB	0.781	0.768	0.735	0.68

Results from the spam assassin dataset examination are shown in Table 12.3. For the HOA approach, feature selection and classification are made using HOA and SVN methods, respectively, and the results are shown in Table 12.3. In addition, the HOA approach uses grey wolf optimizer (GWO) to identify features and the SVN method to classify those features once they have been selected. Instead of making feature selection, as is the case with SVM, PSO, and NB, the suggested technique classifies data without executing this step.

It is recommended that a feature selection strategy that increases accuracy, precision, kappa statistics, and RMSE while simultaneously reducing runtime be used. As a result of eliminating unnecessary or duplicated characteristics, actions are conducted on the most important ones in an optimum feature selection process. As a result of this change, the algorithm's execution times will be slashed while kappa statistics and the RMSE are improved. While executing this experiment, in all feature choices, KNN remained the same. It was decided to combine KNN with the suggested technique for a second time, with the results shown in Table 12.3.

Figure 12.3 shows the assessment results. By using the feature selection technique, HOA has higher accuracy, precision, kappa statistics, R squared, and RMSE than the other methods. According to the findings, the MOBHOA technique operating on the UCI dataset outperforms other conventional meta-heuristic methods regarding classification accuracy. According to the study, this method detected spam emails with a higher degree of accuracy than different approaches. This is because of HOA, a very efficient optimization method that excels at tackling high-dimensional issues. It is also possible to incorporate a feature selection step in addition to the classification phase. Reduced computing complexity and improved classification accuracy may be achieved by eliminating redundant characteristics.

One of the most effective ways to tackle a wide range of issues is through machine learning. However, computational complexity is an issue that plagues the majority of machine learning methods.

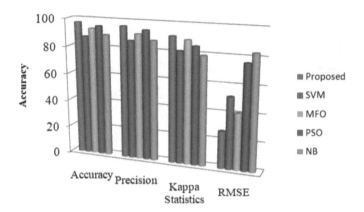

FIGURE 12.3   Accuracy comparison with different methods.

We employed the HOA method to enhance calculation speed and accuracy. We need to apply more current methodologies and calculations to develop exactness further and lessen the intricacy and mistake rate in proving spam distinguishing. There are new improvements being realized, which demonstrate how they can be utilized to tackle spam location issues – only a few concentrate on the viability of deep learning calculations for recognizable spam proof. The majority of datasets are likewise of a hidden or falsely created size, which makes them unusable. Future exploration is therefore expected to consider huge information arrangements, massive datasets, and profound learning calculations to construct more powerful methodologies for spam identification. Furthermore, this examination zeroed in on email spam recognition and other spam location strategies; for example, person-to-person communication spam was not explored in this study. Future research may apply this method to identify spam on other platforms.

12.5 CONCLUSION

Users of the internet and data centers have been concerned about the amount of storage and other resources used by spam and unwanted emails, which is why spam filters have been implemented. In addition, spam provides a means for penetration, cyber-attacks, and access to user content. It is possible to identify spam and remove it using various methods and procedures. Despite the improvements made, spam detection methods have yet to be shown to be successful on their own in the majority of the approaches offered so far. We wanted to develop a robust meta-heuristic algorithm that could be utilized in email services to identify spam messages. We used the new HOA algorithm, a nature-inspired meta-heuristic optimization method created for addressing challenging optimization problems, to accomplish this goal. It takes time to pinpoint a single solution to the complex challenge of spam detection. HOA was binarized and then changed into a multi-objective opposition-based method to address the feature selection issue in spam detection so that it could be used for this task. HOA was originally a continuous algorithm. Experimental evaluation of the suggested technique for spam detection using the spam dataset informational index from the UCI information vault was completed to evaluate the exhibition of an original calculation, an MOBHOA method.

To put it another way: compared to other comparable techniques, such as SVM, PSO, and NB, the new methodology outperforms the previous methods concerning order exactness and accuracy. The results show that the clever strategy outperforms nearly identical meta-heuristic arrangements revealed in writing; thus, it could be used for highlight selection in spam recognition frameworks. SVN was compared against SVM, MFO, PSO, and NB classifiers in terms of accuracy, precision, kappa statistics, and root mean square error in identifying spam emails.

CONFLICT OF INTEREST

The authors declare no potential conflict of interest.

REFERENCES

Abualigah, L. M., Khader, A. T., & Hanandeh, E. S. (2018). A combination of objective functions and hybrid krill herd algorithm for text document clustering analysis. *Engineering Applications of Artificial Intelligence*, *73*, 111–125.

Batra, J., Jain, R., Tikkiwal, V. A., & Chakraborty, A. (2021). A comprehensive study of spam detection in emails using bio-inspired optimization techniques. *International Journal of Information Management Data Insights*, *1*(1), 100006.

El Aassal, A., Baki, S., Das, A., & Verma, R. M. (2020). An in-depth benchmarking and evaluation of phishing detection research for security needs. *IEEE Access*, *8*, 22170–22192.

Emary, E., Zawbaa, H. M., & Hassanien, A. E. (2016). Binary ant lion approaches for feature selection. *Neurocomputing*, *213*, 54–65.

Guo, D., & Chen, C. (2014). Detecting non-personal and spam users on geo-tagged Twitter network. *Transactions in GIS*, *18*(3), 370–384.

Hosseinalipour, A., Gharehchopogh, F. S., Masdari, M., & Khademi, A. (2021). A novel binary farmland fertility algorithm for feature selection in analysis of the text psychology. *Applied Intelligence*, *51*(7), 4824–4859.

Hu, H., & Wang, G. (2018). Revisiting email spoofing attacks. *arXiv preprint arXiv:1801.00853*.

Karim, A., Azam, S., Shanmugam, B., Kannoorpatti, K., & Alazab, M. (2019). A comprehensive survey for intelligent spam email detection. *IEEE Access*, *7*, 168261–168295.

Méndez, J. R., Cotos-Yañez, T. R., & Ruano-Ordás, D. (2019). A new semantic-based feature selection method for spam filtering. *Applied Soft Computing*, *76*, 89–104.

Mirjalili, S. (2015). Moth-flame optimization algorithm: A novel nature-inspired heuristic paradigm. *Knowledge-based Systems*, *89*, 228–249.

Mirjalili, S. (2016). Dragonfly algorithm: A new meta-heuristic optimization technique for solving single-objective, discrete, and multi-objective problems. *Neural Computing and Applications*, *27*(4), 1053–1073.

Mirjalili, S., Mirjalili, S. M., & Hatamlou, A. (2016). Multi-verse optimizer: A nature-inspired algorithm for global optimization. *Neural Computing and Applications*, *27*(2), 495–513.

Mostafa, R., Norizan, M. Y., & Gazi, M. A. (2010). Impact of spam advertisement through email: A study to assess the influence of the anti-spam on the email marketing. *African Journal of Business Management*, *4*(11), 2362–2367.

Naik, K. J., Pedagandam, M., & Mishra, A. (2021). Workflow scheduling optimisation for distributed environment using artificial neural networks and reinforcement learning. *International Journal of Computational Science and Engineering*, *24*(6), 653–670.

Papa, J. P., Rosa, G. H., de Souza, A. N., & Afonso, L. C. (2018). Feature selection through binary brain storm optimization. *Computers & Electrical Engineering*, *72*, 468–481.

Rajamohana, S. P., & Umamaheswari, K. (2018). Hybrid approach of improved binary particle swarm optimization and shuffled frog leaping for feature selection. *Computers & Electrical Engineering*, *67*, 497–508.

Saab, S. A., Mitri, N., & Awad, M. (2014, April). Ham or spam? A comparative study for some content-based classification algorithms for email filtering. In *MELECON 2014-2014 17th IEEE Mediterranean Electrotechnical Conference* (pp. 339–343). IEEE.

Saleh, A. J., Karim, A., Shanmugam, B., Azam, S., Kannoorpatti, K., Jonkman, M., & Boer, F. D. (2019). An intelligent spam detection model based on artificial immune system. *Information*, *10*(6), 209.

Sankhwar, S., Pandey, D., & Khan, R. A. (2019). Email phishing: An enhanced classification model to detect malicious URLs. *EAI Endorsed Transactions on Scalable Information Systems*, *6*(21), 1–12.

Saremi, S., Mirjalili, S., & Lewis, A. (2017). Grasshopper optimisation algorithm: Theory and application. *Advances in Engineering Software*, *105*, 30–47.

Shajideen, N. M., & Bindu, V. (2018, March). Spam filtering: A comparison between different machine learning classifiers. In *2018 Second International Conference on Electronics, Communication and Aerospace Technology (ICECA)* (pp. 1919–1922). IEEE.

Sharaff, A., & Srinivasarao, U. (2020, January). Towards classification of email through selection of informative features. In *2020 First International Conference on Power, Control and Computing Technologies (ICPC2T)* (pp. 316–320). IEEE.

Srinivasan, S., Ravi, V., Alazab, M., Ketha, S., Al-Zoubi, A. M., & KottiPadannayil, S. (2021). Spam emails detection based on distributed word embedding with deep learning. In *Machine intelligence and big data analytics for cybersecurity applications* (pp. 161–189). Springer, Cham.

Srinivasarao, U., & Sharaff, A. (2021). Sentiment analysis from email pattern using feature selection algorithm. *Expert Systems*, e12867, 1–13.

Srinivasarao, U., & Sharaff, A. (2022). Email thread sentiment sequence identification using PLSA clustering algorithm. *Expert Systems with Applications*, 193, 116475.

Srinivasarao, U., Sharaff, A., & Sinha, G. R. (2021). Introduction to data science: Review, challenges, and opportunities. *Data Science and Its Applications*, 1–13.

Wang, M., & Lu, G. (2021). A modified sine cosine algorithm for solving optimization problems. *IEEE Access*, 9, 27434–27450.

Zhang, Y., Gong, D. W., Gao, X. Z., Tian, T., & Sun, X. Y. (2020). Binary differential evolution with self-learning for multi-objective feature selection. *Information Sciences*, 507, 67–85.

13 A Blockchain Model for Land Registration Properties in Metro Cities

Rohan Sawant, Deepa A. Joshi, and Radhika Menon
Savitribai Phule Pune University, Pune, India

CONTENTS

13.1　INTRODUCTION

The process of land registry in India along with many areas of the planet is an exceptionally sluggish, problematic, and drawn-out process. There are many difficulties involved with this cycle; for example, finding the proprietor of various segments of a property is testing when you have a large number of land records to keep up with. Subsequently changing the proprietorship becomes tedious and troublesome. There are likewise numerous go-betweens engaged in the process of land enlistment. Presently individuals have to trust an outsider, that is, government organizations, but which are at risk when monitoring the proprietorship of data. Accordingly, such an outsider has to save all the records in a concentrated dataset.

In contrast to private and business structures, for land there is no field assessment by specialists [1]. This paper-based system is not only difficult to access and maintain, but it is also vulnerable to natural and man-made disasters. Therefore, we will need to look for the most up-to-date procedures that aid in resolving the issues raised by partners during land registration and also eliminate the intermediaries who resemble real estate agents. First are the requirements to confirm that the land records existed prior to change of possession [2]. Digitization of land records assists with lessening the weakness of single or duplicate paper-based titles, and it increases the validity, unwavering quality, and straightforwardness of the land enlistment technique [3].

Nonetheless, this framework strengthens the land enlistment cycle and reduces cases of misrepresentation, while the implementation of enhancements in the responsibility for records remains a significant challenge for the current frameworks [4, 5]. The most recent machine improvements, for example, block chain innovation, have arisen as promising advancements to conquer these issues. The straightforward idea of blockchain innovation is to follow how property changes hands. Data that have been entered once can never be deleted [6]. A few countries, such as Sweden [7], the Netherlands, Honduras [8], and Dubai [9], have wanted to move the land registry framework into a blockchain-based framework.

India and countless other agricultural countries, so far as that is concerned, come up short in areas of strength for property liberties. This is the rationale for why a two-thirds greater share of each and every prospective court case involves property-related issues.

To resolve this issue, the Indian government has started the digitization of land records in the Digital India Land Records Modernization Program (DILRMP), a first step to digitizing old land records, and setting a trend for guaranteeing a genuine, government supported record of exchanges. The public authority plans to use an innovative drone system to plan land packages in country regions, covering nearly 620,000 towns over the following five years. Prime Minister Narendra Modi sent off a property card on Sunday, October 11, 2020 whichhe promised would give clarity regarding property freedom in towns and empower ranchers to involve their property as guarantee for credit from monetary institutions.

The currently used land record title storage system raises major issues about data fraud, the security of highly sensitive data, and the risk of system failure due to natural disasters, such as the server used for data storage going down [10].

The basic and most important aspect of blockchain technology is that it is a decentralized network in which all data supplied by a single node are confirmed by all other available nodes, and only after a consensus is obtained can the shared data be saved to the blockchain [11]. There are various platforms being used for the creation of reliable, decentralized, transparent, immutable, and secure blockchain-based land registration and management systems. Smart contracts based on the Ethereum blockchain are gaining traction among these systems. Being a public blockchain platform, it allows anyone to participate in the blockchain ecosystem [12].

The Dubai Land Record Authority was one of the first government agencies to put its land titles on a blockchain [13]. However, in developing countries like Pakistan access to land records as well as the management of data has been a serious concern. In Pakistan, out of four major provinces, that is, Sindh, KPK, Baluchistan, and Punjab, only Punjab Province land record data has been stored to a computer in Pakistan. In some provinces, land data are still stored and managed typically by a central person known as a *"patwari"*, who saves this crucial data on big paper-based registries. In this regard, the Punjab government took important measures and built an information system known as the Punjab Land Record Management Information System, to simplify the complex process of saving and managing land records [14].

In Maharashtra, land registration involves a lot of paper work. Checking the documents and the identity of the people who signed them must be done manually. There is an increasing number of fraud cases; human intervention takes a significantly long time to complete land registrations; and there is poor handling of the processes. The existing land records available in the country are not clear. This chapter addresses these issues by listing the challenges in property registration and developing an appropriate procedure using blockchain technology to address these issues in Maharashtra Region. Various stakeholders are involved in the land registration process in Maharashtra. We will use one case study: Gujarat land registration and the proposed hybrid blockchain model for land registry in Maharashtra, Pune.

13.1.1 Land Registration Types

1. Purchase Letter Registration;
2. Heir Registration;

3. Prize Letter Registration;
4. Will Registration.

13.1.2 Issues or Challenges in Land Registry, Maharashtra, India

In order to list the issues or challenges in land registry, in Maharashtra, discussions were carried out with the various stakeholders of this field. Meetings and discussions were held with people working in the Talathi office and Maha E-Seva Kendra.

1. In the Maharashtra land registration process relatives can file an objection within 21days; if there has been no objection then it is registered on the land registry.
2. There are so many entries, when registering land, the clerk is usually over-worked, so the complete process of land registration is slow.
3. In this course of the process, many middlemen are involved.
4. Lack of administration: a talathi has the work of all villages in the entire taluka, so has a lot of work. Therefore, they do not submit the land survey application to the process and it remains pending. If it is submitted, it is recorded within 21 days.
5. 7/12 extract is also known as Saat Baara Utara, Record of Land Rights. The 7/12 extract or Utara is an extract from that land register and includes complete information about agriculture land in a rural area of Maharashtra. 7/12 Utara serves as proof of ownership of the land.
    When the transfer of an old man's 7/12 to the internet happened, so many mistakes occurred due to time, such as one man having different khata numbers, e.g., individual, mixed, and general khata numbers.
6. There are several issues with the current land registration process that must be addressed. Even though digitalization has been implemented to some extent, the process is not yet complete, so it is critical to investigate the issues with the current land registration process. The management of Maharashtra's land markets is impacted by improper land transaction and record keeping procedures, issues with coordination between the land records, the courts, bank surveys, and registration department agencies.
7. Existing land records in the country are vague, poorly maintained, and usually do not fully represent reality on the ground.
8. Various departments at the district or town level are updated and store the data. As a consequence of the absence of regular synchronization between these divisions, there are errors in the records and frequent mismatches between both the information on the report and the ground location.
9. Land registry takes up a significant portion of the day to complete title enrollments. There could be months between fruition and enlistment.
10. Many legitimate issues can also arise during this lengthy period.
11. Lack of support for land records. Historically, land enrollment and record keeping were done physically. The Revenue Department typically houses the archives, which are closed to the public. When attempting to establish communication in order to attract property deals, this makes it difficult and time-consuming to obtain data pertaining to land.
12. Records do not accurately reflect the position on the ground. Inaccuracy has also resulted from poor maintenance of land records. Historically, states have ignored changing records through surveys. Actual ground boundaries have not been established using maps. As a result, the spatial records do not match the material records. The difference between spatial and material records likewise emerges because of land moving and parceling, whether through a legacy or deal, which are not caught by studies. For instance, once the land is given to the heir, records may not be updated if a landowner passes away.

13. There are some inconsistencies between land registration and records. Land records combine three kinds of information records: resolutions, maps, and transaction deeds. All property record information is managed by three separate state divisions. It is difficult to ensure that study maps, bibliographical information, and enrollment data are integrated and revised in the presence of many agents responsible for enrollment and record management. Furthermore, citizens must be compelled to move toward various organizations in order to provide all information for land records. The vast majority of those divisions add storehouses, and any of them changing their records renders the records of the others obsolete.

14. To begin, it might be necessary to check that all of the existing area records are accurate and free of obstructive documents. Land records frequently contain errors, are inadequate, and do not accurately reflect the actual situation. A time-consuming and resource-intensive strategy would be to compare these records to every previous transaction and the current situation.

15. Second, it might be necessary to present all information pertaining to land through a single window. At the moment, land records are spread out among various divisions. Land record changes in one office typically don't show up in other divisions' records.

16. The problem is over the state, since there is, so to say, one clerk for the explanation at the monitor general of enlistment (IGR) office in Pune.

17. Survey and settlement don't come to completion in ordinary time spans; in numerous countries, the overview task has not been done in many years.

18. Many landholders can't get the record of the privileges of their landholdings because of the absence of question settlements or the absence of rights reviews.

Other investigations have confirmed the enormous potential of blockchain in property management [15]:

1. "A blockchain is a massively strong widely shared infrastructure that will transfer value and reflect property ownership" [16].

2. "Blockchain encoding property transforms into sensible property that may be transferred via smart contracts" [17].

3. "It will be viewed as information and communications technology (ICT) to record the ownership of on-platform and off-platform properties, as well as the powers and responsibilities emerging from contracts" [18].

4. "It is straightforward to undertake title exchange for any property, both physical and immaterial, whose ownerships are regulated by the blockchain" [19].

5. "Blockchains will be employed to trace tangible assets, permitting a record of ownership to be preserved for each object" [20].

13.1.3 Use of Blockchain Technology for These Issues

The proposed model of using blockchain for the land registration process has benefits over the process consistent with today's version of the land register: each stakeholder will digitally store their documents and information without worrying about losing it, due to localized information management with larger transparency and a good deal of security, resilience, and flexibility. Digital signatures provides a better level of security than manual document filing (fraud decreases and the risk of errors) for the duration of the entire method, usually for five to six months, though two weeks is possible. There exist automatic alerts of possible changes or changes within the land document. There is no single cause of failure due to the simple fact that keep isn't held in a single centralized spot; it's unthinkable to lose keep information since information is available and stays linked to each node on the system.

Citizens will verify the ownership details and total history of the property before entering into for purchase of the property.

The system is clear and integrated because every record is joined to the previous one using a cryptographic hash, so forming a chain of blocks. Records are incorruptible, changeless, and can't be duplicated without human intervention or a positive irrefutable digital signature.

All technology has challenges in implementation, no matter its boundaries. Written land accounts with blockchain technology additionally might face a few challenges. An attempt is made here to list these challenges.

The land registration method with blockchain as a new technology would take time for people to simply accept. The biggest problem with it is that no information can be modified once it's fed into the distributed ledger. Keeping an up-to-date and correct land registry is one of the biggest challenges for land governance in developing countries. Land registry with blockchain technology needs advanced engineering and additionally much manpower. Land registry with blockchain technology is an automatic method and is tough for people to simply accept because of security concerns. Most people are not aware of blockchain technology or a distributed ledger system. In spite of the challenges, considering the advantages, the adoption of blockchain technology for land registration in cities with immediate results is inevitable.

13.1.4 STRUCTURE OF BLOCKCHAINS

A blockchain is an associated series of circulated records that can be customized to store and track anything of significant worth. These blocks can't be changed whenever they are included in a chain, which makes the chain of exchanges freely verifiable and unhackable [21]. A blockchain can be considered as an associated rundown of blocks which contain a set of exchanges in each block and are distinguished by their own hashtags. Each block is associated with the preceding block, known as the parent block, subsequently making a "chain" back to the principal block. Therefore every block has a reference to no less than one ancestor; hence the term "blockchain" [22]. A blockchain verifies, collects, executes, and stores smart contracts in blocks, which facilitate transaction-related requests for automated procurement and payment. Also title transfers for tangible and intangible properties can be easily executed, whose ownerships are controlled by a blockchain.

The thought is to have most of the members in the framework to check the content of each block. When a block has been placed and confirmed the data can't be eradicated or changed. Each block could be characterized as an encoded snippet of data. In principle anybody inside the framework can add information to the chain of blocks, audit the information whenever, yet nobody can change the information without satisfactory approval. Thus all of the "blocks" generate a total and unchanging history of the organization's events, which is imparted to all members in the framework.

13.1.5 THE VARIOUS KINDS OF AGREEMENT CONVENTIONS UTILIZED FOR APPROVING EXCHANGES ON THE BLOCKCHAIN

- Confirmation of Work (PoW)
  Verification of work is an agreement convention that endeavors to forestall digital assaults like communicated forswearing of administration assaults, which may deplete the assets of a PC framework with numerous phoney solicitations. Verification of work: the mining challenge is open to anyone. Each digger competes with the other to add the following block. It is a method for characterizing a costly and unwieldy PC computation called mining and consumes much computing power [24].
- Confirmation of Stake
  In verification of work agreement calculations, the excavators who tackle the numerical issues are compensated by making new blocks and approving exchanges. It is a typical choice

of PoW. Here, the validators are select in light of the small number of coins they own in the framework [23].

Evidence of the stake demands basically less energy, so it is smart when contrasted with the confirmation of the work calculation.

Moreover, there is less prerequisite to deliver an excessive number of coins for boosting excavators to deal with the organization.

- Designated Proof of Stake
  Designated verification of stake (DPoS) is an elective agreement technique where every hub with a stake in the organization can appoint the confirmation of exchanges to one more hub by the common way of casting a ballot [25].
- Evidence of Elapsed Time (PoET)
  In Proof of Elapsed Time, the organization involves a lottery capable of carrying out the agreement. A lottery calculation is utilized for looking through the pioneers from a bunch of hubs. In this way, the validators are chosen haphazardly from the pool [23]. Artist is one of the productive agreement calculations utilized for permissioned blockchains where you really want consent to get to the organization. Writer calculation involves a particular method to cover straightforwardness in the entire organization and guarantees a protected login.
- Viable Byzantine Fault Tolerance (PBFT)
  PBFT expects that specific hubs are exploitative or broken and was intended to be an elite execution agreement calculation that depends on a bunch of confided in hubs in the organization [26]. The hubs in PBFT are requested in a successive way with one being the pioneer and different hubs going about as reinforcements [27].

The characteristics of blockchain technology are the essential components of the land registration process. Thus, implementation of blockchain technology for land registration brings all stakeholders on a single platform and provides the best fit solution of a secure, authentic, and transparent process.

13.2 CURRENT LAND REGISTRATION PROCEDURE

The land registration procedure is well established and is being followed by the government sector. In order to list the process in the proper sequence with all the details, discussions were carried out with the various stakeholders of this field. Meetings and discussions took place with people working in the Talathi office and Maha E-Seva Kendra. Also, to understand the exact implementation at the ground level, interaction with the Talathis of the two villages was carried out. The other resources utilized were the related research papers and discussions with experienced engineers in the construction industry.

The current land registration procedure in India, with the adoption of the Digital India Land Records Modernization Programme, is explained below (see also Figure 13.1).

1. Title verification of the property
   The documentation of property varies depending on whether or not the property has been bought from a developer or is a secondary sale. In the last case, due diligence would be less complicated because the initial owner could have the property documents ready for the registration. The commitment for the verification of the property title, however, lies on the buyer before the registration.
2. Estimation of the property value
   Estimate the value of the property in line with the circle rates within the given space. This can cause deep trouble when paying tax. The tax prices are computed as a portion of the higher of the specific value paid for the property or the circle rate within the provided location.
3. Buying stamp papers
   Obtain the non-judicial stamp papers for that fee after the computation is done.

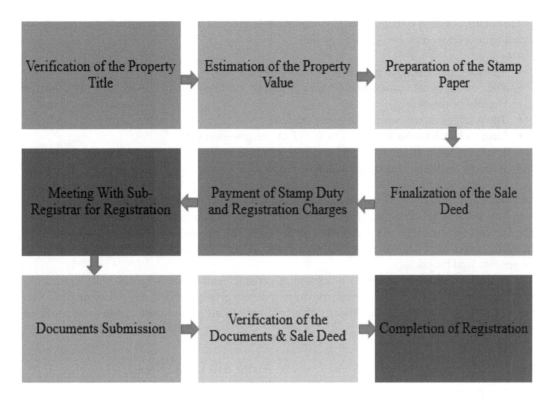

FIGURE 13.1 Current land registration procedure.

The stamp papers will be purchased by person or online. One should purchase all these papers from the authorized stamp vendors, whereas e-stamps are purchased online from shcilestamp.com. The customer pays the fee to the Treasuries and Accounts Department either online or in person after raising the Challan using eGRAS (the government receipt strategy for bookkeeping, though this does not function in many states, especially in the geographical regions of Rajasthan, Haryana, and Jharkhand).

4. Preparation of the deed

The deed should be ready and written on stamp papers. The topic matter varies according to whether it is a lease, mortgage, sale, power of professional person, etc.

5. Document submission

Along the edge of the deed for the deal, you are expected to present the imperative archives like a No Objection Certificate (NOC) in the event that the structure is found inside the town authority's territory, ID and address confirmation, cash or a certificate for the installment of the visa-sized pictures of the gatherings inside the managing, charge, and so on.

Approach the sub-registrar for registrationBook a meeting with the sub-registrar for the registration of the sale deed. The transacting parties attend the sub-registrar's workplace to effect registration of the deed, attended by two witnesses. Everyone involved in the approach has to bring their identity papers, many pictures, etc. A creative copy of the deed, together with two photocopies of identical paperwork, need to be carried.

6. Completion of registration

The sub-registrar's office checks the identity and map of the property and registers it. Once the sale deed is registered, one gets a receipt. After two to seven days the sub-registrar's office is again visited to obtain the sale deed. The sub-registrar can hand over all the original documents but hold on to a copy of each document.

The central issues that encompass the obtaining of land in India are more difficult than those connected with developed property. These include:

- Various deals which have not been recorded as expected;
- The vowing of land to neighborhood cash banks;
- Divided possessions;
- The need for money while managing venders;
- Lands which have been allowed to SC/ST by the government;
- Land roof regulations;
- Extreme resettlement and restoration regulations.

As things stand currently, land securing has turned into a way for many middlemen to rake in serious cash. This is on the grounds that the guidelines and intricacies connected with obtaining land today give colossal exchange to such individuals. In the event that the government becomes involved in the cycle, agents can be killed, lessening the expense of the exchange and passing the advantage to the genuine land proprietors.

Until that occurs, the accessibility of idiot-proof arrangements concerning land will remain scant on the ground. In case it wasn't already obvious, a decent arrangement is one where one can purchase, in one go, a spotless title property that conforms to all government designs and specified utilizations.

13.2.2 Measures which Should be Taken to Avoid Bad Land Deals

- Involve experienced legal advisors for the exchange;
- Perform a definite and expected level of effort;
- Utilize the administration of an established land expert with top to bottom market information.

The goal of purchasing land for improvement ought to get a spotless, secure title and have the option to develop the plot without having to confront any future difficulties at the improvement stage, and inside a specified time.

13.2.3 Types of Blockchain Technology for Land Registration

From the literature, the suggested types of blockchains are those that are usually employed for land enlistment in the location described in this sector. On the hidden blockchain, there's no complete open and regulated network that is a state machine generated by crypto-monetary science (e.g., verification of work, proof of stake). In a very private blockchain, there's one or a constrained assortment of performers that approve the hashes that are to be maintained inside the blockchain, applying computeriszd markers.

It's feasible to shape a framework with extra firmly controlled admittance consents, and change privileges and authorization to peruse (certain components).

One of the biggest benefits of a private blockchain is the chance to modify the standards of the blockchain and swap deals. In the case of a public blockchain, there are no constraints on who will participate and obtain the data; however, transactions are substantial merely via a constrained arrangement of hubs designated by the host.

There's additionally the opportunity to frame cross-chain trade layers among public and private blockchains. By utilizing these blends, very surprising types of cross-breed mixes are frequently completed and extra accommodating.

The attributes of a crossover blockchain innovation are suited to the land enrollment plan area unit stated below.

13.2.4 Hybrid Blockchains

The applicability of a land registration approach when using a crossover blockchain for the Land Register, a constrained assortment of substances or persons, is a component of the blockchain.

Authorized conveyancers or notaries can work with approved registrars in a true land register blockchain. When the mining is finished, the deal is done. Within the confidential land register blockchain the assessment of dispersed trust might be confounded, since the blockchain isn't open to everybody.

A crossover form of a blockchain enables trade to be private, though there are certain hubs in an incredibly open chain like the Bitcoin organization (e.g., hashes of key reports are stored on a public chain) [30]. Except for that, the diggers (notaries and recognized conveyancers) may sort a specific set, thus having circumspection over the standards that verify transaction validity.

In such a circumstance, all members need to carry out and implement the new guidelines in exactly the same manner. Once the current land register framework gets supplanted by a mixture of blockchains utilized by the current partners inside the chain of resources, there can be an errand for each of the notaries and registrars, bailiffs, or potentially various others.

The job of these partners needs to be considered. Figure 13.2 shows all the partners involved in the land enrollment technique. This suggests that (authorized) conveyancers should check the ID of the people concerned and furnish them with an electronic character by which they can proceed in the deal (a deed of transport or a seizure, a move of possession).

13.2.5 Case Study: Gujarat Land Registration

In India, this work has been initiated within states like Gujarat and Andhra Pradesh. These models are studied well and thought of as a base for the projected work. The main points of the method are on the official website of the Government Revenue Department of Gujarat (Computerization of Land Records and E-Dhara; https://revenuedepartment.gujarat.gov.in/computerization-of-land-records).

In Gujarat, a complete framework consisting of (1) the supply of an automated Record of Right (RoR) from a dedicated counter in a Taluka work environment and (2) receiving a transformation

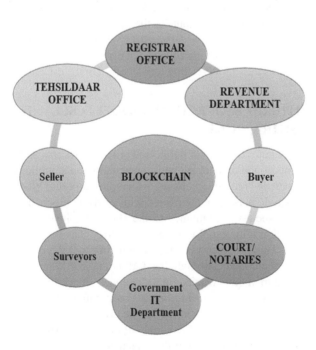

FIGURE 13.2 Stakeholders in the land registration process.

application and cycling it in online mode was visualized *in situ* instantly. The important aspect of providing a mechanized RoR, in view of the fact that the sole authentic record was great, was to stop all manual records. A preparatory activity of free duplicate dispersal for the general population check prior to stopping physically keeping up with land records at town level was taken up. The e-Dhara Land Records Management System was developed to deal with all land records via the use of IT. The illustrated framework was meant to enable the quick issuance of automated RoR over the counter and via online updating of land records.

The work was carried out initially within a controlled design, at Junagadh locality on a pilot basis. At that pilot area, Vanthali Taluka was picked as the pilot taluka, so that a location-wide carry-out of e-Dhara was done. The framework not only enhances the technique for record archiving but also delivers a few assurance advantages.

RoR reports demonstrate the essential concerns of review assortment, land ownership, the kind of land, water system methodology, crop subtleties, and so on. This report is used by ranchers for land swaps (changes), collecting crop credits, negotiating concessions connected to the components of the land holding, and so on. Income organizations contain and maintain all the data required to offer RoR.

The applicant submits their application at the e-Dhara Centre. Then records are evaluated first. The administrator inputs vital details in the PC from the program and generates two duplicates of the acknowledgment receipt. Someone receives a duplicate receipt. E-Dhara Dy Mamlatdar examines the application details, supporting records, and basic subtleties entered by the operator within the framework and validates them biometrically. The framework provides an amazing transformational assortment. Frameworks create change notices. Administrators generate views from the framework and store them with the mutation case document. Talati collects the transformation paperwork from the e-Dhara Centre. Talati follows the transformation technique, obtains affirmations from the party, and watches for 30 days. The document is changed when the skilled power's endorsement is sent to the e-Dhara Centre for the next procedure. A similar competent authority supports this print of the S-structure. This is, in many situations, the specific component of the e-Dhara framework. Checking of the working environment requires a duplicate of the notice carrying the markings of all the khatedars and the S-structure transformation request, which are needed before the biometrically identifiable evidence for altering the area records. One duplicate printout for the town record of each and every updated land record (8A, 7/12), and automated change, is delivered to Talati. In towns, previous land records are superseded by refreshed ones. Past records are solid and in distinct documents. The plan-accomplished transformation document turns into a long-lasting record stored in the e-Dhara record room.

13.3 PROPOSED HYBRID BLOCKCHAIN MODEL FOR LAND REGISTRY IN MAHARASHTRA, PUNE

A hybrid blockchain consolidates features of public and private blockchains: an application or office is enabled on a short permissioned blockchain while speculation on a public blockchain is for security and settlement. With cross-breed blockchains, we employ a public blockchain to produce the record available for each single person on the planet, with a private blockchain operating within the foundation which enables executive admittance to the alterations inside the record. Gujarat state has integrated land registration utilizing blockchain technology. The first test is allocated inside the district of Vanthali Taluka. This procedure is entirely done through the e-Dhara site of the Gujarat Government using an RoR technique. The state has further enforced land registration using block-chain technology. Complete method is carried on official web site (http://registration.ap.gov.in/) of state Government. Currently Maharashtra additionally coming up with for making one-stop site for land registration. I has been announced that initial it'll be given for big town. The one-stop site also will help the management keep the spies off from the all method. A person will check all information connected to property [32]. Considering of these factors, a plan has been proposed for the train towns in Maharashtra. The model is given here within the style of can in Figure 13.3.

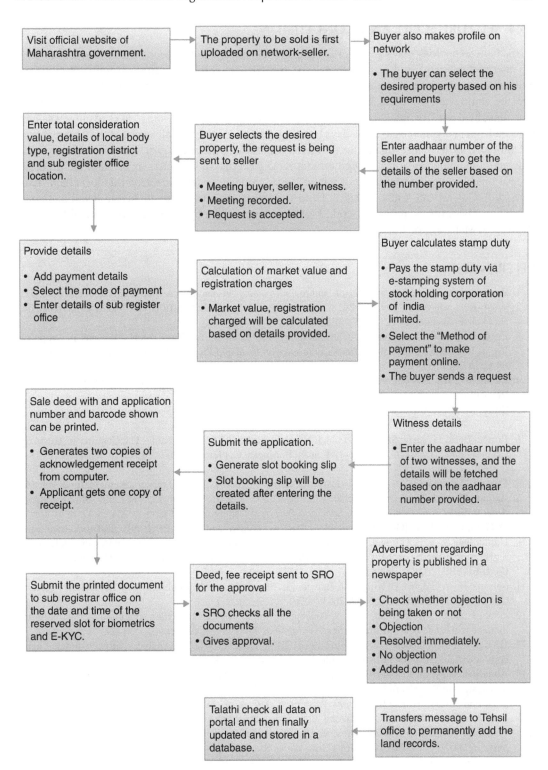

FIGURE 13.3 Proposed model.

13.4 FUTURE SCOPE AND CONCLUSION

Blockchain technology plays an important role in the land registration process because it eliminates the intermediaries involved in the process and provides numerous security and immutability features. The fact that a blockchain can't be changed and can't be hacked is making governments all over the world want to use blockchain decisions in the land registry process. In addition to taking a long time, land registry fraud is common in India. The total amount of time it takes to close a sale is reduced from many months to a few days by using digital signatures at all stages of the land registry. Additionally, we have investigated the problems with the current land registration procedure in India following the implementation of Digital India Land Records, stakeholders involved in the process, and various blockchain technologies for land registration before selecting a hybrid blockchain. Two case-study Gujarat and Andhra Pradesh Land Registration models were studied in detail and considered as a base for the proposed work. Finally we proposed a hybrid blockchain model for Land Registry in Maharashtra, Pune.

REFERENCES

1. Zevenbergen, Jaap. 2002. Systems of land registration aspects and effects. *Publications on Geodesy*, 51.
2. Wüst, Karl, and Arthur Gervais. 2018. Do you need a Blockchain?. 2018 Crypto Valley Conference on Blockchain Technology (CVCBT). IEEE.
3. Dobhal, A., and M. Regan. 2016. Immutability and Auditability: The Critical Elements in Property Rights Registries. *Annual World Bank Conference on Land and Property. Annual World Bank Conference on Land and Property*.
4. Ratan, N. 2018. *Blockchain: The next innovation to make our cities smarter*. India: Price Water Cooper Pvt. Ltd.
5. Swan, M. 2017. Anticipating the economic benefits of blockchain. *Technology Innovation Management Review*, 7(10) October 2017.
6. Roman Beck, IT, Jacob Stenum Czepluch Nikolaj Lollike. 2016. Blockchain – The Gateway to Trustfree Cryptographic Transactions, Twenty-Fourth European Conference on Information Systems (ECIS), İstanbul, Turkey.
7. Chavez-Dreyfuss, G. 2016. Sweden tests blockchain technology for land registry, Reuters, June, vol. 16.
8. Anand, M. McKibbin, and F. Pichel. Colored Coins: Bitcoin, Blockchain, and Land Administration. *Annual World Bank Conference on Land and Poverty*, Washington DC, March 20–24, 2017.
9. D. Govt. Dubai land. [Online]. Available: https://www.dubailand.gov.ae/English/Pages/Blockchain.aspx
10. Humdullah, S., S. H. Othman, M. N. Razali, and H. K. Mammi. Secured data storage framework for land registration using blockchain technology. *2021 3rd International Cyber Resilience Conference (CRC)*, pp. 1–6, IEEE, 2021.
11. Sharma, R., Y. Galphat, E. Kithani, J. Tanwani, B. Mangnani, and N. Achhra. Digital land registry system using blockchain, SSRN 3866088, 2021.
12. Ullah, F., and F. Al-Turjman. 2021. A conceptual framework for blockchain smart contract adoption to manage real estate deals in smart cities. *Neural Computing and Applications*, 35, 1–22.
13. UAE government launches blockchain strategy 2021 — cointelegraph, Available at: https://cointelegraph.com/news/uae-government-launches-blockchain-strategy-2021
14. Abdullah, M., Walter Timo De Vries, and Zahir Ali 2020. Assessing the performance of land administration system in Punjab after land records computerization. *Conference: 2020 World Bank Conference on Land and Poverty At: The World Bank-Washington DC*, pp. 1–24, Washington.
15. San, Kiu Mee, Chia Fah Choy, Wong Phui Fung. 2019. *The Potentials and Impacts of Blockchain Technology in the Construction Industry: A Literature Review. IOP Conference Series: Materials Science and Engineering, Volume 495, 11th Curtin University Technology, Science and Engineering (CUTSE) International Conference 26–28 November 2018*, Sarawak, Malaysia
16. Ramage, M. "From BIM and Blockchain In Construction: What You Need To Know," *Trimble Inc.*, 2018. [Online]. Available: https://constructible.trimble.com/construction-industry/frombim-to-blockchain-in-construction-what-you-need-to-know. [Accessed: 30-Jul-2018].

17. Swam, M. 2015. *Blockchain blueprint for a new economy*, First Edition. United States of America: O'Reilly Media.
18. Aste, T., P. Tasca, and T. Di Matteo. 2015. "Blockchain Technologies: The Foreseeable Impact on Society and Industry," *IEEE Computer Society*, 50(9), pp. 18–28.
19. Wang, J., P. Wu, X. Wang, and W. Shou. 2017. "The outlook of blockchain technology for construction engineering management," *Frontiers of Engineering Management*, 4(1), pp. 67–75.
20. Abeyratne, S. A. and R. P. Monfared. 2016. "Blockchain ready manufacturing supply chain using distributed ledger," *International Journal of Research in Engineering and Technology*, 5(9), pp. 1–10.
21. Taylor, D. 2017. *Construction And Blockchain: How Can It Help the Industry? Published In Capterra Construction Management Blog.* http://Blog.Capterra.Com/Construction-And-Blockchain-How-Can-Ithelp-The-Industry/
22. Bocek, T., B. B. Rodrigues, T. Strasser and B. Stiller, *Blockchains everywhere: A use-case of blockchains in the pharma supply-chain*, IFIP/IEEE Symposium on Integrated Network and Service Management (IM), Lisbon, Portugal, 2017, pp. 772–777, doi: 10.23919/INM.2017.7987376
23. www.cybrosys.com, Blockchain EBook, Cybrosys Limited Edition, www.blockchainexpert.uk 7
24. Mark gates 2017. Blockchain: Ultimate guide to understanding blockchain, bitcoin, cryptocurrencies, smart contracts and the future of money.
25. Larimer, D. 2014. "Delegated proof-of-stake (dpos)," Bitshare whitepaper.
26. Cachin, C. 2016. "Architecture of the hyperledger blockchain fabric," *Journal of Computer and Communications*, 8(4), April 24, 2020.
27. Zheng, K., Y. Liu, C. Dai, Y. Duan, and X. Huang. 2018. "Model checking pbft consensus mechanism in healthcare blockchain network," in *2018 9th International Conference on Information Technology in Medicine and Education (ITME)*. IEEE, 2018, pp. 877–881.
28. Telia Company. 2016. The Land Registry in the blockchain A development project with Lantmäteriet (The Swedish Mapping, cadastre and land registration authority).
29. Ølnes, S., Ubacht, J., & Janssen, M. (2017). "Blockchain in government: Benefits and implications of distributed ledger technology for information sharing." *Government Information Quarterly* 34(3), pp. 355–364. https://doi.org/10.1016/j.giq.2017.09.007
30. Graglia, J. M., and C. Mellon 2018. "Blockchain and Property in 2018: At the End of the Beginning," *Innovations: Technology, Governance, Globalization* 12(1–2), pp. 90–116.
31. Benbunan-Fich, R., and Castellanos, A. Digitization of Land Records: From Paper to Blockchain, Thirty-Ninth International Conference on Information Systems, San Francisco, 2018.
32. TOI, Nisha Nambiar. 2020. Maharashtra: One-stop portal proposal to integrate property dealings, https://timesofindia.indiatimes.com/city/pune/one-stop-portal-proposal-to-integrate-property-dealings/articleshow/74232746.cms

14 A Review of Sentiment Analysis Applications and Challenges

Ulligaddala Srinivasarao and R. Karthikeyan
Vardhaman College of Engineering Hyderabad, Raipur, India

Aakanksha Sharaff and K. Jairam Naik
National Institute of Technology Raipur, Raipur, India

CONTENTS

14.1   INTRODUCTION

Many corporations, government agencies, and non-profit organizations use sentiment analysis daily. As a result of its increasing popularity, the internet has risen to the status of primary source of global knowledge. Many people utilize numerous internet sites to convey their thoughts and ideas and employ user-generated data to monitor public opinion in real time, which may then be used for decision-making purposes. Due to this, sentiment analysis has been more prevalent recently in academic settings. Sentiment analysis is a subset of this, often referred to as "opinion analysis" or "opinion mining" (Sánchez-Rada and Iglesias, 2019). Our team has recently noticed a rise in sentiment analysis usage. Opinion mining has already been detailed in numerous sentiment analysis studies (Ligthart et al., 2021). Piryani et al. (2017) studied data from 2000 to 2015 with the primary purpose of extracting viewpoints and determining emotions. Some recent surveys (Yousif et al., 2019; Birjali et al., 2021) have discussed the issue of sentiment analysis and proposed various possibilities. For sentiment classification, decision-making, and the identification of phone reviews and suggestions, Jain et al. (2021) discuss machine learning methods that use internet reviews. Many studies on assessing social media have used cutting-edge machine-learning techniques (Balaji et al., 2021).

It is necessary to thoroughly investigate several real-world applications, such as analyzing a product's components or attributes, to determine which ones are most appealing to buyers. The findings of a current literature review on opinion mining are presented in the work of Zhao et al. (2021). Additionally, this covers how to convey information in opinions, categorize them, and extract textual characteristics from views with noise or ambiguity. Mowlaei et al. (2020) suggested adaptive aspect-based lexicons for sentiment categorization. The authors outlined an algorithmic and a statistical approach for creating two dynamic lexicons for categorizing attitudes according to their features. A unique vocabulary might be naturally refreshed and give a more definite evaluation of thoughts connected to the setting (Naresh Kumar and Uma, 2021). They used different lexicons from different dictionaries to structure the various studies. This has been employed in multiple industries in the past, including hotels, airlines, hospitals, and the stock market (Zvarevashe and Olugbara, 2018). Hotel ratings have utilized sentiment analysis to understand client preferences and dislikes better. It has also been used to predict the stock market's direction and the value of cryptocurrencies. Valencia et al. (2019). For example, consumer opinion surveys (Ruffer et al., 2020; Cortis and Davis, 2021) and studies of customer satisfaction (Baashar et al., 2020; Miotto et al., 2018) are becoming more popular in the healthcare industry. Sentiment analysis has long been used in business to help it grow and succeed more efficiently.

The reader is introduced to the concept of sentiment analysis in this chapter, which outlines the various problems researchers encounter while performing aspect-level sentiment classification and some of the most recent solutions. The chapter will provide an in-depth look at these techniques, which have been used, modified, and expanded by researchers in recent years to handle sentiment analysis. The major subjects in a group of unstructured texts can be found using topic models, which are probabilistic approaches. In this chapter, which focuses on broader applications, new techniques for sentiment analysis are reviewed and explained.

14.2   SENTIMENT ANALYSIS: AN OVERVIEW

Feature, phrase, and document studies have been done on sentiment analysis levels, including aspect, sentence, and document (Figure 14.1).

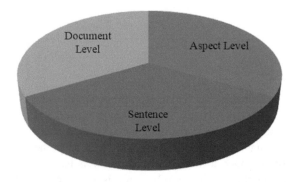

FIGURE 14.1   Level of sentiment analysis.

14.2.1 LEVEL OF ASPECT

Sentiment analysis is conducted at the aspect level. Sentences may have numerous sides. Hence phrase-level sentiment analysis is required. Primary attention is given to all of the sentence's components, and polarity is assigned to each one, resulting in an overall sentiment calculation (Schouten and Frasincar, 2015). Wang et al. (2019) and Yang and Cardie (2014) introduce the concept of aspect-level sentiment capsules (AS-capsules). This model uses the association between specific characteristics and the related feelings that go along with them.

14.2.2 LEVEL OF SENTENCE

Each phrase is assessed at this level of analysis and confirmed to have the same polarity. While useful when working with materials that cover a wide range of emotions, this could also be misused. We'll use the same techniques for documents for each sentence but with additional training data and processing power. To influence the tone of a document, corrections can be concatenated or used alone. Sentiment analysis at the document level can be sufficient in some cases (Behdenna et al., 2018). Previous efforts at sentence-level research aimed at identifying subjective claims.

14.2.3 LEVEL OF DOCUMENT

The entire document is subjected to sentiment analysis at the document level, and just one polarity is given to it. Using this technique, it is possible to categorize different book parts as positive, harmful, or neutral. Using supervised and unsupervised techniques, the document can be classified at this level (Bhatia, Ji, and Eisenstein, 2015). Two of the most significant challenges in document-level sentiment analysis are cross-domain sentiment analysis. This position is well-known as "document-level sentiment categorization". According to this level of analysis, each document expresses a viewpoint about a specific individual or organization (e.g., a single product). Accordingly, it can't be utilized for reports that evaluate or analyze various substances.

14.3 CHALLENGES

Several significant issues with sentiment analysis, commonly known as "opinion mining", show why AI systems sentiment analysis opinion mining needs to be fuzzy.

14.3.1 UNSTRUCTURED DATA

Plain-text reviews of each item by contributors are the text input. Writing semi-structured data from unstructured input data like written reviews takes a lot of work. Semi-organized information has labels or different markers to recognize semantic pieces. However, this is neither crude information nor conforms to the conventional design of information models related to social datasets or other kinds of information.

14.3.2 ASPECT IDENTIFICATION

In previous research, sophisticated approaches to aspect-level SAOM have focused on identifying aspects and pinpointing sentiments. Determining which features the object contributors have strong feelings about is the purpose of the aspect identification step in the analysis process. The literature dealing with aspect identification is divided into two categories:

- Automated extraction: The reviews automatically generate the aspects; no prior knowledge is necessary (Farhadloo and Rolland, 2013; Zang and Wan, 2017).

- (Semi-) manual extraction: Subcategories in this area may be classified as supervised or unsupervised. A subset or the entire set of desired traits is known a priori. When they are known ahead of time, specific subsets are used as seeds and grown differently (Areed et al., 2020).

14.3.3 Sentiment Identification

The method of determining the text based analysis is known as sentiment identification. There are many ways to communicate one's emotional state. Rating scales are commonly used online to indicate customer views on items. Several websites, such as TripAdvisor, flipchart, and Epinions, use the five-star overall rating system. Rotten Tomatoes has a five-star rating system, whereas IMDb has a 1–10 rating system for movies.

In SAOM, coping with unpleasant feelings is very tough. According to Tolstoy, every person in a miserable family in Anna Karenina is unhappy, just as all joyful families have members with similar emotions. In SAOM, the same can be stated for both positive and negative feelings. To be polite (even on the internet), some individuals opt to qualify their comments, but generally people are more inventive when describing what they don't like about a product. All of these factors hamper the automatic resolution of the issue. Rather than relying on hand-crafted solutions, automated approaches use machine learning algorithms to detect patterns in data and learn from practice instances. How difficult would it be to extract patterns if there needed to be more working-out instances or if the working-out examples were restricted in diversity?

14.3.3.1 Sentiment Recognition Using Supervised Methods

There are several ways to think about sentiment categorization. Various categorization algorithms from machine learning have been used in the SAOM literature, for instance to detect attitudes used or to detect moods. One such has been designed by Zhao et al. (2022) to classify sentiments based on aspects of personality. It is possible to conduct research using aspect-based sentiment analysis, as discussed by Trisna and Jie (2022). A novel method proposed in a paper by Gaye has changed sentiment analysis on Twitter (Gaye et al., 2021) that integrates the advantages of a lexical dictionary and machine learning models. Al Amrani et al. (2018) employed a hybrid technique that used both SVM and Random Forest for sentiment classification to detect Amazon product reviews. The researchers found that classifier model accuracy was improved using a mixed method rather than distinct algorithms. For their excellent classification capacity, Vinodhini and Chandrasekaran (2016) utilized back propagation and probabilistic neural networks. The authors of "A Hierarchical Neural-Network-Based Document Representation Approach for Text Classification" (Zheng et al., 2018) incorporated progressive brain design into traditional brain network approaches, showing that their suggestions outperformed the corresponding brain network models for record order. Most of the researchers working on neural networks and reinforcement learning methods have techniques that are working effectively (Naik et al., 2021). According to Sharaff and Srinivasarao (2020), naive Bayes using binary characteristics appeared to perform better in various text categorization tests.

14.3.3.2 Sentiment Recognition Using Unsupervised Methods

After extracting the dogmatic fragment, its sentiment orientation should be detected in the subsequent stage. As a result of utilizing probabilistic latent semantic analysis text clustering, Srinivasarao and Sharaff (2022) extracted information for various uses, such as finding common emotions in email threads and recognizing the sequence of characteristics in the emails. For example, Srinivasarao and Sharaff (2021) developed sentiment clustering using email patterns, and their proposed method has achieved 97% accuracy, which is greater than other current methodologies. It was shown that the exact number of Twitter sentiment groups might be used by combining the k-means algorithm with the density-based clustering method (Rehioui and Idrissi, 2019).

14.3.3.3 Lexical Analysis for Sentiment Recognition

Opinion lexicons have been employed by much research in the literature to determine the sentimental tenor of the relevant portion. Dictionary-based procedures track down the feeling direction of a stubborn expression of interest by scanning their current vocabulary for the expression. The dictionary age process ordinarily starts with a seed rundown of assessment words whose assessment directions are known ahead of time. Afterward, different techniques are used to extend the seed list and add additional opinion words. Dictionary-based and corpus-based procedures are the most common ways to increase the original seed list of opinion terms. Dictionary-based methods rely on online dictionaries like WordNet (Andreevskaia and Bergler, 2006; Aung and Myo, 2017) and extra information (such as their glosses) to enlarge the original seed set. Better lists may be generated using these methods, which use word connections like synonyms and antonyms and some machine learning. The vocabulary created from online dictionaries is an opinion lexicon devoid of context. Corpus-based approaches have developed a domain-specific language that captures the opinion words in a specific domain. This approach uses specific syntactic criteria and co-event designs to supplement the initial seed breakdown of assessment words (Srinivasarao and Sharaff, 2021; Esuli and Sebastiani, 2006). The seed set develops rules for employing and associating concepts like And, Or, But, Neither-Or, and Neither-Nor. It is feasible to produce domain-specific lexicons using a specific corpus of interest.

14.3.4 Topic Model-Based Approaches

What are point models? They are probabilistic methodologies given by variously leveled Bayesian organizations for identifying the significant points in a massive assortment of unstructured materials. The issue of SAOM is often addressed in two stages: first, by identifying aspects and then by identifying sentiments (Mowlaei, 2020; Pla and Hurtado, 2014). One of the benefits of topic modeling approaches is that they can detect both aspects and feelings concurrently. These algorithms can identify the themes from text analysis alone without labeled training data.

Comparisons with classic Latent Dirichlet Allocation (LDA) were made to examine how well customary LDA performed on angle extraction without change for short texts by Ozyurt and Akcayol (2021). Joint viewpoint-based feeling points (JABST) were created by Tang et al. (2019) to extricate multi-grained viewpoints and suppositions simultaneously by displaying angles, conclusions, and feeling extremities and granularities simultaneously. Latent dirichlet allocation (LDA) was introduced to find succinct portrayals of the individuals in an assortment. Characterization, curiosity recognition, outline, and decisions of closeness and pertinence are all made more accessible by LDA's ability to analyze big datasets quickly while maintaining significant statistical associations (Schweighofer, 2022). Using LDA, it is assumed that a combination of themes created each document. As a result, to construct a document, it is essential to distinguish the fraction of each subject represented in that document and the topic to which each document's words belong. Hasan, 2021) is an abbreviation for LDA generation process. Table 14.1 shows different abbreviations in detail.

14.4 APPLICATIONS OF SENTIMENT ANALYSIS

Among the various uses for sentiment analysis are gauging client satisfaction and monitoring patient well-being through social media. Technology breakthroughs like the cloud, big data, blockchain, and the IoT have further increased its applicability, enabling sentiment research in virtually every industry. Figure 14.2 shows some of the most commonly used sentiment analysis applications. Sentiment analysis is used in a variety of sectors and disciplines, including:

TABLE 14.1

Various Descriptions of Abbreviations

Abbreviation	Description of Abbreviation
ABSA	Aspect Based Sentiment Analysis
AGCN	Aggregated Graph Convolutional Network
AHICM	Adaptive Hybridized Intelligent Computational Model
CNN-LSTM	Convolutional Neural Network Long Short-Term Memory
JABST	Joint Aspect Based Sentiment Topic
LDA	Latent Dirichlet Allocation
MLA	Machine Learning Algorithms
NLP	Natural Language Processing
PLSA	Probabilistic Latent Semantic Analysis
SAOM	Sentiment Analysis, or Opinion Mining
SVM	Support Vector Machine

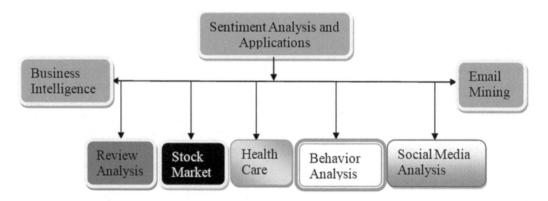

FIGURE 14.2 Applications of sentiment analysis.

14.4.1 BUSINESS INTELLIGENCE

The discipline of business intelligence reaps various benefits from using sentiment analysis. In addition, companies may use sentiment analysis data to enhance their goods, study customer comments, and design a new marketing plan. Customer sentiment analysis is the greatest mutual usage of sentiment analysis in the business intelligence area. Product manufacturers may utilize these studies, but customers may also use them to assess products and make better-educated selections. In corporate intelligence, sentiment analysis offers several advantages. Many businesses may benefit from its findings by using the data to improve their products or analyze the opinions of their customers (Zhao et al., 2021). Customer impressions of goods and services are often the focus of sentiment analysis in business intelligence. As a result, customers may utilize these studies to compare products and make better-informed decisions. Service meal reviews on amazon.com have been posted over the last eight years (Bose et al., 2020). There are eight distinct emotions in the Emotion Lexicon and two moods (positive and negative). Sentiment analysis may be used to detect consumer behavior and potential dangers and improve customer happiness.

14.4.2 REVIEW ANALYSIS

Sentiment analysis of hotel and restaurant reviews may assist consumers in making better decisions and also enable the establishments themselves to grow and develop. The feature that obtains more favorable or unfavorable assessments, according to sentiment analysis of hotels and restaurants, may be identified so that proprietors can focus their efforts on improving this component. In the words of Sann and Lai, this is one of the most enticing sectors, as determined by sentiment research (Sann and Lai, 2020). When consumers read evaluations of hotels and restaurants, they can make better decisions for themselves and the businesses themselves (Zhao et al., 2017). Hotels and restaurants may benefit from aspect based sentiment analysis (ABSA) (Akhtar et al., 2017), which analyses online reviews to determine which aspects have received the most favorable and unfavorable feedback. Service providers stand to gain the most by taking the element that generates the most negative feedback and making improvements.

14.4.3 THE STOCK MARKET

Stock price forecasting may be done using sentiment analysis. This can be carried out by analyzing all stock market news and foreseeing stock price trends (Correia et al., 2022). Information can be obtained from various sources, including blogs, Twitter, and news articles. The overall polarity of news articles regarding a certain company can be determined using sentence-level sentiment analysis. Xing et al. (2018) employed this technique to determine whether the trend would rise or fall.

In contrast to negative news, which was more likely to result in a downward trend, positive news was more likely to do so. Bitcoin and other digital cryptocurrencies are based on blockchain technology. Participants in a blockchain validate digital transactions using peer-to-peer consensus techniques. Sentiment analysis is still a rare research subject in the context of blockchain technology. Still, when it is, it has been applied to forecast the value of digital cryptocurrencies, as in Kraaijeveld and De Smedt (2020).

14.4.4 HEALTHCARE

Sentiment analysis is now being used in this field, as in many others. Studies, Twitter (Carvalho and Plastino, 2021), blogs, stories in the news, and reviews are just a few examples of the many places researchers might get data. A formal review and analysis of new medical updates are possible applications of this data, which may be studied for different uses. Experts in the field are always looking for new ways to incorporate sentiment analysis and other natural language processing applications in their work (Ebadi et al., 2021). Apps like this allow healthcare practitioners to gather and analyze data about patients' feelings and illnesses to enhance their services. Jiménez-Zafra et al. (2019) found that using sentiment analysis was hard because the language used in healthcare is different and unique.

14.4.5 BEHAVIOR ANALYSIS

Many people use Facebook to freely express their opinions on a wide range of subjects, as Abutiheen et al. (2022) have shown. We can learn more about the way people process and interpret textual information by looking at studies like that done by Chen et al. (2022). For example, Mahmoudi (2021) used a behavior-based method to improve sentiment analysis by detecting biased participants on online social networks.

14.4.6 SOCIAL MEDIA ANALYSIS

Using social data sentiment analysis, a company can monitor customer sentiment around the clock, seven days a week. This allows the company to respond quickly to negative publicity and boost its

TABLE 14.2
Most Popular Applications of Sentiment Analysis

References	Applications	Method	Dataset	Result
Zhao et al. (2021)	Consumer product	AHICM	Online reviews (e-commerce)	Accuracy ratio = 90%
Akhtar et al. (2017)	Hotel reviews	LDA	Crawl customer reviews	Sentiment (positive, negative)
Correia et al. (2022)	Stock market	CNN-LSTM	Stock dataset	Accuracy = 53%
Ebadi et al. (2021)	Healthcare	MLA	Coronavirus disease 2019	Topics-wise analysis
Chen et al. (57)	Behavior analysis	SVM	Chinese microblog	Accuracy of (3-class) = 42%
Abutiheen et al. (2022)	Social media analysis	SVM	Facebook	Accuracy = 85%
Srinivasarao and Sharaff (2022)	Email mining	PLSA	Enron (email dataset)	Accuracy = 89%

public image. For the decision-making process, this also provides constant, trustworthy information about customers that can be tracked over time. People often say what they think about products, services, and businesses in their social media posts since they don't have to be asked.

14.4.7 EMAIL MINING

People have to communicate their sentiments to the rest of humanity. Unlike such analyses based on publicly available information, we have found that intimate conversations often convey the true feelings of individuals. Sending heartfelt notes like "I'm very happy for you" or "I'm sorry for your loss" by email is a common way to express feelings about significant events in one's life, such as getting engaged or having a baby. Thus, sentiment analysis of personal email archives is a viable avenue to investigate. Email sentiment pattern detection using a trajectory representation is a new approach to solving sentiment analysis tasks introduced by Liu and Lee (2018). The most common uses of sentiment analysis are listed in Table 14.2.

14.5 PERFORMANCE EVALUATION PARAMETERS

Modern sentiment analysis relies heavily on accuracy, F1-scores, and precision metrics. Recall and accuracy are used as performance criteria in the study of sentiment analysis using deep learning architectures.

The metrics include the following:
The number of reviews that have been appropriately classified as "good".

True Negative (TN): The percentage of negative evaluations.
FP: The percentage of correct forecasts.
False Negative (FN): The number of false negative reviews.

Accuracy is the most frequently cited criterion to measure performance among all categorization exercises. The model's accuracy is measured by the percentage of correct forecasts. Using a balanced dataset, accuracy is an appropriate statistic for sentiment categorization.

$$\text{Accuracy} = \frac{\text{Number of Correct Predictions}}{\text{Total Number of Predictions}} \qquad (14.1)$$

"Perfection" is defined as the percentage of positive samples accurately identified compared to the total number of anticipated positive samples. This statistic can help you determine your confidence in your forecast. If a model has 100% accuracy, all pieces assessed as positive may be considered certain.

$$\text{Precision} = \frac{\text{True Positive}}{\text{True Positive} + \text{False Positive}} \qquad (14.2)$$

Sensitivity: Recall is also known as the ability to remember. Percentage of Positive Instances Compared to Total Positive Instances in the Classification This metric tracks the model's misclassification rate. When it comes to accuracy and recall, the two are directly correlated. This means that increasing precision also with increasing recall is possible. Most of the time, a recall should be used when a class is being captured.

$$\text{Recall} = \frac{\text{True Positive}}{\text{True Positive} + \text{False Negative}} \qquad (14.3)$$

A person's F1-score is calculated by averaging their Recall and Precision scores. After accuracy, this is the most often used metric – a compromise solution to the impasse between precision and recall. The F1-score manages recall and accuracy.

$$\text{F1 Score} = 2 * \frac{\text{Precision} * \text{Recall}}{\text{Precision} + \text{Recall}} \qquad (14.4)$$

14.6 CONCLUSIONS

Computational intelligence techniques, which are crucial to sentiment analysis, can be used to gather information about customers' perceptions of goods and services. There has been a lot of progress on this subject, but much work still needs to be done. Since the beginning of this work, most of our efforts have gone toward figuring out how to decode written text semantics. Despite this, previous research has been able to offer methodologies that identify attitudes, views, and attributes and that these correlate quite well with customer satisfaction levels. How far the probabilistic computational intelligence methodologies can be generalized to other contexts or domains is still being determined. Because of this, there are several possibilities for future study, which significantly impact how businesses perceive and assess their consumers and the goods and services themselves.

14.7 FURTHER RESEARCH

Despite the advancements in sentiment and aspect identification studies, context-specific information is still needed to be included in the analysis. Another option is to provide additional details about the reviewer since this information is typically accessible (many frameworks contain possibly valuable commentator data). Similarly, one could incorporate detailed area data (retagging) to improve the comprehension of feelings and conclusions, as well as quantitative or subjective data associated with non-literary media (such as pictures or recordings) to improve the scientific abilities of opinion investigation. Moreover, sentiment analysis's dynamic component requires more attention in the future. The way we feel and think, as well as the way we use technology, all change over time. We emphasize that the computing efforts involved with sentiment analysis must be efficient enough to handle big datasets dynamically. Lastly, improving our knowledge of information quality will be critical to the success of sentiment analysis, such as the one described here. If you throw trash in, you might get garbage out. There are many new ways to study information quality in the future, some of which may have much to do with sentiment analysis.

CONFLICT OF INTEREST

The authors declare no potential conflict of interest.

REFERENCES

Abutiheen, Z. A., Mohammed, E. A., & Hussein, M. H. (2022). Behavior analysis in Arabic social media. *International Journal of Speech Technology*, 25, 1–8.

Akhtar, N., Zubair, N., Kumar, A., & Ahmad, T. (2017). Aspect based sentiment oriented summarization of hotel reviews. *Procedia Computer Science*, *115*, 563–571.

Al Amrani, Y., Lazaar, M., & El Kadiri, K. E. (2018). A novel hybrid classification approach for sentiment analysis of text document. *International Journal of Electrical & Computer Engineering (2088-8708)*, 8(6).

Andreevskaia, A., & Bergler, S. (2006, April). Mining wordnet for a fuzzy sentiment: Sentiment tag extraction from wordnet glosses. In *11th Conference of the European Chapter of the Association for Computational Linguistics* (pp. 209–216).

Areed, S., Alqaryouti, O., Siyam, B., & Shaalan, K. (2020). Aspect-based sentiment analysis for Arabic government reviews. In *Recent Advances in NLP: The Case of Arabic Language* (pp. 143–162). Springer, Cham.

Aung, K. Z., & Myo, N. N. (2017, May). Sentiment analysis of students' comment using lexicon based approach. In *2017 IEEE/ACIS 16th International Conference on Computer and Information Science (ICIS)* (pp. 149–154). IEEE.

Baashar, Y., Alhussian, H., Patel, A., Alkawsi, G., Alzahrani, A. I., Alfarraj, O., & Hayder, G. (2020). Customer relationship management systems (CRMS) in the healthcare environment: A systematic literature review. *Computer Standards & Interfaces*, *71*, 103442.

Balaji, T. K., Annavarapu, C. S. R., & Bablani, A. (2021). Machine learning algorithms for social media analysis: A survey. *Computer Science Review*, *40*, 100395.

Behdenna, S., Barigou, F., & Belalem, G. (2018). Document level sentiment analysis: A survey. *EAI Endorsed Transactions on Context-Aware Systems and Applications*, 4 (13), 154339.

Bhatia, P., Ji, Y., & Eisenstein, J. (2015). Better document-level sentiment analysis from rst discourse parsing. *arXiv preprint arXiv:1509.01599*.

Birjali, M., Kasri, M., & Beni-Hssane, A. (2021). A comprehensive survey on sentiment analysis: Approaches, challenges and trends. *Knowledge-Based Systems*, *226*, 107134.

Bose, R., Dey, R. K., Roy, S., & Sarddar, D. (2020). Sentiment analysis on online product reviews. In *Information and Communication Technology for Sustainable Development* (pp. 559–569). Springer, Singapore.

Carvalho, J., & Plastino, A. (2021). On the evaluation and combination of state-of-the-art features in Twitter sentiment analysis. *Artificial Intelligence Review*, *54*(3), 1887–1936.

Chen, X., Mao, J., Liu, Y., Zhang, M., & Ma, S. (2022). Investigating human reading behavior during sentiment judgment. *International Journal of Machine Learning and Cybernetics*, 1–14.

Correia, F., Madureira, A. M., & Bernardino, J. (2022). Deep neural networks applied to stock market sentiment analysis. *Sensors*, *22*(12), 4409.

Cortis, K., & Davis, B. (2021). Over a decade of social opinion mining: A systematic review. *Artificial Intelligence Review*, *54*(7), 4873–4965.

Ebadi, A., Xi, P., Tremblay, S., Spencer, B., Pall, R., & Wong, A. (2021). Understanding the temporal evolution of COVID-19 research through machine learning and natural language processing. *Scientometrics*, *126*(1), 725–739.

Esuli, A., & Sebastiani, F. (2006, May). Sentiwordnet: A publicly available lexical resource for opinion mining. In *Proceedings of the Fifth International Conference on Language Resources and Evaluation (LREC'06)*.

Farhadloo, M., & Rolland, E. (2013, December). Multi-class sentiment analysis with clustering and score representation. In *2013 IEEE 13th International Conference on Data Mining Workshops* (pp. 904–912). IEEE.

Gaye, B., Zhang, D., & Wulamu, A. (2021). A Tweet sentiment classification approach using a hybrid stacked ensemble technique. *Information*, *12*(9), 374.

Hasan, M., Rahman, A., Karim, M., Khan, M., Islam, S., & Islam, M. (2021). Normalized approach to find optimal number of topics in Latent Dirichlet Allocation (LDA). In *Proceedings of International Conference on Trends in Computational and Cognitive Engineering* (pp. 341–354). Springer, Singapore.

Jain, P. K., Pamula, R., & Srivastava, G. (2021). A systematic literature review on machine learning applications for consumer sentiment analysis using online reviews. *Computer Science Review*, *41*, 100413.

Jiménez-Zafra, S. M., Martín-Valdivia, M. T., Molina-González, M. D., & Ureña-López, L. A. (2019). How do we talk about doctors and drugs? Sentiment analysis in forums expressing opinions for medical domain. *Artificial Intelligence in Medicine*, *93*, 50–57.

Kraaijeveld, O., & De Smedt, J. (2020). The predictive power of public Twitter sentiment for forecasting cryptocurrency prices. *Journal of International Financial Markets, Institutions and Money, 65*, 101188.

Ligthart, A., Catal, C., & Tekinerdogan, B. (2021). Systematic reviews in sentiment analysis: A tertiary study. *Artificial Intelligence Review, 54*(7), 4997–5053.

Liu, S., & Lee, I. (2018). Discovering sentiment sequence within email data through trajectory representation. *Expert Systems with Applications, 99*, 1–11.

Mahmoudi, A. (2021). Identifying biased users in online social networks to enhance the accuracy of sentiment analysis: A user behavior-based approach. *arXiv preprint arXiv:2105.05950.*

Miotto, R., Wang, F., Wang, S., Jiang, X., & Dudley, J. T. (2018). Deep learning for healthcare: Review, opportunities and challenges. *Briefings in Bioinformatics, 19*(6), 1236–1246.

Mowlaei, M. E., Abadeh, M. S., & Keshavarz, H. (2020). Aspect-based sentiment analysis using adaptive aspect-based lexicons. *Expert Systems with Applications, 148*, 113234.

Naik, K. J., Pedagandam, M., & Mishra, A. (2021). Workflow scheduling optimisation for distributed environment using artificial neural networks and reinforcement learning. *International Journal of Computational Science and Engineering, 24*(6), 653–670.

Naresh Kumar, K. E., & Uma, V. (2021). Intelligent sentinet-based lexicon for context-aware sentiment analysis: Optimized neural network for sentiment classification on social media. *The Journal of Supercomputing, 77*(11), 12801–12825.

Ozyurt, B., & Akcayol, M. A. (2021). A new topic modeling based approach for aspect extraction in aspect based sentiment analysis: SS-LDA. *Expert Systems with Applications, 168*, 114231.

Piryani, R., Madhavi, D., & Singh, V. K. (2017). Analytical mapping of opinion mining and sentiment analysis research during 2000–2015. *Information Processing & Management, 53*(1), 122–150.

Pla, F., & Hurtado, L. F. (2014, August). Political tendency identification in twitter using sentiment analysis techniques. In *Proceedings of COLING 2014, the 25th International Conference on Computational Linguistics: Technical Papers* (pp. 183–192).

Rehioui, H., & Idrissi, A. (2019). New clustering algorithms for twitter sentiment analysis. *IEEE Systems Journal, 14*(1), 530–537.

Ruffer, N., Knitza, J., & Krusche, M. (2020). # Covid4Rheum: An analytical twitter study in the time of the COVID-19 pandemic. *Rheumatology International, 40*(12), 2031–2037.

Sánchez-Rada, J. F., & Iglesias, C. A. (2019). Social context in sentiment analysis: Formal definition, overview of current trends and framework for comparison. *Information Fusion, 52*, 344–356.

Sann, R., & Lai, P. C. (2020). Understanding homophily of service failure within the hotel guest cycle: Applying NLP-aspect-based sentiment analysis to the hospitality industry. *International Journal of Hospitality Management, 91*, 102678.

Schouten, K., & Frasincar, F. (2015). Survey on aspect-level sentiment analysis. *IEEE Transactions on Knowledge and Data Engineering, 28*(3), 813–830.

Schweighofer, E. (2022, January). Semantic search and summarization of judgments using topic modeling. In *Legal Knowledge and Information Systems: JURIX 2021: The Thirty-fourth Annual Conference, Vilnius, Lithuania, 8–10 December 2021* (Vol. 346, p. 100). IOS Press.

Sharaff, A., & Srinivasarao, U. (2020, January). Towards classification of email through selection of informative features. In *2020 First International Conference on Power, Control and Computing Technologies (ICPC2T)* (pp. 316–320). IEEE.

Srinivasarao, U., & Sharaff, A. (2021a). Sentiment analysis from email pattern using feature selection algorithm. *Expert Systems*, e12867.

Srinivasarao, U., & Sharaff, A. (2021b). Email sentiment classification using lexicon-based opinion labeling. In *Intelligent Computing and Communication Systems* (pp. 211–218). Springer, Singapore.

Srinivasarao, U., & Sharaff, A. (2022). Email thread sentiment sequence identification using PLSA clustering algorithm. *Expert Systems with Applications, 193*, 116475.

Subhashini, L. D. C. S., Li, Y., Zhang, J., Atukorale, A. S., & Wu, Y. (2021). Mining and classifying customer reviews: A survey. *Artificial Intelligence Review, 54*(8), 6343–6389.

Tang, F., Fu, L., Yao, B., & Xu, W. (2019). Aspect based fine-grained sentiment analysis for online reviews. *Information Sciences, 488*, 190–204.

Trisna, K. W., & Jie, H. J. (2022). Deep learning approach for aspect-based sentiment classification: A comparative review. *Applied Artificial Intelligence, 36*, 1–37.

Valencia, F., Gómez-Espinosa, A., & Valdés-Aguirre, B. (2019). Price movement prediction of cryptocurrencies using sentiment analysis and machine learning. *Entropy, 21*(6), 589.

Vinodhini, G., & Chandrasekaran, R. M. (2016). A comparative performance evaluation of neural network based approach for sentiment classification of online reviews. *Journal of King Saud University-Computer and Information Sciences, 28*(1), 2–12.

Wang, Y., Sun, A., Huang, M., & Zhu, X. (2019, May). Aspect-level sentiment analysis using as-capsules. In *The World Wide Web Conference* (pp. 2033–2044).

Xing, F. Z., Cambria, E., & Welsch, R. E. (2018). Natural language based financial forecasting: A survey. *Artificial Intelligence Review, 50*(1), 49–73.

Yang, B., & Cardie, C. (2014, June). Context-aware learning for sentence-level sentiment analysis with posterior regularization. In *Proceedings of the 52nd Annual Meeting of the Association for Computational Linguistics (Volume 1: Long Papers)* (pp. 325–335).

Yousif, A., Niu, Z., Tarus, J. K., & Ahmad, A. (2019). A survey on sentiment analysis of scientific citations. *Artificial Intelligence Review, 52*(3), 1805–1838.

Zang, H., & Wan, X. (2017, September). Towards automatic generation of product reviews from aspect-sentiment scores. In *Proceedings of the 10th International Conference on Natural Language Generation* (pp. 168–177).

Zhao, J., Xue, F., Khan, S., & Khatib, S. F. (2021). Consumer behaviour analysis for business development. *Aggression and Violent Behavior*, 101591.

Zhao, M., Yang, J., Zhang, J., & Wang, S. (2022). Aggregated graph convolutional networks for aspect-based sentiment classification. *Information Sciences, 600*, 73–93.

Zhao, W., Guan, Z., Chen, L., He, X., Cai, D., Wang, B., & Wang, Q. (2017). Weakly-supervised deep embedding for product review sentiment analysis. *IEEE Transactions on Knowledge and Data Engineering, 30*(1), 185–197.

Zheng, J., Guo, Y., Feng, C., & Chen, H. (2018). A hierarchical neural-network-based document representation approach for text classification. *Mathematical Problems in Engineering*, 1–10.

Zvarevashe, K., & Olugbara, O. O. (2018, March). A framework for sentiment analysis with opinion mining of hotel reviews. In *2018 Conference on Information Communications Technology and Society (ICTAS)* (pp. 1–4). IEEE.

15 Handling Skewed Datasets in Computing Environments
The Classifier Ensemble Approach

Uma R. Godse
MIT Art, Design and Technology University, Pune, India

Darshan V. Medhane
Savitribai Phule Pune University, Nashik, India

CONTENTS

15.1 BUILDING A CLASSIFIER ENSEMBLE

Classifier ensembles are also called multiple classifier systems in which a set of learning models are constructed. These learning models are used to generate the individual predictions which can be combined with a specific approach in order to enhance the classification accuracy. Further, the final prediction is generated by combining the decisions of individual models in an intelligent way. The generated ensemble model is used for predicting the unseen test data. Thus, multiple opinions are taken into account before making the final decision on the class label. This approach has been proved beneficial in dealing with imbalanced datasets and has improved the probability of correct classification provided that ensemble construction is carried out cleverly. To be precise, the various factors play a critical role in enhancing the performance of a classifier ensemble. This chapter gives a detailed discussion of the design factors that affect the performance of a classification algorithm. Basically, the classifier ensemble formation involves two major phases. The initial phase is concerned with generating a set of individual classification algorithms. The major design factors that are to be considered at this stage are as follows.

Incorporating diversity among different classifiers. The classifier ensemble that combines multiple individual learning models is capable of improving the performance only if the selected member classifiers are diverse in nature. If the member classifiers with similar behaviour are combined, it is not likely to improve the performance. The more the disagreement between the members of an ensemble, the more is the performance improved. The reason behind this is the probability that the incorrect behaviour of a few members may be ignored as most of the remaining members do not agree with the decision. Therefore, a systematic approach to generating a diverse set of individual learning models is needed. The various schemes to create a diverse set of member classifiers are discussed in Section 15.1.1.

Base classifier selection. Another important design consideration is the selection of the proper base classification algorithm. The learning model performing well on one dataset may not give such favourable results on another dataset. Moreover, the changes in the initial values of different parameters or environmental changes may also result in a varying performance. Some classification algorithms are stable in nature where changes in some of the input parameters do not much affect the generated learning model. Such models may not be suitable for the classifier ensemble because the ensembles are created with the combination of diverse learning models.

Considering all these facts, the base classifier selection plays a major role in the success of a classifier ensemble. A careful study and analysis of the different individual learners used in the literature is carried out in order to pick the appropriate individual classification algorithms.

15.1.1 Diversity among Different Classifiers

As discussed in the above section, the diversity introduced among the base classifiers of an ensemble ensures the improved performance of the classifier ensemble. Various techniques are designed in order to introduce diversity in the construction of an ensemble. Approaches to form the classifier ensemble are categorized according to the manner in which the diversity is introduced [1–3]. There are four different methods to incorporate diversity among the classifiers:

1. Different training datasets;
2. Different feature sets;
3. Different classification models;
4. Different parameters.

The details of each approach are elaborated as follows.

Different training datasets. The first commonly used method to introduce diversity in the classifier ensemble construction involves employing different training datasets to build different learning models. The original training dataset D is used to generate a set of training subsets which are dissimilar. Training dataset D is applied with sampling with or without replacement in order to generate $D_1, D_2, \ldots, D_n$ training subsets as an output [4, 5]. The value of n is based on the number of base classifiers to be generated. Each subset will be used to train and build a different classifier model. Thus, base classifiers $C_1, C_2, \ldots, C_n$ are trained on $D_1, D_2, \ldots, Dn$ respectively. The individual prediction of each Ci is then combined using the appropriate combining method. The output of the combined model is treated as the final prediction. Figure 15.1 shows the classifier ensemble formation using different training datasets.

Different feature sets. Another approach of ensemble creation involves introducing diversity in the base classifiers with the help of different feature sets [6–8]. In this case, the diversity of features is exploited instead of the diversity of instances. Each member classifier of an ensemble is trained on a different subset of the available input features. The original feature set F is used to generate $F_1, F_2, \ldots, Fn$ as output subsets of features. Each subset of features will be used to train and build a different classifier model. That is, base classifiers $C_1, C_2, \ldots, Cn$ are trained on feature subsets F1, $F_2, \ldots, Fn$ respectively. As every individual classifier is trained on different features, they will probably work in a different fashion. Individual prediction of each Ci is then combined using a combining method. The output of the combined model is treated as a final prediction. Figure 15.2 shows the process of ensemble creation using different feature sets.

Although the dataset used for training base classifiers remains same, the attributes used for training them are different. Therefore, the behaviour of generated classifiers is likely to be different and

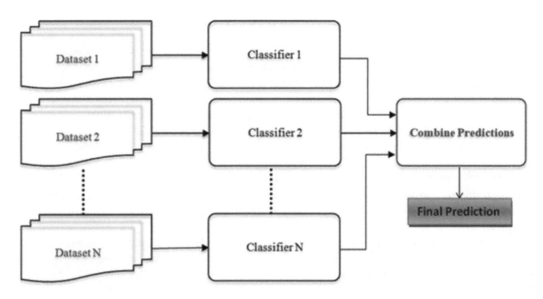

FIGURE 15.1   The classifier ensemble formation.

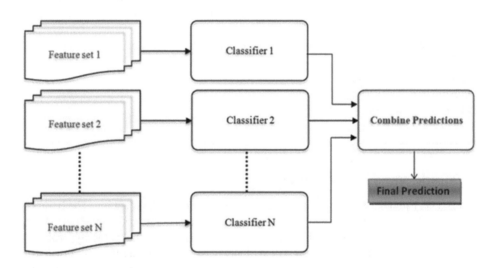

FIGURE 15.2   The process of ensemble creation.

consequently the probability of correct classification is increased. A random subspace ensemble is created using this approach where predictions of base classifiers trained on different feature subsets are combined using a majority vote rule. It is recommended to use half of the original features in order to get good results.

Different classification models. In this category, the base classifiers are diversified using different learning algorithms. The diverse learning algorithms trained on the same dataset will behave in a different way due to the unique characteristics of each algorithm. The StackingC algorithm is representative of this group.

Different parameters. In this group, diversity is introduced by varying the parameters of the classification model. That is, each base learner is generated by changing the parameters of the learning model.

15.2 BASE CLASSIFIERS FOR CLASSIFIER ENSEMBLES

The individual classification algorithms that are treated as members of the classifier ensemble are called base classifiers. The predictions of the base classifiers are combined by the ensemble combination method in order to generate the final prediction of the classifier ensemble. That is, the combination of base classifiers forms the classifier.

The usage of a suitable base classifier plays a crucial role in the performance of the constructed classifier ensemble. The generated classifier ensemble model improves the classification performance provided that the base classifiers used as members of the ensemble are diverse in nature. More precisely, the diverse classifiers that disagree with each other are less likely to agree on the incorrect class label for the given instance. Therefore, their combination has less probability of misclassifying the instance. One approach to generate the diverse classifiers is to train the individual classifiers with different training data. The bagging ensembles are representatives of this category.

The learners that are sensitive to the changes in the training data are treated as unstable learners. That is, minor changes in the training dataset may significantly affect the generated learning model. Consequently, the diverse learning models can be created with smaller changes in the training datasets. As a result, individual classification models are diverse in nature and their combination is helpful to improve the performance of classification. Due to this reason, many research studies recommend the use of unstable classification algorithms to form the classifier ensemble. It has been observed that decision tree and neural networks are unstable in nature. Therefore, the base classifier pool used to construct the proposed classifier ensemble consists of the decision tree and multilayer perceptron (MLP) learning model [9].

The three base classifiers used in the experimentation of this work are:

1. Support vector machine;
2. Decision tree;
3. Multilayer perceptron.

A brief description of the selected classification algorithms is given in the following sections.

15.2.1 Support Vector Machine (SVM)

The SVM is a very popular and widely used learning algorithm for classification. The basic concept behind it is to obtain the hyperplane which segregates the samples into different classes so that the margin between the classes is at the maximum [10–12]. Figure 15.3 shows the hyperplane of the SVM. The distance between the nearest instance of any class and the hyperplane is known as a margin. As this distance increases, the chances of misclassifying the instance of one class as belonging to the opposite class are decreased. The SVM classifier is recommended due to its low generalization error which helps it to perform efficiently on unseen data as well [13]. For linearly separable data where instances of different classes are on opposite sides of the hyperplane, SVM proves to be excellent.

The data that are not linearly separable cannot be separated with such a hyperplane. However, SVM deals with this situation by transforming the non-separable data into a higher dimensional space. As a result, the data that were non-separable become linearly separable. The function that maps the lower dimensional space onto the higher dimensional space is known as the kernel function, and the derived feature space is known as reproducing kernel Hilbert space. This satisfies

$$K\left(x_i, x_j\right) = \left(\varnothing\left(x_i\right), \varnothing\left(x_j\right)\right)$$

(15.1)

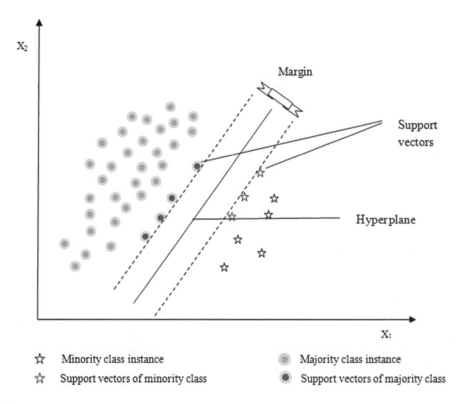

FIGURE 15.3 The hyperplane of the SVM.

where K is the kernel function and Φ is the mapping function that maps the original feature space to the higher dimensional space that SVM offers, which has many advantages such as its capacity to handle outlier instances that are located far from the instances of the same category. It has been found that SVM can deal with the high dimensional space in an efficient manner. SVM is good for the data that are not in structured form. The available kernels of SVM allow us to solve critical problems as well. On the other hand, SVM suffers from a few limitations also.

For instance, direct probability estimates are not generated as an output of SVM. As the size of the dataset increases, very lengthier training times are observed. If the number of attributes of the dataset is much larger than the size of the dataset, this may lead to over-fitting of the data. The model suffering from an over-fitting issue is specific to the instances on which it has been trained. As a result, it may not classify the unseen instances correctly resulting in the increased generalization error.

15.2.2 DECISION TREE

A decision tree is one of the popularly used classification algorithms in the machine learning community. The decision tree model has a tree-like structure made up of various nodes that are generated in recursive fashion. The divide and conquer strategy is used in this process. The nodes are either internal or leaf nodes where the internal nodes have outgoing branches while leaf nodes do not have such branches. Each node represents the test on split attribute that partitions the input instances into a number of sub-paths depending on the possible outcomes of the test condition. The condition checked at each node is known as the decision rule. The terminating nodes test the split condition and the possible values of that attribute represent the different classes. Figure 15.4 shows a sample decision tree for the identification of risky customers.

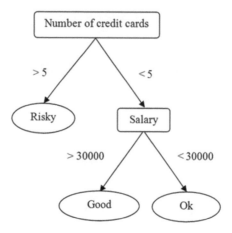

FIGURE 15.4 Sample decision tree for identification of risky customers.

The major concern while constructing the decision tree is the selection of the attribute that should be tested at each node. The choice of proper attribute may prove beneficial while inappropriate selection may not generate the optimum tree. For instance, if some important attribute is missing then the path corresponding to its outcome will be missing which in turn may produce a wrong prediction. The attribute should be selected such that the purest node is produced. The purity of a node can be quantified with various measures. Entropy is one of the measures used for quantifying the impurity at the node.

$$\text{Entropy} = \sum_i P_i \log P_i \tag{15.2}$$

where P_i signifies the probability that the random selection chooses the ith value. Another measure used for this purpose is information gain, where the attribute having the highest information gain is selected as the splitting attribute for the particular node. This expresses the expected amount by which entropy gets declined when a particular attribute is used to partition the space of the instances. To be specific, when a parent node is partitioned into subsets, the entropy of parent node is different than its child nodes. This change in entropy is quantified as information gain. Let T be a set of instances, attribute A be a splitting criterion at a particular node, and T_{A_i} be the subset of instances for attribute value A_i. Then the information gain at that node can be calculated as

$$\text{Information Gain} = \text{Entropy}\left(\text{parent } T\right) - \sum_{i=1}^{n} W_i \, \text{Entropy}\left(\text{child } T_{A_i}\right) \tag{15.3}$$

where

$$W_i = \frac{|T_{A_i}|}{|T|}$$

Let

T be the set of all instances

$$A = \{A_1, A_2, \ldots. A_k\}$$

A be the set of attributes

$$C = \{C_1, C_2, \ldots C_n\}$$

C be the set of classes

$$\text{Val}_{Aj} = \{A_{j1}, A_{j2}, \ldots A_{jm}\}$$

and Val_{Aj} be the possible outcomes for attribute A_j.

The construction of the decision tree involves the following steps being executed in a top-down manner:

1. Start from a root node.
2. If all instances belong to the same class C_i then
   (a) Return the leaf node labelled with class C_i.
3. Else
   (b) Compute the value of measure as for information gain.
   (c) Select the best attribute A_j for splitting the node.
4. Split the dataset *T* into m subsets T_{Aj1}, T_{Aj2} T_{Ajm} based on the values of attributes A_j.
5. $A = A - A_j$.
6. Repeat the steps 2 to 5 for all partitions T_{Aji} generated in the above step.

The decision tree constructed in this way is further used to classify unseen test instances. The test instance is applied with the test condition at the root node. The outcome defines the subsequent path to be followed. If the next node in the path is an internal node, then repeat the same process. Otherwise, apply the final decision rule and its outcome will specify the final class label. The decision tree offers many advantages which has led to its wide usage in the existing literature. The main feature of the decision tree is its simple and self-explanatory nature. Moreover, the time to construct the tree is relatively shorter. Trees are capable of handling both numerical and categorical attributes. Even the data containing missing values can be handled. On the other hand, decision trees are sensitive to changes in the training data and noisy data.

In this work, the most popular variant of the decision tree, namely C4.5, has been used for the experimentation. The Waikato Environment for Knowledge Analysis (WEKA) implementation of C4.5 is known as J48. The best attribute for the splitting condition is chosen according to the normalized information gain.

15.2.3 Multilayer Perceptron (MLP)

MLP is a kind of artificial neural network that comprises a network of simple neurons known as perceptrons [14, 15]. The perceptron is a node or unit that takes a set of inputs and generates the output by taking into account the weights associated with each input. The function that does this transformation is known as an activation function. Figure 15.5 shows an MLP with one hidden layer [16–21].

The input In1 … InN is transformed by the input layer to the hidden layer. The hidden layer executes the activation function on the input in order to perform the required computations. The output of the activation function becomes the input for the next layer. The number of layers in MLP depends on the number of hidden layers. The network with zero hidden layers is known as a single layer perceptron and is capable of learning only linear functions. The network that can learn nonlinear functions and consist of more than one hidden layer is known as a multilayer perceptron. The activation function *F* is defined as

$$F = \sum_{i=1}^{N} \text{In}_i W_i + b \tag{15.4}$$

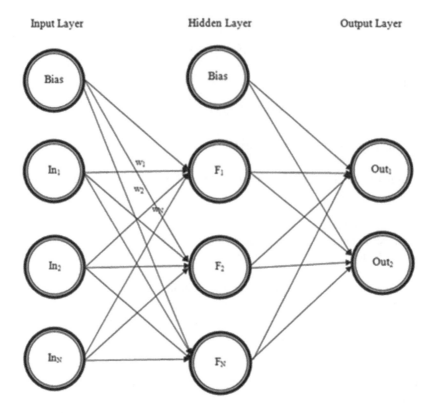

FIGURE 15.5   MLP with one hidden layer.

The term b in Equation (15.4) represents bias that is equal to 1 and defines the threshold value for the perceptron. The learning process in the case of an MLP is executed with the help of a back propagation algorithm. The steps involved in the learning phase of the MLP are as follows:

1. Initialize the weight values w_1, w_2, ..., w_N with random values.
2. Process the input training example with the activation function and initialized weight values. That is, the input is processed through hidden layers, and the output of the hidden layer is processed by the output layer to generate the final output.
3. The objective is to make the predicted value closer to the actual prediction of the instance. To accomplish this, the total error that signifies the loss associated with the randomly initialized model is computed.
4. The loss function is propagated in a backward direction in order to revise the random values of weights in such a way that the predicted values with the generated model move closer to the desired prediction. To be precise, the used optimization technique updates the weights in order to minimize the loss.
5. The above steps are executed iteratively until the stopping criteria are satisfied. The main advantage of MLP is its ability to learn nonlinear and complex relationships. The MLP learning model can be used for both classification and regression. However, it faces some limitations such as the lengthier training time required to build the model. Also, the number of hidden neurons for MLP must be set by the user. If the value set by user is lower, then it may cause under-fitting while a higher value may generate an over-fitted model.

15.3 ENSEMBLE COMBINATION STRATEGY

As discussed in Section 15.1.1, the classifier ensemble model integrates the multiple individual classification models and generates a final prediction depending on the multiple predictions given by them. Thus, the prediction generated by consulting the variety of learners helps to increase the generalization capacity of the final model. The individual decisions are combined by using a strategy in which the final decision reflects the decisions of individual learners. Figure 15.6 represents the categorization of the combination methods used to combine the predictions of base classifiers in order to generate the final prediction of the classifier ensemble [9–11]. Basically, the combination methods can be categorized into two groups on the basis of whether selection or merging of individual learners' predictions is done [22–24]:

1. Classifier fusion;
2. Classifier selection.

The commonly used combination methods for forming the ensemble belong to the fusion category which merges the individual decisions. The classifier fusion approaches can be again grouped into two classes based on the type of predictions merged by them. The category that combines the numerical outputs is known as an algebraic combiner. Various operations such as mean, product, sum, and average are used to merge the individual predictions. Another category of fusion does the merging of the nominal outputs. Voting is the well-known and commonly used technique where each base classifier has to vote for a particular class. The final prediction is generated according to the number of votes received by each class.

The following subsections briefly discuss the various methods that are commonly used to combine the predictions of members of the classifier ensemble.

15.3.1 CLASSIFIER FUSION

The combination methods of this category make use of the decisions of all the individual learning models. Initially, all the base classifiers of the ensemble are trained on different datasets. This creates a set of diverse classifiers. The predictions of the individual classifiers are merged to generate

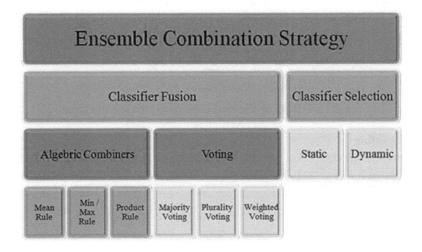

FIGURE 15.6 Categorization of the combination methods.

a final prediction of the class label. Thus, each member of the classifier ensemble contributes to the final decision-making process. A variety of combination rules such as sum, voting, average, and product is available. The well-known and commonly used method for combining categorical predictions is voting [25, 26].

15.3.1.1　Voting

Many applications of classifier ensembles make use of the voting combination mechanism. In this method, each base classifier predicts the class label for the given instance and votes for that class. Then the votes gained by each class are computed. The final label is predicted according to the votes achieved by each class. Further, the voting methods can be classified into the following groups on the basis of the criterion that is used to decide the final class label:

   a. Majority voting;
   b. Plurality voting;
   c. Weighted voting.

To discuss the aforementioned techniques in brief, let us assume that

C is the set of classes

$$C \leftarrow \{C_1, C_2, \ldots C_{C\_CNT}\}$$

L is the set of base classifiers of the ensemble

$$L \leftarrow \{L_1, L_2, \ldots L_{B\_CNT}\}$$

The function $P_{i,j}(x)$ specifies whether the base classifier L_i classifies the given instance x as a member of the class C_j and is defined as

$$P_{i,j}(x) = 1 \quad \text{if } x \in C_j = 0 \tag{15.5}$$

otherwise the function P is applied on x using all the base classifiers $L_1, L_2, \ldots, L_{B\_CNT}$. Then the variable sum_j which indicates the number of votes received by class C_j is calculated as

$$\text{sum}_j = \sum_{i=1}^{B\_CNT} P_{i,j}(x) \tag{15.6}$$

The variable sum_j is used for deciding the final class label for the instance x.

   a. **Majority voting**

      In the case of majority voting, the class that has retrieved more than half the votes is predicted as the final class label. The variable $\text{sum}j$ is used to compute the total number of votes received by all the classes.

$$\text{Total\_votes} = \sum_{j=1}^{C\_CNT} \text{sum}_j \tag{15.7}$$

The final class label is the class C_j that satisfies the condition:

$$\text{sum}_j > \frac{1}{2}\text{Total\_votes} \tag{15.8}$$

If none of the class gets more than half of the total votes, then the classifier ensemble can use a reject option for decision making. Thus, the final class must get at least half of the total votes.

b. **Plurality voting**
   In plurality voting, the criterion for the final class label is the class with the highest votes among all the classes. Therefore, if a class gets less than half of the votes but there is a maximum value of votes, then that class represents the final prediction. The final class label is the class C_j that satisfies the condition:

$$\text{argmax}_{j\in\{1,2...C_{\text{CNT}}\}}\text{sum}_j \tag{15.9}$$

c. **Weighted voting**
   In the above two voting mechanisms, all the base classifiers are assigned equal weights. In some scenarios, the base classifiers have varying performance and should not contribute equally in the decision-making process. In such scenarios, a base classifier with good performance can be given more weight, while the weaker is given less weight. Therefore, the formula to calculate sum$j$ needs to be modified as:

$$\text{sum}_j = \sum_{i=1}^{B_{\text{CNT}}} W_i P_{i,j}(x) \tag{15.10}$$

where W_i is the weight assigned to each base classifier L_i depending on its performance. The final class prediction is the class C_j that satisfies:

$$\text{argmax}_{j\in\{1,2...C_{\text{CNT}}\}}\text{sum}_j \tag{15.11}$$

15.3.2 CLASSIFIER SELECTION

Classifier fusion involves training each base classifier on the whole feature set. On the other hand, classifier selection involves generating a set of learning models where each of them learns from a subset of features. Whenever a new instance is to be classified, the data located in the locality of this instance are searched. The learner trained using these data is selected for making the final decision of the class to which the new instance belongs. Classifier selection can be done in either of the following ways [27–29]:

1. Static selection. Initially, the different base classifiers are assigned the responsibility of different regions. Whenever any new instance is to be classified, the region to which it belongs is searched. Subsequently, the classifier that is best for that region is used to classify the new instance. Thus, the regions and the classifiers suitable for them are defined statically.
2. Dynamic selection. The base classifier to classify the new instance is selected in a dynamic fashion. Different methods of adapting the classifiers have been suggested in the literature. For example, the dynamic classifier selection based on local accuracy (DCS LA) method selects the classifier based on local accuracy [30, 31]. The classifier that is confident in the locality of the given instance is selected.

15.4 CONCLUDING REMARKS

To deal with the class imbalance issue faced by many real-world applications, several classification approaches are available in the literature. In this regard, the first concern is to reduce the imbalance between the classes with the help of a resampling technique. Subsequently, the resampled training data with a reduced degree of imbalance are used to build the classifier ensemble that is diverse in nature, optimal in size, and performs significantly well. This chapter has detailed the basics of the classifier ensemble approach for handling the skewed datasets and various design factors that are considered during the construction phase of the proposed classifier ensemble model. This was followed by the conclusions drawn on the basis of the experimental analysis. Finally, a few avenues for further research in the area of imbalanced data classification were discussed. The conclusions presented in this chapter are based on the pre-processing of the imbalanced data and classification using a classifier ensemble technique by applying borderline under-sampling (BLUS), the selection of base classifier (SBC), the construction of mini-ensembles (CME), and OptDCE.

REFERENCES

1. Kuncheva, L. I. (2001). Combining classifiers: Soft computing solutions. In S.K. Pal and A. Pal (Eds), *Pattern Recognition: From Classical to Modern Approaches* (pp. 427–451). World Scientific.
2. Gutiérrez-López, A., González-Serrano, F. J., & Figueiras-Vidal, A. R. (2023). Optimum Bayesian thresholds for rebalanced classification problems using class-switching ensembles. *Pattern Recognition*, 135, 109158.
3. Wang, Y., Liu, D., Ma, S., Wu, F., & Gao, W. (2020). Ensemble learning-based rate-distortion optimization for end-to-end image compression. *IEEE Transactions on Circuits and Systems for Video Technology*, 31(3), 1193–1207.
4. Marqués, A. I., García, V., & Sánchez, J. S. (2012). Two-level classifier ensembles for credit risk assessment. *Expert Systems with Applications*, 39(12), 10916–10922.
5. Emil Richard Singh, B., & Sivasankar, E. (2019). Enhancing prediction accuracy of default of credit using ensemble techniques. In *First International Conference on Artificial Intelligence and Cognitive Computing* (pp. 427–436). Singapore: Springer.
6. Rahman, A., & Verma, B. (2011). Novel layered clustering-based approach for generating ensemble of classifiers. *IEEE Transactions on Neural Networks*, 22(5), 781–792.
7. Dong, X., Yu, Z., Cao, W., Shi, Y., & Ma, Q. (2020). A survey on ensemble learning. *Frontiers of Computer Science*, 14(2), 241–258.
8. Cruz, R. M., Sabourin, R., & Cavalcanti, G. D. (2018). Dynamic classifier selection: Recent advances and perspectives. *Information Fusion*, 41, 195–216.
9. Godase, U. R., Medhane, D. V. (2022). OptDCE: An optimal and diverse classifier ensemble for imbalanced datasets. *International Journal of Computer Information Systems and Industrial Management Applications*, 14, 151–161.
10. Zhou, Z. H. (2012). *Ensemble methods: foundations and algorithms*. CRC Press.
11. Li, J., Cheng, K., Wang, S., Morstatter, F., Trevino, R. P., Tang, J., & Liu, H. (2017). Feature selection: A data perspective. *ACM computing surveys (CSUR)*, 50(6), 1–45.
12. Dong, X., Yu, Z., Cao, W., Shi, Y., & Ma, Q. (2020). A survey on ensemble learning. *Frontiers of Computer Science*, 14(2), 241–258.
13. Aburomman, A. A., & Reaz, M. B. I. (2016). A novel SVM-kNN-PSO ensemble method for intrusion detection system. *Applied Soft Computing*, 38, 360–372.
14. Alpaydin, E. (2020). *Introduction to machine learning*. Cambridge, MA: MIT Press.
15. Zhou, Z. H. (2012). *Ensemble methods: foundations and algorithms*. CRC Press.
16. Castro, C. L., & Braga, A. P. (2013). Novel cost-sensitive approach to improve the multilayer perceptron performance on imbalanced data. *IEEE Transactions on Neural Networks and Learning Systems*, 24(6), 888–899.
17. Haixiang, G., Yijing, L., Shang, J., Mingyun, G., Yuanyue, H., & Bing, G. (2017). Learning from class-imbalanced data: Review of methods and applications. *Expert Systems with Applications*, 73, 220–239.

18. Branco, P., Torgo, L., & Ribeiro, R. P. (2016). A survey of predictive modeling on imbalanced domains. *ACM Computing Surveys (CSUR)*, 49(2), 1–50.
19. Windeatt, T. (2006). Accuracy/diversity and ensemble MLP classifier design. *IEEE Transactions on Neural Networks*, 17(5), 1194–1211.
20. Yu, Z., Li, L., Liu, J., & Han, G. (2014). Hybrid adaptive classifier ensemble. *IEEE Transactions on Cybernetics*, 45(2), 177–190.
21. Rahman, A., & Verma, B. (2011). Novel layered clustering-based approach for generating ensemble of classifiers. *IEEE Transactions on Neural Networks*, 22(5), 781–792.
22. Parikh, D., & Polikar, R. (2007). An ensemble-based incremental learning approach to data fusion. *IEEE Transactions on Systems, Man, and Cybernetics, Part B (Cybernetics)*, 37(2), 437–450.
23. Ganaie, M. A., & Hu, M. (2021). Ensemble deep learning: A review. arXiv preprint arXiv:2104.02395.
24. Polikar, R. (2012). Ensemble learning. In *Ensemble machine learning* (pp. 1–34). Boston, MA: Springer.
25. Kuncheva, L. I. (2003). "Fuzzy" versus "nonfuzzy" in combining classifiers designed by Boosting. *IEEE Transactions on Fuzzy Systems*, 11(6), 729–741.
26. Ren, Y., Zhang, L., & Suganthan, P. N. (2016). Ensemble classification and regression-recent developments, applications and future directions. *IEEE Computational Intelligence Magazine*, 11(1), 41–53.
27. Kuncheva, L. I. (2002). Switching between selection and fusion in combining classifiers: An experiment. *IEEE Transactions on Systems, Man, and Cybernetics, Part B (Cybernetics)*, 32(2), 146–156.
28. Polikar, R. (2006). Ensemble based systems in decision making. *IEEE Circuits and Systems Magazine*, 6(3), 21–45.
29. Du, P., Bai, X., Tan, K., Xue, Z., Samat, A., Xia, J., ... & Liu, W. (2020). Advances of four machine learning methods for spatial data handling: A review. *Journal of Geovisualization and Spatial Analysis*, 4(1), 1–25.
30. Xiao, J., Xie, L., He, C., & Jiang, X. (2012). Dynamic classifier ensemble model for customer classification with imbalanced class distribution. *Expert Systems with Applications*, 39(3), 3668–3675.
31. Branco, P., Torgo, L., & Ribeiro, R. P. (2016). A survey of predictive modeling on imbalanced domains. *ACM Computing Surveys (CSUR)*, 49(2), 1–50.

16 Diagnosis of Dementia Using MRI
A Machine Learning Approach

Aaishwarya Ashish Gaikwad and Swati V. Shinde
Pimpri Chinchwad College of Engineering, Pune, India

CONTENTS

DOI: 10.1201/9781003359456-16

16.1   INTRODUCTION

Archie and Donald are two 78-year-old men who are neighbours. Both wake up feeling moody, but the cause of Archie's moodiness is the fact that he could not get a good night's sleep while Donald's cause is that he is feeling very depressed and anxious. During the day while Archie was doing his daily tasks, he faced some challenges while trying to complete them; but when Donald tried to fill in a cheque, he was not able to do so. He could not remember the procedure to be followed, which led him to feel very frustrated and confused as he did not know the reason why he could not fill out the cheque when he has been doing it his whole life. In the evening, they decided to go for a walk. Archie was able to navigate his way back to his home correctly, but Donald was not able to remember his way back. Later he had to ask fellow pedestrians to help him reach his home.

On diagnosis, it was found that Donald was suffering from dementia. Mental fogginess, struggling with day-to-day tasks, wearing clothes in the wrong order and seasonally inappropriate, feeling frustrated and moody most of the time due to not being able to remember how to perform daily tasks are some of the signs of dementia onset. Memory impairment; hallucinations; depression; paranoia; difficulty communicating, reasoning, and handling complex tasks are some of the common effects of dementia on an individual. It is a disorder that is progressive in nature and has no cure for the time being. Only treatment can be provided, to reduce the risk factors.

It is estimated by the World Health Organization (WHO) that in the coming years 55 million will suffer worldwide from dementia, with more than 60% living in low-income nations. It is anticipated that these values will increase to 139 million by 2050 since the elderly population is rising in almost every country. Alzheimer's causes memory loss and is fatal. It along with similar types of dementia cause one in three elderly deaths. Alzheimer's disease is now responsible for 145% more deaths than breast and prostate cancer put together.

Dementia is caused by the destruction or impairment of the connections and nerve cells in the brain. Here, depending on which area of the brain is affected, dementia affects each person variably and shows different signs. These are typically categorized using the traits of dementia, such as the proteins that build up in the brain or the portion of the brain that is impacted.

The different categories of dementia are Alzheimer's, Vascular, Lewy Body, Frontotemporal, and mixed.

16.1.1   Alzheimer's Disease (AD)

This is a neurological condition brought on by intricate brain changes following cellular damage. It causes dementia symptoms, which progressively get worse over time. The primary gene that boosts the likelihood of AD is apoprotein E4 (APOE). The brains of AD sufferers have acquired plaques and tangles. Tau protein creates fibrous bundles known as tangles, and beta-amyloid protein creates clumps known as plaques. Alzheimer's disease can cause memory loss, trouble understanding problems, difficulty finishing routine chores, confusion about time and place, among other symptoms. The disease has the following three stages.

16.1.1.1   Early-stage Alzheimer's (Mild)

A person with Alzheimer's may be able to function on their own in the early stages. Despite this, the individual could experience memory lapses, such as forgetting familiar words or where everyday objects are located. A few examples of difficulties are losing a priceless item, having trouble remembering names, and struggling to complete tasks in social or professional contexts.

16.1.1.2   Middle-stage Alzheimer's (Moderate)

Symptoms of dementia are more noticeable in the intermediate stage of Alzheimer's. The individual might mispronounce phrases, lose their temper, or act in unpredictable ways, including refusing to take a shower. It may be tough for the individual to express their thoughts and carry out simple tasks without assistance if there is damage to the brain's nerve cells.

Symptoms include forgetting recent events or details about one's past, feeling moody, and having trouble remembering details about oneself, such as one's address or phone number.

16.1.1.3 Late-stage Alzheimer's (Severe)

Dementia symptoms are bad when the disease is in its latter stage. People start to lose their ability to react to their surroundings, communicate, and eventually regulate their mobility. Even if they may still use words or phrases, it gets harder for them to express their pain. People may have substantial personality changes and require intensive care as their memory and cognitive abilities continue to deteriorate. Individuals may need 24/7 support with individual daily care at this point, have trouble talking, and/or experience changes in their daily activities.

16.1.2 VASCULAR DEMENTIA (VD)

The brain's blood vessels are harmed in this situation. Strokes and other adverse consequences on the brain, like the destruction of the white matter fibres, can result from blood vessel problems. Problem-solving challenges, slow thinking, inattentiveness, and disarray are some of the most prevalent signs of VD.

16.1.3 LEWY BODY DEMENTIA (LBD)

People who have this problem, a progressive kind, have abnormal protein aggregates called Lewy bodies in their brains. Rapid eye movement (REM) dysfunction, hallucinations, difficulties focusing and paying attention, uncontrolled movement, tremors, and parkinsonism are just a few of the telltale signs of Lewy body dementia.

Some of the symptoms of AD are present in people with LBD, but they are more likely to have the start or early stages of sleep difficulties, well-formed ocular hallucinations, and visual–spatial dysfunction. These symptoms may vary significantly from hour to hour or day to day. Additionally typical are issues with motor coordination that resemble Parkinson's disease. They may happen even when there is not a serious memory loss, but memory loss frequently happens at some stage of the illness, particularly when the brain abnormalities associated with other dementia causes are present.

16.1.4 FRONTOTEMPORAL DEMENTIA (FTD)

This is caused by the deterioration of the nerve fibers of the brain's frontal and temporal lobes and their interconnections. Language, conduct, and personality traits are changed. Common symptoms include behavior, personality, reasoning, and judgement problems, in addition to speech and movement.

Early signs typically include pronounced personality and behavioral changes as well as challenges with language production or comprehension. Memory is not so much hampered in its beginning stages, unlike Alzheimer's.

16.1.5 MIXED DEMENTIA

AD, VD, and LBD are only a few of the disorders that affect patients with the syndrome known as mixed dementia. Huntington's disease (HD), traumatic brain injury (TBI), Creutzfeldt–Jakob disease, and Parkinson's disease are a few other conditions connected to dementia:

- Progressive brain nerve cell death is a symptom of the rare hereditary condition HD. This illness, which frequently results in motor, intellectual, and psychological problems, has a substantial impact on a person's functional capacities.

- Frequent head traumas cause the disease recognized as TBI. This is more common in boxers, footballers, and military personnel. Depending on the hampered region, this illness might cause dementia. Signs and symptoms include depression, hyperactivity, memory loss, and difficulty speaking. It also contributes to parkinsonism. The effects of the trauma may not manifest for years.
- Creutzfeldt–Jakob disease is an uncommon brain disorder that mainly affects people without any known risk factors. Proteins called prions may have developed because of this illness. Typically, this fatal condition shows signs and symptoms beyond age 60. It is heritable even if there is no known cause for it. Additionally, exposure to cerebral or nervous system tissue that has been damaged, such as tissue after a corneal transplant, may be the root of the problem.
- Parkinson's disease is a gradually developing ailment which impairs both the nervous system's ability to function and the nervous system itself. The symptoms appear over time. One hand may tremble slightly as the first symptom. Although tremors are common, the illness may also cause stiffness or make you move more slowly. Parkinson's disease dementia is a common symptom that many patients experience over time.

16.2 LITERATURE SURVEY

This work is connected to several areas in dementia detection using machine learning (ML) models, with each area containing a large amount of related work.

Shih-Yi Chien et al. [1] provided a deep understanding of dementia's underlying principles and psychosocial contributors, as well as how these characteristics regulate the risk of dementia across various user scenarios.

Etminani K. et al. [2] aimed to build and authenticate a 3D deep learning (DL) model that uses fluorine 18 fluorodeoxyglucose PET (18F-FDG PET) to predict the final identification of dementia and contrast the model's execution with that of the specialist's work; 90% of the data was applied for training the newly presented 3D Convolutional Neural Network (CNN) and 10% was used for external testing.

For Helaly et al. [3] the major objective is to build an early detection model for AD and the categorisation of medical images for different stages of it. This work employs a deep learning methodology, more especially CNNs. The AD spectrum has four multi-classified stages. Between every two-pair class of AD phases, distinct binary image classifications are also used. Two methodologies are employed to categorise the medical photos to find AD. The initial procedure uses 2D and 3D CNN models to work on the structural brain scans in 2D and 3D from the Alzheimer's Disease Neuro Imaging (ADNI) database. The second approach makes use of VGG19 along with pretrained classification models by utilizing the transfer learning principle. The 3D multi-class AD categorization had an accuracy of 95.17%. The accuracy produced by the second approach was 97.00%.

CNN and long short term memory machine learning (LSTMML) methods in Python were used by Diskin et al. [4] to classify dementia using MRI and demographic data. The CNN is a computer vision model that can extract 2D features through kernel convolution and pooling procedures in addition to thick layers of interconnected vectors that contain individual elements known as neurons and may predict classes. A recurrent neural network made up of separate computational cells with the purpose of analyzing sequential data is called an LSTM. The algorithm was trained using nine factors, including sexual preference, age, educational status, social class, and mini-mental state examination (MMSE). The demographic data was preprocessed using selective variable removal and null value replacement. Additionally, both models were improved by modifying the model's hyper-parameters. Final accuracy, precision, and recall for the CNN model were 89.5, 87.3, and 86.8%; for the LSTM they were 82.3, 71.7, and 75.8%. Given that the model was able to discern broad distinctions between brains with dementia and brains in good health, it may be assumed that the CNN's improved efficacy was due to its larger dataset, which allowed for better abstraction and fit.

With the centre of attention on neuroimaging and mostly academic papers since 2016, Golrokh Mirzaei and Hojjat Adeli [5] note that this work covers the most recent research on ML approaches used for the identification and categorization of AD. The SVM algorithm, Random Forest, CNNs, and K-means are a few of these methods. This review reveals that there is no one ideal method, but DL procedures like CNN seem to have promise for the detection of AD, where transfer learning could be used.

The creation of an effortlessly repeatable and dependable CAD means utilizing the clinical and MONAI frameworks – which were created to promote standards in medical imaging. These were accessible by Termine et al. [6]. To ensure reliability, a DL system was trained to recognize FTD using information from the NIFD database. The model performed similarly to existing FTD classification methods, reaching 80% accuracy. To comprehend AI behavior and locate areas of the photos where the DL model does not work, explainable AI algorithms were used. It was revealed that attention maps are influenced by brain regions that are characteristic of FTD and which provided insight into how to enhance FTD detection. For a benchmark comparison in FTD categorization, the suggested standardized methodology may be helpful.

A CNN architecture was suggested by Abedinzadeh et al. [7] to categorize AD based on MRI scans. Our main goal is to categorize and predict the severity of dementia using pretrained CNNs, and to provide doctors with a useful decision-support tool for establishing the severity of AD focused on the degree of dementia. The classification model for dementia is trained and assessed using the common Kaggle dataset. Synthetic minority oversampling technique (SMOTE) addresses the dataset's main issue, which is a gap between classes. Compared to existing methods, VGGNet16 with ReduceLROnPlateau achieves an accuracy of 98.61% and a specificity of 99% by utilizing testing data that includes four phases of dementia.

The assumption firmness considering the effectiveness of algorithms for dementia diagnosis is examined by Faouri et al. [8]. Two feature reduction algorithms, seven ML models, Information Gain (IG), and principal component analysis (PCA) were used in a vast number of tests to achieve this. For the IG and PCA dimension, feature selection criteria were raised from 20 to 100%, and 2 to 8%, respectively, to test the robustness of these techniques. As a result, there have been $7 \times 9 + 7 \times 7 = 112$ experiments. Different classification evaluation results were obtained for each experiment. According to these results, of the seven methods, the SVM and Naïve Bayes are highly reliable algorithms when the selection limit is changed. Additionally, it was discovered that IG appeared to be more effective than PCA for diagnosing dementia.

The categorization of dementia using MRI, clinical records, and ML algorithms is discussed by Bharati et al. [9]. The authors have transformed univariate feature selection into a filter-based feature extraction during the MR data preprocessing stage. To approximate the critical features for attaining high classification accuracy, bagged decision trees are also utilized. For the diagnosis of dementia, several ensemble learning-based ML techniques – including XGB, gradient boosting (GB), voting-based, and random forest (RF) classifiers – are taken into consideration. Voting-based classifiers usually outperform the others; therefore, the potential is evident for distinguishing dementia from imagery along with medical data.

A model of logistic regression with an efficiency of 81% was created by Chedid et al. [10] to overcome many of the issues with earlier efforts. No other study, to our knowledge, has concurrently addressed the following issues: (1) the deficiency of mechanization and objective artefact removal, (2) the reliance of experience, (3) the requirement for enormous sample sizes, and (4) the use of black box ML approaches like deep neural network (DNN) with illogical feature selection. In addition to traditional neuropsychological testing, this work demonstrates the likelihood of an automated and expansible system that may be used to identify AD in clinical settings, improving the accuracy, quantification, and usability of AD diagnosis.

Tran Anh Tuan and others [11] present two steps of segmentation and classification, both utilizing DL, as an effective technique for diagnosing AD using MRI data. To categorize AD based on segmented brain tissues, a novel framework combining XGBoost and SVM is utilized. This new model combines Gaussian mixture model (GMM) and CNN to segment the brain tissues.

Broman et al. [12] showed that the relevant features to identify the disease at its earliest stages can be improved, and accurate predictions can be generated, with the aid of an ML system. The datasets for Alzheimer Features and Exploratory Data Investigation for Predicting Dementia were used to conduct this analysis. The dataset was processed using the following ML algorithms: naive Bayes, Decision Trees, KNN, and Fully Connected Neural Networks. Confusion matrices for both naive Bayes and Decision Trees were shown to produce the best outcomes among the models when accuracy scores were evaluated.

When used to identify dementia from clinical datasets, SVM, ANN, Bayes, Decision Trees, logistic regression (LR), Random Forest, and KNN all perform differently, according to a comparison study by Yunus et al. [13]. SVM and Random Forests have been found to work efficiently on open-access repository datasets.

First, we use a variety of previously trained models, including Vision Transformer (ViT), which provide the best evaluation results, as stated in Ilias et al. [14]. Next, we recommend multimodal models. To manage the effect of each modality on the final categorization and to capture the links between the two modalities practically, our introduced models more explicitly comprise a gated multimodal unit and cross-modal attention. Extensive tests performed on the ADReSS Challenge database show how well the suggested models perform and how they outperform cutting-edge techniques.

Ghosh et al. [15] have provided examples of DL usages and related methodologies that may be used to identify dementia stages more broadly and perhaps direct therapy for multiclass picture identification in the future. Each of the 6400 pictures of MRI included in the study datasets is divided into the four classifications of AD severity: mild, very mild, non, and moderate. Employing the CNN technique, these four image requirements were used to categorize the dementia phases for every affected individual. The authors effectively identified and forecast the various AD stages with a 97.19% accuracy rate using the CNN-based in silico model. In addition, ML methods like SVMs and extreme gradient boosting were used. Once more, ANN, SVM, XGB, and KNN provided accuracies of 96.62, 96.56, 94.62, and 89.88%, respectively.

Rutkowski et al. [16] created a digital biomarker for dementia to predict it as early onset. The research presents promising initial findings of EEG-wearable-based signal evaluation and categorization using fractal dimension detrended fluctuation analysis (MFDFA) in training and evaluation activities. We investigate shallow and DL ML algorithm for biomarker detection. In both the experimental tasks, an accuracy of 90% was obtained for RF and fully convolutional neural network (FCNN) classifier models. In the current study, which focuses on the development of straightforward wearable EEG-based objective dementia biomarkers, 35 senior volunteers take part.

Deepa et al. [17] emphasize DL methods for age degradation AD dementia in order to determine the different phases of damaged areas and stages of dementia. Principal component analysis (PCA) is the primary method used to forecast the state of elderly people in order to emphasize the seriousness. Datasets such as ADNI and Oasis have provided innovation for detecting the segment of patients afflicted at the mild cognitive impairment (MCI) stage, which would result in losing recollection of actions such as cycling, walking, and remembering known items. The MRI brain image is classified to determine the perpendicular shapes that will be utilized to determine the matrix worth of the imaging's damaged regions. The correlation is then created by comparing training examples with eigenvalues generated by covariance by utilizing the integer data of grid points delivering the accurate prediction as t. Overfitting can be avoided by making specific mathematical hypotheses, and the amount can be adjusted to obtain the best output when PCA is used with the CNN model for classification.

Taeho et al. [18] used tau positron emission tomography (PET) data to construct a DL-based design for classifying AD. The 3D CNN among normal participants attained an accuracy of 90.8%. The layer-wise relevance propagation (LRP) model revealed the areas of the mind in tau PET images that were important for CNN categorization of AD. The hippocampal, Para hippocampal, thalamic, and fusiform areas were the four most substantially discovered regions. Using a DL approach that integrates 3D CNN and LRP procedures, tau PET images can be used to identify desirable traits for AD categorization and have applications for initial identification during whole prodromal phases.

Zhu et al. [19] developed and validated a new ML-based technique to assist in screening tests of healthy people. An informant-based questionnaire was used to assess cognitive deficits, very mild dementia (VMD), and dementia. A 37-item questionnaire was completed by 5272 participants. Three alternative feature selection strategies were evaluated to choose the most crucial traits. Then, the diagnostic models were created using the top attributes together with six classification methods. IG outperformed the other two feature selection approaches. Naive Bayes was the most effective algorithm.

The goal for Dale et al. [20] was to create an automated gait evaluation technique based on frequent, unobtrusive gait data collection and computer vision method analysis. On a specialist dementia ward over the course of two weeks, 1066 walking movies of 31 dementia-related older adults walking spontaneously in a hallway were recorded. These walking videos were then subjected to an existing pose estimate technique. Gait characteristics were generated from stride-about monitoring film. Using monitored location data, and their relationship with medical agility, evaluation scores and knowledge on future potential falls were studied. The number of upcoming falls and retrieved gait parameters were found to be significantly correlated, providing contemporaneous and prospective confirmation of this strategy.

Basaia et al. [21] created and evaluated a DL approach relying on a structural MRI scan to predict the prognosis of patients proceeding to AD (c-MCI). CNNs were built on 3D weighted images from ADNI and patients at the Centre. The ability of CNN to differentiate between AD, c-MCI, and s-MCI was studied. The AD vs HC classification tests achieved the highest rates of accuracy, utilizing both the ADNI dataset separately (99%) and the combination of ADNI and non-ADNI database (98%). CNNs are a strong tool for computer-aided screening for every participant all over the AD spectrum.

Using the WEKA tool, Bansal et al. [22] applied J48 Naïve Bayes, Random Forest, and Multilayer Perceptron on the OASIS dataset's cross-sectional and longitudinal MRI data. Age, sex, education, socioeconomic status, clinical dementia grade, the atlas scale parameter, and additional variables exposed to the attribute selection approach utilizing CFSSubsetEval included the expected intracranial and normalized whole-brain volume. The categorization accuracy for J48 was the highest at 99.52%.

A 2017 study by Alam et al. [23] involved a non-invasive biomarker called MRI which shows morphometric variations and structural alterations in the brain. The major variables from MRI transaxial segments, LDA, and a twin SVM are presented as elements of a novel technique for distinguishing AD from HC. The proposed method's prediction accuracy ranged from 92.65 to 1.18 over the ADNI dataset, with 92.19 to 1.56 for specificity, and 93.11 to 1.29 for sensitivity. The suggested method produces precision, sensitivity, and specificity that are on a par with or better than those produced by different established AD prediction techniques.

Chudhey et al. [24] developed a model that uses several ML algorithms to aid in the early identification of dementia. An SVM classifier, LR, Decision Tree, and KNN are among the models employed in the proposed work. These classifiers are employed to choose the best model and predict dementia. To further attain the best results, an ensemble learning predictor, also known as a stacking classifier, is strategically combined with all the classifiers stated above. The results revealed a 20% improvement over the most recent ML models, and as a result, they were able to achieve a maximum accuracy of 93.33%.

An early detection instrument, the Functional Activities Questionnaire (FAQ), was investigated by Thabtah et al. [25], using an information strategy based on the selection of features and categorization. The goal is to identify the critical FAQ points that could lead to AD development. The proposed research-based methodology was used to process real data observations from ADNI research to accomplish the goal. On data subsets of the demographic FAQ items, the suggested approach produced ML algorithms with accuracy, sensitivity, and precision that were all above 90%.

Herzog and Magoulas [26] focused on the application of ML and computational methods to detect the initiation of degenerative diseases. Leveraging functional MRI from the ADNI database and imagery analysis tools, asymmetry is found. Asymmetry levels are investigated using statistical features generated from segmented asymmetry images, making use of CNN and SVM. This suggests that imaging disequilibrium attributes or fragmented MRI pictures of asymmetry can provide knowledge into early dementia diagnosis, and it shows very promising results in distinguishing cognitively intact participants from those with early MCI and AD.

Garcia-Gutierrez et al. [27] started out to construct cognitive tests applied to train ML models for diagnosis. Evolutionary algorithms motivated by natural selection were used to perform both traditional single and multi-objective categorization and feature selection. A meta-model approach was also applied, along with traditional algorithms like naive Bayes and SVMs. More than 84% of diagnoses for AD, by FTD, and their differential diagnosis were correct. The quantity of examinations and scores required could be greatly decreased by algorithms. The most significant assessments included the Addenbrooke's Cognitive Examination, verbal fluency, and the Free and Cued Selective Reminding Test

Adeli et al. [28] adapted the complete framework for Alzheimer's diagnosis by adopting a simple 3D CNN and applying the network's model parameters. Accuracy was 94.1%, and the model beats the prior futuristic in diagnosing AD. We discovered illness biomarkers depending on the trained model, and the findings were consistent with the literature. The learnt framework is then used to predict medium cognitive impairment (MCI), a precursor to AD, outperforming alternative solutions.

Zhang et al. [29] offer a method for detecting brain diseases that uses landmark-based deep multi-instance learning (LDMIL). To be more explicit, we use an information driven learning technique to distinguish abnormal feature points as well as neighboring image patches in brain MR images. Furthermore, using the structural information supplied by all identified landmarks, our LDMIL framework constructs an image categorizer that receives both the local spatial information communicated by texture features detected by landmarks and universal knowledge. The suggested method outperforms cutting-edge techniques when evaluated on 1500 people from three public ADNI datasets.

Taeho et al. [30] present a unique three-step process (SWAT-CNN) for DL-based genomic variant identification to uncover phenotypic variation single nucleotide polymorphisms (SNPs) that could be utilized to develop precise sickness categorization models. They employed a CNN to choose regions associated with phenotypes by dividing the complete genome into non-overlapped, optimal-sized bits. The second phase involved running the CNN on the selected segments to use a Sliding Window Association Test (SWAT). In the third phase, we used CNN to develop a classification model from all found SNPs. GWAS data from the ADNI, which included (N = 981; control older people (CN) = 650 and to evaluate our methods, we used GWAS data from the ADNI, which includes. Using our technique, we discovered that the most relevant genetic location for AD is an APOE region. Our classification model has an AUC of 0.82, which is suitable for usage with XGBoost, Random Forest, and traditional ML approaches. SWAT-CNN, a new genomic sequence technique that employs deep learning to detect infomercial SNPs and a categorization model for AD, has the potential for a wide range of biomedical applications.

Li and Liu [31] offer a classification technique that uses multi-cluster DenseNets to study the many local attributes of MRI scans that are incorporated for AD categorization. To extract a lot of 3D spots from each region, the full brain image is divided into small regions first. Then, the patches are separated into small groups utilizing the K-means clustering technique. A DenseNet is constructed to establish attributes for categorization. Results are combined to enhance the final answer. The proposed technique for the classification task may start by learning the MRI parameters from clusters to the global picture level. Rigid segmentation and synchronization are not required for MRI image preparation. The ADNI dataset includes T1-weighted MRIs. According to experimental data, the proposed technique has promising classification capabilities, with accuracy values of 89.5 and 92.4% for AD vs NC and 73.8 and 77.5% for MCI vs NC classification, respectively.

Gunawardena et al. [32] conducted a study in which two experiments were modelled on the ADNI dataset. The accuracy attained with the first approach, SVM, was 84.4%, which is not very high, thus the second method, CNN, was utilized, which had an accuracy of roughly 96%. In the dataset, the CNN model remains impartial.

Kim et al. [33] suggested a unique technique for distinguishing Alzheimer patients from healthy individuals that uses dual-tree complex wavelet transforms (DTCWT), LDA, and twin SVM. This innovative technique achieved an accuracy of 93% on the ADNI database and 97% on the OASIS dataset. These precision values outperform those obtained by previous AD prediction systems.

Vichianin et al. [34] used SVM to study the beneficial aspects of Alzheimer patients using MRI. A T1-weighted MRI scans both sides of the brain. As an evaluation metric, receiver operating characteristic (ROC) analysis was performed. SVM was used to calculate hippocampal relative volumes, amygdala relative volumes, entorhinal cortex thicknesses, and hippocampus and amygdala relative volumes. The findings revealed that all traits are required for diagnosis.

16.3 ALGORITHMIC SURVEY

The various algorithms used and studied in this research are as follows.

16.3.1 SUPPORT VECTOR MACHINE (SVM)

SVM is utilized for categorization problems. It is used to construct a hyperplane that can distinguish between the several categories of easily available data points. Each data point is transformed by the SVM method into a point in an n-D field, characteristics, and a value for each feature. Finding the hyperplane that divides the two classes completes the categorization. Because it is built on statistical learning frameworks, it is one of the most reliable prediction methods.

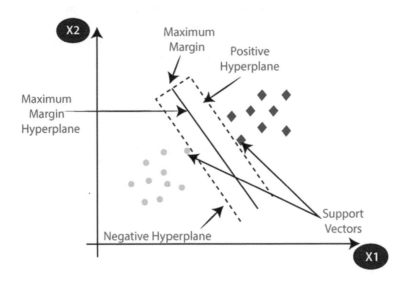

FIGURE 16.1 Support vector machine.

16.3.2 Convolutional Neural Network (CNN)

A CNN, often known as ConvNets, is a feed-forward ANN whose network structure is modelled after how the visual cortex of animals is organised. Because it has input data, an output layer, a number of hidden layers, and a wide range of parameters, a CNN is capable of learning complex objects and patterns. It subsamples the input utilising convolution and pooling methods before employing an activation function. The output unit is the last fully linked layer after all of the hidden units, which are initially only partially connected. The input image's dimensions and the output shape's dimensions are similar.

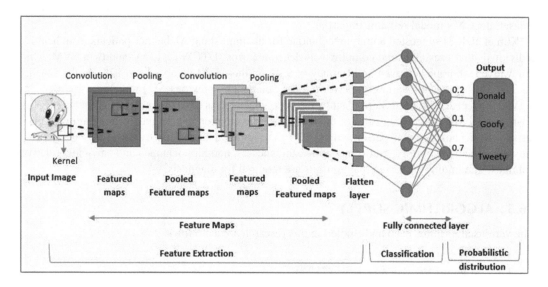

FIGURE 16.2 Convolutional neural network.

16.3.3 Naïve Bayes

Based on Bayes theorem, the Naive Bayes algorithm is a supervised learning technique for categorization problems. It provides results built on the possibility that an object will occur since it is a probabilistic classifier. The classifier's theoretical underpinning is the Bayes theorem. The predictor and features are thought to be independent in this situation. To put it another way, the presence of one feature does not alter the behavior of another. The result is the phrase "naive" Sentiment analysis, spam detection, recommender systems, and other uses for naive Bayes algorithms are common. Utilizing it is simple and quick.

$$Likelihood \qquad Class\,Prior\,Probability$$

$$P(c\,|\,x) = \frac{P(x\,|\,c)\,P(c)}{P(x)}$$

$$Posterior\,Probability \qquad Predictor\,Prior\,Probability$$

$$P(c\,|\,X) = P(x_1\,|\,c) \times P(x_2\,|\,c) \times \cdots \times P(x_n\,|\,c) \times P(c)$$

FIGURE 16.3 Mathematical formula for Naïve Bayes.

16.3.4 DECISION TREE

This is a method for using supervised learning to solve difficulties with categorization and regression. Every leaf node in a decision tree corresponds to a class label because the core node of the tree includes the qualities required to solve the problem. One type of supervised ML method is decision tree algorithms. This tactic aims to create a framework in which the decision tree uses a tree structure to predict the values of the desired variables that offers a resolution to the problem.

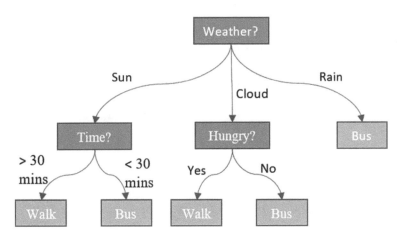

FIGURE 16.4   Decision tree example.

16.3.5 LOGISTIC REGRESSION

The logistic regression model presupposes that the input variables and the event's log-odds have a linear connection. The natural logarithm of the chance of the event divided by the probability that it won't happen is known as the log-odds, commonly referred to as the logit function. The log-odds are then transformed using the logistic function into a range [0, 1] that represents the probability of the event.

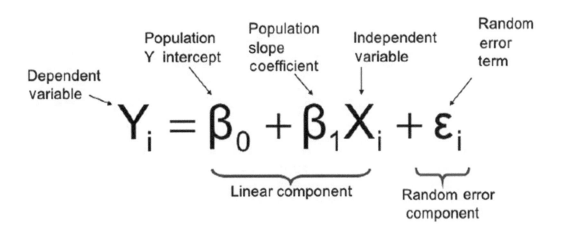

FIGURE 16.5   Mathematical formula for logistic regression.

16.3.6 Multilayer Perceptron (MLP)

This is composed of layers that are dense and flawlessly coupled, and which can transform any input dimension into any required dimension. An MLP is a neural network that has many layers. We connect neurons so that a portion of their outcomes is also their input; this is to create a neural network. With one neuron (or node) for each input, one for each output, and hidden layers with any quantity of neurons on each hidden layer, an MLP has one input, one output layer, and one node for each output. It benefits from sigmoid activation. The sigmoid activation function accepts real values as input and converts them into numbers ranging from 0 to 1.

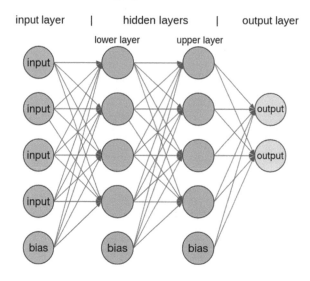

FIGURE 16.6 Multilayer perceptron.

16.3.7 Voting Based Classifiers

Voting classifiers are ML models that anticipate an outcome (class) depending on the class that has the highest possibility of being the output. They gather expertise by training on a variety of models.

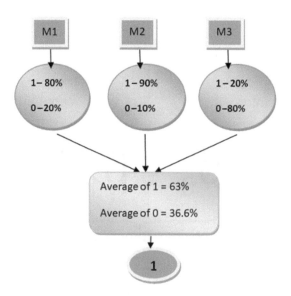

FIGURE 16.7 Voting based classifiers.

The findings of each classifier that was submitted into the voting classifier are simply averaged to forecast the output class with the most votes. Here, the idea is to develop a model which learns from several other algorithms and forecasts output based on their cumulative majority of polling for each output class.

16.3.8   K-Nearest Neighbour

This is a simple supervised learning ML methodology. It puts the new object in the group that is most like the existing categories, presuming that the new case and the previous cases are comparable. It falls under the area of supervised learning and has a wide range of uses in pattern recognition, data mining, and intrusion detection. It is commonly discarded in real-world situations owing to its non-parametric character, which implies that it holds no intrinsic ideas about the distribution of data.

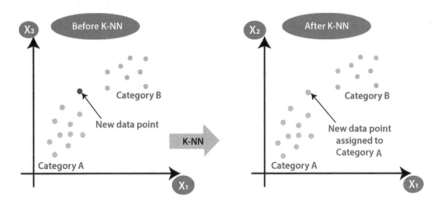

FIGURE 16.8   K-nearest neighbour.

16.3.9   Extreme Gradient Boosting (XGB)

A global, expandable, gradient-boosted decision tree (GBDT) ML framework is called Extreme Gradient Boosting (XGBoost). It provides parallel tree boosting and is the best ML package for regression, categorization, and ranking problems. The open-source program XGBoost effectively

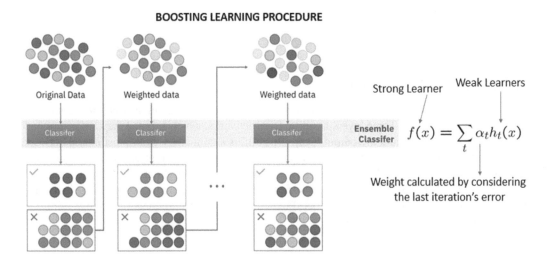

FIGURE 16.9   Extreme gradient boosting (XGB) procedure.

implements the gradient boosted trees method. Gradient boosting attempts to forecast a target variable by combining the predictions of numerous, weaker, simpler models. This is the efficiency, reliability, and viability of this algorithm. It includes both linear model solvers and tree learning techniques. Therefore, what makes it speedy is its capacity for parallel processing on a unified system.

16.3.10 KERNEL SUPPORT VECTOR MACHINE

Data can be entered and then converted utilizing a kernel function into the format required for processing. The word "kernel" is used because an SVM's window for data manipulation is given by a series of mathematical operations. A kernel function frequently modifies the training set of data to convert a non-linear decision area into a linear equation in a greater number of dimension spaces. It basically returns the integral between two locations in an appropriate feature dimension.

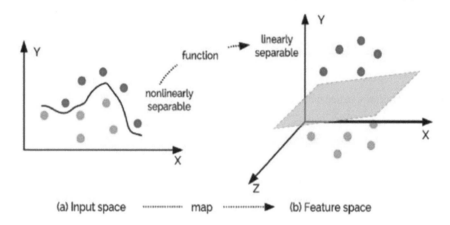

FIGURE 16.10   Kernel SVM.

16.3.11 RADIAL BASIS FUNCTION

A specific kind of artificial neural network utilized for function approximation issues are radial basis function (RBF) networks. Three layers make up RBF networks, which are feed-forward neural networks: the input, hidden, and the output layer. This differs significantly from most neural network architectures, which have several layers and generate non-linearity by repeatedly using non-linear activation functions. The hidden layer is where computation takes place after receiving input data from the input layer. The RBF neural network's hidden layer is its most potent and distinctive feature compared to other neural networks. Prediction tasks like classification or regression are reserved for the output layer.

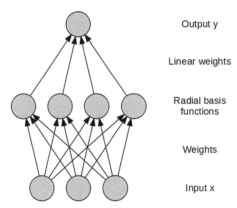

FIGURE 16.11   Radial basis function.

16.3.12   GAUSSIAN MIXTURE MODEL

A function called a Gaussian mixture is made up of several Gaussians, each of which is denoted by the string K, where K is the number of clusters in our dataset. It is a widely used model for clustering or generative unsupervised learning. It is based on the optimization approach and is also known as expectation-maximisation clustering, or EM clustering. Sub-populations within a larger population that are normally distributed are represented using Gaussian mixture models. There are two peaks, and the data appear to be rising and falling three or four times, depending on your perspective. However, if more than one Gaussian distribution can adequately represent the data, we can create a Gaussian mixture model.

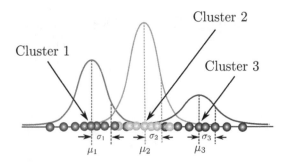

FIGURE 16.12   Gaussian mixture model.

16.4   PROPOSED METHODOLOGY

16.4.1   INTRODUCTION

The general topic of this section is: How to detect dementia? The method is depicted schematically in Figure 16.13. An explanation of the processing flow is provided below.

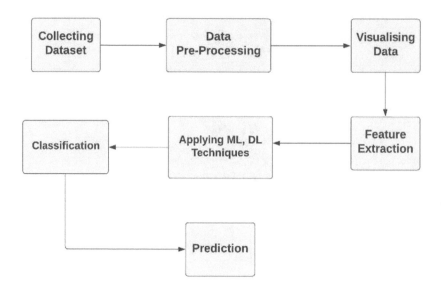

FIGURE 16.13   Flowchart of methodology.

16.4.2 DATASET

The dataset consists of about 5000 MRI images in total, each of which is divided based on the stage of AD. The data file is separated into four classes, each including test and training data: mild, moderate, very mild, and non-demented. This information was obtained over several years under different circumstances. On Kaggle, this dataset is accessible.

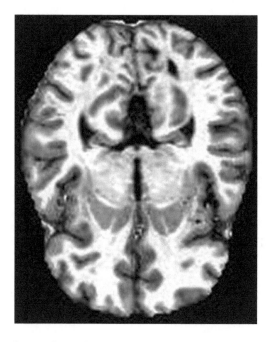

FIGURE 16.14   MRI scan for non-dementia.

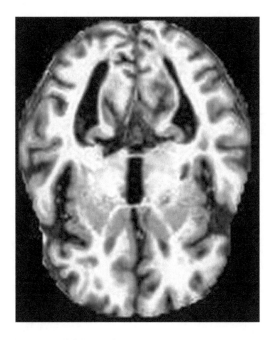

FIGURE 16.15   MRI scan for very mild dementia.

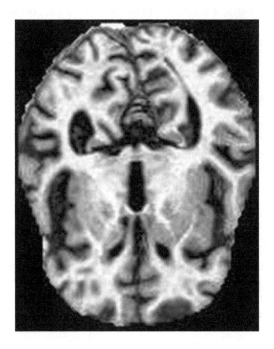

FIGURE 16.16   MRI scan for mild dementia.

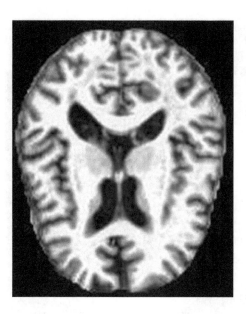

FIGURE 16.17   MRI scan for moderate dementia.

16.4.3 DATA PRE-PROCESSING

Before being used for model training and inference, pictures must first undergo image pre-process-ing. This encompasses, but is not limited to, adjustments to the size, orientation, and color. At this stage, the image is checked for areas of low intensity, and the appropriate methods for converting the data to the desired format are also used, including geometric adjustments, image filtering, and segmentation.

16.4.4 VISUALIZING DATA

The visual display of data and information offers an easy approach to observe and analyze trends, anomalies, and patterns in data by utilizing visuals like charts, infographics, and maps. Additionally, it offers a great tool for staff members or business owners to clearly deliver data to non-technical audiences. In this scenario, the data were visualized using several Python tools, such as matplotlib and seaborn. Box plots, scatter plots, line plots, heat maps, and other types of plots were available.

16.4.5 FEATURE EXTRACTION

Here, the raw, unedited data are transformed into numeric values that may be handled while preserv-ing the authenticity of the original information set's content. The dimensionality reduction method, which eliminates the redundant and unnecessary data, makes the dataset more efficient and increases accuracy. As a result, processing will be simpler.

16.4.6 Applying ML and DL Techniques

The properties of the set of data that were collected in this step were subjected to a variety of approaches, including ML and DL, along with their multiple techniques and algorithms. A program that uses a dataset that has never been seen before to detect patterns or make choices is known as an ML model. A network with numerous layers can also be used to train DL models.

16.4.7 Classification

A classification model will then be developed using classifiers such naive Bayes, Decision Trees, ANN, and SVM. These classifiers categorize training data according to the class label. This supervised ML technique called classification asks the model to guess the appropriate label for some input data. When performing classification, the algorithm is fully trained using the training data, assessed using test data, and then utilized to make predictions on fresh, unused data.

16.4.8 Prediction

Once the data are classified, the model may produce precise predictions, which will help us achieve our objective. The most accurate method from the collection of techniques, such as voting-based classifiers, multilayer perceptron, and kernel SVM, will be used to perform these.

16.5 RESULTS

Table 16.1 compares the effectiveness of the various algorithms used in this study to diagnose dementia.

According to the plot shown in Figure 16.18, generated on the basis of the results, Kernel SVM has the highest accuracy while Random Forest has the least.

TABLE 16.1
Comparison of Results

Algorithm	Accuracy (%)
Kernel Support Vector Machine	94
Radial Basis Function (RBF)	93
Multilayer Perceptron (MLP)	91
Voting Based Classifier	89
Support Vector Machine (SVM)	87
Decision Tree	84
Extreme Gradient Boosting (XGB)	80
K-Nearest Neighbour (KNN)	76
Naïve Bayes	76
Logistic Regression	76
Random Forest	74

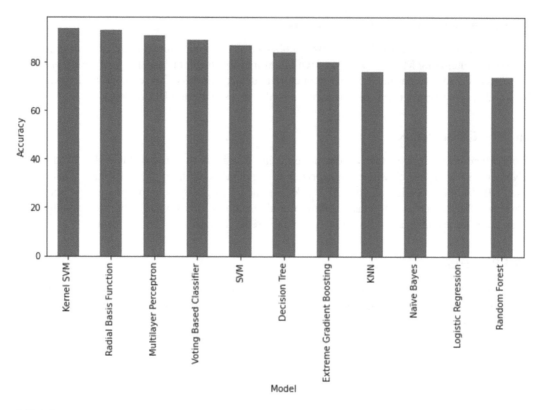

FIGURE 16.18 Comparison of models used.

16.6 CONCLUSION AND FUTURE WORK

Dementia can be diagnosed using a process that involves several tests, including cognitive and neurological, brain scans, psychiatric evaluation, genetic, and blood testing. The patient may find this operation to be exceedingly time and labour intensive. Therefore, we have suggested a technique to lessen the difficulty of this process. Even 15 years prior to a current diagnosis, dementia can be identified, and future risk factors can be minimized with merely an MRI of the patient's brain. This is conceivable because dementia is a gradual illness, and the first signs of the neurodegenerative condition can be seen up to 20 years before it reaches its final stage.

For the prediction of several forms of dementia, such as mild, moderate, very mild, and none, several models were used. The Kernel SVM method produced the highest results, achieving an accuracy of 94%. MLP and voting based classifiers came in second and third, respectively, with accuracies of 91 and 89%.

We intend to work on a dataset in the future that contains a variety of assessments, including cognitive tests like the Mini MMSE and MoCA, as well as checks for the presence of biomarkers in cerebrospinal fluid. Patients will be able to diagnose a particular stage of dementia while sitting in the comfort of their home.

ACKNOWLEDGEMENT

I would like to express my gratitude to Dr. Swati Shinde for her constant support, encouragement, and guidance as I prepared this chapter.

REFERENCES

[1] Shih-Yi Chien, Shiau-Fang Chao, Yihuang Kang, Chan Hsu, Meng-Hsuan Yu, and Chan-Tung Ku; "Understanding Predictive Factors of Dementia for Older Adults: A Machine Learning Approach for Modeling Dementia Influencers"; *International Journal of Human-Computer Studies*, Volume 165, p. 102834; 2022.

[2] K. Etminani, A. Soliman, A. Davidsson et al.; "A 3D Deep Learning Model to Predict the Diagnosis of Dementia with Lewy Bodies, Alzheimer's Disease, and Mild Cognitive Impairment Using Brain 18F-FDG PET"; *European Journal of Nuclear Medicine and Molecular Imaging*, Volume 49, pp. 563–568; 2022.

[3] H.A. Helaly, M. Badawy, and A.Y. Haikal; "Deep Learning Approach for Early Detection of Alzheimer's Disease"; *Cognitive Computation*, Volume 14, pp. 1711–1727; 2022.

[4] Jack Diskin and Alison Huenger. "Machine Learning For Alzheimer's Disease Diagnosis: Computer Vision and Recurrent Neural Networking."; *Journal of Dawning Research*, Volume 4; 2022.

[5] Golrokh Mirzaei and Hojjat Adeli; "Machine Learning Techniques for the Diagnosis of Alzheimer's Disease, Mild Cognitive Disorder, and Other Types of Dementia"; *Biomedical Signal Processing and Control*, Volume 72, Part A; 2022.

[6] A. Termine, C. Fabrizio, C. Caltagirone, and L. Petrosini; "A Reproducible Deep-Learning-Based Computer-Aided Diagnosis Tool for Frontotemporal Dementia Using MONAI and Clinical Frameworks"; *Life*; 2022.

[7] Farhad Abedinzadeh Torghabeh, Yeganeh Modaresnia, and Mohammad Mahdi Khalilzadeh; "Effectiveness of Learning Rate in Dementia Severity Prediction Using VGG16"; Elsevier; 2022.

[8] Faouri Sinan, AlBashayreh Mahmood, and Azzeh Mohammad; "Examining the Stability of Machine Learning Methods for Predicting Dementia at Early Phases of the Disease"; *arXiv*; 2022.

[9] S. Bharati, P. Podder, D.N.H. Thanh et al.; "Dementia Classification Using MR Imaging and Clinical Data with Voting-Based Machine Learning Models"; *Multimedia Tools and Applications*; 2022.

[10] N. Chedid, J. Tabbal, A. Kabbara et al.; "The Development of an Automated Machine Learning Pipeline for the Detection of Alzheimer's Disease"; *Scientific Reports*, Volume 12, 18137; 2022.

[11] Tran Anh Tuan, The Bao Pham, Jin Young Kim, Manuel R. João, and S. Tavares; "Alzheimer's Diagnosis Using Deep Learning in Segmenting and Classifying 3D Brain MR Images"; *International Journal of Neuroscience*; 2022.

[12] S. Broman, E. O'Hara, and M. L. Ali, "A Machine Learning Approach for the Early Detection of Dementia"; *IEEE International IOT, Electronics and Mechatronics Conference (IEMTRONICS)*; 2022.

[13] Miah Yunus, Prima Chowdhury, Seema Sharmeen, Mahmud Mufti, and Kaiser M. Shamim; "Performance Comparison of Machine Learning Techniques in Identifying Dementia from Open Access Clinical Datasets". In Saeed, F., Al-Hadhrami, T., Mohammed, F., & Mohammed, E., editors, *Advances on Smart and Soft Computing*, of *Advances in Intelligent Systems and Computing*, pp. 79–89, Singapore, Springer; 2021.

[14] L. Ilias, D. Askounis, and J. Psarras; "Detecting Dementia from Speech and Transcripts using Transformers"; *arXiv.*; 2021.

[15] Robin Ghosh, et al.; "Application of Artificial Intelligence and Machine Learning Techniques in Classifying Extent of Dementia Across Alzheimer's Image Data"; *IJQSPR*; Volume 6, 2; 2021.

[16] Tomasz M. Rutkowski et al.; "Neurotechnology and AI Approach for Early Dementia Onset Biomarker from EEG in Emotional Stimulus Evaluation Task."; *43rd Annual International Conference of the IEEE Engineering in Medicine & Biology Society (EMBC)*; 2021.

[17] N. Deepa and S.P. Chokkalingam; "An Age Impairment Ad Dementia on Various Stages Depicting the Severity on Patient Using a Deep Learning Model"; *Annals of the Romanian Society for Cell Biology*; 2021.

[18] Jo Taeho, K. Nho, S.L. Risacher et al.; "Deep Learning Detection of Informative Features in Tau PET for Alzheimer's Disease Classification"; *BMC Bioinformatics*, Volume 21; 2020.

[19] Fubao Zhu, Xiaonan Li, Haipeng Tang, Zhuo He, Chaoyang Zhang, Guang-Uei Hung, Pai-Yi Chiu, and Weihua Zhou; "Machine Learning for the Preliminary Diagnosis of Dementia", *Scientific Programming*; 2020.

[20] Kimberly Dale Ng, S. Mehdizadeh, A. Iaboni, A. Mansfield, A. Flint, and B. Taati; "Measuring Gait Variables Using Computer Vision to Assess Mobility and Fall Risk in Older Adults With Dementia"; *IEEE Journal of Translational Engineering in Health and Medicine*, Volume 8, pp. 1–9; 2020.

[21] Silvia Basaia, Federica Agosta, Luca Wagner, Elisa Canu, Giuseppe Magnani, Roberto Santangelo, and Massimo Filippi; "Automated Classification of Alzheimer's Disease and Mild Cognitive Impairment Using a Single MRI and Deep Neural Networks"; *NeuroImage: Clinical*, Volume 21; 2019.

[22] Deepika Bansal, Rita Chhikara, Kavita Khanna, and Poonam Gupta; "Comparative Analysis of Various Machine Learning Algorithms for Detecting Dementia"; *Procedia Computer Science*, Volume 132, 2018.

[23] S. Alam, R. Kwon, I. Kim, and S. Park; "Twin SVM-Based Classification of Alzheimer's Disease Using Complex Dual-Tree Wavelet Principal Coefficients and LDA"; *Journal of Healthcare Engineering*; 2017.

[24] A.S. Chudhey, H. Jindal, A. Vats, and S. Varma; "An Autonomous Dementia Prediction Method Using Various Machine Learning Models"; S. Tiwari, M.C. Trivedi, M.L. Kolhe, K. Mishra, and B.K. Singh (eds.) *Advances in Data and Information Sciences. Lecture Notes in Networks and Systems*, vol 318; Springer; 2017.

[25] Fadi Thabtah, Swan Ong, and David Peebles; "Detection of Dementia Progression from Functional Activities Data Using Machine Learning Techniques"; 2022.

[26] N.J. Herzog and G.D. Magoulas; "Machine Learning-Supported MRI Analysis of Brain Asymmetry for Early Diagnosis of Dementia"; A.E. Hassanien, R. Bhatnagar, V. Snášel, and M. Yasin Shams (eds.) *Medical Informatics and Bioimaging Using Artificial Intelligence. Studies in Computational Intelligence*, vol 1005. Springer; 2022.

[27] F. Garcia-Gutierrez, A. Delgado-Alvarez, C. Delgado-Alonso, et al.; "Diagnosis of Alzheimer's Disease and Behavioural Variant Frontotemporal Dementia with Machine Learning-aided Neuropsychological Assessment Using Feature Engineering and Genetic Algorithms"; *International Journal of Geriatric Psychiatry*, Volume 37, Issue 2; 2021.

[28] S. Esmaeilzadeh, D.I. Belivanis, K.M. Pohl, and E. Adeli; "End-To-End Alzheimer's Disease Diagnosis and Biomarker Identification"; Y. Shi, H.I. Suk, and M. Liu *Machine Learning in Medical Imaging. MLMI Lecture Notes in Computer Science*, vol 11046. Springer; 2018.

[29] Mingxia Liu, Jun Zhang, Ehsan Adeli, and Dinggang Shen; "Landmark-Based Deep Multi-instance Learning for Brain Disease Diagnosis"; *Medical Image Analysis*, Volume 43; 2018.

[30] Taeho Jo, Kwangsik Nho, Paula Bice, and Andrew J Saykin; "For The Alzheimer's Disease Neuroimaging Initiative, Deep learning-based identification of genetic variants: application to Alzheimer's disease classification"; *Briefings in Bioinformatics*, Volume 23, Issue 2, March; 2022.

[31] Fan Li and Manhua Liu; "Alzheimer's disease diagnosis based on multiple cluster dense convolutional networks"; *Computerized Medical Imaging and Graphics*, Volume 70; 2018.

[32] K. A. N. N. P. Gunawardena, R. N. Rajapakse, and N. D. Kodikara, "Applying convolutional neural networks for pre-detection of alzheimer's disease from structural MRI data," *2017 24th International Conference on Mechatronics and Machine Vision in Practice (M2VIP)*, Auckland, New Zealand, 2017.

[33] S. Alam, R. Kwon, I. Kim, and S. Park (2017). Twin SVM-Based Classification of Alzheimer's Disease Using Complex Dual-Tree Wavelet Principal Coefficients and LDA. *Journal of Healthcare Engineering*, 2017.

[34] C. Jongkreangkrai, Y. Vichianin, C. Tocharoenchai, H Arimura, and for the Alzheimer's Disease Neuroimaging Initiative; "Computer-aided classification of Alzheimer's disease based on support vector machine with combination of cerebral image features in MRI"; *Journal of Physics*, Volume 694, 2016.

17 Optimized Student's Multi-Face Recognition and Identification Using Deep Learning

Avadhoot Autade
Pimpri Chinchwad College of Engineering, Pune, Maharashtra, India

Pratik Adhav
Savitribai Phule Pune University, Nashik, Maharashtra, India

Abhimanyu Babar Patil, Aditya Dhumal, Sushma Vispute, and K. Rajeswari
Pimpri Chinchwad College of Engineering, Pune, Maharashtra, India

CONTENTS

17.1 INTRODUCTION

Higher education institutions place a greater emphasis on developing students' independent ability. But students frequently engage in the practice of missing or even replacing classes, which results in subpar training and negatively impacts on the development of their professional level. The standard procedure for such occurrences is to have a roll call or the timetable signed. These two approaches are a time and energy waste. When there are many pupils in the class, they will use a lot of class time and be unable to address the issue of signing. Face recognition does not require active input from the subject.

Numerous applications heavily rely on face identification and recognition. It is primarily utilized in systems for home security, criminal detection, and attendance tracking. Facial recognition is a technique for identifying someone or confirming their identity by using their face. Facial recognition technology can identify people in real time as well as in still photos and movies [1].

Detection, alignment, feature extraction, and task recognition are the phases in face recognition. Deep learning models first approached then surpassed human performance in facial recognition tests. Face recognition using a convolutional neural network (CNN) algorithm is more efficient and reliable.

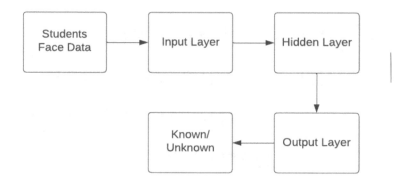

FIGURE 17.1 Basic block diagram of CNN for face recognition.

The CNN is a method of deep learning that can take into account an input image, assign priority to different parts and objects in the image, and be able to differentiate between them. In comparison to other classification methods, a ConvNet requires significantly less pre-processing. Contrary to fundamental approaches, where filters must be hand-engineered, ConvNets can learn these filters and attributes [2].

The organization of the visual cortex and the connectivity network of neurons in the human brain both have an influence on the design of a ConvNet. Individual neurons only respond to stimuli in this restricted region of the visual field, known as the receptive field. The entire visual field is covered by a series of such fields that overlap [2].

The basic visual representation of the CNN model for face recognition is shown in Figure17.1.

The input layer of the model contains the data. The number of characteristics and neurons in the input layer are equal. Depending on the model and volume of data, there could be numerous hidden layers. There are a specific number of neurons in each buried layer. The output of the hidden layer is fed into the logistic processes. The output of each class is converted into the likelihood score for each class using the logistic function.

The model uses Python's face_recognition library for recognizing faces. The backend of this library utilizes deep learning and cutting-edge facial recognition from Dlib. High quality code, machine learning algorithms, numerical algorithms, image processing, networking, testing, data compression, and threading are some of Dlib'skey features.

17.2 THE LITERATURE

17.2.1 TECHNICAL SURVEY

Chacua et al. [3] developed a people identification model through facial recognition using deep learning. Table 17.1 shows the common findingsof the evaluation of the system suggested by the authors in two different environments: one controlled (a room with sufficient light and small postural adjustments on the face) and the other uncontrolled (stairs and halls with various front camera distances, consistent light, and significant face pose variations) [3].

TABLE 17.1
Evaluation of the System (%) [3]

Overall Results	Accuracy	Error Rate	Sensitivity	Specificity
Controlled environment	96	4	96	0
Uncontrolled environment	71.43	28	72	86.67

The performance measures used by the author [4] are the kappa score represented in Figure 17.1, which is 99.82%, and which is used to determine the cross-reliability. Precision shows the ratio of correctly predicted beneficial assumptions to all predicted beneficial assumptions. Recall shows the percentage of real positives that are clearly predicted, which is 99.8743%. In terms of precision, 99.8611% of affirmative recognitions were truly accurate. The average value of precision and recall, or the F1-score, is 99.864%. The proportion of accurate predictions to all predictions is referred to as accuracy. The overall accuracy is 99.8671% and the average accuracy is 99.874%.

Figure 17.2 shows the accuracy comparison between the multi-task cascaded convolutional neural network (MTCNN) and Viola Jones. If the model is run in a multitask fashion, it yields results that show the model performed well [5].

Figure 17.3 displays how CNNs performed in terms of the quantity of enhanced pictures. Five known post-CNNs were evaluated. It turns out that the DenseNet121 model has the best average accuracy (99.76%) out of the five models [6].

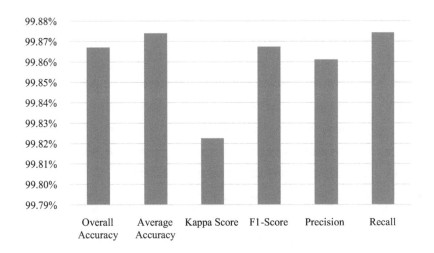

FIGURE 17.2 Summary of classification accuracy by Kakarla et al. [4].

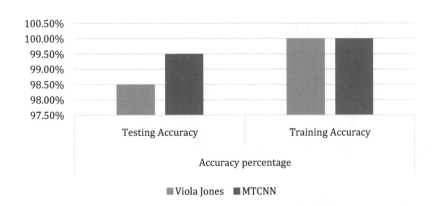

FIGURE 17.3 Accuracy comparison between MTCNN and Viola Jones [5].

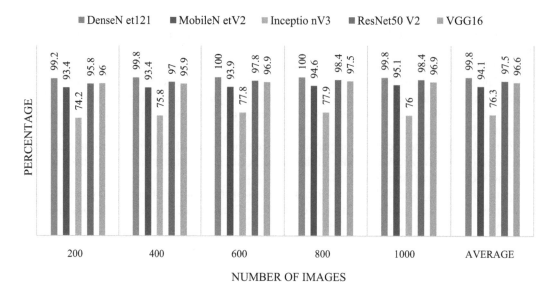

FIGURE 17.4 Performance of CNN models [6].

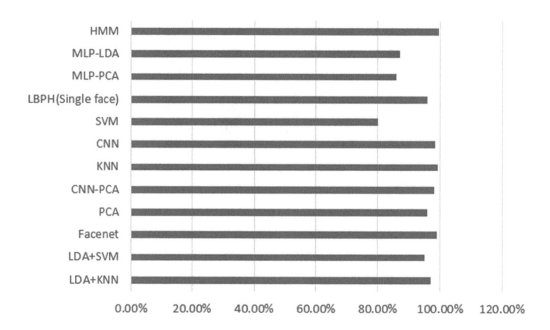

FIGURE 17.5 Different algorithms with 12 horizontal bars showing percentage of the accuracy [7].

The graph between the algorithms and their accuracy is shown in Figure 17.4. The Hidden Markov Model (HMM), K-Nearest Neighbour (KNN), and CNN are more accurate in the graph than other algorithms [7].

17.2.2 Non-Technical Survey

A portable device made by Bhattacharya et al. [8] may be utilized even when the sessions are in progress and perform effectively. To evaluate the quality of a face, the authors used posture estimation, sharpness, picture size or resolution, and brightness. Additionally, they discussed how to compute the parameters and normalize them. The weights were applied to the parameters to determine the final score. To extract low-dimensional unique characteristics from the facial photos, they employed the CNN algorithm. For face detection, they made use of the Viola Jones method.

Using motion-based detectors and a camera that records video and uses HMM to identify faces, the method proposed by Yadav etal. [9] employed these to track attendance. It logs attendance and maintains track of whether a student attended the entirety of a lecture or not.

Harish et al. [10] created an application that uploads photos shot by faculty members'phones to Google Drive. These are retrieved by a system for FACENET recognition before attendance is recorded. This model's accuracy was 100%. The FACENET algorithm and system integration with Google Drive were addressed by the authors. Due to the fact that the data are saved in Google Drive, the storage needs are quite minimal.

A model with a camera for collecting student photographs was proposed by Patil et al. [11]. Features are obtained using Linear Discriminant Analysis (LDA) and identified using KNN, and Viola Jones is used to identify the face. The photos'contrast was improved by the authors using a technique called histogram equalization. The accuracy of this model is 97%.

A thorough examination of a number of edge detection methods, including Prewitt, Sobel, Canny, Roberts, and Laplacian of Gaussian, was performed by Ansari et al. [12]. These methods were created using MATLAB R2015a, and the effectiveness of each edge detection methodology was evaluated using Peak Signal-to-noise Ratio (PSNR) and Mean Square Error (MSE). Following an experimental examination, the authors discovered that the Canny edge detector outperforms other methods.

A model based on a Raspberry PI system was created by Nagoriya et al. [13] to swiftly and correctly detect and identify human faces. To make it simple to identify student faces, this project used the eigen matrix idea. This system is independent of both hardware and software because it was built using an open-source image processing library.

A method was created by Zeng et al. [14] that uses deep-learning-related concepts to enhance the AlexNet CNN and the WebFace dataset to enhance network training and evaluation. They used this concept to create a strong facial-recognition-based tracking system in the classroom, combining it with Radio Frequency Identification (RFID) card scanning technology. According to the research, the approach is reliable and successful in cutting the expenses associated with student absences.

With the use of video, Patil et al. [15] conducted a comparative evaluation of facial recognition models. The models that were examined were CNN, Viola Jones, Haar Cascade, and Histogram Oriented Gradients. For face detection and recognition, they made use of CNN and Haar Cascade. The accuracy of this model for the attendance system is 94.6%.

A distinct CNN architecture, which includes the process of collecting student face data, was proposed by Kakarla et al. [4]. They discovered that the suggested CNN design offered 99% accuracy. They also created a web-based application called a clever attendance tracking method that used facial recognition to give real-time attendance data for pupils.

Using a DNN-based face detector, Damale et al. [16] demonstrated three distinct methods for face recognition, including SVM, MLP, and CNN. For feature extraction in the SVM and MLP algorithms, they employed Principal Component Analysis (PCA) and LDA. Comparing CNN's performance rating to other methods, it is favorable.

Mathew et al. [5] discussed a technique for reidentifying people from surveillance camera footage. Face detection from movies and person prediction using CNN models created using the cropped face pictures from the face detection stage are crucial tasks in this approach. They determined the variables influencing the model's performance.

A CNN-based face detection and recognition algorithm was suggested by Khan et al. [17] which beats conventional methods. A smart classroom with face recognition technology for tracking student attendance has been suggested as a way to verify the effectiveness of the proposed algorithm. The publicly accessible Labeled Faces in the Wild (LFW) dataset is used to train the facial recognition algorithm. From a single shot of 40 students, the system can distinguish 30 out of the 35 faces that it can detect. On the test data, the suggested system had an accuracy rate of 97.9%.

TABLE 17.2
Different Categories of Work Done

Category	Dataset	Algorithms Used	Results
Deep learning person recognition data set analysis for threat avoidance and crime detection	Video dataset is used	MTCNN, Viola Jones (Haar Cascade)	Accuracy between 96 and 99%. MTCNN outperforms all other networks.
Deep-learning-based attendance tracking method for single-face data	Video dataset is used	CNN, SVM, MLP, CNN-PCA, and HOG	Accuracy between 95 and 98%. CNN-PCA performs better than others
Deep-learning-based student face recognition model with multiple face image data	Student photo dataset with several faces	CNN.Python'sface_ recognition module	99.38% accuracy rate.

17.3　COMMON FINDINGS FROM THE SURVEY

Table 17.2 shows a comparative analysis of three different categories of work done by existing authors for face recognition with different datasets. It includes face recognition to avoid crime; anattendance tracking method for single-face data; and face recognition model with multiple face image data.

17.4　RESULTS AND DISCUSSION

This work uses the dataset Labeled Faces in the Wild (LFW) to examine the issue of unchecked face recognition. The LFW database operates with 13,233 images, 5749 people, and 1680 people with two or more images to get the required results. This model has an accuracy of 99.38% on the marked faces in the LFW database.

Table17.3 displays the model's accuracy with various tolerance values and various face counts of 1, 3, 4, and 7. Results indicate that the average accuracy is 76.04% for a tolerance value of 0.6. The model provides 89.45% accuracy for a tolerance value of 0.4. The model with the tolerance value 0.5 gives the highest accuracy of 98.70%. As shown in the table, with tolerance values 0.4 and 0.6, as the count of faces increases, accuracy decreases. But with the tolerance value 0.5, for the increased count of faces, accuracy increases. So the tolerance value 0.5 gives the optimized model with the average accuracy of 98.7% with multiple faces in the image (see Figures 17.6 and 17.7).

TABLE 17.3
Comparison of Accuracy with Different Tolerance Values (%)

Tolerance Values	0.4	0.5	0.6
No. of Faces in Image			
1	99.38	99.38	99.38
3	99	99	99
4	61.43	98.5	61.43
7	98	98	44.35
Average accuracy (%)	89.45	98.70	76.04

FIGURE 17.6 Face recognition using Python's face_recognition library for four-face image data.

FIGURE 17.7 Face recognition using Python's face_recognition library for seven-face image data.

17.5 CONCLUSION

A deep learning-based method for face identification has been proposed in this study. Deep learning and cutting-edge facial recognition technology from Dlib are used in the system's back-end. The model's facial recognition accuracy on a real-time database was 99.38% with a single face image dataset. With a tolerance value of 0.5, the model produces more precise results. The error rate increases over a tolerance threshold of 0.6. The suggested model performs better than the established methods. The use of facial recognition in numerous applications has also been evaluated.

REFERENCES

[1] S. Kadambari, G. Prabhu, D. Mistry and M. Khanore, "Automation of Attendance System Using Facial Recognition," *2019 International Conference on Advances in Computing, Communication and Control (ICAC3)*, 2019, pp. 1–5, doi: 10.1109/ICAC347590.2019.9036819

[2] I. Rao, P. Shirgire, S. Sanganwar, K. Vyawhare and S.R. Vispute, 2022. "An Overview of Agriculture Data Analysis Using Machine Learning Techniques and Deep Learning", *Second International Conference on Image Processing and Capsule Networks. ICIPCN 2021.* Lecture Notes in Networks and Systems, vol. 300. Springer, Cham. https://doi.org/10.1007/978-3-030-84760-9_30

[3] B. Chacua, "People Identification through Facial Recognition usingDeep Learning," *2019 IEEE Latin American Conference on Computational Intelligence (LA-CCI)*, 2019, pp. 1–6, doi: 10.1109/LA-CCI47412.2019.9037043

[4] S. Kakarla, P. Gangula, M. S. Rahul, C. S. C. Singh and T. H. Sarma, "Smart Attendance Management System Based on Face Recognition Using CNN," *2020 IEEE-HYDCON*, 2020, pp. 1–5, doi: 10.1109/HYDCON48903.2020.9242847

[5] V. Mathew, T. Toby, A. Chacko and A. Udhayakumar, "Person Re-identification through Face Detection from Videos Using Deep Learning," *2019 IEEE International Conference on Advanced Networks and Telecommunications Systems (ANTS)*, 2019, pp. 1–5, doi: 10.1109/ANTS47819.2019.9117938

[6] F. P. Filippidou and G. A. Papakostas, "Single Sample Face Recognition Using Convolutional Neural Networks for Automated Attendance Systems," *2020 Fourth International Conference On Intelligent Computing in Data Sciences (ICDS)*, 2020, pp. 1–6, doi: 10.1109/ICDS50568.2020.9268759

[7] Sushma Vispute, K. Rajeswari, Pratik Adhav, Avadhoot Autade, Abhimanyu Babar Patiland Aditya Dhumal, "A Comprehensive Review for Smart Attendance Monitoring System Using Machine Learning and Deep Learning", *International Research Journal of Engineering and Technology (IRJET)*, 08(12), 432–437, December 2021.

[8] S. Bhattacharya, G. S. Nainala, P. Das and A. Routray, "Smart Attendance Monitoring System (SAMS): A Face Recognition Based Attendance System for Classroom Environment," *2018 IEEE 18th International Conference on Advanced Learning Technologies (ICALT)*, 2018, pp. 358–360, doi: 10.1109/ICALT.2018.00090

[9] M. Yadav, A. Aggarwal and N. Rakesh, "Motion Based Attendance System in Real-Time Environment for Multimedia Application," *2018 8th International Conference on Cloud Computing, Data Science & Engineering (Confluence)*, 2018, pp. 332–336, doi: 10.1109/CONFLUENCE.2018.8442813

[10] M. Harish, P. Chethan, Syed Abdul Azeem and M. G. Veena, "A Smart Attendance System Based on Machine Learning," *2019 Global Conference for Advancement in Technology (GCAT)*, 2019, pp. 1–7, doi:10.1109/GCAT47503.2019.8978324

[11] V. Patil, A. Narayan, V. Ausekar and A. Dinesh, "Automatic Students Attendance Marking System Using Image Processing And Machine Learning," *2020 International Conference on Smart Electronics and Communication (ICOSEC)*, 2020, pp. 542–546, doi:10.1109/ICOSEC49089.2020.9215305

[12] Mohd Aquib Ansari, Diksha Kurchaniyaand Manish Dixit, "A Comprehensive Analysis of Image Edge Detection Techniques", *International Journal of Multimedia and Ubiquitous Engineering*, 2017, doi:10.14257/ijmue.2017.12.11.01

[13] Harsh Nagoriya, "Attendance System using Face Recognition utilizing OpenCV Image Processing Library," *International Journal for Research in Applied Science and Engineering Technology (IJRASET)*, 2020, ISSN: 23219653.

[14] W. Zeng, Q. Meng and R. Li, "Design of Intelligent Classroom Attendance System Based on Face Recognition," *2019 IEEE 3rd Information Technology, Networking, Electronic and Automation Control Conference (ITNEC)*, 2019, pp. 611–615, doi: 10.1109/ITNEC.2019.8729496

[15] P. Patil and S. Shinde, "Comparative Analysis of Facial Recognition Models Using Video for Real Time Attendance Monitoring System," *2020 4th International Conference on Electronics, Communication and Aerospace Technology (ICECA)*, 2020, pp. 850–855, doi: 10.1109/ICECA49313.2020.9297374

[16] R. C. Damale and B. V. Pathak, "Face Recognition Based Attendance System Using Machine Learning Algorithms," *2018 Second International Conference on Intelligent Computing and Control Systems (ICICCS)*, 2018, pp. 414–419, doi: 10.1109/ICCONS.2018.8662938

[17] M. Z. Khan, S. Harous, S. U. Hassan, M. U. GhaniKhan, R. Iqbal and S. Mumtaz, "Deep Unified Model for Face Recognition Based on Convolution Neural Network and Edge Computing," *IEEE Access*, vol. 7, 2019, pp. 72622–72633, doi: 10.1109/ACCESS.2019.2918275

18 Impact of Fake News on Society with Detection and Classification Techniques

Saroj Kumar Chandra
Jindal University, Raigarh, India

CONTENTS

18.1 INTRODUCTION

Fake news is one of the most critical elements for spreading positivity or negativity in society [1, 2]. Its detection and classification covers many fields of study such as computer science, social science, economics, psychology, and journalism. In current scenarios, people are shifting from traditional newspapers, tabloids, and magazines to social media websites like Facebook, Twitter, news blogs, and online newspapers. Real-time news is possible within seconds due to social media and its higher degree of ease of use [3]. It has been found that, in 2016, 62% of US adults were seeking news from social media, while only 49% were reported seeing news on online platforms in 2012 [4]. Facebook allows users to share, discuss, and debate issues such as health, education, and democracy. It has been reported that 70% of internet traffic is due to news websites [5]. Social media has been a double-edged sword for news consumption.

Despite the fact that online news is much easier to access, is faster and cheaper, the quality of news-on-news blogs or social media is much lower that of the traditional news communities and therefore a huge volume of fake or false news is being circulated on social media for a variety of purposes, such as political or financial gain, for fabricating mindsets, changing the opinions of people, and spreading absurdity or satire [6]. The threat of fake news emerged on a large scale during the 45th US presidential election in 2016 [7]. The problem of fake news has serious threats to the ethics of journalism and has also created disruption in the political world. According to one estimation, over 1 million tweets were related to fake news by the end of 45th US presidential election. The *Macquarie Dictionary* declared "fake news" as the term of the year in 2016. One recent case concerns the widespread and novel COVID-19 virus, where fake or false news was spread over the world through the internet about the nature, origin, and behavior of the virus. Due to this the circumstances worsened as more people read false or fake content online.

DOI: 10.1201/9781003359456-18

Detecting fake news or misinformation on social media or online platforms is an extremely important and challenging task. The main struggle arises because the human eye cannot accurately discriminate true from false news; for example, a survey found that, when a fake news article was shown, the interviewee found it very or somewhat accurate 75% of the time, while another survey found that 80% of high school students had a difficult time analyzing fake news [8]. Many fact-inspecting sites have been deployed to confirm or expose the leading confusion and misinformation, for example, snopes.com and PolitiFact. These sites play a major part in combating fake or false news, but they need expert analysis, which hampers real-time analysis of news; also, these fact-checking websites are domain dependent (e.g., political) and are not generalized for analyzing fake news from several fields such as technology, sports, and entertainment. To raise public awareness and provide tips on distinguishing true from false news, numerous blogs and articles have been written. The World Wide Web accommodates data in different formats such as audios, videos, and documents. The news published online in a heterogeneous format (such as articles, audios, videos, and news) is comparatively difficult to encounter and classify, as this rigorously demands human proficiency. However, computational methods such as machine learning and natural language processing (NLP) can be used to detect and separate fake or false news articles from articles that are based on true news. This chapter deals with the analyzing of news articles, that is, whether the article is fake or not by using NLP. Various preprocessing steps are applied to clean the textual data; classification algorithms are then applied.

The rest of the chapter is organized as follows. Section 18.2 briefs on the research methodology and algorithm design. In this section, machine learning models are used for fake news detection; classification is also briefly described. Results and discussion are presented in Section 18.3.

18.2 RESEARCH METHODOLOGY AND ALGORITHM DESIGN

The flow of the present work in shown in Figure 18.1. It is divided into sub-tasks such as dataset loading, preprocessing of data (normalization and standardization), dataset division for training and testing, and implementation of machine learning (ML) models for fake news detection and classification. A brief description of each of the ML models used is presented below. The most important resource for training ML systems nowadays is social media datasets. We have used the fake and real news dataset from Kaggle [9]. This includes text which features news published on social media or any kind of information that is related to world politics, religion, events, and so on. Unstructured data is what Twitter data is. The amount of information of this kind is expanding daily. To obtain clean, accurate, and consistent data, data preparation is essential. A text is full of different views as to the facts it reflects. Raw texts are very unstructured and include redundant information when they are not first processed. Preprocessing of tweets is done in many ways to address these problems.

18.2.1 MACHINE LEARNING MODELS

In the present work, Logistic Regression, Naive Bayes Classifier, Random Forest, Excessive Gradient Boosting, and Long Short-Term Memory (LSTM) have been used for fake news detection and classification. A brief description of each is presented in this section.

Random Forest Classifier: Random Forest uses an ensemble technique to classify the data points. In this approach, the results of multiple decision trees are combined to label new points. The performance of Random Forest is better when compared to other models but takes longer time due to the calculation of multiple decision trees.

Excessive Gradient Boosting: XGBOOST is an excessive gradient boosting technique where decision trees are generated sequentially. Weights play a very important role in this method. Weights are assigned to independent variables before being used in decision trees.

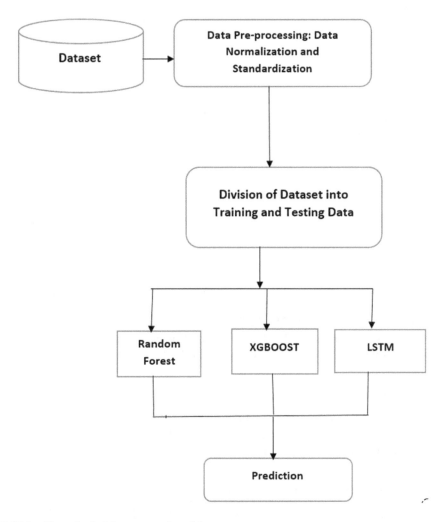

FIGURE 18.1   Flow chart of the proposed model.

The independent variables which are misclassified by the classifier are given more weight in the next decision tree model. Finally the results of all the sequentially generated decision trees are combined to produce final classification outcomes. XGBOOST has been used in many problems for solving regression, classification, ranking, and custom prediction. The two decision trees attempt to complement one another, as seen by the sum of their separate prediction scores. The model can be mathematically given as

$$y_i = \sum_{k=1}^{K} fk(xi) \quad fk \in F \tag{18.1}$$

where K is the number of trees, F is the set of potential CARTs, and f is the functional space of F. The objective function for the above model can be given as

$$Obj(\theta) = \sum_{k=1}^{K} l(y - \hat{y}) + \sum_{k=1}^{K} \varnothing(fk) \tag{18.2}$$

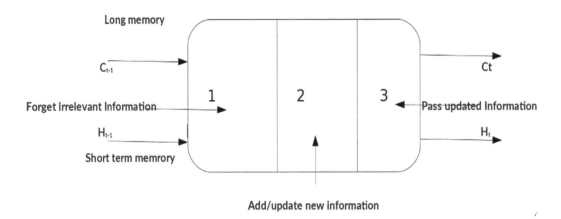

FIGURE 18.2 LSTM classification model.

Here the first term is defined as the loss function and the second term is defined as a regularization parameter.

Long Short-Term Memory (LSTM): LSTM is an extension of a recurrent neural network (RNN) and a sequential network [10]. Its major advantage is that it can handle vanished component problems that occur in an RNN. Figure 18.2 shows the architecture of LSTM.

18.2.2 MACHINE LEARNING MODEL EVALUATION

In the present work, ML models such as Logistic Regression, Naive Bayes, Random Forest, XBOOST, and LSTM are applied for the detection and classification of fake news. Precision, Recall, F1-score, and accuracy score are used for a quantitative comparative study.

18.2.3 ALGORITHM DESIGN FOR PROPOSED MODEL

In order to anticipate and categorize suicidal emotion, Algorithm 18.1 is provided. The nature of this algorithm is self-explanatory. In the first step, the dataset is loaded. Normalization and standardization are applied in the second step. In the third step, the dataset is divided into a 70:30 ratio. The ML models are applied on the divided dataset for the detection and classification of fake news. Precision, Recall, and F1-score are all computed in the final stage.

ALGORITHM 18.1: Fake News Analysis (*Dataset*, Fake/Real News)

```
Input: TwitterDataset
Output: Class labels
 begin
 DF:Loading of dataset Normalized
 DF= normalize(DF)
 Standardized DF= normalize(Normalized DF)
 Divide dataset into training and testing with ratio of 70:30
 training XGBoot, Random Forest, and LSTM
 testing XGBoot, Random Forest, and LSTM
 Compute Precision, Recall and F1-Score for each of the models
 end
```

18.3   RESULTS AND DISCUSSION

All the experimental work was performed on Windows 11 with an 8GB RAM, a 1.60GHz CPU clock speed, and 256KB, 1MB, 6MB, L1, L2, and L3 cache memories respectively.

The hardware configuration of the machine used is shown in Table 18.1. The performance of different classifiers used for fake news analysis are tested using a confusion matrix. A confusion matrix is a 2 × 2 matrix which has entries for True Positive (TP), False Positive (FP), False Negative (FN), and True Negative (TN). TP and TN represent exact matches between the predicted and actual class, whether positive or negative. FP represents the observation where negative data points are falsely classified as positive, whereas FN denotes the observation where positive data points are falsely classified as negative. The confusion matrix is shown in Table 18.2.

The experimental work was performed on the Kaggle dataset. It has five features: title, text, subject, date, and target. In order to make it easier for our machine to learn goal values, news is labeled as either 0 for false news or 1 for authentic news. The dataset is preprocessed for achieving higher accuracy and for reduced complexity. It was also divided in the ratio 70:30. Hence, 70% of the data is used for training and the remaining 30% is set aside for model testing. The dataset is randomly shuffled when it goes through the models in order to improve learning and understanding of the data by the models.

The models were quantitatively evaluated using Precision, Recall, and F1-score [11]. Precision gives the percentage of the relevant data out of the total obtained data. Recall gives the percentage of relevant data out of the total relevant data. Quantitative data gathered using various ML algorithms is shown in Table 18.2. It can be seen from the table that 99% accuracy was obtained by the LSTM classifier, which is more when compared to other models such as Random Forest and XGBOOST. It was also found that LSTM has a higher performance ratio in Precision, Recall, and F1-score.

TABLE 18.1
Hardware Configuration Used

Hardware	Capacity
CPU clock speed	1.60Ghz
RAM	8GB
L1 Cache Memory	256KB
L2 Cache Memory	1MB
L3 Cache Memory	6MB

TABLE 18.2
Quantitative Evaluation of Proposed Work

Models	Accuracy	Precision	Recall	F1-score
Random Forest	0.85	0.87	0.86	0.86
XGBoost	0.85	0.82	0.88	0.85
LSTM	0.99	0.99	0.99	0.99

18.4 CONCLUSION

In the current work, three different ML models were used for fake news identification and classi-fication. The models used were Random Forest, XGBOOST, and LSTM. Quantitative evaluations of the presented work were performed using accuracy score, Precision, Recall, and F1-score. It has been found that LSTM gives a higher performance in the detection and classification of fake news.

REFERENCES

[1] S. Raja, "Fake news detection using voting ensemble classifier", *International Conference on Inventive Computation Technologies (ICICT)*, 2022, pp. 1241–1244.

[2] T. Mladenova, I. Valova, "Research on the ability to detect fake news in users of social networks", *International Congress on Human-Computer Interaction, Optimization and Robotic Applications (HORA)*, 2022, pp. 01–04.

[3] R. Behera, M. Jena, S. Rath, S. Misra, "Co-lstm: Convolutional lstm model for sentiment analysis in social big data", *Information Processing Management*, 58, 2021, p. 102435.

[4] R. C. Gonzalez, *Digital Image Processing*. Upper Saddle River, NJ: Pearson Prentice Hall, Third Edition, 2014.

[5] Digital Scholar, available at https://digitalscholar.in/pros-and-cons-of-social-media/

[6] H. Ahmed, I. Traore, S. Saad, Detection of online fake news using n-gram analysis and machine learning techniques, *International Conference on Intelligent, Secure, and Dependable Systems in Distributed and Cloud Environments*, 2017, pp. 127–138.

[7] M. Bovet, A. H. Makse, "Influence of fake news in twitter during the 2016 us presidential election", *17th International Computer Conference on Wavelet Active Media Technology and Information Processing (ICCWAMTIP)*, 2019, pp. 205–208.

[8] T. Jiang, J. P. Li, A. U. Haq, A. Saboor, "Fake news detection using deep recurrent neural networks", *17th International Computer Conference on Wavelet Active Media Technology and Information Processing (ICCWAMTIP)*, 2020, pp. 205–208.

[9] Fake and Real News Dataset, n.d. available at https://www.kaggle.com/datasets/clmentbisaillon/fake-and-real-news-d

[10] G. S. N. Murthy, S. R. Allu, B. Andhavarapu, M. Bagadi, M. Belusonti, "Text based sentiment analysis using LSTM", *International Journal of Engineering Research Technology (IJERT)*, 9(5), pp. 1–5.

[11] S. K. Chandra, M. K. Bajpai, "Fractional mesh-free linear diffusion method for image enhancement and segmentation for automatic tumor classification", *Biomedical Signal Processing and Control*, 58, 2020, p. 101841.

19 Neurological Disorder Detection Using Computer Vision and Machine Learning Techniques

Deepali Ujalambkar
Savitribai Phule Pune University, Pune, India

Amol Bhawarthi
Cognizant Technology Solutions, Pune, India

CONTENTS

19.1 INTRODUCTION

The brain is a unique organ with very flexible and sensitive tissues. It is referred to in technical terms as the body's central processing unit. This processing unit receives information in the form of nerve signals from sensory organs connected to the nervous system. Our brain merely assists us in expressing our thoughts, carrying out our activities, and exchanging opinions, feelings, and emotions. It assists us in regulating, maintaining, and controlling many bodily systems under challenging environmental situations. However, under some different circumstances, brain cells develop and reproduce indiscriminately [1]. This aberrant growth of brain cells results in an increase in the total volume of the brain's nerve tissues, which puts more pressure on other nearby tissues. As a result, the brain's surrounding tissues move and are lifted up against the skull. Tumors are abnormal increases in tissue mass, and when they occur inside the brain, they are referred to as brain tumors. Some tumors are malignant and some are non-malignant. New blood vessels tend to grow in tumors. It can be challenging to find a malignant tumor inside a mass of tumors. A 3D brain model and a 3D analyzer tool are required for the precise detection of malignant tumors [2]. Typically, cerebral spinal fluid (CSF) is impacted by brain tumors. This results in strokes. Therefore, timely and accurate early detection and diagnosis are essential.

Now, only timely, accurate detection and diagnosis will allow for the treatment of such tumors. For the precise identification and treatment of a brain tumor, innovative techniques like image processing are used. Using computer technology, such as image recognition, the targeting machine recognizes a tumor and its shape. In general, image recognition is a way of comprehending and examining captured digital images for particular information like coloration and sharpness. Brain tumors are found using the scan-based imaging method known as magnetic resonance imaging (MRI) [3]. This technique can monitor the entire human body's internal organs to detect any tumors, not just those in the brain. This method has the distinct advantage of not employing ionized radiation, which is used in X-rays and has numerous negative effects. Instead, it creates images of the internal body structure using a magnetic field and radio waves.

The development of this image processing technology has allowed us to improve images' clarity to the point where it is simple to identify brain tumors. Segmentation is one of the techniques used in computer vision to divide an image into many segments of pixels. It is then simple to distinguish the tumor-positive brain area from the adjacent, healthy brain components. By giving distinct labels to pixels while segmenting, a difference can be readily made. Labeling is used to show how pixels with the same label have a similar feature, allowing us to cover the entire required image of the area affected collectively. The main objective is to identify brain tumors using a segmentation methodology in MRI images.

19.2 LITERATURE REVIEW

In [4], an attempt is made to estimate the degree of a brain tumor to define its level of severity. Image processing algorithms are employed to estimate the size of the glioma. The extent and stage of a brain tumor can be accurately estimated using Fuzzy C-Means and K-Means clustering techniques. This overcomes the shortcomings of the region-growing and thresholding methods. Using the output of the K-Means algorithm, the Fuzzy C-Means (FCM) algorithm is utilized to precisely determine the tumor's edge [4].

The authors of [5] proposed a neural network (NN) and fuzzy logic (FL) based method for classifying and analyzing brain tumors. This is one of the methodological approaches used to assess, retrieve, and transform the concealed information in brain tumor procedures so as to devise classifier software.

In [6], a technique based on computer-aided image processing for detecting brain tumors and calculating the tumor's surface area and location is suggested. MRI scans of the brain are processed by an integrated binarization, anatomical, and histogram-based technique to recognize brain tumors. The detection precision of the suggested method is 86.84%.

In [7], a system for the identification and categorization of brain tumors is proposed. The method employs computer-based methods to identify tumor blocks in MRI images of various individuals with brain tumors of the astrocytoma type. It categorizes the type of tumor using an artificial neural network (ANN). Image processing methods like image enhancement and segmentation, equalization of histograms, and extraction of features have been used to identify brain tumors by utilizing MRI images.

In [8], a developed and fully automated methodology that performs both localization and characterization is put forward. The technique makes use of multivariate discriminative features taken from brain MRI images.

In [9], an image segmentation-based brain tumor detection method is proposed. Brain and other medical images are diagnosed using MRIs. The system uses a method which helps to optimize feathers through entropy for accurate classification of images.

FCM segmentation, which can improve the segmentation of medical images, was suggested in [10]. The approach employed in this paper includes the cleaning, categorization, and extraction of features, as well as tumor recognition from MRI scanned brain images. The simulation is deployed in MATLAB.

In [11], the authors suggested an improved edge detection technique for segmenting cerebrum tumors. The suggested approach combines the Sobel method with the picture independent threshold method. The use of the close contour approach lowers the incidence of spurious edges. The tumor is finally retrieved from the image based on the pixel intensity inside closed outlines. MRI is the preferred imaging method for research on brain malignancies. A single MRI scan can yield a vast amount of information. When a radiologist needs to make a diagnosis, there are more sources of information available but fewer testing tools [12]. So an automated data-driven tumor recognition method is recommend in this paper, where the identification (signature) process uses both localization (segmentation) and characterization.

Multiple attempts have been made to quantify the information content of the organ's afflicted area using multi-parameter statistical MRI data. However, these have been far less effective than conventional MRI investigations [13]. There are two possible strategies for managing their variation and accuracy:

- By calculating the region of interest;
- By automating the quantitative extraction of features.

They typically comprise two phases:

1. Localization;
2. Characterization.

Most methods depend on one of the opposing points of view. Traditional methods of segmentation are concentrated on a few simple MRI scans, whereas more advanced extraction feature techniques are given a preliminary manual region of interest definition. The extent of the brain tumor is determined using image processing techniques. The effective application of K-Means and FCM to predict the location and level of a brain tumor resolves the shortcomings of thresholding and region based algorithms. By feeding back on the effectiveness of the K-Means method, the FCM algorithm achieves accuracy for the detection of the edge of the tumor. This demonstrates how brain tumors can be identified and categorized using FL and NN [14].

The comprehensive platform for assessment and categorization of brain tumors is one example of a layered structure that may be built using the latent facts that can be discovered using the brain tumor approach to analyze, extract, and convert them into software artifacts [15]. The method cannot be utilized to treat newly identified tumor types; it can only be applied to tumors that are comparable to one another. Therefore, we have decided that in order to improve tumor identification accuracy, we need to train the system with a diversity of tumor kinds. Other systems, like ANN, have used different deep learning neural networks to get reliable results, but such strategies and methods have necessitated a significant amount of hardware computation, which produces subpar outcomes [16].

19.3 METHODOLOGY

A client–server application based approach is proposed. The application takes an MRI image into account and produces a precise report. Figure 19.1 depicts the lesion and the probable diagnosis of the tumor which will be included in the outcome that the machine produces.

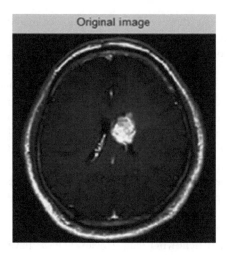

FIGURE 19.1 Image prior to thresholding.

19.3.1 THRESHOLDING

In this approach, intensity values are assigned as threshold values. The values below the threshold values are set as 0 (black); those above the set threshold are marked as 1 (white). This is the easiest way to threshold. The values using the thresholding method are calculated as shown in Equation 19.1 [13].

$$\text{global\_image}(x, y) = f(x) = \begin{cases} -1, \text{image}(x, y) \geq t \\ 0, \text{otherwise} \end{cases} \quad (19.1)$$

where t is the threshold value.

Figure 19.1 shows the image prior to thresholding. After preprocessing and applying the thresholding to the image, the image is converted and appears as shown in Figure 19.2. This depicts the image after thresholding

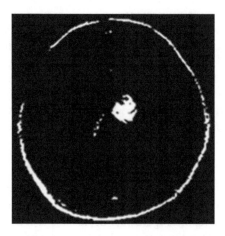

FIGURE 19.2 After thresholding image.

19.3.2   Segmentation

Thresholding is done using the Sauvola algorithm. This is useful for images where the background is not uniform. The mean and standard deviation of the immediate neighborhoods are taken into account while computing numerous thresholds for each pixel rather than a single global threshold, as shown in Equation 19.2 for the entire image:

$$t(x,y) = mn(x,y).\left[1 + c.\left(\frac{sd(x,y)}{d} \right) - 1 \right]$$

(19.2)

where $mn(x, y)$ is the mean of the neighborhoods; c is a constant value in the range 0.2…0.5 and has the default value 0.5; $sd(x, y)$ is the standard deviation of the neighborhoods; and d is the dynamic range of standard deviation and where the default value is 128.

Since the image is binarized, and all the pixels are taken into consideration while comparing with the global threshold, this method provides much better accuracy than the simple thresholding technique. We binarize an image using these algorithms and compare it to a common global thresholding value as shown in Equation 19.2.

19.3.3   Edge Based Segmentation Method

An edge filter is deployed to the image during edge-based segmentation. Based on how effectively the filter functions, pixels are then classified as edge or non-edge pixels. The same group is assigned to pixels that are not divided by an edge. According to the theory of edge-based image segmentation, the position of an edge can be established by a maximum of the first-order derivative or a zero crossing in the second-order derivative. Irrespective of the reference frame the only factor used to identify a pixel as an object pixel is its Gray value. Before the approach converges into a coherent result, to optimize the findings, component analysis and segmentation might be repeated [17].

19.3.4   Region-Dependent Segmentation Approach

Region-dependent segmentation techniques work repeatedly by isolating pixel categories with different values from each other and grouping adjacent pixels together to provide identical values.

"Segmentation" is a term that refers to spatial clustering. When a pixel is grouped together with other pixels with comparable values, the spatial component frequently unites to form a homogeneous related element within that pixel that belongs to a similar category.

19.3.5   Convolution Neural Networks (CNNs)

A CNN is a type of feed-forward neural network (FFNN). Dependencies within and between the series can be quickly learned. By significantly reducing the number of parameters, the local perception and weight sharing of CNNs can increase the effectiveness of model learning [18]. A pooling layer and convolution layer make up the majority of CNNs. Figure 19.3 depicts a typical CNN architecture.

Convolutional layers serve as characteristic extractors. As part of the training phase, the convolution filter kernel weight parameters are established. Deep convolution layers are able to extract local attributes. They restrict the convolution layers of the hidden layers to local ones. The convolutional layers' weights are utilized to extract functions during training; the fully connected layers are utilized for classification.

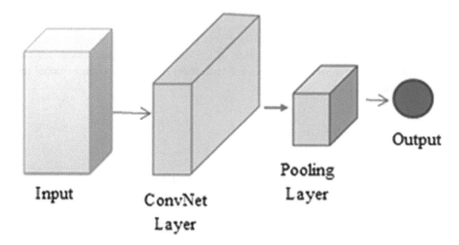

FIGURE 19.3 CNN architecture.

We can utilize the neural network method to classify the entire tumor by first training it with balanced categories and then refining it with portions that are close to the initial binary CNN.

19.3.6 KNN Algorithm

The KNN algorithm is an iterative and evolutionary approach. It aims to divide the dataset into several non-overlapping sub-categories called "clusters", which are specified by K (a predefined value). In each cluster, a particular category (data point) correlates to every additional data point. This enables data points to be kept within the same category or cluster, while also keeping them within the other categories or clusters as separate from one another [5]. This distributes the data points of a cluster so that their sum over the square distance from the cluster's center (the arithmetical mean of all the cluster's data points) is at least the same. The data point that belongs to the same category is calculated using the distance formula.

19.4 SYSTEM ARCHITECTURE

The modules involved in the system are shown in Figure 19.4.

1. Image preprocessing;
2. Boundary approach (thresholding);
3. Edge based segmentation approach;
4. Region based segmentation approach;
5. The CNN algorithm;
6. Calculate region of interest and area.

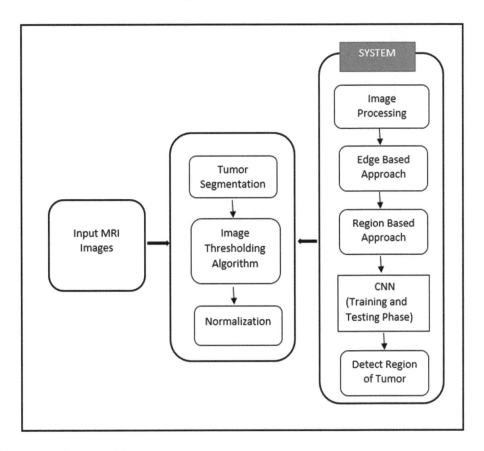

FIGURE 19.4   System architecture.

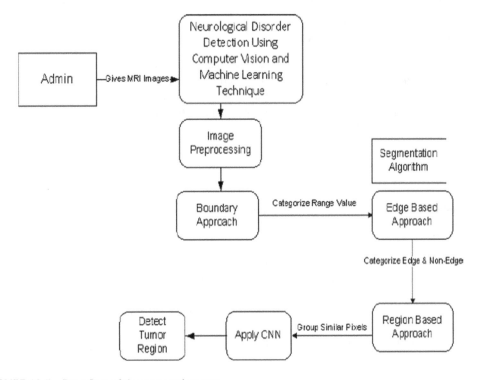

FIGURE 19.5   Data flow of the proposed system.

1. Accepts a volume of size $W1 \times H1 \times D1$
2. Requires four hyper parameters:
        i. Number of filters K
        ii. Their spatial extent F
        iii. The stride S
        iv. The amount of zero padding P

3. Produces a volume of size $W2 \times H2 \times D2$ where:

     i. $W2 = (W1 - F - 2P)/S + 1$

     ii. $H2 = (H1 - F + 2P)/S + 1$ (i.e. width and height are computed equally by symmetry)

     iii. $D2 = K$

With parameter sharing, it introduces $F*F*D1$ weights per filter, for a total of $(F*F*D1)*K$ weights and K biases. (i.e. width and height are computed equally by symmetry)

4. In the output volume, the d-th depth slice (of size $W2 \times H2$) is the result of performing a valid convolution of the d-th filter over the input volume with a stride of S, and then offset by d-th bias.

5. A common setting of the hyper parameters is $F=3, S=1, P=1$

FIGURE 19.6   Working steps of proposed algorithm.

The details of the working of the algorithm as elaborated in Section 19.3 is shown in Figure 19.6.

19.5   RESULTS AND DISCUSSION

The testing of the proposed model is checked against the test cases listed in Table 19.1. The system is designed using a simple graphic user interface (GUI).

The brain tumor dataset includes 3678 MRI scans from 253 people. Amongst them, 15,766 glioma and 840 pituitary tumors are available. The images used for study have a resolution of 512×512.

TABLE 19.1
Test Cases

Name of Test Case	Description	Expected Result
MRI preprocessing	OpenCV image (apply preprocessing on input image	Grey scale and edge detection is done
Edge based segmentation	Apply edge based segmentation algorithm	Pixels segregated as edge or non-Edge
Region based segmentation	Grouping of pixels which are near and have similar values	Regional maxima applied
Apply SVM	Apply SVM algorithm on training and testing data	Identify tumor
Calculate Region Of Interest	Apply K-means algorithm	Highlight Region Of Interest

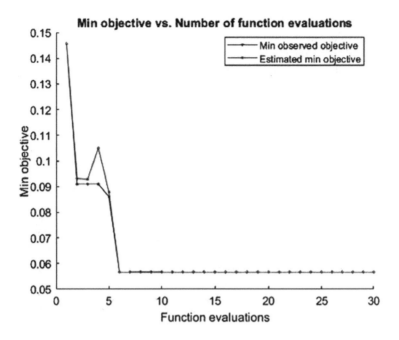

FIGURE 19.7   Output of k-nearest neighbor clustering algorithm.

True class		Meningioma	Glioma	Pituitary	True Positive Rate	False Positive Rate
	Meningioma	96%	1%	3%	96%	4%
True class	Glioma	2%	96%	2%	96%	4%
	Pituitary	2%		98%	98%	2%
		Meningioma	Glioma	Pituitary	True Positive Rate	False Positive Rate

Predicted Class

FIGURE 19.8   Confusion matrix using an SVM classifier.

The results of the k-nearest neighbor (KNN) algorithm are shown in Figure 19.7. There are 30 functions that have been evaluated. The lowest observed objective for a function evaluation of 30 is 0.057. The algorithm's precision is 0.98.

Figure 19.8 depicts the confusion matrix for the class's pituitary, glioma, and meningioma, which are regarded as a check of the accuracy of the proposed method.

The confusion matrix for using the SVM method on test data is shown in Figure 19.9. If the anticipated output matches the targets, this confusion matrix shows a maximum accuracy of 96.12%. Figure 19.9 depicts the confusion matrix for the KNN algorithm, where the accuracy is 97%.

Figure 19.10 depicts the GUI of the proposed system using a computer vision and machine learning technique (Figures 19.11–19.13).

	Meningioma	Glioma	Pituitary	True Positive Rate	False Positive Rate
Meningioma	97%	1%	2%	97%	3%
Glioma	3%	96%	1%	96%	4%
Pituitary	2%		98%	98%	2%

True class

Predicted Class

FIGURE 19.9 Confusion matrix using KNN.

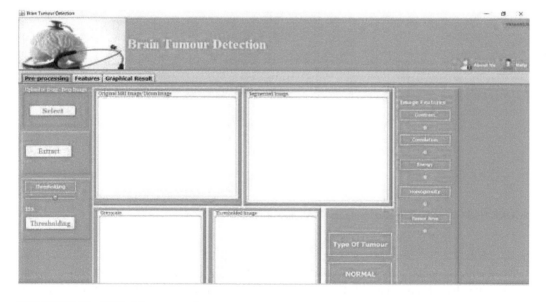

FIGURE 19.10 GUI of the proposed system.

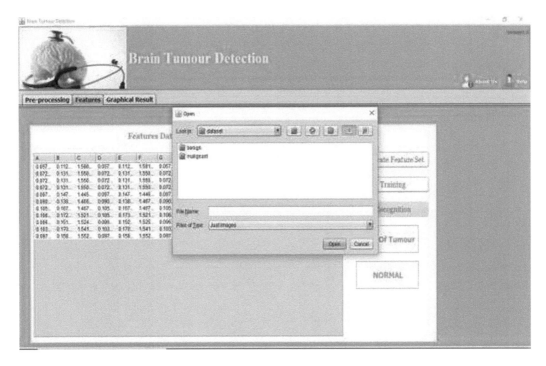

FIGURE 19.11 Select the image as input.

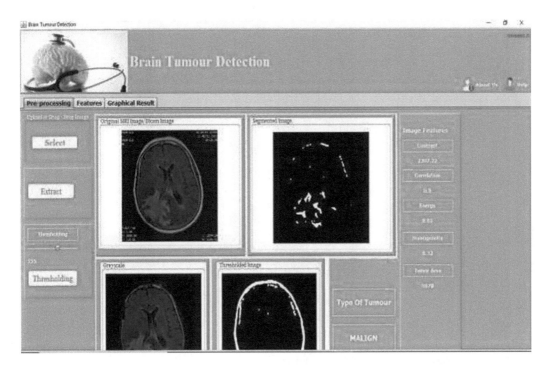

FIGURE 19.12 MRI image preprocessing.

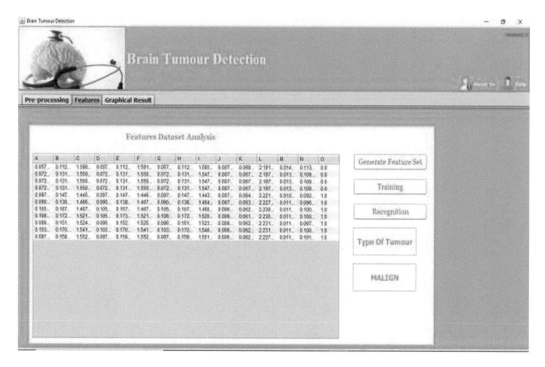

FIGURE 19.13   Featured analysis.

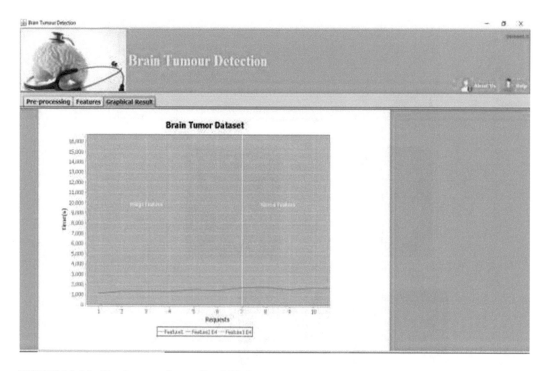

FIGURE 19.14   Result: normal or malign MRI image.

19.6   CONCLUSION

Even for experienced doctors, identifying brain tumors takes time and demands high specificity and accuracy, making it a major problem in the medical community. Consequently, this work has proposed a system for automatically diagnosing brain tumors using MRI data. An algorithm resembling CNN-based segmentation approaches has been designed for the identification of brain tumors from MRI brain images by using several techniques, such as edge detection and thresholding followed by segmentation. Edge-based segmentation and region-based segmentation are employed in this instance to separate the digital image into several parts of pixels. By first training it with balanced classes and then refining it with proportions that are near to the initial binary CNN, a neural network approach can be used to detect the entire tumor. Even though we have achieved very high diagnostic rates, the proposed method needs to be evaluated on larger datasets with individuals of diverse age groups and races in order to expand its scalability and adapt it in the future to other medical applications.

REFERENCES

1. Arnaud A, Forbes F, Coquery N, Collomb N, Lemasson B, Barbier EL, "Fully Automatic Lesion Localization and Characterization: Application to Brain Tumors using Multi parametric Quantitative MRI Data", *IEEE Transactions on Medical Imaging*, 37(7): 1678–1689, 2018.
2. Pereira S, Pinto A, Alves V, Silva CA, "Brain Tumor Segmentation using CNN in MRI Images", *IEEE Transactions on Medical Imaging*, 35(5): 1240–1251, 2016.
3. Malhotra Hema, Naaz Sameena, "Analysis of MRI Images Using Data Mining for Detection of Brain Tumor", *IJARCS*, 9, 2018. 10.26483/IJARCS.V9I2.5369.
4. Shrivastava Pallavi, Upadhayay Akhilesh, Khare Akhil, "Devising Classifiers for Analyzing and Classifying Brain Tumor using Integrated Framework PNN", *International Conference on Energy Systems and Applications*, 1–6, doi: 10.1109/ICESA.2015.7503303, 2015.
5. Nalbalwar R, Majhi U, Patil R, Gonge S, "Detection of Brain Tumor by Using ANN", *International Journal of Research in Advent Technology*, 3(4): 272–279, 2014.
6. Sharif M, Amin J, Nisar MW, Anjum MA, Muhammad N, Shad SA, "A unified patch based method for brain tumor detection using features fusion", *Cognitive Systems Research*, 59: 273–286, 2020.
7. Joseph RP, Singh CS, Manikandan M, "Brain tumor MRI image segmentation and detection in image processing", *International Journal of Research in Engineering and Technology*, 3, eISSN: 2319-1163, pISSN: 2321-7308, 2014.
8. Salunkhe PB, Patil PS, Bhamare DR, "Brain tumor detection and area calculation of tumor in brain MRI mages using clustering algorithms", *IOSR-JECE*, 4: 34–38.
9. Saba T, Mohamed AS, El-Affendi M, Amin J, Sharif M, "Brain tumor detection using fusion of hand crafted and deep learning features", *Cognitive Systems Research*, 59: 221–230, 2020.
10. Samriti Paramveer Singh, "Brain tumor detection using image segmentation", *International Journal of Engineering Research and Development*, 4(2): 1923–1925, 2016.
11. Suhag Sonu, Saini LM, "Automatic detection of brain tumor by image processing in Matlab", *International Journal of Advances in Science, Engineering and Technology*, 3(3): 114–117, 2015.
12. Amin J, Sharif M, Yasmin M, Fernandes SL, "A distinctive approach in brain tumor detection and classification using MRI", *Pattern Recognition Letters*, 139: 118–127, 2020.
13. Shelkar R, Thakare MN, "Brain tumor detection and segmentation by using thresholding and watershed algorithm", *IJACT*, 1(3): 321–324, 2014.
14. Lemée JM, Corniola MV, Da Broi M., Joswig H, "Extent of resection in meningioma: Predictive factors and clinical", *Scientific Reports*, 9(1): 5944, 2019.
15. Heo S, Lee H, "Fault detection and classification using ANN", *IFAC*, 51(18): 470–475, 2018.
16. Hossam Sultan H, Nancy Salem M, Al-Atabany W, "Multi-classification of brain tumor images using DNN", *IEEE Access*, 7: 2169–3536, 2019.

17. Latif G, Butt M, Khan AH, Butt O, Iskandar DNFA, "Multiclass brain Glioma tumor classification using block-based 3D Wavelet features of MR images", *4th International Conference on Electrical and Electronics Engineering ICEEE*, 5: 333–337, 2017.

18. Sayali Jadhav D, Channe HP, "Comparative study of K-NN, naive bayes and decision tree classification", *The International Journal of Science and Research*, 5(1): 1842–1845, 2016.

20 Deep Learning for Tea Leaf Disease Classification
Challenges, Study Gaps, and Emerging Technologies

Swati V. Shinde and Sagar Lahade
Pimpri Chinchwad College of Engineering, Pune, India

CONTENTS

20.1 INTRODUCTION

In both exporting and developing nations, tea is a consequential cash crop and has a noteworthy impact on poverty reduction, rural expansion, and food safety. For millions of agriculturalists, it is their main source of income. In many countries, tea has cultural value as well. Tea consumption has numerous health advantages, including anti-inflammatory, antioxidant, and effects on weight loss. The produced beverage that people drink the most worldwide is tea (*Camellia sinensis*). It was one of the world's first libations when it was found in approximately 2700 BC.

The annual worldwide tea trade is projected to be roughly $9.5 billion, despite the fact that annual global tea output surpasses $17 billion. China generated the largest revenue from the tea industry in 2022, totaling $99.81 billion. India brought in $15.67 billion, ranking it second in income behind

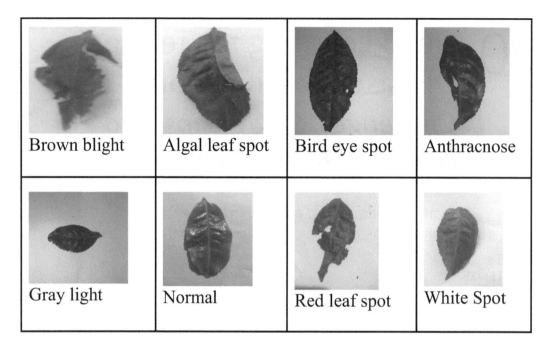

| Brown blight | Algal leaf spot | Bird eye spot | Anthracnose |
| Gray light | Normal | Red leaf spot | White Spot |

FIGURE 20.1 Tea leaf diseases.

China. India is one of the five best tea-exporting nations in the world, contributing 10% of all exports. There is a 2.1% growth rate projected for India's consumption. Over 1 million people in India have direct employment as a result of the tea industry. Due to its forward and backward interconnections, another 10 million people rely on tea for their livelihood.

The production of tea contributes significantly to India's agricultural output and GDP. Due to more land becoming unrestricted China has lately surpassed India as the world's top producer of tea which it had held for close to a century. In addition to this, tea leaf diseases are a significant factor in the losses experienced by the tea business. Since tea has such a high export value, the pathogen directly impedes the economic development of the countries that grow it by attacking the delicate leaves of the plant. Leaf infections are a challenging task since immature tea plant shoots are supplied to manufacture tea. Any challenges to the yield are quite important given the economic importance of tea. Due to the wrath of insect pests, tea crops lose anywhere from 6 to 14% of their production. Tea leaf diseases must be precisely diagnosed and identified in order to be prevented and controlled.

Figure 20.1 lists the most typical ailments that affect tea leaves. The following diseases have been identified and categorized:

a. Brown Blight: A disease characterized by the presence of brown lesions or spots on tea leaves. It can negatively impact the health and productivity of tea plants.
b. Algal Leaf Spot: This disease is characterized by the appearance of greenish or yellowish spots caused by the growth of algae on tea leaves. It can affect the photosynthetic capacity of the plant.
c. Bird Eye Spot: A tea leaf disease distinguished by the presence of small, dark spots resembling bird eyes. It can lead to leaf discoloration and reduced leaf quality.
d. Anthracnose: A fungal disease causing dark, sunken lesions on tea leaves. It can lead to defoliation and reduced yield if not managed effectively.
e. Gray Light: This disease is marked by the development of grayish patches or spots on tea leaves. It can be caused by various factors, including fungal pathogens or environmental

stress. f) Red Rust: A disease characterized by the appearance of reddish-brown rust-like spots on tea leaves. It is caused by fungal pathogens and can have detrimental effects on tea plant health and yield.

f. Red Leaf Spot: A disease characterized by the appearance of red or reddish-brown spots on tea leaves. It can indicate fungal or bacterial infections and may impact the overall health of the plant.

g. White Spot: This disease is identified by the presence of small, white spots on tea leaves. It can be caused by fungal or viral pathogens and may affect leaf quality.

Figure 20.1 provides valuable insights into the diverse tea leaf diseases encountered in the study.

The field of artificial intelligence (AI) and computer science known as machine learning (ML) focuses on the use of raw facts and algorithms to mimic human learning, progressively increasing the precision of the system. A subsection of machine learning, which is a subdomain of AI, is deep learning (DL). DL algorithms are aimed to match human judgements by frequently examining data with a given logical system. To accomplish this, DL utilizes multi-layered networks of algorithms known as neural networks.

Measures of how well DL/ML models and methods can detect and classify illness in tea leaves use accuracy, precision, recall, F1, and other scores. These measures are useful for evaluating the models' performances in illness detection and classification and by pinpointing areas where more refinement is needed. The models' efficacy and behavior are measured using a number of different graphical representations, including Receiver Operating Characteristic (ROC) curves, confusion matrices, and precision-recall plots. These metrics may be used to evaluate the efficacy of various models and procedures, allowing for the selection of the most suitable one for each specific application.

By addressing the challenges, leveraging suitable techniques, and employing appropriate deep learning models, tea leaf disease classification using deep learning aims to improve accuracy, speed up diagnosis, and enable effective management strategies in tea cultivation. Figure 20.2 illustrates the major components of tea leaf disease classification using deep learning, including challenges, techniques, and models. These components are crucial for accurate disease classification in tea cultivation.

Figure 20.3 depicts the techniques utilized in tea leaf disease classification using deep learning, addressing critical challenges faced in the field. To combat the issue of insufficient dataset, transfer learning leverages pre-trained models. Variation in symptoms is tackled through deep learning models, such as CNNs, that capture subtle disease variations. Complex image backgrounds are handled by preprocessing techniques and data augmentation, enhancing focus on disease-related features. These techniques collectively enhance the accuracy and robustness of tea leaf disease classification using deep learning

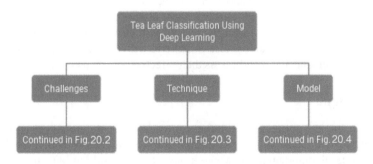

FIGURE 20.2   Tea leaf disease classification in DL.

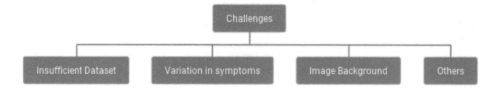

FIGURE 20.3   Challenges in tea leaf disease classification.

FIGURE 20.4   DL techniques used for tea leaf classification.

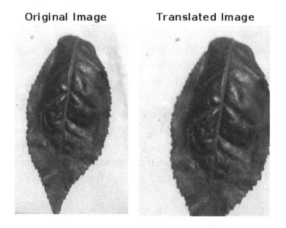

FIGURE 20.5   DL models used for tea leaf classification. and performance metric

Figure 20.4 presents an overview of the key techniques employed in deep learning for tea leaf disease classification, including Ensemble Learning, GAN (Generative Adversarial Network), and Data Augmentation. Ensemble Learning combines multiple models to improve classification accuracy and robustness. GANs generate synthetic tea leaf images, aiding in data augmentation and enhancing disease identification. Data Augmentation techniques, such as image rotation and scaling, increase the diversity and size of the training dataset, improving model performance. These techniques collectively contribute to more precise and reliable tea leaf disease classification using deep learning.

Figure 20.5 showcases models used for tea leaf disease classification, including LeNet, Merge Model, and ResNet. These models capture disease patterns with varying strengths. Performance measures like accuracy, precision, and recall assess their effectiveness in accurate disease identification.

20.2   MOTIVATION

The motivation for implementing a DL solution for tea leaf disease classification is rooted in the economic and social significance of the tea industry. Tea is a major cash crop, not only in exporting nations but also in developing countries, where it plays a crucial role in reducing poverty, promoting rural expansion, and ensuring food security. Millions of agriculturalists depend on tea as their primary source of income, and in many cultures, tea holds significant cultural value. Despite its importance, the tea industry is facing significant challenges, including the impact of tea leaf diseases on production and exports. Tea leaf diseases can cause significant losses, with estimates of up to 14% of production being lost due to insect pests. These diseases not only impede the economic development of countries that grow tea but also threaten the livelihoods of those who depend on it.

The key to successfully avoiding and managing these diseases is an accurate diagnosis and identification of the problem. Classifying diseases in tea leaves has traditionally been done by hand examination, which may be laborious, costly, and error-prone. Here, DL comes into play since it has the ability to increase productivity and precision when classifying tea leaf diseases. It can help the tea business and advance plant disease classification at the same time by investigating the use of DL in the classification of diseases affecting tea leaves.

20.3 LITERATURE REVIEW

The literature review table presents a comprehensive overview of the studies conducted in the field. The Table 20.1 provides a valuable summary of the existing body of knowledge, enabling a comprehensive understanding of the subject matter

TABLE 20.1
Literature Review Table

Reference	Year	Description	Advantage	Disadvantage	Result
[1]	2020	Convert RGB image to Hue-Saturation-Intensity format, isolate green pixels, perform segmentation, use LeNet.	Better accuracy than traditional backpropagation network	Less sensitive to detect red leaf spot (85%).	Overall accuracy 90.23%.
[2]	2022	By combining multiple CNN modules (ResNet network and Inception-v3), MergeModel can pull out a wide range of distinguishing features and improve its ability to identify diseases.	Training may take place with less data than usual, yet recognition performance is improved thanks to this strategy.	Increasingly complicated.	MergeModel is 13% better at identifying disease than Inception v3, and it is 5% better than ResNet34 on the small-size dataset.
[3]	2021	Apply a model based on CNN with seven layers.	Some images are taken with a camera right in the field.	Most of the time, either 64 or 128 filters are used in the convolution layers.	94.45% accuracy.
[4]	2021	Training samples made better by C-DCGAN.	In order to identify and isolate disease spots in tea leaf pictures, SVM analysis is performed.	Without data augmentation, VGG16 has a big problem with over fitting, and the accuracy drops a lot.	90% accuracy.
[5]	2018	In order to train the network, raw pictures were first subjected to preprocessing methods including image segmentation and data improvement.	CNN is more efficient than SVM and Backpropagation.	CNN works well with massive datasets.	CNN's rate of correct recognition is 93.75%.

(Continued)

TABLE 20.1 (Continued)

Reference	Year	Description	Advantage	Disadvantage	Result
[6]	2020	In order to identify illnesses in tea leaves, they retrained models that had previously been developed using imageNet data.	Transfer learning with full fine-tuning accuracy improved.	Evaluation of transfer learning and tuning on small-footprint architectures ResNet, VGGNet, and Xception.	Accuracy is improvedwith respect to training from scratch. Accuracy obtained by ResNet is 94.05%, by VGGNet 91.26% and by Xception 91.27%.
[7]	2021	Images taken in natural settings aren't very accurate because of things like changing light, shadow, different shapes, and leaves that cover each other.	To improve the base photos, the Retinex technique was included. Faster region-based Convolutional Neural Network helped with the identification of faint, obscured, and diminutive ill days. To achieve severity grading, diseased leaves are fed into VGG16 networks.	Dataset images were taken from a specific location in China, and different locations may have different light intensities.	In comparison to traditional ML methods, the suggested methods' detection average precision and severity grading accuracy has increased by more than 6% and 9%, respectively.
[8]	2019	In addition, features are gathered and exploited using the dense scale-invariant feature transform. Make a model incorporating the multi-layer perceptron and the support vector machine to categorize diseases on the basis of descriptions provided by a bag of visual words.	Local characteristics taken from pictures that remain unchanged by translation, scaling, or rotation.	While certain diseases only appear at specific periods of the year, others can affect tea plants at any time. The timing of disease diagnosis could therefore vary throughout the year, which would have an impact on how accurately diseases are identified.	LeafNet accuracy is 90%. SVM is 60%. Multilayer Perceptronis is 70%.
[9]	2022	In this research, they reveal a DL modified Mask R-CNN for fully independent segmentation as well as tracking of tomato plant leaf disease.	Optimizing the Region Proposal Network's anchor fractions and indeed the architecture of feature extraction to uplift detection performance and metric computation effectiveness.	—	Accuracy is 98%.

20.4 CHALLENGES IN DL FOR TEA LEAF DISEASE CLASSIFICATION

Insufficient Dataset: The DL network requires a huge amount of data to work efficiently. But in this area, most of the datasets are private and not available for public usage. That makes it difficult to work in this area, unless researchers have the resource and time to collect data from the ground. Otherwise, there is a dataset available under CC BY-SA 4.0 license known as the "tea sickness dataset"[10], which contains more than 800 images of tea leaf disorder images arranged under eight classes.

The mechanism of developing effective new training samples from the ones that are already present is referred to as image augmentation. Researchers alter the original image just enough to create a fresh sample. Researchers could, for instance, alter the original image's brightness a little, chop off a portion of it, or mirror it, to create a new image.

Geometric Transformation: The safety of image augmentation plays a very critical role in the success of the model. The safety of image augmentation is nothing but the capability of the augmentation process to sustain the class label after the process. For example, flipping of an image does not have any effect if the model is going to predict whether a given image belongs to a cat or a dog, but the same operation may have negative implications on the number recognition model because flipping of number 6 change the class label, because it will represent number 9 after flipping operation.

Rotation: When using rotation augmentations, the image is rotated either to the right or left around an axis that may be adjusted from 1 to 359°.

Translation: A highly useful transformation to prevent positional bias in the data is to shift pictures to the left, right, up, or down. Suppose someone developed a model to recognize their family members based on the image provided but, while training, all faces were properly center aligned. Therefore in testing proper, center-aligned images would be needed.

The Figure 20.6 illustrates the image translation process,

The Figure 20.7 presents essential geometric transformation operations applied to tea leaf images. Flipping horizontally or vertically modifies the orientation and enhances symmetry in tea leaf images. Rotation allows adjusting image angles for improved alignment and viewing purposes. Cropping enables the extraction of specific regions of interest from tea leaf images, facilitating feature extraction and background removal.

Color Space Transformation: One of the most commonly encountered barriers to solving image recognition problems is illumination bias. A very easy and simple solution is to visit each and every pixel value of the input image and update the pixel value with current pixel values plus or minus a

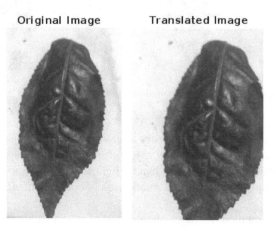

Original Image   Translated Image

FIGURE 20.6   Image translation.

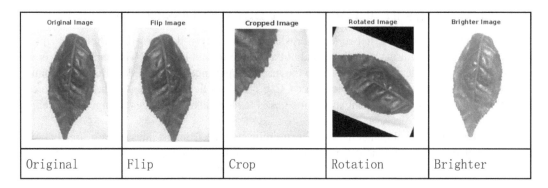

| Original | Flip | Crop | Rotation | Brighter |

FIGURE 20.7 Geometric transformation.

FIGURE 20.8 A few examples of color augmentations.

constant. Simply converting the image's intensity level values (pixel values) to other intensity level values (pixel values) that lie between the new range of minimum and maximum values is another option. So many techniques are available to handle lightness and darkness problems using color space transformation. Figure 20.8 showcases a collection of color augmentation techniques applied to tea leaf images.

Another cutting-edge method for data augmentation is generative modeling. In generative modeling, artificial instances are created from datasets while maintaining their original attributes. The extremely intriguing and very-well-liked generative modeling system known as Generative Adversarial Network was developed using adversarial training [11].

20.4.1 VARIATIONS IN SYMPTOMS

Practitioners often believe that a disease's symptoms won't alter while looking for it in leaves. The interactions between illnesses, plants, and the environment lead to the symptoms of tea leaf disorders. Changes in any one of the three can result in variations in illness symptoms, as will be covered below. The two main variants of tea leaf diseases are:

a. Distinct symptoms may be present at different phases of the illness's development. Figure 20.9 illustrates the different phases involved in the development of blister blight on tea leaves. The figure provides a comprehensive visual representation of the progression of this fungal disease

b. Several diseases may be present on the same tea leaf leaves at the same time. The symptoms of several diseases may alter dramatically if they are grouped together, making it difficult to distinguish between them. In addition, distinct diseases may have similar symptoms, thus complicating disease categorization. While this is going on, it could be challenging to identify plant illnesses because of the age, genotype, and healthy tissue color changes (and resulting contrast variations) of the tea leaf itself. Figure 20.10 portrays the occurrence of both grey blight and brown blight on the same tea leaf. The figure visually captures the coexistence of these two distinct types of blights, each characterized by unique visual symptoms.

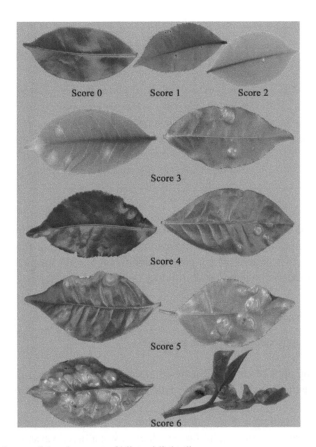

FIGURE 20.9 All phases of development of blister blight disease.

FIGURE 20.10 Grey blight and brown blight occurring in the same leaf.

TABLE 20.2
Interclass Similarities

Disease Name	Symptom of Disease
Blister blight	Small, pinhole-size spots on young leaves
Red rust	Lesions on leaves, spread to branches and fruit
Brown blight	Small, oval, pale yellow-green spots on leaves
Grey blight	Small, oval, pale yellow-green spots on leaves
Twig die back, stem canker	Browning and drooping of leaves, dieback of shoots, cankers on branches
Brown root rot	Yellowing and wilting of leaves, death of the plant, longitudinal cracks on roots
Red root rot	Yellowing of leaves, wilting and sudden death of bush

Other elements, like temperature, humidity, wind, soil quality, and sunshine, may also affect a particular disease's symptoms. A variety of symptom changes may result from the interplay of illnesses, plants, and the environment, which present significant hurdles for picture capture and annotation. Table 20.2 showcases the interclass Similarity between various tea leaf diseases.

20.4.2 Interclass Similarities

There are two ways to approach solving this issue:

a. Gathering photographs of certain illnesses that show the whole spectrum of variety;
b. Continually updating the richness of the database in real-world applications.

The first approach is impracticable since gathering photos of the whole range of variations requires a lot of work and money, and it is uncertain if researchers have gathered variants entirely. The alternative approach is far more practical, and researchers already utilize it widely to significantly broaden the diversity of data.

20.4.3 IMAGE BACKGROUND

Most image-based techniques for leaf analysis begin with leaf segmentation. This operation may often be carried out automatically without too many issues if some sort of panel (ideally white or blue) is placed below the leaf. However, segmentation may be difficult if the backdrop includes vegetation, foliage, dirt, and other objects. When the backdrop has a sizable quantity of green, segmenting the leaf is quite challenging. It can also be challenging to appropriately segment the region of interest where the symptoms are present since the backdrop frequently contains factors that might make this difficult.

For segmenting leaves, there are generally five ways that may be employed. which are explained below.

a. **The Threshold Segmentation**: The threshold segmentation approach has a significant drawback. It divides the foreground by establishing a certain threshold. Most of the time, the same threshold is applied to all pixels, which might result in inaccurate holes or even split the object into many parts. The succeeding step, such as picture categorization, will suffer as a result of this drawback. It is challenging to choose a fair threshold, which is often chosen manually.

b. **K-means Clustering**: K-means clustering is automated and effective in the majority of situations, but time-consuming and inappropriate for fast-moving scenarios.

c. **Otsu Technique**: For picture segmentation, Otsu, an efficient and adaptable thresholding technique, has been extensively employed. The Otsu approach is threshold adaptive and works well in terms of time consumption, but it won't create the right threshold when the gray-level histogram resembles a unimodal distribution.

d. **Deep Learning Fully Convolutional Network (DL FCN)**: There is also Deep Learning Fully Convolutional Network (DL FCN) To classify pictures at the pixel level, FCN undergoes pixel-by-pixel semantic segmentation training. The FCN approach may segment pictures of arbitrary size if time and memory constraints are ignored, but it has significant downsides, such as improperly taking into account the connection between pixels.

e. **Watershed Segmentation**: The last technique is watershed segmentation, which is successful. To solve the main flaw of this method, over-segmentation, three revised watershed algorithms have been developed.

There is no one segmentation method that solves all problems. Combining many different strategies could be a smart move. Figure 20.11 demonstrates the image segmentation operation

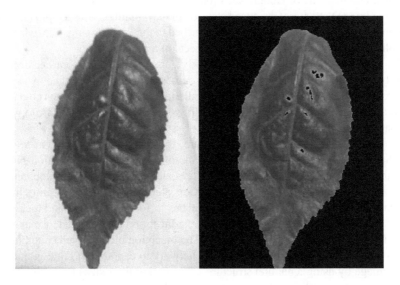

FIGURE 20.11 Image segmentation.

applied to tea leaf images. Image segmentation is a critical process that partitions an image into distinct regions or objects of interest.

20.4.4 OTHER PROBLEMS

The difficult-to-control capture settings might result in photos with unpredictable properties, making illness detection more difficult. The majority of symptoms gradually blend into healthy tissue rather than having sharp borders, making it challenging to distinguish between healthy and sick areas [12]. In traditional DL issues, researchers frequently and presumptively assume that the samples of the testing and training sets are identical. Typically, they use the training set to train the model and the test set to evaluate it. The test situation, nevertheless, is frequently unpredictable in the real application. Due to a number of variables, including the impact of the season and climate, the distribution of the test set is significantly different from the training set. The over-fitting problem that occurs in these situations causes the trained model to under-perform in real-world applications. Mohanty et al. validated this non-ideal robustness problem using the Plant Village dataset to train and test deep CNN (DCNN) models; the greatest accuracy they were able to attain was 99.35%. When the DCNN models were tested on a collection of images taken under various conditions from the training set, the accuracy decreased to 31% [13]. The reliability of CNN models may be increased in three different ways. Simpler-parameter compressed models provide more resilience and less over fitting. Compressed models perform poorly when dealing with sophisticated recognition. Unsupervised-based DL techniques are also effective at achieving more stable results. Unsupervised models frequently perform significantly worse than supervised DL models overall. Multi-condition training is an additional strategy (MCT).

20.5 A REVIEW OF RECENT CNN ARCHITECTURES FOR TEA LEAF DISEASE CLASSIFICATION

20.5.1 GOOGLENET

Inception-v1 is another name for the CNN architecture GoogleNet, which was created by Google researchers in 2014. The network was created with the intention of enhancing the precision and effectiveness of image classification tasks, and it has subsequently been used in a number of computer vision applications. One of GoogleNet's main benefits is its increased accuracy. When it was first released, the ImageNet dataset produced state-of-the-art findings, with a top-5 error rate of only 6.67%. This outstanding outcome may be partly ascribed to the Inception module, which enables the network to collect both fine-grained and coarse aspects of a picture.

GoogleNet processes digital images more quickly and effectively than earlier deep neural network designs because of its efficient use of CPU resources. This is accomplished by using 1 × 1 convolutional layers, which lower the network's computational cost and parameter count. In addition, GoogleNet is scalable because of the way it is built, which enables the network to grow in layers without dramatically raising processing costs.

A key component of the GoogleNet architecture, the Inception block, is made to effectively gather both the fine- and coarse-grained components of a picture. The Inception block gives the network the ability to gather properties on multiple scales by fusing several convolutional layers with different filter sizes into a parallel structure. Concatenating the output feature maps from the block's branches along the depth axis join the branches to form the Inception block's output. The common filter sizes used in the various branches of the Inception block include a max-pooling layer in addition to 1 × 1, 3 × 3, and 5 × 5 convolutions. The Inception block is well suited for a variety of computer vision applications because it allows the network to capture both fine-grained and coarse features of an image by using a parallel structure with varying filter sizes [13]. Figure 20.12 showcases the basic Inception module utilized in the GoogleNet architecture.

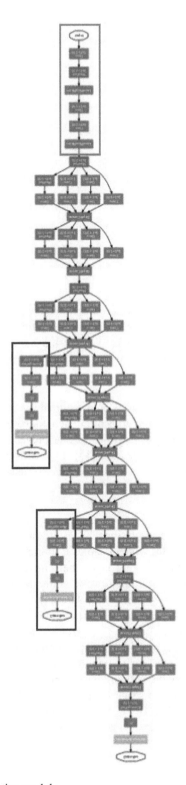

FIGURE 20.12   GoogleNet inception module.

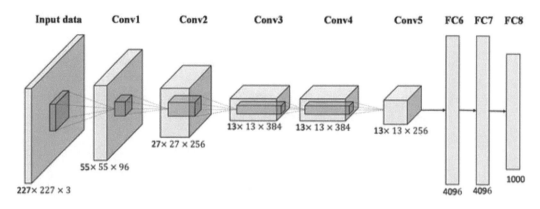

FIGURE 20.13   AlexNet architecture.

20.5.2   ALEXNET

There are five convolutional layers in the AlexNet architecture. Three fully connected layers and a softmax layer are used for classifying. After an initial convolutional layer with 96 filters of size 11 × 11 and stride 4, a max-pooling layer of size 3 × 3 and stride 2 is used; 256 filters of size 5 × 5 with stride 1 make up the second convolutional layer, which is followed by a max-pooling layer of size 3 × 3 with stride 2. Convolutional layers three through five use 384, 384, and 256 3 × 3 filters with a stride of 1, respectively.

Each of the linear layers has 4096 neurons, and the final one is linked to the softmax layer for classification. Using ReLU activation functions after each convolutional and fully linked layer, the network's architecture introduces nonlinearity. To further prevent overfitting, the linear layers are additionally subjected to dropout regularization [13]. Figure 20.13 illustrates the architecture of AlexNet, a deep convolutional neural network (CNN) used for tea leaf disease classification.

20.5.3   VGG16

The 16-layer architecture consists of convolutional layers (13) and linear layers (3). In part, VGG16's efficacy may be attributed to its depth, which enables it to gradually discern increasingly intricate details in the input image. The max pooling layers help in reducing the spatial dimensions and broadening the receptive field, while the miniature 3 × 3 filters with a stride of 1 and padding further enhance the network in taking up fine-grained information in the image. VGG16's structure is likewise simple and easy to understand. The modular structure of its convolutional and pooling layers makes it easy to modify or repurpose.

VGG16 may have drawbacks, such as high computational cost and memory limits. Due to the extensive computational resources required to train the VGG16 network from scratch on a massive dataset, it may be difficult to deploy the network on low-power devices or in real-time applications. As a result, researchers have considered several approaches, such as model compression and architectural modifications, to enhance VGG16 [4]. Figure 20.14 presents the architecture of VGG-16, a deep convolutional neural network (CNN) widely used in tea leaf disease classification.

20.5.4   RESNET50

This design is fairly sophisticated, with a total of 50 layers consisting of 49 convolutional layers and 1 fully linked layer. The network's enhanced capability to learn from input data is largely attributable to ResNet50's use of residual connections. If the network is given the option to learn residual

VGG-16

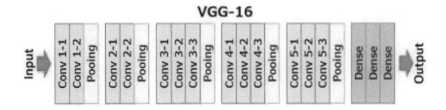

FIGURE 20.14 VGG-16 architecture.

ResNet50 Model Architecture

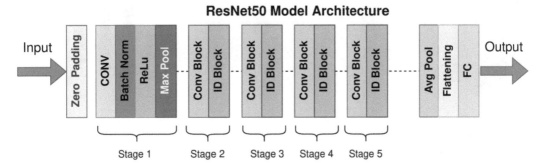

FIGURE 20.15 ResNet50 architecture.

functions without having to discover an exact mapping between input and output, it may do so by including a residual link that bypasses one or more convolutional layers.

ResNet50's structure is rather complex, with blocks of convolutional layers and residual connections adding further layers. Nonetheless, the network is able to detect more nuanced elements in the input image because to its complexity. One other advantage of ResNet50 is its ability to handle vanishing gradients, a typical problem in multi-layer deep neural networks. As a result, residual connections may help prevent gradients from becoming too small to be useful for learning by carrying the gradient signal more effectively. Figure 20.15 presents the architecture of ResNet (Residual Neural Network), a deep convolutional neural network (CNN) widely utilized in tea leaf disease classification

20.5.5 LEAFNET

The LeafNet ConvoNet was designed to recognize diseases within tea leaves. The architecture is comprised of five convolutional layers, two linear layers, and a final classification layer. The number of kernels used in the first, second, and fifth convolutional layers is reduced by half as compared to the AlexNet design. After resizing the image to 227 × 227 pixels, the network instantly begins processing all three color channels.

LeafNet is built on a foundation of convolutional and linear layers. Convolutional layer 1 uses a rectified linear unit activation function, which comes after a sequence of 24 filters with a kernel size of 11 × 11 pixels. After the sub-sampling layer, use a 3 × 3 kernel to normalize the local responses. Researchers use 64 filters with 5 × 5 kernel sizes and the rectified linear unit activation function in the second convolutional layer. The pooling layer's kernel size is the same as that of the first pooling layer, and it employs local response normalization. The third and fourth convolutional layers each include 96 filters with a rectified linear unit activation function and a kernel size of 3 × 3 pixels. In the fifth convolutional layer, they utilize 64 filters with 3 × 3 pixel kernel sizes and the rectified linear unit activation function. In the sub-sampling layer, a 3 × 3 pixel kernel is used.

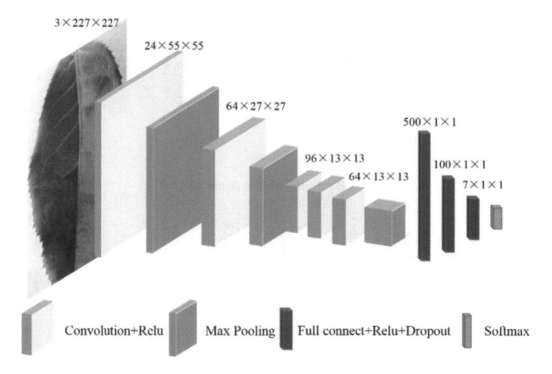

FIGURE 20.16 LeafNet architecture.

The first layer is fully linked, and consists of 500 neurons, a rectified linear unit based activation function, and a dropout operation. A hundred neurons are followed by rectified linear unit and dropout operations in the fully linked second layer. The seven kinds of neurons found in the last connected layer might be read as the various illnesses indicated by the tea leaves. The output layer, which determines the input image's label, receives the results from the last fully connected layer. As the total of the outputs equals 1, with the aim of restricting the output to a value between 0 and 1, the softmax activation function is used.

With LeafNet's unique design and layers, tea leaf disease classification is simplified. Dropout approaches, local response normalization, and ReLU activation functions are the ways to improve the model's generalization and robustness against overfitting [8]. Figure 20.16 presents the architecture of LeafNet, a deep convolutional neural network (CNN) widely utilized in tea leaf disease classification

20.5.6 MERGEMODEL

MergeModel improves identification accuracy by combining two prominent DL frameworks, ResNet34 and Inception-v3. Because of its capacity to train hundreds of layers without performance saturation, ResNet34 is selected as the fundamental network. To extract more detailed characteristics from tea leaf photos, Inception-v3 is employed. MergeModel broadens the network by using the Block module and deepens the network by using ResNet. MergeModel's structure incorporates convolution and pooling layers before the Block module to minimize computation and generate more precise feature mappings. Overall, MergeModel performs well in detecting tea

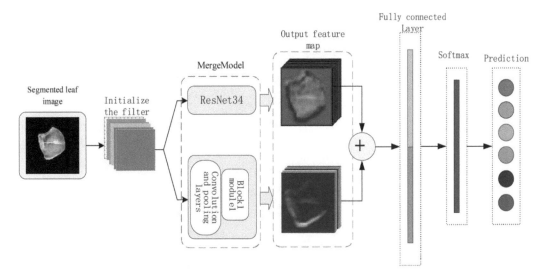

FIGURE 20.17   MergeModel.

leaf illnesses [2]. Figure 20.17 presents the architecture of Merge model, a deep convolutional neural network (CNN) widely utilized in tea leaf disease classification

20.5.7   XIAOXIAO SUN1'S CNN ARCHITECTURE

Figure 20.18 presents the architecture of Xiaoxiao SUN1's CNN, a deep convolutional neural network (CNN) widely utilized in tea leaf disease classification.

The convnet utilized in the experiment has an aggregate of nine layers: two convolution layers, two maximum pooling layers, two partial response normalization layers, two linear layers, and one classification output layer.

20.5.8   LENET

Yann LeCun built the LeNet-5 CNN architecture in 1998 to interpret handwritten digits. It encompasses two convolutional layers, two average sub-sampling layers, two linear layers, a single flattened layer, and one softmax classification layer. A $24 \times 55 \times 55$ pixel RGB picture is generated by convolving a $3 \times 11 \times 11$ kernel filter with a $3 \times 227 \times 227$ RGB image. Then sub-sampling is applied to reduce the picture dimensions to $64 \times 27 \times 27$ pixels. The network is then refined with additional convolutional and pooling-sub sampling layers. Output probabilities for ten classes of handwritten digits are calculated using a softmax classification layer, which is fed 500 1×1 feature maps from the linear layer and 10 1×1 feature maps from the linked layer (0–9). Overall, LeNet-5 was a milestone point in the advancement of CNN and continues to serve as a foundational architecture for image classification applications [1]. Figure 20.19 presents the architecture of LeNet, a deep convolutional neural network (CNN) widely utilized in tea leaf disease classification.

The Table 20.3 showcases a comparison of the accuracy achieved by Architecture's.

Figure 20.20 presents a bar graph illustrating the accuracy comparison of different architectures in tea leaf disease classification.

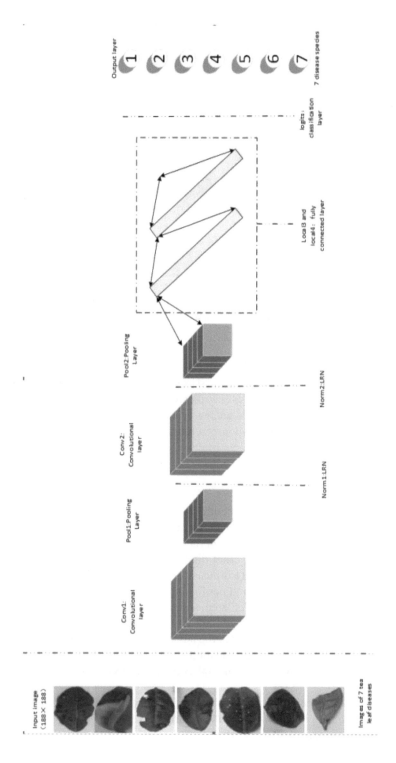

FIGURE 20.18 Xiaoxiao SUN1's CNN architecture.

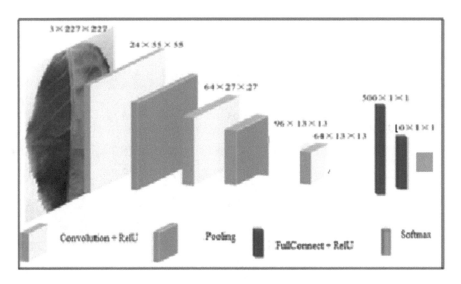

FIGURE 20.19 LeNet architecture.

TABLE 20.3
Architecture Accuracy

Architecture	Accuracy
GoogleNet	98.21
AlexNet	80.00
VGG16	90.00
ResNet50	92.00
MergeModel	94.00
Xiaoxiao SUN1's CNN	93.75
LeNet	90.23
LeafNet	90.16

20.6 TRENDING MODELS AND TECHNIQUES USED IN THIS FIELD

In 2019, [5] developed a CNN model with nine layers, including two convolution layers, two maximum pooling layers, two layers that partially normalized responses, two complete connection layers, and one layer that outputs classifications. A dropout mechanism is used in experiments after the completely linked layer to lessen over-fitting. The experiment is primarily compared to the SVM and BP algorithms, and it was shown that when feature extraction and classifier training are combined with DL technology, the accuracy of illness detection and learning efficiency are significantly improved.

It should be emphasized that the two SVM and BP algorithms need to preprocess the image using a variety of ways before classifying the image of tea leaf sickness and extracting its tone, design, and structure components. Following that, recognition and classification are performed using these feature selection classifiers. However, the lengthy experimental procedure associated with feature extraction and the intricate process of parameter tuning will somewhat skew the recognition results. In contrast to SVM and BP, CNN may input the actual picture directly into the network without the preprocessing step of feature extraction, drastically lowering the time and the constraints of artificial design features.

Accuracy vs. Architecture

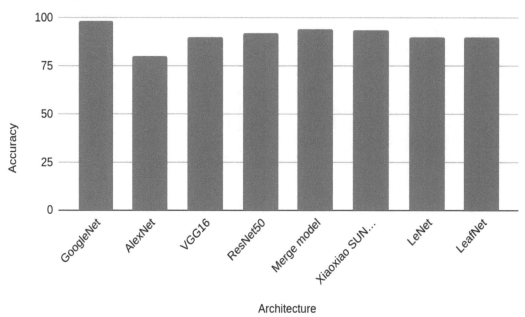

FIGURE 20.20 Architecture accuracy comparison.

The network can achieve high recognition accuracy by modifying the learning rate, the number of iterations, and the addition of dropouts, which is helpful for the detection and categorization of tea illnesses. Since it would take a long time to modify the learning rate throughout the experiment, a mechanism for figuring out the right learning rate needs to be devised, which calls for more study. The number of experimental datasets is unequal because of the different times and levels of tea sickness prevalence. Therefore, a fix for the dataset's imbalance is required. Results of the experiment revealed that CNN's memory accuracy is 93.75%.

In [8], the indications of tea leaf ailments are automatically extracted from photos using a CNN architecture called LeafNet with a changeable-sized feature extractor kernel. This architectural design was produced using a combination of two linear layers, a classification layer, and five convolutional layers. Additionally, the linear layer has 500, 100, and 7 neurons, respectively, instead of the typical AlexNet architecture's use of 100.

The scale-invariant feature transform (SIFT) algorithm, which is invariant to picture rotation, scaling, and affine transformations, is used to extract local characteristics from images. The SIFT technique is therefore rated as the most reputable and trusted invariant feature descriptor for digital image processing. Support vector machine and multi-layer perceptron classifiers are then employed to identify illnesses using the dense scale-invariant feature transform (DSIFT) features that were also extracted. The three classifiers' performance in identifying diseases was then assessed on an individual basis. The ConvoNet known as LeafNet distinguished tea leaf illnesses with an overall classification precision of 90.16%, followed by the SVM algorithm at 60.62%, and the MLP algorithm at 70.77%. Compared to the MLP and SVM algorithms, LeafNet was unquestionably more effective in identifying tea leaf illnesses.

The number of convolution operators used to build the first, second, and fifth convolution layers is intended to be equivalent to 50% of the filters used in AlexNet. DL systems must be trained using a tremendous volume of data, as is universally acknowledged. But if it is attainable at all, the questionnaire method is extremely expensive. Using models that have been trained on a big dataset in the target domain with a smaller dataset is a sensible approach to dealing with the limited data issue.

For transfer learning, their research indicates that because our task differs from ImageNet's, just using transfer learning on their data may not be beneficial. It has been discovered that it is successful to apply fine-tuning to DCNN models that have already been trained. Fine-tuning routinely outperforms that of employing simply transfer learning or only some of the fine-tuning. Additionally, it is superior to training the model from scratch, that is, without utilizing pre-trained models. [6].

LeNet-5, a well-known model of convolutional networks, is selected to perform tea leaf classification. In this LeNet-5 model, there are two convolution layers, two average pooling layers also known as subsampling, followed by one flattening convolution layer, two fully connected layers, and one softmax classification layer. Receiver Operative Curve (ROC) was used to assess the accuracy of CNN classifiers in determining the illness state of different tea leaves from the picture collection. Due to its visible phytopathological signs and ease of caution, blight leaf disease produces the greatest accuracy level among other illnesses. The next most precisely categorized illness is tea red scab, with a yield of 94%; the next illnesses are all categorized between 84 and 93%. When compared to traditional backpropagation networks, which generate 85% accuracy for the blister blight disease, this model is believed to produce a high accuracy level based on the established accuracy levels.

The computational complexity which is needed for using a standard neural network is greatly decreased when adopting this approach. The great internal failure adaptability of CNNs allows the use of erroneous or partial foundation photos, hence adequately enhancing the accuracy of picture recognition. The findings of the current investigation highlight the potential for using CNNs in the detection and evaluation of diseases affecting tea plants, which might significantly increase disease recognition for tea ranch horticulture. LeNet's diagnosis of the illness isn't 100% accurate, but improvements to the current method may be put into practice in subsequent tests despite this [1].

In this investigation, the effects of lighting shifts, shadows, varying leaf architectures, and mutual leaf blockage has resulted in poor accuracy in photos of tea leaf blight collected under realistic conditions. To remedy the source photographs and lessen the impact of lighting variations and shadows, a Retinex method is used. The usage of a DL framework called Faster Region-based CNN is used to identify tea leaf blight leaves, which improves the detection capabilities of unclear, blocked, and small parts of sick leaves. The leaves of tea plants infected with tea leaf blight are identified and fed into VGG16 networks that have been trained to rate and analyze disease severity. According to their results [7], the suggested method increases accuracy in severity grading by more than 9% and the average detection score by more than 6%.

According to the proposed investigation, the ConvNet was constructed with a single input layer, four convolution layers, and two linear layers. The image data is sent to the input layer. The input picture from the dataset is parsed by the convolution layers, and the output layer assigns it to one of eight categories [3].

20.7   CONCLUSION

DL approaches are currently frequently employed in the identification and classification of tea leaf diseases. The issues associated with traditional ML algorithms have been resolved or substantially resolved by DL, a sub-field of ML, which is typically used for image classification, target identification, and picture segmentation. The use of DL for tea leaf disease classification has emerged as a promising method in recent years. However, a number of obstacles remain, including limited data availability, the need for more robust image preprocessing procedures, and the need for more advanced models.

Despite these challenges, modern technologies such as CNNs, image processing, and transfer learning have been successfully employed in tea leaf disease classification, with models such as ResNet, VGG, and Inception demonstrating good performance. In recent years, researchers have fused numerous models to develop hybrid versions, and they have achieved high accuracy.

Additionally, the survey has also highlighted the need for more research in this field to address the study gaps, to overcome current challenges, and to improve the accuracy and efficiency of the classification process. Overall, the future of tea leaf disease classification using DL looks promising with the potential for even better results in the future.

REFERENCES

[1] Gayathri, S. et al., *"Image Analysis and Detection of Tea Leaf Disease using Deep Learning"*, https://doi.org/10.1109/ICESC48915.2020.9155850

[2] Hu, Gensheng et al., *"Using a Multi-convolutional Neural Network to Automatically Identify Small-sample Tea Leaf Diseases"*, https://doi.org/10.1016/j.suscom.2022.100696

[3] R. S. Latha et al., *"Automatic Detection of Tea Leaf Diseases Using Deep Convolution Neural Network"*, https://doi.org/10.1109/ICCCI50826.2021.9402225

[4] Hu, Gensheng et al., *"A Low Shot Learning Method for Tea Leaf's Disease Identification"*, https://doi.org/10.1016/j.compag.2019.104852

[5] Sun, X. *"Image Recognition of Tea Leaf Diseases Based on Convolutional Neural Network"*, https://doi.org/10.1109/SPAC46244.2018.8965555

[6] Ramadan, Ade *"Transfer Learning and Fine-Tuning for Deep Learning-Based Tea Diseases Detection on Small Datasets"*, https://doi.org/10.1109/ICRAMET51080.2020.9298575

[7] Hu, Gensheng et al., *"Detection and Severity Analysis of Tea Leaf Blight Based on Deep Learning"*, https://doi.org/10.1016/j.compeleceng.2021.107023

[8] Chen, Jing et al., *"Visual Tea Leaf Disease Recognition Using a Convolutional Neural Network Model"*, https://doi.org/10.3390/sym11030343

[9] Kaur, Prabhjot et al., *"An Approach for Characterization of Infected Area in Tomato Leaf Disease Based on Deep Learning and Object Detection Technique"*, https://doi.org/10.1016/j.engappai.2022.105210

[10] Kimutai, Gibson; Förster, Anna (2022), "Tea Sickness Dataset", *Mendeley Data*, V2, https://doi.org/10.17632/j32xdt2ff5.2

[11] Shorten, Connor et al, *"A survey on Image Data Augmentation for Deep Learning"*, https://doi.org/10.1186/s40537-019-0197-0

[12] Barbedo, Jayme Garcia Arnal, *"A Review on the Main Challenges in Automatic Plant Disease Identification Based on Visible Range Images"*, https://doi.org/10.1016/j.biosystemseng.2016.01.017

[13] Mohanty, S.P.; Hughes, D.P.; Marcel, S. 2016, "Using Deep Learning for Image-Based Plant Disease Detection", *Frontiers in Plant Science*, 7, 141, https://doi.org/10.3389/fpls.2016.01419

Index

Pages in **bold** refer to tables.